W9-CZU-306

The Ways of the Poem

The Ways of the Poem

Edited by Josephine Miles

University of California

Prentice-Hall, Inc., Englewood Cliffs, New Jersey

64894

PRENTICE-HALL ENGLISH LITERATURE SERIES

Maynard Mack, Editor

© 1972 by Prentice-Hall, Inc., Englewood Cliffs, New Jersey
This volume is a revised edition of *The Ways of the Poem* by
Josephine Miles © 1961 by Prentice-Hall, Inc.

All rights reserved. No part of this book may be
reproduced in any form, by mimeograph or any other means,
without permission in writing from the publisher.

13–946319–4
Library of Congress Catalog Card Number 78–146676
Printed in the United States of America

Current printing (last digit):
10   9   8   7   6   5   4   3   2   1

Prentice-Hall International, Inc., London
Prentice-Hall of Australia, Pty. Ltd., Sydney
Prentice-Hall of Canada, Ltd., Toronto
Prentice-Hall of India Private Limited, New Delhi
Prentice-Hall of Japan, Inc., Tokyo

Acknowledgment is made to the following publishers, agents, and
individuals who have granted permission to reprint selections from copy-
righted publications.

EARLE BIRNEY
for "World Winter." Reprinted by permission of the author.

CURTIS BROWN LTD
from *Pansies* by D. H. Lawrence, "Fidelity," copyright 1929 by Frieda Lawrence
Ravagli. Reprinted by permission of the author's estate.

CALDER AND BOYERS, LTD.
from *Poems, 1950–1965*, by Robert Creeley, "Fancy," "The Rhythm," "The Shame."
Copyright 1966.

CITY LIGHTS POCKET BOOKSHOP
from *Howl and other poems* by Allen Ginsberg, "Sunflower Sutra." Copyright 1956.
from *Pictures of the Gone World* by Lawrence Ferlinghetti #26 ("Reading Yeats").
Copyright 1955.

THE CLARENDON PRESS
for "London Snow" and "Nightingales" by Robert Bridges. Reprinted by permission of The Clarendon Press, Oxford.
from *The Shorter Poems of Robert Bridges*, "When First We Met." Reprinted by permission of The Clarendon Press, Oxford.

CORNELL UNIVERSITY PRESS
from *Selected Poems* by A. R. Ammons, "Hardweed Path Going." Copyright 1968.

DOUBLEDAY & COMPANY
from *The Waking: Poems 1933–1953* by Theodore Roethke, "The Waking." Copyright 1953 by Theodore Roethke. Reprinted by permission of Doubleday & Company, Inc.
from *Rewards and Fairies* by Rudyard Kipling, "The Way Through the Woods," copyright 1910 by Rudyard Kipling. Reprinted by permission of Mrs. George Bambridge and Doubleday & Company, Inc.

FOUR SEASONS FOUNDATION
from *In Cold Hell, In Thicket* by Charles Olson, "La Torre." Copyright 1967.
from *The Pill Versus the Springhill Mine Disaster* by Richard Brautigan, "Chinese Checker Players" and "All Watched Over by Machines of Loving Grace." Copyright 1968.

FULCRUM PRESS
from *A Range of Poems* by Gary Snyder, #10, "Amitabha's Vow." Copyright 1966.

THOMSON GUNN
for "Sunlight."

HANDY BROTHERS MUSIC CO., INC.
for "Joe Turner Blues." Copyright 1915 by W. C. Handy. Copyright renewed 1942 by W. C. Handy. Published for U.S.A. by Handy Brothers Music Co., Inc., 1650 Broadway, New York, N.Y. 10019. Rights outside the U.S.A. controlled by Robbins Music Corporation, 1540 Broadway, New York, N.Y. 10036. Reprinted by permission.

HARCOURT, BRACE AND COMPANY
from *Ceremony and other Poems* by Richard Wilbur, "Ceremony," copyright 1948, 1949, 1950, by Richard Wilbur. Reprinted by permission of Harcourt, Brace and Co., Inc.
from *Things of This World* by Richard Wilbur, "All These Birds," copyright 1956, by Richard Wilbur. Reprinted by permission of Harcourt, Brace and Co., Inc.
from *Collected Poems 1909–1935* by T. S. Eliot, "The Love Song of J. Alfred Prufrock," "Ash Wednesday," and "The Hollow Men," copyright 1936, by Harcourt, Brace and Co., Inc. Reprinted by permission of the publishers.
from *Good Morning America* by Carl Sandburg, "Redhaw Rain," copyright 1928, renewed 1955, by Carl Sandburg. Reprinted by permission of Harcourt, Brace and Co., Inc.
from *Slabs of the Sunburnt West* by Carl Sandburg, "Hoof Dusk," copyright 1922, by Harcourt, Brace and Co., Inc., renewed 1950 by Carl Sandburg. Reprinted by permission of the publishers.
from *Lord Weary's Castle* by Robert Lowell, "Colloquy in Black Rock," copyright 1944, 1946, by Robert Lowell. Reprinted by permission of Harcourt, Brace and Co., Inc.
from *Poems 1923–1954* by e. e. cummings, copyright 1940 by e. e. cummings. Reprinted by permission of Harcourt, Brace and Co., Inc.

HARMS INC.
for "You're the Top" by Cole Porter, copyright 1934, by Harms Inc. Reprinted by permission.

HARPER AND ROW

from *The Rescued Year* by William Stafford, "At the Bomb Testing Site" and "Walking West." Copyright 1966.

from *Traveling through the Dark* by William Stafford, "Traveling through the Dark." Copyright 1962.

HARVARD UNIVERSITY PRESS

from *The Poems of Emily Dickinson,* T. H. Johnson, editor, "Under the Light, Yet Under," "To Flee from Memory," and "To Make a Prairie," copyright 1955, by the President and Fellows of Harvard College. Reprinted by permission of the publishers.

THE HOGARTH PRESS LTD

for "Hunter," by F. Garcia Lorca, tr. by Stephen Spender and J. L. Gili. Reprinted by permission of The Hogarth Press Ltd.

HOLT, RINEHART AND WINSTON, INC.

from *A Shropshire Lad* by A. E. Housman, Poem XL, and Poem XLIII. Reprinted by permission of the publishers.

from *Complete Poems of Robert Frost,* "Design," "The Oven Bird," "Reluctance," and "The Pasture." Copyright 1930, 1949, by Henry Holt and Co., Inc., copyright 1936, by Robert Frost. Reprinted by permission of the publishers.

HOUGHTON MIFFLIN COMPANY

from *Poems: North and South* by Elizabeth Bishop, "The Fish." Published 1955, by Houghton Mifflin Company. All rights reserved. Reprinted by permission of the publishers.

from *Collected Poems: 1917–1952* by Archibald MacLeish, "Empire Builders," "The End of the World," and "Memory Green," published 1952, by Houghton Mifflin Company. All rights reserved. Reprinted by permission of the publishers.

INDIANA UNIVERSITY PRESS

from *New Negro Poets U.S.A.* by Langston Hughes, "Each Morning" by LeRoi Jones. Copyright 1964.

ALFRED A. KNOPF

from *Collected Poems of Wallace Stevens,* "Connoisseur of Chaos," copyright 1942, 1954, by Wallace Stevens, "The Pediment of Appearance," copyright 1947, 1954, by Wallace Stevens, "The Idea of Order at Key West," copyright 1935, 1954, by Wallace Stevens, and "The Snow Man," and "Anecdote of Men by the Thousand," copyright 1931, 1954, by Wallace Stevens. Reprinted by permission of Alfred A. Knopf, Inc.

from *Selected Poems* by John Crowe Ransom, "Piazza Piece," copyright 1927, 1945, by Alfred A. Knopf, Inc. Reprinted by permission of the publishers.

from *The Weary Blues,* by Langston Hughes, "The Negro Speaks of Rivers," Copyright 1926.

LITTLE, BROWN & COMPANY

for "After Great Pain, A Formal Feeling Comes" by Emily Dickinson, copyright 1929, by Martha Dickinson Bianchi. Reprinted by permission of Little, Brown & Co.

from *Verses from 1929 On* by Ogden Nash, "More About People," copyright 1931, by Ogden Nash. Reprinted by permission of Little, Brown & Co.

LITTLE SQUARE REVIEW

for "from the Songs of the Masked Dancers," from *Twenty-one Versions of American Indian Texts.* Copyright 1968 by John Skinner.

LIVERIGHT PUBLISHING CORPORATION

from *The Collected Poems of Hart Crane,* "At Melville's Tomb," "Voyages," (I, II, and III), copyright 1933, by Liveright, Inc. Reprinted by permission of Liveright Publishers, New York.

THE MACMILLAN COMPANY

from *Collected Poems* by William Butler Yeats, "To the Rose Upon the Rood of Time," "The Lover Mourns for the Loss of Love," "He Bids His Beloved Be at Peace," "The Folly of Being Comforted," "Adam's Curse," "The Wild Swans at Coole," "Her Praise," "A Dialogue of Self and Soul," "The Cat and the Moon," "Byzantium," and "Sailing to Byzantium." Reprinted by permission of the Macmillan Company.

from *Collected Poems* by Marianne Moore, "Wood Weasel" and "The Mind Is an Enchanted Thing." Reprinted by permission of The Macmillan Company.

from *A Treasury of Russian Verse*, Yarmolinsky, editor, "Improvisation," by Boris Pasternak, tr. Babette Deutsch. Reprinted by permission of The Macmillan Company.

from *Collected Poems* by Thomas Hardy, "The Oxen," and "Her Dilemma." Reprinted by permission of The Macmillan Company.

from *Collected Poems* by Vachel Lindsay, "The Eagle That Is Forgotten." Reprinted by permission of The Macmillan Company.

NEW DIRECTIONS

from *The Teeth of the Lion* by Kenneth Patchen, "The Origin of Baseball," copyright 1942, by New Directions. Reprinted by permission of New Directions.

from *The Selected Writings of Paul Valery*, "Helen, the Sad Queen," tr. Janet Lewis, copyright 1950, by New Directions. Reprinted by permission of New Directions.

from *Selected Poems* by Muriel Rukeyser, "Who in One Lifetime," copyright 1951, by Muriel Rukeyser. Reprinted by permission of New Directions.

from *Personae* by Ezra Pound, "A Pact," and "The Spring" copyright 1926, by Ezra Pound. Reprinted by permission of New Directions.

from *The Cantos* by Ezra Pound, "Canto XVII," copyright 1934, 1937, 1940, 1948, by Ezra Pound. Reprinted by permission of New Directions.

from *Collected Earlier Poems of William Carlos Williams*, "The Yachts" and "Flowers by the Sea," copyright 1938, 1951, by William Carlos Williams. Reprinted by permission of New Directions.

from *Collected Poems* by Dylan Thomas, "The Force That Through the Green Fuse Drives the Flower," "Fern Hill," "In My Craft or Sullen Art," "A Refusal to Mourn the Death, by Fire, of a Child in London," and "Do Not Go Gentle into That Good Night," copyright 1952, 1953, by Dylan Thomas. Reprinted by permission of New Directions.

from *The Giant Weapon* by Yvor Winters, "By the Road to the Air-Base," copyright 1943, by New Directions. Reprinted by permission of New Directions.

from *The Sorrow Dance* by Denise Levertov, "The Wings" and "Living." Copyright 1967.

from *Bending the Bow* by Robert Duncan, "My Mother Would Be a Falconress." Copyright 1968.

W. W. NORTON COMPANY

from *Translations from the Poetry of Rainer Maria Rilke*, tr. M. D. Herter Norton, Co., Inc. Reprinted by permission of the publishers.

OXFORD UNIVERSITY PRESS

from *Undercliff:* Poems 1946–1953 by Richard Eberhart, 1953, "The Horse Chestnut Tree." Reprinted by permission of Oxford University Press, Inc.

from *Selected Poems* by Richard Eberhart, 1951, "The Fury of Aerial Bombardment." Reprinted by permission of Oxford University Press, Inc.

NORMAN HOLMES PEARSON

for "Evening" by H. D. Reprinted by permission of Norman Holmes Pearson, owner of copyright.

RANDOM HOUSE

from *The Edge of Being* by Stephen Spender, copyright 1949 by Stephen Spender. Reprinted by permission of Random House, Inc.

from *Such Counsels You Gave to Me* and Other Poems by Robinson Jeffers, "Oh, Lovely Rock" and "All the Little Hoofprints," copyright 1937, by Random House, Inc. Reprinted by permission of Random House, Inc.

from *Poems 1940–1953* by Karl Shapiro, "The Twins," copyright 1942, by Karl Jay Shapiro. Reprinted by permission of Random House, Inc.

from *The Collected Poetry of W. H. Auden,* "In Memory of W. B. Yeats," copyright 1940, by W. H. Auden, and "Nothing is given; we must find our law," copyright 1945, by W. H. Auden. All reprinted by permission of Random House, Inc.

from *Glad and Sorry Seasons* by Leonard Nathan.

RICE, STANLEY

from *Forty-three Poems* by Stanley Rice, "The Bicycle," "On the Murder of Martin Luther King."

ROMAN BOOKS, INC.

from *The Anatomy of Love* by J. W. Corrington, "Algerien Reveur." Copyright 1964.

JAMES SCHEVILL

for "A Guilty Father to His Daughter." Reprinted by permission of the author.

CHARLES SCRIBNER'S SONS

from *The Children of the Night* by Edwin Arlington Robinson, "Luke Havergal." Reprinted by permission of Charles Scribner's Sons.

THE SOCIETY OF AUTHORS

for "The Listeners" by Walter de la Mare. Reprinted by permission of the Literary Trustees of Walter de la Mare and The Society of Authors as their representative.

for Poems XL and XLIII by A. E. Housman. Reprinted by permission of the Society of Authors as the Literary Representative of the Trustees of the estate of the late A. E. Housman's Collected Poems.

SOUTHERN REVIEW

for "Before an Old Painting of the Crucifixion" by N. Scott Momaday.

VANGUARD PRESS

from *Collected Poems* by Edith Sitwell, "Heart and Mind," copyright 1946, 1954, by Dame Edith Sitwell. Reprinted by permission of the publishers.

THE VIKING PRESS

from *Last Poems* by D. H. Lawrence, "Trees in the Garden," copyright 1933, by Frieda Lawrence. Reprinted by permission of The Viking Press.

VINTAGE BOOKS, INC.

from *Snaps* by Victor Cruz, "Walking on the Lips of the Bronx" and "latin & soul." Copyright 1969.

A. P. WATT & SON

for "Lovers in Winter," "Through Nightmare," and "Counting the Beats" by Robert Graves. Reprinted by permission of A. P. Watt & Son.

WESLEYAN UNIVERSITY PRESS

from *Poems: 1957–1967* by James Dickey, "The Shark's Parlor." Copyright 1967.

WILLIAMSON MUSIC

for "It Might As Well Be Spring," by Oscar Hammerstein, copyright 1945, by Williamson Music Inc. Reprinted by permission of Williamson Music Inc., New York.

YALE UNIVERSITY PRESS

from *The Lost Pilot* by James Tate, "The Lost Pilot." Copyright 1967.

NOBUYUKI YUASA

for "New Moon" by Basho, translated by Nobuyuki Yuasa. Reprinted by permission of the translator.

Contents

64894

АĒ8Аꓛ

Preface

To like a poem is to want to talk about it, to learn more about it, to hear it over and think about what is heard. This book begins with the ways and terms of such hearing. Then it proceeds to an abundance of poems of all kinds, composed from different points of view by more than a hundred poets of five centuries in England and America, including in its revision new poets of the mid-twentieth century.

Many critical readings of the book have made its completion possible: readings by Maynard Mack of Yale University, George P. Elliott of Syracuse University, Richard Worthen of Diablo Valley College, Roberta Holloway of San Jose State College, Robert Beloof of the Rhetoric Department and Mark Schorer of the English Department of the University of California. The ideas of students in 143, 149, 247 at the University of California have aided in the making. Harriet Polt helped in the beginning and Elizabeth Kaupp immeasurably in the completion of the work. Beverly Wilson assisted in the preparation of the first revision, Rita Fattaruso and Elin Stetz in this revision. To all of these, I make grateful acknowledgment.

Josephine Miles

The Ways of the Poem

I

Ways of the Poem: Whole Tone, Component Parts

WAYS OF POETRY NOW

The ways of poetry are many, and in our time they are vibrant with a sense of strong resources and demands. Around us we hear the words of old and new ballads, blues, sutras, haiku, shouts, meditations, chants, songs, and observations. It is a vocal world. Poetry keeps moving from the page to films, to records, and stages; poetry is read at births, deaths, marriages, protests, and be-ins. Trying to exemplify and contain it within the quiet frame of the covers of a book helps give a more steady view of its life and times.

A collection is the result of choices; the basis of choice in *Ways of the Poem* is a variety of values; enough of Renaissance, Romantic, and Modern work, enough of each of the major tones, enough of individual poets, so that the patterns of development become clear and the patterns of the present speak out in their richness of variety.

Poetry now is not just one voice, not just one poetic present; rather, it is a welter of individual voices from which may gradually emerge, when one listens, certain chief tones of concern and ways of expression drawing on precedents past and worldwide. Consider the poetry of rock, for example, with its variations upon the strongly accented English and Spanish ballad tradition; or the poetry of meditation, drawing upon the metaphysical poets of the seventeenth century; or the poetry of ode and chant, drawing upon eighteenth century resources and Milton, Whitman, India; or the poetry of observation, photographic accuracy and selectivity, of the imagist tradition, French or Japanese, objective and reportorial.

From the sixteenth to the twentieth century, from young Wyatt of King Henry's court to young Cruz of New York's East Side, poetry has had its say. Ginsberg claims as ancestors Milton and the Bible as well as Whitman; Levertov, Ammons, Creeley, and LeRoi Jones use great reportorial delicacy; compare Momaday's Indian control to that of the anonymous Indian poem earlier quoted or the perspectives of Al Young and Victor Cruz.

As in the first part of the twentieth century poetry felt the energy of its own English heritage, now in the second half it is moved by the excitement of tones beyond the European scene, older in time and more distant in place and so closer to home, whether home be Snyder's California, Stafford's Iowa and Oregon, Corrington's New Orleans, Dickey's Georgia, Creeley's New Mexico, Jones' New Jersey, or Levertov's New York. Place, time, modes of music, ways of seeing and speaking, all work together at the poem's center.

The discussion which follows is for those who enjoy observing how poems work. The simplest terms for naming the parts of a poem and how they relate to the whole are discussed in general and in relation to certain basic sorts of wholes, with a survey of how these basic sorts have developed in our history. The poems themselves appear in chronological order by birthdate of the poet, so that they may be followed by the reader in the stream of time, or dipped into anywhere, backwards or forwards, as a line speaks out to him. Renaissance, Romantic, and Modern poetry provide three historical centers; the moderns are presented most fully, especially in poets under forty, because they are least known.

STRUCTURE, SOUND, AND SUBSTANCE

Talking becomes poetry as walking becomes dancing. It takes on a form to give shape to a mood or idea. As the steps in dance do not merely follow one after another but are grouped, accented, and repeated, so the words in poetry are grouped by stresses, the stresses by lines. The foot, or the beat, is a measure for verbal lines as for spatial ones. Such measure in language designs a close, formal pattern. When you measure so closely what you are saying, by stresses or feet, you are probably not setting out on the long progress of the novel, event by event; not undertaking the conflict of drama, scene by scene; rather, you are focusing on the structure of sound, as in song, where the beat and the phrase and the verse-line provide the units of emphasis, and what is said, because it seems valuable, is made memorable in closely organized pattern.

Poetry, like history and science, is a way of using language. Like drama and story, it is a way of using language as art, giving it significant shape. Like music and dance, but characteristically in its own materials of language, it is an art of significant shape in harmony and sound. So the poem accentuates in the substance and structure of language, in the sentences and what they refer to, the special pattern of their sound.

As poetry is an art of language, its component parts are the parts of language: *structure*, the way the words and sentences are put together; *substance*, what they refer to; *sound*, their rhythm and tone-quality. From a simple sentence to a complex combination of sentences, the interrelationship of structure, sound, and substance is based upon tone. A tone natural for a *structure* of argument will differ from one for a *structure* of exclamation. A tone suitable for one kind of *substance* or subject matter will not be identical with that for another *substance*. And in *sound*, a stressed tone or a sharp tone will vary markedly from an unstressed or a flat tone. Tone may apply to single components and to the poem as a whole. When referring to the whole, it describes the poem's character and entity. If you listen to a poem read aloud at a distance, you may not hear the words, but you will be able to catch from its whole tone its character.

The traditional division of poetry into narrative, dramatic, and lyric is based upon the emphasis of the whole tone. The narrative is objective: the speaker stands apart and tells what happens, what he sees. The dramatic involves conflict, the argument or dialogue of more than one point of view. The lyric, because it centers in the first person, can afford the simplicity of a melody which dominates both substance and structure. In our day, most poetry is lyrical—the narrative having become prosaic as in the novel and short story, the drama having turned to prose on stage and screen—but still among lyrics we may distinguish these differing emphases of tone: the direct candor and judgment of narrative representation, the logical argumentation of implied or direct dialogue, the fervor of exclamation.

On the printed page, it is not the print but the heard tone of the speaking poem that counts; in the brief lyric that follows, for example, the *I* and his exclamation:

> Western wind, when wilt thou blow?
> The small rain down can rain,—
> Christ, if my love were in my arms
> And I in my bed again!

To read this poem is to hear its whole tone. What do we hear? The *sound* is built from the repetition of words and syllables, as if to intensify the mind's turning upon a single thought, and from swift rhythms that throw the repetitions into relief by bringing them back upon the ear with speed. The *structure* is that of an implied prayer to the natural forces of wind and rain and love. And the *substance* or subject is the power of the personal *my arms, my bed*—the warmth of love—to sustain the storm. If we disagree about any of these statements, we can look again, in more detail, at the sound, structure, substance, to see what they are and how they fit together. And what we shall come up with, finally, is a revised or renewed sense of this anonymous medieval poem's whole tone.

Or again,

> I'm going out to clean the pasture spring;
> I'll only stop to rake the leaves away
> (And wait to watch the water clear, I may):
> I sha'n't be gone long.—You come too.
>
> I'm going out to fetch the little calf
> That's standing by the mother. It's so young,
> It totters when she licks it with her tongue.
> I sha'n't be gone long.—You come too.

The tone here is mild in comparison to that of the "Wind." It is deliberate, familiar; someone is being spoken with, and an answer is implied. The natural details are simple and serene—leaves, spring-water, calf—an easily accepted *substance*. The *sound* shows a pattern of regular, and thus easily acceptable, rhyme and stress within the natural accents of speech. The *structure* begins with declarative statements and moves to imperatives which have the effect of petition. There may be intensity of desire in this poem, too, then; Robert Frost's speaker may be very eager for the companionship he asks; but he speaks in a tone of voice different from the anonymous speaker's; he appears to be a different sort of person, less able to speak his feeling with lyrical directness of exclamation, more involved in the hesitancies and expectancies of a dramatic situation for which the setting is his planned trip to the pasture. The animals and even *you* seem the object of his tenderness and responsibility, while for the anonymous poet the forces of nature are larger than he, stormy and passionate as well as tender.

Then hear how much more cool and aloof, how precise, how objectively centered, is the tone of William Carlos Williams's poem "Flowers by the Sea." These lines neither exclaim nor invite, but carefully and exactly observe and describe.

> When over the flowery, sharp pasture's
> edge, unseen, the salt ocean
>
> lifts its form—chickory and daisies
> tied, released, seem hardly flowers alone
>
> but color and the movement—or the shape
> perhaps—of restlessness, whereas
>
> the sea is circled and sways
> peacefully upon its plantlike stem

What is Williams's view? That flowers beside the sea seem an embodiment of restlessness, the sea itself seems so stabilized and peaceful. The tone is one of careful and patient and absorbed discrimination in the making of this contrast between flowers of the land and the flower of the sea. The *structure* is one of logical declarative statement: *When* the ocean lifts its form . . . daisies seem hardly flowers alone, but restlessness, *whereas* the sea sways peacefully. So that the patterns of *sound* may not interfere with the delicate sight, there is no rhyme or other shaping pattern of repetition, and no regular pattern of stress or beat, but rather an ordered progression and balancing of phrases which is called *cadence*. (See Index of

Terms for further explanation of all such unfamiliar terms.) The one strong quality of the sound is *onomatopoeia,* an echoing of the sense: the three end words, *ocean, alone, stem,* make in their *n* and *m* sounds the same contrast to the *s* of *pasture's, daisies, shape, whereas, sways,* that the calm ocean makes to the restless flowers, in Williams's way of seeing them. Sound and structure both serve to emphasize the precisions of a third-personal, objective observation of *substance,* of sharp pasture's edge, salt ocean, chickory, daisies.

We have heard in these three brief poems three different tones of voice established by three different relationships of *sound* to *substance* to *structure.* The first cries aloud in intense personal feeling, using rhyme, repetition, and exclamation to help convey in lyric *sound* a feeling that is indicated in the simple substance. The second speaks gently and directly to another person; the natural facts are fully given and the sounds are richly repetitive, not for the projection of an inner state so much as for the speaker's effect upon the hearer: in this poem it is the *structure* of persuasion that is stressed. The third poem is most impersonal, in that the poet—and there is no other speaker implied—gives over his self to the observed object; in this poem, *substance* dominates, conditioning both the structure, which is one of contrast, and the contrasting sounds. The whole tone of any poem is given distinction by one of these emphases of component parts. Theoretically, perhaps, all could carry equal weight and power, but the tendency then might be to pull apart. Some subordination of one power of language to another is effective in the composition of the whole. A dominant substance will draw sound to its service; a rich sound-pattern will override structure; a complex structure will alter the features of substance in new ways. Conflicting elements will make for tension and ambiguity of tone; collaborating elements, for a simpler unity. The art of combining the elements, of using all the powers of language, is the art of making the poem.

COMPONENTS IN FAMILIAR FORMS

Let us look at more poems, almost all anonymous like "Western Wind," for more examples of ways of combination. Nursery rhymes, ballads, hymns, popular songs, all are part of the tradition of poetry in our language, composed perhaps by

one individual and preserved by voice through many generations, or perhaps composed by successive individuals, each
altering the pattern a bit, so that we have many versions of
one basic theme or thought. All, being oral, are closely connected with song, so that sound is closely organized in each of
them; but note to what different effects. First in three nursery
rhymes, then in three ballads, three popular songs, and three
hymns, note the varieties of whole tone, the special emphatic
composition of each work.

THE HOUSE THAT JACK BUILT

This is the house that Jack built.

This is the malt
That lay in the house that Jack built.

This is the rat,
That ate the malt   5
That lay in the house that Jack built.

This is the cat,
That killed the rat,
That ate the malt
That lay in the house that Jack built.   10

This is the dog,
That worried the cat,
That killed the rat,
That ate the malt
That lay in the house that Jack built.   15

This is the cow with the crumpled horn,
That tossed the dog,
That worried the cat,
That killed the rat,
That ate the malt   20
That lay in the house that Jack built.

This is the maiden all forlorn,
That milked the cow with the crumpled horn,
That tossed the dog,
That worried the cat,   25

That killed the rat,
That ate the malt
That lay in the house that Jack built.

This is the man all tattered and torn,
That kissed the maiden all forlorn, 30
That milked the cow with the crumpled horn,
That tossed the dog,
That worried the cat,
That killed the rat,
That ate the malt 35
That lay in the house that Jack built.

This is the priest all shaven and shorn,
That married the man all tattered and torn,
That kissed the maiden all forlorn,
That milked the cow with the crumpled horn, 40
That tossed the dog,
That worried the cat,
That killed the rat,
That ate the malt
That lay in the house that Jack built. 45

This is the cock that crowed in the morn,
That waked the priest all shaven and shorn,
That married the man all tattered and torn,
That kissed the maiden all forlorn,
That milked the cow with the crumpled horn, 50
That tossed the dog,
That worried the cat,
That killed the rat,
That ate the malt
That lay in the house that Jack built. 55

This is the farmer sowing his corn,
That kept the cock that crowed in the morn,
That waked the priest all shaven and shorn,
That married the man all tattered and torn,
That kissed the maiden all forlorn, 60
That milked the cow with the crumpled horn,
That tossed the dog,
That worried the cat,
That killed the rat,
That ate the malt 65
That lay in the house that Jack built.

THE SILVER STY

There was a lady loved a swine,
    Honey, quoth she,
Pig-hog wilt thou be mine?
    Hoogh, quoth he.

I'll build thee a silver sty,   5
    Honey, quoth she,
And in it thou shalt lie.
    Hoogh, quoth he.

Pinned with a silver pin,
    Honey, quoth she,   10
That thou may go out and in.
    Hoogh, quoth he.

Wilt thou have me now,
    Honey? quoth she.
Speak or my heart will break.   15
    Hoogh, quoth he.

WHEN I WAS A LITTLE BOY

When I was a little boy I lived by myself,
And all the bread and cheese I got I laid upon a shelf;
The rats and the mice they made such a strife,
I had to go to London-town and buy me a wife.

The streets were so broad and the lanes were so narrow,   5
I was forced to bring my wife home in a wheelbarrow.
The wheelbarrow broke and my wife had a fall,
Farewell wheelbarrow, little wife and all.

We can see that "The House That Jack Built" is marvelously focussed upon *substance*. As in the old song "The Twelve Days of Christmas," sound-pattern and structure are fixed in simple, repetitive form to provide a frame for the building up of substance. A story is told, but it is told through added substance, not through the standard narrative procedure of *then, and then, and then,* in active clauses. Add rat to malt, and cat to rat, and eventually you get romance and marriage in the house that Jack built.

"The Silver Sty," on the other hand, is a dramatic rhyme: the conflict is greater, and the outcome not so gradual. What is a lady doing, loving a swine? Evidently she knows, for she proposes a generous compromise: his own environment, freely controlled, but improved with silver. Evidently he is not so flexible of mind, for while hers is the varied and persuasive thought and substance of the poem, his is the inarticulate and steadily repeated refrain. In the *structure* lies the drama of the poem, the contrast between two characters, the lady with her imploring adaptability of rich substance, the swine with his steady, impervious response of rough sound.

Of the three nursery rhymes, it is the first-personal "Little Boy" which is, as we might have supposed, most "subjective" or inward. This speaker is not telling us all he knows: the connection between streets, wheelbarrow, fall, and farewell is never clarified. He might have made the same point with different substance and structure entirely; both are cryptic, suggesting more than they reveal. But the *sound* is clear and emphatic in making the point: that the speaker feels the reasonableness of his story. The sound is steady, downright, regularly rhymed, conclusive. This was a man not happily suited to marriage, neither alert like the man all tattered and torn, nor taciturn like the swine. The whole tone of his poem is neither constructive nor dramatic, but lyrically self-involved.

In reading the ballads that follow, consider the difference between the straightaway narrative progression of "Barbara Ellen," the dramatic revelations of "The Two Corbies," and the lyrical concentration on personal feeling in "Springfield Mountain." The Indian song has a more communal anonymity. In reading the popular songs, notice in "You're the Top" how the identifications provide the feeling of superlatives, emphasizing substance in description rather than in interaction; in "Spring," how the comparisons are subordinated to a complexity of restless sound expressive of a much more inward feeling; and how "Goin' Away Blues" moves farther than the others toward the actual dramatizing of relationship. Recent writers like Dylan, Lennon, and Cohen move toward a similar range.

Finally, try to distinguish the powerfully different whole

tones of the hymns. First, the objective and emphatic controlling force of the substance of the "Spacious Firmament," wherein regularly measured sound subserves the main effect produced by the words for great cosmic materials, *shining frame, unwearied sun, moon, stars, planets, dark terrestrial ball, radiant orbs,* and the *divine hand* that made them. Then, in contrast to this objective and descriptive view, the more melodious and subjective one of "O God, Our Help," in which personal feeling makes a thousand ages as one evening, time is suspended as in a dream, and God is called upon in an instant as in eternity. Each poem has its own characteristic entity, in mood, in formal combination of qualities, and in resultant effect.

BONNY BARBARA ELLEN

"In Scotland was I bred and born;
In Yorkshire was my dwelling;
And there I fell in love with a pretty fair maid,
    And her name was Barbara Ellen.

"I sent a boy down to her house,   5
    To the house that she did dwell in;
I sent him to her father's house.
    Her name was Barbara Ellen.

"Look up, look up at my bed-head,
    You'll see a napkin hanging;   10
In that you'll find a gold watch and chain,
    And that's for Barbara Ellen.

"Look down, look down at my bed-foot,
    You'll see a trunk a-standing;
It's full of gold and jewelry,   15
    And that's for Barbara Ellen.

"Look down, look down at my bed-side,
    You'll see a bowl o'erflowing;
And in that bowl there's my heart's blood,
    That's shed for Barbara Ellen."   20

So slowly she put on her clothes;
    So slowly she went walking;

So slowly, as she crossed the field,
She met the corpse a-coming.

"Oh, lay him down, oh, lay him down,   25
That I may gaze upon him."
The more she gazed, and still she gazed,
She could not keep from smiling.

The young men cried out, "Oh fie! for shame
Hard-hearted Barbara Ellen!   30
There's many a wealthy squire died
For cruel Barbara Ellen."

She went down into yonder vale;
She could hear the dead-bell's knelling,
And every toll it seemed to say,   35
"Hard-hearted Barbara Ellen!"

"Oh, father, father! dig my grave,
And dig it deep and narrow;
For a young man died for me to-day,
I'll die for him to-morrow."   40

On the one was buried a red rose bud,
On the other, a sweet brier;
And they grew and they grew to the church-steeple top,
Till they could grow no higher.
There they twined in a true-lover's knot,   45
For all true lovers to admire.

THE TWO CORBIES

As I was walking all alone
I heard two corbies making a moan;
The t'one unto the t'other say,
"Where shall we go and dine to-day?"

"In behind yon old fail dike,   5
I wot there lies a new slain knight;
And nobody kens that he lies there,
But his hawk, his hound, and lady fair.

corbies—crows
fail—fallen

12

"His hound is to the hunting gone,
His hawk to fetch the wild-fowl home,   10
His lady's ta'en another mate,
So we may make our dinner sweet.

"Ye'll sit on his white house-bone,
And I'll pick out his bonny blue een;
With a lock of his golden hair   15
We'll thick our nest when it grows bare.

"Many a one for him makes moan,
But none shall ken where he is gone;
O'er his white bones, when they are bare,
The wind shall blow for evermair."

SPRINGFIELD MOUNTAIN

On Springfield Mountain there did dwell
A likely youth and known full well—
A likely youth of twenty one,
Leftenant Curts's only son—
   Only son, only son, only son—   5
   Leftenant Curts's only son.

One Monday morning he did go
Down to the meadow for to mow.
He mowed all day. At last he feels
A pison sarpent bite his heels.   10
   Bite his heels, bite his heels, bite his heels—
   A pison sarpent bite his heels.

He laid his scythe upon the ground—
He laid it down and looked around
To see if nobody he couldn't espy   15
To carry him home that he might die—
   That he might die, that he might die, that he might die—
   To carry him home that he might die.

He looked around, but looked in vain—
No one was there to ease his pain;   20
So he made up his mind his time had come,
And laid his head on a cold stun—

On a cold stun, a cold stun, a cold stun—
And laid his head on a cold stun.

So this young man gave up the ghost,   25
And forth to Abraham's bosom did post
Out of the meadow he came to mow,
With nobody by to see him go,
    To see him go, see him go, see him go,
With nobody by to see him go.

from THE SONGS OF THE MASKED DANCERS

APACHE
(From a translation by Pliny Earle Goddard, *Astrov, 215*)

The day broke in slender rain,
East, where the dawn strikes,
West, where lightning water stands,
North, south, east, west,
Day dawns with life.   5

I am there and go
Among the sky boys.
One came to me
With long life,
Prayed over   10
My body with
His longest life:
His life given to me.

The holy sky boy
Spoke four times,   15
Prayed in thunder
Over my body.

Thunder spoke
Four times until
His speaking   20
Became my breathing.

YOU'RE THE TOP

COLE PORTER

You're the top, you're the Coliseum,
You're the top, you're the Louvre Museum,
You're a melody
      From a symphony   5
        By Strauss,
You're a Bendel Bonnet
    A Shakespeare sonnet,
        You're Mickey Mouse!
You're the Nile,   10
      You're the Tower of Pisa,
You're the smile
      Of the Mona Lisa,
I'm a worthless check,
      A total wreck,   15
        A flop,
But if, baby, I'm the bottom, you're the top!

IT MIGHT AS WELL BE SPRING

OSCAR HAMMERSTEIN

I'm as restless as a willow in a windstorm,
I'm as jumpy as a puppet on a string!
(I'd say that I had spring fever,
But I know it isn't spring.)
I am starry-eyed and vaguely discontented,   5
Like a nightingale without a song to sing.
(Oh, why should I have spring fever
When it isn't even spring?)

I keep wishing I were somewhere else,
Walking down a strange new street,   10
Hearing words that I have never heard
From a man I've yet to meet.

I'm as busy as a spider, spinning daydreams,
I'm as giddy as a baby on a swing.
I haven't seen a crocus or a rosebud   15
Or a robin on the wing,
But I feel so gay—in a melancholy way—
That it might as well be spring . . .
It might as well be spring.

JOE TURNER BLUES

W. C. HANDY

You'll never miss the water till your well runs dry,
Till your well runs dry.
You'll never miss Joe Turner till he says "Good Bye."

Sweet Babe, I'm goin' to leave you, and the time ain't long,
No, the time ain't long.   5
If you don't b'lieve I'm leavin' count the days I'm gone.

You will be sorry, be sorry from your heart,
Sorry to your heart,
Someday when you and I must part.

And ev'ry time you hear a whistle blow,   10
Hear a steamboat blow,
You'll hate the day you lost your Joe.

THE SPACIOUS FIRMAMENT ON HIGH

JOSEPH ADDISON

The spacious firmament on high,
With all the blue ethereal sky,
And spangled heav'ns, a shining frame,
Their great Original proclaim.
Th' unwearied sun, from day to day,   5
Does his Creator's pow'r display,
And publishes to every land
The work of an Almighty hand.

Soon as the evening shades prevail,
The moon takes up the wondrous tale,   10
And nightly to the list'ning earth
Repeats the story of her birth;
Whilst all the stars that round her burn,
And all the planets, in their turn,
Confirm the tidings as they roll,   15
And spread the truth from pole to pole.

What, though in solemn silence all
Move round the dark terrestrial ball;
What, though no real voice or sound
Amidst their radiant orbs be found;   20

In Reason's ear they all rejoice,
And utter forth a glorious voice,
For ever singing as they shine:
"The hand that made us is Divine."

O GOD, OUR HELP IN AGES PAST

ISAAC WATTS

O God, our help in ages past,
  Our hope for years to come,
Our shelter from the stormy blast,
  And our eternal home;
Beneath the shadow of Thy throne   5
  Thy saints have dwelt secure;
Sufficient is Thine arm alone,
  And our defence is sure.

Before the hills in order stood,
  Or earth received her frame,   10
From everlasting Thou art God,
  To endless years the same.
A thousand ages in Thy sight
  Are like an evening gone;
As short the watch that ends the night   15
  Before the rising sun.

Time, like an overflowing stream,
  Bears all its sons away:
They fly forgotten, as a dream
  Dies at the opening day.   20
Our God, our help in ages past,
  Our hope for years to come,
Be Thou our guard while troubles last,
  And our eternal home.

THE PILLAR OF THE CLOUD

JOHN HENRY NEWMAN

Lead, Kindly Light, amid the encircling gloom,
  Lead Thou me cn!
The night is dark, and I am far from home—
  Lead Thou me on!

Keep Thou my feet; I do not ask to see   5
The distant scene—one step enough for me.

I was not ever thus, nor prayed that Thou
    Shouldst lead me on.
I loved to choose and see my path; but now
    Lead Thou me on!   10
I loved the garish day, and, spite of fears,
Pride ruled my will; remember not past years.

So long Thy power hath blessed me, sure it still
    Will lead me on,
O'er moor and fen, o'er crag and torrent, till   15
    The night is gone;
And with the morn those angel faces smile
Which I have loved long since, and lost awhile.

COMPONENTS IN FOREIGN FORMS

In varying ways, our tradition of common song shows us that even the words sung by many people, whole groups or generations of people, are composed to give a single unified tone, a whole sense drawn from the combination of the powers of language, its substance in reference, its structure, and its sound. The hearing of poems in a foreign language shows us this same unity of composition, by reminding us how the powers of one language differ from those of another, so that we may understand and even translate substance, for example, but lose the basic effect of the sound, or keep something of the sound but lose the particular structure of the foreign idiom.

The following examples of poems in another language are preceded by English translations, so that each different language may be heard with some simple sense of its meaning.

HUNTER

(TR. STEPHEN SPENDER AND J. L. GILI)

Above the pine trees:
four pigeons go through the air.

Four pigeons
fly and turn round.

They carry wounded   5
their four shadows.

Below the pine trees:
four pigeons lie on the earth.

CAZADOR

F. GARCIA LORCA

¡Alto pinar!
Cuatro palomas por el aire van.

Cuatro palomas
vuelan y tornan.
Llevan heridas   5
sus cuatro sombras.

¡Bajo pinar!
Cuatro palomas en la tierra están.

PRELUDE

(TR. M. D. HERTER NORTON)

Whoever you are: at evening step forth
out of your room, where all is known to you;
last thing before the distance lies your house:
whoever you are.
With your eyes, which wearily   5
scarce from the much-worn threshold free themselves,
you lift quite slowly a black tree
and place it against the sky: slender, alone.
And you have made the world. And it is large
and like a word that yet in silence ripens.   10
And as your will takes in the sense of it,
tenderly your eyes let it go . . .

19

EINGANG

RAINER MARIA RILKE

Wer du auch seist: am Abend tritt hinaus
aus deiner Stube, drin du alles weisst;
als letztes vor der Ferne liegt dein Haus:
Wer du auch seist.
Mit deinen Augen, welche müde kaum   5
von der verbrauchten Schwelle sich befrein,
hebst du ganz langsam einen schwarzen Baum
und stellst ihn vor den Himmel: schlank, allein.
Und hast die Welt gemacht. Und sie ist gross
und wie ein Wort, das noch im Schweigen reift.   10
Und wie dein Wille ihren Sinn begreift,
lassen sie deine Augen zärtlich los . . .

HELEN, THE SAD QUEEN

(TR. JANET LEWIS)

Azure, 'tis I, come from Elysian shores,
To hear the waves break on sonorous steps,
And see again the sunrise full of ships,
Rising from darkness upon golden oars.

My solitary arms call on the kings   5
Whose salty beards amused my silver hands.
I wept; they sang of triumphs in far lands,
And gulfs fled backwards upon watery wings.
I hear the trumpet and the martial horn
That wield the rhythm of the beating blade,   10
The song of rowers binding the tumult.

And the gods! exalting on the prow with scorn
Their ancient smile that the slow waves insult,
Hold out their sculptured arms to my sad shade.

HÉLÈNE

PAUL VALÉRY

Azur! c'est moi . . . Je viens des grottes de la mort
Entendre l'onde se rompre aux degrés sonores,
Et je revois les galères dans les aurores
Ressusciter de l'ombre au fil des rames d'or.

Mes solitaires mains appellent les monarques   5
Dont la barbe de sel amusait mes doigts purs;
Je pleurais. Ils chantaient leurs triomphes obscurs
Et les golfes enfouis aux poupes de leurs barques,

J'entends les conques profondes et les clairons
Militaires rythmer le vol des avirons;   10
Le chant clair des rameurs enchaîne le tumulte,

Et les Dieux, à la proue héroïque exaltés
Dans leur sourire antique et que l'écume insulte
Tendent vers moi leurs bras indulgents et sculptés.

IMPROVISATION

(TR. BABETTE DEUTSCH)

A flock of keys I had feeding out of my hand,
To clapping of wings and croaking and feathery fight;
On tiptoe I stood and stretched out my arm, and the sleeve
Rolled up, so I felt at my elbow the nudging of night.

And the dark. And a pond in the dark, and the lapping of
    waves.   5
And the birds of the species I-love-you that others deny
Would be killed, so it seemed, before the savage black
    beaks,
The strong and the strident, were ever to falter and die.

And a pond. And the dark. And festive the palpitant flares
From pipkins of midnight pitch. And the boat's keel   10
    gnawed
By the wave. And always the greedy noise of the birds
Who fighting over the elbow fluttered and cawed.

21

The gullets of dams were agurgle, gulping the night.
And the mother birds, if the fledglings on whom they dote
Were not to be fed, would kill, so it seemed, before   15
The roulades would die in the strident, the crooked throat.

YA KLÀVISHEY STÀYU KORMÌL S RUKÌ

BORIS PASTERNAK

Pod hlòpanye krỳlyev, plesk i klyòkot
Ya vỳtyanul rùki, ya vstàl na noskì,
Rukàv zavernùlsya, noch tyòrlas' o lòkot'.
I bỳlo temnò. I èto byl prùd
I volny.—I ptìts iz poròdy lyublyùvas,   5
Kazàlos', skorey umertvỳat, chem umrùt
Kriklìvyye, chòrnyye, krèptkiye klyùvy.

I èto byl prùd. I bỳlo temnò.
Pylàli kubỳshki s polùnochnym dyògtem.
I bỳlo volnòyu obglòdano dnò   10
U lòdki. I grỳzlisya ptìtsy o lòkte.

I noch poloskàlas v gortànyakh zaprùd.
Kazàlos, pokàmest ptenèts ne nakòrmlen,
I sàmki skorèy umertvyàt, chem umrùt
Rulàdy v kriklìvom iskrìvlennom gòrle.

HAIKU

(TR. NOBUYUKI YUASA)

New moon in the sky
And on the earth the faintly
White flowers of wheat.

HAIKU
BASHŌ

Mikazuki ya,
chi wa oboronaru
soba batake.

22

Reading a poem in another language most vividly brings home to us the integration of sound with substance and structure in the art of poetry, for if it is a language strange to us or even partially strange, the uncertainty of one reference or one connective or one pronunciation may throw the whole off balance. And translators, much as they may know of both tongues, are unable wholly to convey integration in one language into another: if they recapture the sound, they may lose exact meaning; and if they follow meaning with word for word exactness, they may lose the shaping of the whole. However little you know of the languages here, you will have been able to catch in the original poems many shades of quality which are missing from the translations, helpful and wise as these may be. See, for example, in Lorca's "Cazador," how the substance has been translated more fully than the sound: pines, pigeons, air, earth, the consequences of the hunter. Lorca used parallels in sound and structure to convey more fully the idea of consequence, *before* the hunter and *after*, and these are almost impossible to carry over into English. Hear how ¡Alto Pinar! sounds sustained, as it should, in contrast to the bumpiness of "Above the pine trees!" And how the sound and structure of "van" is repeated by "tornan" and, sadly, "están," in a strongly meaningful parallel at which "air," "turn around," and "earth" do not even hint.

So too in Rilke's "Eingang," to mention just one point, the light, rippling phrasing of "Whoever you are" cannot rightly convey the necessary upright stability of the monosyllables in "Wer du auch seist." If sense were all of poetry, or if sound were, or structure, then we could create more successful substitutes in another language; it is the interworking complex of all these, the full use of language in its manifold resources of sound and meaning, that makes a poem an entity for which neither analysis nor summary nor translation can provide a substitute, but for which all can help to reveal the parts working in the whole.

DESCRIPTIVE TERMS AND DETAILS

Traditionally, because poetry is as old as any art we have, and because people have enjoyed talking about and labelling its details of construction, just as they do for contemporary sports like baseball and arts like photography, we have built up a stock of descriptive terms for poetic techniques. We may usefully sort and clarify these in their relation to the components of the poem, first in summary form, then with further explanations:

FOR WHOLE TONE

    lyric—tone of exclamation, invocation, unity of mood

    dramatic—tone of question, argument, conflict

    narrative—tone of observation and representation of essentials

FOR STRUCTURE

    Kinds of sentence

    first person—exclamatory, invocative

    second person—questioning, argumentative

    third person—declarative, objective

    Kinds of development

    repetitive, circular

    argumentative, subordinative

    sequential, progressive

FOR SUBSTANCE

    Kinds of words, diction

    archaisms, coinages, clichés, borrowings, variations in dialects and levels of usage

    Kinds of literal reference as subject matter

    denotative-connotative

    concrete-abstract

    specific-general

    Kinds of extensions from literal reference

    symbolic

    metaphoric

    evaluative

FOR SOUND

    Kinds of stress or quantity

    in syllables, feet, phrases, pauses, lines, stanzas

    Kinds of quality

    sounds smooth, rough; sharp, blunt; open, closed; high, low; long, short; hard, soft; sound suiting sense—onomatopoeia

    Kinds of repetitions

    alliteration, assonance and consonance, rhyme, refrain

64894

The elements of sentence-making, of statement-making, are the elements of *structure*. The way a language constructs its sentences is the way it constructs its poems, the characteristics of the sentences giving character to the whole statement. Sentences in English may be declarative; they may be turned into questions or imperatives, involving a second person in a query or command; they may be exclamatory, neither telling nor asking but calling out or invoking. Of the parts of speech in the sentence, the subject-pronouns may be closely related to the type of statement: first person, often exclamatory; second, often interrogative or imperative; third, often declarative. We find, too, that exclamatory statements are apt to use adjectives—"Oh, what a beautiful morning!"—while imperative and second-personal sentences are more apt to use verbs and clauses—"Don't throw bouquets at me"—and declaratives stand between extremes.

In addition to this grammatical function, words have a referential force to name and label *substance*. *Green* not only modifies *grass* grammatically, it labels a whole range of color. In this realm of reference, *green* may extend itself in three possible directions away from the literal or direct naming of a certain range of color: first, toward the symbolic, the green that may stand for *envy,* for example; second, toward the metaphoric, the *green* that parallels inexperience as green wood parallels youth; third, toward the evaluative or superlative—the *really green,* the *greenest.* Much descriptive and imagist poetry tends to use evaluative reference—"out in the west where men are *men,*" or "just one cub, but that a *lion!*" Much medieval and modern poetry uses symbolic reference, the naming of some object or quality of sense which stands for a less definable whole, either by convention or by context —"the lion of Judea!" Much metaphysical and romantic poetry uses metaphoric reference—"Richard the lion-hearted" —finding courage in man as in animal. Firmly implied by all of these extensions of meaning is their basis in usual and accepted reference. The literal states an *is.* The evaluative extends it to a norm or an *ought;* the symbolic to an association, a *may be;* the metaphoric to an *as if,* or *in a way.* Each deepens the literal by limiting it in a special way and thus focussing on certain of its potentialities, the evaluative by *intensification,* as in Gertrude Stein's "a rose is a rose is a rose"; the symbolic by *implication,* as in Eliot's sacred rose; the figurative or metaphoric by *interchange,* as in Burns' love like a red, red rose. (See Index of Terms.)

The literal base itself may vary in diction. The literal terms may refer to objects, actions, persons (*trees, to run, children*), in which case they are called concrete, or to concepts (*truth, democracy*), in which case they are called abstract. They may refer to trees or truth in general, or to a specific tree or truth. They may simply refer to or denote a specific item, *that tree,* or connote also its general connections and associations, *Christmas* or *cross,* or associations more individual, less shared. They may be drawn from various languages, those from Latin sources often seeming more dignified and learned than the shorter, blunter Anglo-Saxon and Germanic terms. Remember Macbeth's "No, this my hand will rather / The multitudinous seas incarnadine, / Making the green one red." They may be coinages and neologisms, invented for special purposes, as *jazz* was for the new product in music, or they may be renewed from a distant past, like *deem* or *bedight,* to give a special antique or literary flavor, called archaism. Just as the quality of speech of one friend of ours may be blunt, brief, specific, colorful, rough, another's may be refined, elaborate, archaic, abstract, and another's may be some combination of these two. The quality of personal style depends not only on *what* is referred to but also on *by what* it is referred to: not only on what topic but on which of its many possible labels or appellations is used.

The quality of personal style rests in *sound,* as well as in *structure* and *substance.* The main characteristics of sound in English poetry are quantitative or qualitative. Quantity in English is stress, emphasis. Since pronouncing the syllable or single sound-unit *emph* takes more energy than either the *a* or *sis* in the word *emphasis,* we mark the difference thus: emphasis. A sentence will contain a number of stresses usually supported by high pitch and strong pause. "He spoke with emphasis and enthusiasm, but didn't really say much, though he went on and on." Poetry sets this naturally irregular pattern of stress against some regular verse or line pattern; that is, it "measures" the rhythm of what is being said. The measure may be so slight as that of mere *cadence* or phrasal patterns—"He spoke with émphasis / and enthúsi-

asm / but didn't really sáy much / though he went on / and
on." In such a cadenced measure, there is no regular number
of syllables between stresses, but each word-grouping has
one main stress, and approximately the same weight as every
other. So the last phrase in "though he went on / and on" may
be set apart from its predecessor to give it more time, to extend its stress, and thus to indicate its importance. Modern free
verse, verse "free" of exact measure, uses such phrasal groupings, giving to each line an irregular number of emphasized
phrasal units.

A stronger measure is that of a regular number of stresses
per line, as in Anglo-Saxon and much modern verse. "He spoke
with emphasis and enthusiasm / But didn't really sáy much,
though he went / On and on into everybody's dinnertime."
There are four naturally emphasized syllables in each of the
first two lines, and by adding a few more words to "on and
on" we make four stresses in this line too, and begin to set up
and fulfill expectations in a regular measure, a pattern. Such a
line or verse pattern is always potential in prose speech; much
of what we say is naturally measured, since stressed syllables
in words tend to alternate with one or two unstressed. But
prose seeks to move straight forward, to proceed, as its *pro*
suggests; it would be slowed down and overemphasized by
doubling back or turning or re*vers*ing into verses or lines; so it
scatters, swallows, or piles up many of its stresses, while poetry
takes the pains to lay them down carefully. The terms *dimeter,*
trimeter, tetrameter, pentameter, hexameter indicate the number of stresses in the line, from two to six, and the terms
iambic and *anapestic* indicate a rhythm rising from one or
two unstressed to a stressed syllable, while *trochaic* and
dactylic indicate the corresponding falling rhythm. (See Index
of Terms, *Meter.*) *Caesura* indicates a pause in the line, often
marked by punctuation, as by the comma after *much* in the
above example.

The strictest verse measure is by number of syllables per
foot or feet per line, as in French and Latin "octosyllabics"
or "decasyllabics," eight or ten syllable lines. Our lines about
the enthusiastic speaker would have to be shorn of a number
of extra syllables and then more closely stressed, in order to
fit this strictest form: He spóke with emphasís, enthusiásm, /
But didn't réally saý much, though he went / Straight on and

on through people's dinnertime." Sometimes it is the pleasure
of the poem to make the thought and measure exactly coincide,
as here. At other times the value lies in the tension or
contrast between the two; Macbeth's "Tomórrow and tomórrow ánd tomórrow / Créeps ín this pétty páce from dáy to
dáy" sets meaning against measure in the first line, as the
two sets of stresses show, and only after the first two words in
the second gets down to an easy correlation. Some poets like to
make sound support substance at every point; others like to set
up dramatic conflict between them; in any case, the character
of the relationship is what counts.

In addition to quantity of number or stress, sound has quality,
often called tone-color: the character of its vowels and consonants; sharpness in p, t, k, hardness in b, d, g, liquidness in l,
m, n, r, sibilance in s, open or closed quality and length or
shortness of vowels, as in the short closed *i* of *ship*, the long
open *i* of *machine,* or the closed *o*ften, the open *o*pen.
Like stresses, these qualities may be given pattern by regular
repetition. The main sorts of repetition are: alliteration, the
repetition of a single initial. letter (Peter Piper picked pep-
pers); assonance and consonance, the repetition of other
vowels and consonants (grave-grain; grave-grove); rhyme, the
repetition of the final stressed syllable of a line plus any unstressed that may follow (cat-mat, tenderly-slenderly); and
refrain, the repetition of whole phrases or whole lines, commonly at the ends of line-groups or stanzas.

Such patterned, expected repetition is carried over from
sound into substance and structure. Key words are repeated.
Special sentence-forms are repeated. Phrases and statements
are set up in parallel, in balance, or in contrast to one another.
Such close arrangement is part of the character of verse-
making, since the line itself calls attention to its form: its
stresses, its relation to substance and statement, its order of
sound, its emphatic beginning (often capitalized), its middle
(where a break or *caesura* often comes), its end (which may
rhyme), and the parallels and groupings by which it is shaped
into stanzas. As in weaving, small flecks of sound recur to
accent design, and whole strands run parallel to support design. When sound, substance, and structure support and en-
force each other, a whole tone evolves, single and positive like
lyric admiration, for example, or complex and double, like
narrative mockery or dramatic irony.

We have been thinking of the interrelationships of the parts of a poem and its working details, and we have been looking at one sort of combination and then another. Traditionally, categories for whole poems have been established by emphasis on some one component. For example, the line or stanza pattern of a poem has served to categorize it, so that we have *blank* or *free verse, couplets, tercets, quatrains, sestets, octets,* and their combination in *sonnets,* seven-line *rhyme royal,* nine-line *Spenserian stanza,* and longer fixed stanza forms like the *rondeau, rondel, villanelle,* and so on. (See Index of Terms.)

Another traditional basis of classification is substance or subject matter. In the past two centuries, many collections of poems have been grouped as poems on nature, love, the seasons, childhood, holidays, or, more minutely, on stars, fish, forests, rivers; or, more abstractly, on thoughts of friendship, religion, patriotism. A modern version of such classification is that based on the biases given to literal subject matter by its metaphoric, symbolic, or evaluative extensions. So we may speak of seventeenth-century metaphysical poetry as poetry of *metaphor;* we speak of the French *symbolist* poetry of the nineteenth-century; we speak of eighteenth-century *descriptive* and twentieth-century *imagist* poetry. All the while, we are selecting one focus or another for our labels. Note that MacLeish's "End of the World" can appropriately be called a sonnet, for its sound pattern; a circus poem, for its substance; or an imagist poem, for the direct sensory quality of its substance, among other possibilities.

The emphasis on structure in the categories of this anthology should complement those on sound and substance in other anthologies in which either verse form or subject matter provides the traditional bases of classification. The nearest to a traditional emphasis on structure is the classical and medieval one on point of view, on theme: the divisions into poems of sorrow, of celebration, of pithy statement, into elegy, ode, prayer, epigram, and so on. These are to be distinguished among the poems which follow. Structures of declaration, address, and exclamation in the third, second, and first persons involve in their tones of speech the very feelings they are aiming to convey, so that feeling is not merely expressed or carried by the poem but is involved in the grammar and syntax. No more than sound-pattern or subject does the structure of point of view provide air-tight compartments for the grouping of poems. The reader may want to reconsider and rearrange, on this or other bases. But at least this basis is a strong and integral one for poetic categories.

What may be said about the relation of categories in poetry to the goodness or badness of the poem? As we have noted, evaluation is one sort of extension of language, and many critics extend *a* poem to *the* poem, to the best, the ideal poem, on the basis of one or another category. There are many poems, they say, but some are more really poems, better than others because they have more sound-pattern, or more images, or more symbols, or more valuable substance, or more exclamation, or more drama than others. A poem on a serious subject may seem more of a poem than one on a trivial subject. A poem on cabbages, if we like cabbages, may seem better than a poem on kings, if we dislike kings. But such extension of the meaning of "poem" is not the work of this introduction, the intention of which is literal and descriptive. Descriptively, a poem is a poem and a good and beautiful poem if its component parts work together to make a whole entity—one poem, not one-and-a-half or two—if sound, structure, and substance serve mutually.

Further evaluation comes from external relationships—of the poem to other poems and further purposes—and all the poems in this collection reveal such relationships, such purposes. The basic critical statement "I value this" includes not only the thorough description of "this," which is the focus of descriptive understanding, but also the description of "I," which every reader makes for himself, and the description of "value," the criteria of judgment. What is important for critical clarity is to interrelate rather than to confuse these three descriptions. If a poem sets up expectations which it does not fulfill, it is not a good poem in its own terms. If you set up expectations which it does not fulfill, it is not a good poem in your terms. If your standards or criteria for valuing a poem are met by it, but you still do not like it, this is what you may very well say: I know it is a good poem, but I just don't like it; we often experience such discrepancies between general standards and specific instances.

Different kinds of goodness, even different kinds of greatness, provide the bases for different choices by each reader. Yet there are common and prolonged agreements, and most of the poems in this book have been admired, as well as perhaps disliked, by many readers over a number of centuries. Your preferences may disagree with some and agree with others on the combined bases of your own character, your principles of value and those of your time, and the character of the poem itself. The poem itself: the attempt of the person with a sense of design to give specific aesthetic shape and entity to the conceptual forces of language; to join philosophy's meaning with history's event in the steadfast design of art.

Beginners in the writing of poetry may find that the whole tone of a poem comes first to the sense. Later, the components—what measure, what line of thought, what words—clarify themselves, sometimes half-consciously, sometimes not until they get spoken or written down. One may have an idea for a poem a long time before the poem takes shape, and the idea itself may be a belief, a sight, a scrap of conversation, a wordless tune. If you want consciously to try to write a poem, start with any of these and mull it over until more pattern and weight accrue to it; feel, for example, how the sight of a person and the echo of a melody may effectively be combined; how a tone of voice may be caught in a sentence or two. Finding poems you like may strengthen the sense of whole tone and how it is composed; finding poets you like, whole styles of composition. Reading in the present, the current magazines like *Poetry* and the experimental quarterlies, and the new poets published each year, and reading in the past the poets who have meant much to us over many years, gives a sense of the traditions we inherit and the ways we may possibly change or deepen them.

COMPARISONS AND CATEGORIES

This chapter of introduction can do no better than to select a variety of poems, to suggest how manifold are the possibilities and powers of the components of language in their combination toward whole forms. First we may note three poems which are clearly argumentative in tone. We may hear how they involve a second person, with interest in relation to that person, with tightly controlled verse-form and procedure of sentences.

In "Counting the Beats" the hearer feels first of all the shifting beat, the variation of sound and meaning within the strong repetitions. *You, love, and I Counting the beats, Where shall we be, Not there but here,* in their basic two-beat iambic pattern set up a partial conflict with the sense, which would stress *you* and *counting* and *where,* and thereby early establish the uneasiness of tone within the regularity of assertion. The increased number of beats in the second and third lines contributes to this effect. The materials of storm and sky are relevant, but not dominant. Perhaps *here,* in addition to *you* and *I* and *counting,* is the important concept.

COUNTING THE BEATS

ROBERT GRAVES

You, love, and I,
(He whispers) you and I,
And if no more than only you and I
What care you or I?

Counting the beats,   5
Counting the slow heart beats,
The bleeding to death of time in slow heart beats,
Wakeful they lie.

Cloudless day,
Night, and a cloudless day;   10
Yet the huge storm will burst upon their heads one day
From a bitter sky.

Where shall we be,
(She whispers) where shall we be,
When death strikes home, O where then shall we be   15
Who were you and I?

Not there, but here,
(He whispers) only here,
As we are, here, together, now and here,
Always you and I.   20

Counting the beats,
Counting the slow heart beats,
The bleeding to death of time in slow heart beats,
Wakeful they lie.

Schevill plays with a greater variety of odd terms in "A Guilty Father," but still is mostly active and relational—as in *gladfully* and *father my way.* The repetitions are of rhymes and alliterations, many of the references metaphoric rather than literal, as in *twist of time, fox hound, her sun, cement, glad gully* and many more.

A GUILTY FATHER TO HIS DAUGHTER

JAMES SCHEVILL

Why are you always glad to me?
Shouts my daughter gladfully
A twist of time a tuneful word
Happy I roll into the glad gully

High father in my Morning Glory   5
Silk virtue violently in me
I rule my family like an old fox hound
And father my way in fancy

When I curse her she catcalls
And cancels her sparky consent   10
Carnal her sun foams out and her flesh
Firms between us fixed as cement

Prince of Fathers in my glad gully
Hobbledehoy in my fatherly rain
Why are you always glad to me?   15
Demon down the fatherly drain.

Robert Bridges more traditionally uses the shaping forces of repetition to create a tone of formal relation. This poem is in one of the traditional French forms called a triolet—eight lines rhyming ABaAabAB, with the capitals indicating repeated lines. Not only do lines end in rhyme, but whole phrases and lines are repeated, with an effect of great artifice but great compactness.

WHEN FIRST WE MET

ROBERT BRIDGES

When first we met we did not guess
That Love would prove so hard a master;
Of more than common friendliness
When first we met we did not guess.
Who could foretell this sore distress
This irretrievable disaster
When first we met?—We did not guess
That Love would prove so hard a master.

What do you notice most immediately then about "The Definition of Beauty," "More About People," "If All the Seas Were One Sea"?

THE DEFINITION OF BEAUTY

ROBERT HERRICK

Beauty, no other thing is, than a Beam
Flasht out between the Middle and Extream.

MORE ABOUT PEOPLE

OGDEN NASH

When people aren't asking questions
They're making suggestions
And when they're not doing one of those
They're either looking over your shoulder or stepping on your toes
And then as if that weren't enough to annoy you   5
They employ you.
Anybody at leisure
Incurs everybody's displeasure.
It seems to be very irking
To people at work to see other people not working,   10
So they tell you that work is wonderful medicine,
Just look at Firestone and Ford and Edison,
And they lecture you till they're out of breath or something
And then if you don't succumb they starve you to death or some-
          thing.
All of which results in a nasty quirk: 15
That if you don't want to work you have to work to earn enough
          money so that you won't have to work.

IF ALL THE SEAS WERE ONE SEA

ANON.

If all the seas were one sea,
What a *great* sea that would be!
If all the trees were one tree,
What a *great* tree that would be!
And if all the axes were one axe,   5
What a *great* axe that would be!
And if all the men were one man,
What a *great* man that would be!
And if the *great* man took the *great* axe,
And cut down the *great* tree,   10
And let it fall into the *great* sea,
What a splish-splash that would be!

Does not the substance dominate? of *beauty, people, seas, trees, men* and *axes?* Note that they are treated as the subjects of the sentences: that is, the statements are made about them, and are made in an objective, impersonal, general, evaluative way with couplet line-endings to emphasize the clear, general statements that are being made. While there are exclamation marks at the ends of some of the lines in "If All the Seas," they are not necessary to the sense, which is simply establishing a superlative norm.

"Hark, Hark," on the other hand, contains no specific exclamation points, but is, as you can tell from listening to its tone, an exclamatory poem. It suggests, rather than stating or arguing, and it does so in varying line lengths. The dogs and the beggars are clear enough substance, but more than stated substance is to be considered: the implications of, the possible symbolic quality of, the one in a velvet gown. Should we ask who this is, or is the poem happier just to preserve the mystery?

HARK HARK

ANON.

Hark, hark,
The dogs do bark,
The beggars are coming to town;
Some in rags,
And some in jags,
And one in a velvet gown.

Sometimes an object is called upon in order to be drawn into the feelings of the spectator, and does not answer back. Such a relationship is that in Earle Birney's "World Winter": the title itself shows that while the sun is at first addressed, what counts is the quality of winter in the poet's heart, which is also in the wrynecked, woedealing world:

WORLD WINTER

EARLE BIRNEY

Sun
proud Bessemer   peltwarmer beauty
these weeks steer us   to scan sky for you.
The dun droppings blur   we drown in snow.
Is this tarnished chimneyplug   in a tenantless room,   5
this sucked wafer   white simpleton
you?

Not chiefly the months   mold you heartcharmer
to scant hammerdent   on hardiron sky
not alone latitude   to lodgers on this   10
your slantwhirling lackey   lifecrusted satellite,
this your one wrynecked   woedealing
world.

MacLeish's "End of the World" moves in sonnet form from an apparently objective narrative devoted to circus substance to a sudden exclamational mystery in *dazed, starless, vast, canceled,* in the interpreting adjectives contributed by the implied exclaimer. It reaches, too, out to more than can be stated.

THE END OF THE WORLD

ARCHIBALD MaCLEISH

Quite unexpectedly as Vasserot
The armless ambidextrian was lighting
A match between his great and second toe
And Ralph the lion was engaged in biting
The neck of Madame Sossman while the drum   5
Pointed, and Teeny was about to cough
In waltz-time swinging Jocko by the thumb—
Quite unexpectedly the top blew off:

And there, there overhead, there, there, hung over
Those thousands of white faces, those dazed eyes, 10
There in the starless dark the poise, the hover,
There with vast wings across the canceled skies,
There in the sudden blackness the black pall
Of nothing, nothing, nothing—nothing at all.

Thomas's "A Refusal" again suggests, in fuller overtones of ceremony, how much cannot be said except by sound and implication. We note as he speaks how interwoven are the irregular lines and rhymes, to suit the mood of the speaker; how rich are the patterns of sounds, beginning with *never* and confirmed at the end with *no other*. We note how little or sentence structure there is; only never . . . until . . . shall I let pray . . . or murder with truth . . . she lies . . . to no other age. The substance of bird, beast, and flower, seed and Thames are important mainly as they provide the natural world in which the young death has taken place and is not mourned, is secret, is not to be murdered by speech, but to be remembered by this ceremony of sound.

A REFUSAL TO MOURN THE DEATH, BY FIRE, OF A CHILD IN LONDON

DYLAN THOMAS

Never until the mankind making
Bird and beast and flower
Fathering and all humbling darkness
Tells with silence the last light breaking
And the still hour 5
Is come of the sea tumbling in harness

And I must enter again the round
Zion of the water bead
And the synagogue of the ear of corn
Shall I let pray the shadow of a sound 10
Or sow my salt seed
In the least valley of sackcloth to mourn

The majesty and burning of the child's death.
I shall not murder
The mankind of her going with a grave truth 15

Nor blaspheme down the stations of the breath
With any further
Elegy of innocence and youth.

Deep with the first dead lies London's daughter,
Robed in the long friends,   20
The grains beyond age, the dark veins of her mother
Secret by the unmourning water
Of the riding Thames.
After the first death, there is no other.

So the component parts of poetry are combinable in various ways, and each individual poem has its individual combination of the sound, substance, and sentence structure of its language. There are probably, too, as many sorts of tone as there are speaking voices. Yet through certain recurrent patterns of language, certain tones are distinguishable, as we have noted them here: the argumentative and questioning tone of a poem involving speech from one person to another; the exclamatory tone of a person speaking deep or high beyond his own capacities; the more even and generalizing attention to substantial fact and value by the narrator and observer who speaks of things and events in the third person. No one component can necessarily establish a tone, but a number in combination may do so. Indeed, historically we note how basic the tone of argument was to most poetry in the sixteenth and seventeenth centuries, how basic the exclamatory was to the romantic eighteenth, how familiar all three ways of speaking are to our modern poetry.

TONE OF QUESTION AND ARGUMENT: CHIEFLY IN THE SECOND PERSON

The *you* of a poem makes for uncertainty and questioning, often even conflict. What will the *you* reply to what is being said? Will he agree, will he be won over, will he in turn present a divergent view, what is the poetic import of this talk with him? The *you* represents doubts, difficulties, and interests just because he is someone else, and one naturally expects to talk to someone else. This is a talking kind of poem, the poem of the second person: its diction is apt to be characteristically natural and colloquial, its metaphors spontaneous and extreme, as they are in conversation; its structure active and complex, as in conversation; its substance subordinated to relationship. Interplay is expected between speaker and listener, and some common knowledge is assumed, so that there need not be a heavy outlay of substance in information.

Those who believe that poetry-making began in the ceremonies of courting, of praying, or of fighting find this sort of two-person poetry to be the most basic sort, as they find drama to be the basic form of literature. Not always, of course, is it clear-cut and fully developed. Sometimes the *you* seems a mere figment in the poem, not seeming to change the situation much, as Auden's "Look, stranger," does not; or sometimes the *you* is in such agreement that no dramatic change results, or at other times is so stiltedly addressed that no feeling of possible response is given; indeed, ceremonious poems of invocation do not imply a dialogue and are more suitably considered as first-person lyrics. Nevertheless, a strong tradition of the second-person colloquial poem has persisted through all the four centuries of modern English poetry, about sixty examples of which are present here in all their varying shapes and tones.

Often, poems are grouped by the century or place in which they were written, or by their subject-matter and substance, or by their sound-patterns. But point of view, as it most fundamentally establishes tone, is more basic still, because tone provides the synthesis. From sound alone without substance, or from substance alone without structure, we cannot tell the whole tone of the poem; it is their combination that matters, and it is the point of view of the speaker that suggests what the combination will be. We may at least fairly expect, though of course we may never count on, the fact that a second person in a poem, as in life, will make for a tone of interchange, of suspense, of relationship, colloquially phrased and complexly structured. The poems of this kind precede historically and dominate English poetry especially in the sixteenth and seventeenth centuries.

The poets of the Renaissance, among them Wyatt and Surrey in mid-sixteenth-century England, were delighted with the new opportunities they felt for the play of courtship in verse. For the many centuries of the Middle Ages, poetry of address had been religious more than secular; Christ and

Mary had been the very personal *you* of poetry. Now a renewed sense of the enjoyable amorousness of classical Latin
verse, and the convention of paying court to the lady in the
chivalric tradition, the making of pleas which would never
be granted, allowed the poets to play over the French and
Italian variations on the theme of steadfast desire unfulfilled
and warm love coldly returned. Whether or not the lady
explicitly answers the plea in the poem, we know what she is
going to say: *no*. We know her to be a lady necessarily pure
and thus necessarily cruel. Note Wyatt's vivid sense of his
own patience, Gascoigne's carefully rounded argument, and
Raleigh's playful reply to Marlowe's passionate shepherd.
Note, from Donne on, a less light-hearted use of the tradition;
either a more intellectual love-making, or a turning back to
heavenly persons as subjects of address. Note the decrease
of these poems of dramatic relationship in the eighteenth century, and their strong recurrence in the nineteenth and twentieth centuries in somewhat less dramatic form, the speaker
petitioning the listener to hear his personal confidence.

Reading Wyatt's "Forget Not Yet," we see the poetry of
a dramatic personal relationship, a reminder of steadfast
loyalty, patient, boasting, apologetic, paradoxically combining
faith with reason, in an equally steadfast *structure* of address.
Sound supports structure in its steady repetitions, the slight
but significant changes in the "forget not" refrain. *Substance*
is abstract; connections rather than objects are important
here: "intent," "service," "assays," the double meaning of
test and acknowledgment in the word "approved," the simpli-
fying of "steadfast" in "never moved"; the substance we see
is repetitive too, following the sound in emphasizing relationship.

Surrey's sonnet is not so wholly devoted to making its own
point clearly felt. Its substance is more various, devoted to
the traits of the lady as well as to the fidelity of the lover,
and the sonnet rhyming is less close, the five-stress line-length
more ample, to cope with these fuller materials; yet the whole is
still focussed upon the relationship of lover to lady. Sidney,
dramatizing the writing of just such sonnets, adds another
beat to every line, and piles effort upon effort, both literal and
figurative, dramatizing the weight of the substance of effort
itself, until he comes to the simplicity of the last line.

For Gascoigne, the relationship for meditation and some dramatization is that between parents and children. So also it is, more cryptically, in Raleigh's "The Wood, the Weed, the Wag." And note how fondly Ben Jonson draws all into the position of "you"—his book, his friend, even the reader, in that familiarity and closeness of feeling which his contemporaries and successors among the metaphysical poets expressed toward the personal thou and you of God.

The dramatic addresses of such later poets as Byron and Browning and Meredith and Hardy are more impersonal in that often the I and you both become imagined characters as in a play. The I of "Childe Roland" is an example. Or the I and you are treated as we, feeling together, as in Meredith's "Winter Heavens" and in the poems of Frost and Auden, the drama of the universe and their relation to it.

A closer look at Herbert's poems will show the way in which the point of view, the assumption of another's presence, pervades and gives form to structure, sound, and substance. In *Jordan*, the speaker asks a number of questions about something he evidently does not believe in. Who *does* believe that verse needs fictions, twists, artifices, enchantments, decorations, catching the sense at two removes? Who does believe in natural scene as poetic truth? Not the speaker! Let others sing, or riddle, or trick; this speaker wants to speak plainly and rhyme plainly, and his plain substance is the greatest and truest of all subjects, of whom and to whom he can speak. What is false hair, a painted chair, a purling stream, a nightingale, in comparison with My God, My King? From neat but scornful patterns of trivial substance, the speaker draws finally the right substance and the right tone for poetry, profound, natural to the human voice, and true.

There is a fight in this poem. The speaker seriously dislikes this *who* and his poetics, perhaps Marlowe's Passionate Shepherd and many others like him, and wastes no time on decorations of sound or sense. He uses a regularly scannable five-line verse form to tie up his neat packets of questions, and he keeps the sound colloquial: "Who says so? I say rather—" The last line of each stanza is emphasized by its shortness as well as by its position, and serves as a crisp summary, the first with a particular negative, the second with a more general negative, the third with a triumphantly particular yet all-encompassing positive.

In *Virtue,* the speaker condescends to address the very substance of sweet spring, days, and roses which he has considered trivial, but here again he is making an argument, ruefully, to their discredit. "Thou must die." Only the sweetness of the soul survives in strength, the seasoned timber amidst wood rotting to coal. *Coal* is the plain speaking of this poem, in contrast to its *roses,* and the ending is therefore indirect, the metaphor of seasoned timber rather than the direct naming of God, but still plain and colloquial in its argumentative tone of voice.

In "Love," the soul itself is one of the speakers, not in a metaphor like timber but in the personification of a character in a scene. The other speaker is Love; it is the Lord now participating in the dialogue, bidding welcome, observing, persuading, questioning, commanding. Note how the short lines alternate with long, to suggest the changes in speaker, and how the final short line, as in the other poems, is the simplest in its sound and attitude.

As you become familiar with these poems of dialogue and question, of a tone which seems to take into account a feeling or position other than its own, you will recognize how variously they can be composed. The feeling of *you* may be as fully developed as that of Swift's Stella, for whom the couplets serve to balance the perspectives, or as little as the second person of Byron's *So We'll Go No More,* who is assumed to share the speaker's own argument. But when you settle down to absorption in any one of them, you will feel, I think, an action, an interchange, between the persons of the poem, which questioning, metaphor, and stanza all are apt to support. There should be no final answer as to where any single poem must fit; many might effectively read Milton's "When I consider how my light is spent" as dramatic in the way that Herbert's "Love" is, for example. What is important is to consider the speaking tone of each poem as you hear it, the point of view of each speaker in relation to the sound and substance of his speech.

To be considered: poems by Wyatt, Surrey, Gascoigne, Sidney, Marlowe, Raleigh, Jonson, Herbert, Vaughan, Crashaw, Herrick, Lovelace, Taylor, Swift, Burns, Lord Byron, Robert

Browning, Elizabeth Barrett Browning, D. G. Rossetti, Christina Rossetti, Dickinson, Meredith, Hardy, Housman, Kipling, Robinson, Frost, Lindsay, Macleish, Auden, Graves, Ransom, Eberhart, Roethke, Lowell, Young.

TONE OF EXCLAMATION AND INVOCATION: CHIEFLY IN THE FIRST PERSON

Centuries ago, when Aristotle in the *Poetics* distinguished between dramatic and narrative points of view, he suggested also a third, the "dithyrambic." This was the particularly musical and personal mode of poetry, exalted and ceremonious in its tone, neither so colloquial nor so accurate as the other two, but fired with inspiration and implying through musical harmonies what could not always be verbally expressed. Pindar was such a poet, as were prophets like Isaiah, and Longinus was the early critical advocate of such poetry. Today, Ezra Pound, as both poet and critic, makes much the same discrimination as Aristotle did, when he distinguishes musical or melopoeic poetry, including his own, from colloquial logopoeic and observational phanopoeic. "Oh, what a brave hero!" "Oh, what a terrible dream!" "Oh, what a beautiful morning!" are exclamations at the heart of the musical or melopoeic mode, largely and deeply felt, with a minimum of complex reasoning or structure. Translations of the Bible provided English with a strong example of poetic parallelism, the use of cumulative parallel phrase and sentence structures, to take the place of the more rounded arguments of stanzas.

Early users of this "high" style were men especially faithful to Biblical tone: Spenser, who has been called the first great Protestant poet; Sylvester, who translated what was close to Biblical paraphrase; Bradstreet, who brought this style to America; Cowley, who consciously saw the relation to Pindar's odes; Milton, who succeeded beyond the rest in giving the new verse an English sound as well as universal substance. These poets made ready for the use of the revolutionary poets of the eighteenth century—Thomson, and Blake, and later, in the nineteenth century, Whitman—just the free and resonant form they needed to celebrate liberty and democracy: a regularly stressed but irregularly rhymed or unrhymed line, much cosmic substance vastly delineated, and a rolling sound, onomatopoetic and harmonious.

The first of Spenser's sonnets of love, the "Amoretti," gives us a further tone for the Elizabethan sonnet, not personal address and argument, but rather an exclamatory sense of rich qualities, of appreciative intensity in the speaker. The happy leaves are invoked, rather than addressed as real persons, and "leaves, lines, and rhymes" all are important for their sensory or aesthetic association with the lady, through soft bands, starry light, and the mythological sacred brook of Helicon. No attitude or action of the lovers is argued, but rather the qualities of beauty and pleasure are exclaimed, so that the rich references seem more important than the simple serial structure, and sound is especially important in the soft and pleasant combination of open vowels and sibilant and liquid consonants.

Of this sort of ceremonious, harmonious exclamatory poem, Spenser's *Epithalamion*, like Milton's *Lycidas*, is one of the most beautiful examples in English. By the poet himself, as speaker, and with the aid of the Muse which he formally calls upon, a lyrical pattern of ritual is created, by which vagaries of human action are subdued, and even solid substance is chosen for, and blended into, its effects of sound. The sounds are full and open, smoothly connected, and the lines are varied in length, with an effect of improvisation, as if the poet were composing and re-echoing as he goes. "So· I unto myself alone will sing; / The woods shall to me answer, and my echo ring." As his lady wakes, comes forth, comes to the altar and the celebrations, and retires to the bridal bowers, all the powers of heaven are drawn to the marriage ceremony by the poet's song.

So Milton draws these powers to the ceremony mourning Lycidas, his real friend Edward King, as the bride of the *Epithalamion* was Spenser's own bride. Like Spenser, Milton calls on the Muses' aid to heighten the whole ceremony beyond the everyday into the sublime in sound and sense. So Sylvester in his translation of Du Bartas, and Anne Bradstreet in her early American version, treated the "rarest beauties of this Universe."

What about us today? Why do we still employ so high a style, such a rhapsody, when we are celebrating neither

Olympic heroes, nor Biblical prophecies, nor cosmic and political upheavals? Possibly it is the depth and richness of tone that we need, a sense of inner correspondences between sound and substance, imagery which seems to stand for more than itself and thus becomes symbol. Baudelaire is the great exemplar of such verse in French, and Mallarmé after him. And we may note through the poems of Keats, Tennyson, Whittier, Wilde, Henley, Thompson, the growing effect of strong, even fantastic, sense-impressions so powerful that they are not directly described but must be conveyed effectively through sound which echoes sense.

The youthful Hart Crane some years ago made a poetic stir with just such verse; it had a depth of overtone, a light-and-shade or chiaroscuro of sound which seemed thunderous after the tones of Robinson's Havergal or Eliot's Prufrock, men whom readers reacted to dramatically rather than felt with wholeheartedly. After Crane, Dylan Thomas brought not only the full tones of his verse but the full tones of his "bardic" voice to records. Resonant adjectives, phrases, participles, open vowels and assonances, internal rhyming and onomatopoeia, exclamation and invocation, the ceremony of celebration, all characterize this poetry that speaks outward from within.

Ye leaves, ye learnéd sisters, ye laurels are not a part of a dramatic interplay in their respective poems; rather, they are above the action, invoked as part of the ceremony. Much more important than action and argument, in the poems such muses preside over, are the loftiness or depth of harmony and tone: the patterns of vowel sounds, the rich qualities of reference, the implications of much more to be said. Increasingly the emotional and subjective force of the first person has come to be stated, as the I is more and more named: early and restrainedly in Milton's "When I consider how my light is spent," where much of the force of the final *stand* and *wait* is carried in the likeness of their sound to that of *his state*; then later more fully in such a poem as Keats's "Elgin Marbles," where his own feelings are more variously developed in *unwilling sleep, gentle luxury,* and *dizzy pain,* but come to an effectively implicative ending much like Milton's with the sounds of *grandeur, rude, billow, main* all preparing to confirm the suggested force of the final phrase, the *shadow of a magnitude*. In such a complex of traits, the colloquial reasonableness and plainness of Herbert's verse would be out of place, as would its finesse of structure; here the suggestions of sense, rather than the shapes of thought, are dominant.

Do you think Blake's "Tiger" might possibly answer back? If so, you might prefer not to read it as invocative. And what is the difference between Ulysses as speaker and Browning's Bishop? When you come to a poem like D. H. Lawrence's "Trees in the Garden," you can hear through the first exclamation, *how still the trees are!* the tone of inward wonder which is to dominate. The adjectives like *lovely, ghostly, evanescent* give us the mood of the speaker, as they do in Spenser's sonnet, and the sounds of *still* and *stand* prepare us for *strangers*, which carries the culminating feeling. As you read and listen, you hear no argument, but rather the ceremony of personal response, the strain of conveying a wonder beyond individual, especially beyond rational, capacity. Thus the reliance on sound, subjective quality, and exclamation.

One could say of Ezra Pound's "Pact," which follows closely, that it is a very different sort, involving a second person. But does it, or is it all about the feelings of I, and is *let there be* invocative?

To be considered: poems by Spenser, Sylvester, Milton, Bradstreet, Cowley, Thomson, Gray, Collins, Smart, Warton, Countess of Winchilsea, Berkeley, Shenstone, Blake, Keats, Tennyson, Whittier, Henley, Wilde, Thompson, Lawrence, Pound, Moore, Sitwell, Crane, Thomas, Spender, Bishop, Rukeyser, Wilbur, Ginsberg.

TONE OF STATEMENT AND OBSERVATION: CHIEFLY IN THE THIRD PERSON

Many of us enjoy novels so slow and steady-moving that we can "live with them." There is such poetry too, a poetry of prolonged progression and meditation, and we find it in our own day as well as in the past: in "The Waste Land" as well as in the first great Elizabethan work of this kind, "A Mirror for Magistrates." These works are mirrors for their times, as are Rochester's, Dryden's, and Pope's satires, Goldsmith's and Crabbe's "Villages," many classical narratives, and the imagist poetry of the present. Poets have held up mirrors first to officials and courtiers, then to urban society, then to rural society, then to the natural world.

The distinguishing tone of this poetry is in its fidelity to selected fact, the clarity of its reporting of image. *Substance* is its stress; both *sound* and *structure* move along clearly as aids to substance. Neither dramatic suspense nor inner inexpressibility leaves one guessing: the relevancies are spelled out in language that is more literal, more concrete, and at the same time more general than in the other modes of speaking.

Its background is classical Latin, specifically the poetry of Horace and Virgil. They and their followers used the classical style of generalities or norms of things, seeing not just individual objects but classes of events—the way things are in general: a typical son, farm, leader, drink, or friend. About friendship, for example, not its drama nor its inexpressibility so much as the good solid assumptions one can make about it interested these poets. Or, negatively and satirically, the assumptions one ought to be able to make about it, even in the light of facts which don't measure up to the assumptions: for example, the mocking of a false friend. Sometimes this poetry is called "humanistic," because it so thoroughly tries to reflect human norms and values of action and belief.

The happy man for the humanist is the man of the middle road, the classical golden mean. He seeks neither metaphysical nor sublime extremes, feels neither like unworthy dust nor like a god, but like a human being with faults and virtues. In sentences, he tends to balance action in verbs with qualification in adjectives.

Shakespeare's sonnets are among the first to portray man in this way. Unlike other sonnets of his day, such as Sidney's, Spenser's, Daniel's, Drayton's, his are concerned less with the characteristics of the lover than with the characteristics of a man in his many capacities—poet, friend, philosopher, as well as lover. They see the stature of man as serious and effective in the human universe. They balance quality and action, sense and thought. They feel passionately, and at the same time reason aptly, and are smooth in effect because their elements are so closely joined.

This trait of smooth balance tended to be lost in the first half of the seventeenth century, when poets were writing either at the dramatic extreme of Donne or at the sublime extreme of Milton. Edmund Waller in mid-century was hailed as the poet who returned English to an elegant middle ground, or, as Dryden said, found the language brick and left it marble. "Marble" required a cool and level use of Latinate phrases and generous epithets, instead of the rough "brick" monosyllabic and clausal units of speech characteristic of native English. In the nineteenth century, Arnold and Bridges again endeavored to gain that smoothness of sound, that grace of order, mastered by poets of such high seriousness as Virgil. For our own day, Wallace Stevens sometimes offers it, and it is a defining characteristic of much of the poetry of Eliot and of Yeats.

Looking specifically at Sackville's "Induction," or Introduction, to the *Mirrour,* we see how narrative structure often encloses and objectifies both individual vision and dramatic dialogue. After the narrator has given us a view of the season and the sequence of the constellations, to fix the time exactly, he tells us that there breaks into his meditation about the fate of great men a vision of a "piteous wight," Sorrow, with whom he speaks, and who promises to show him the actual histories of princes of renown, beginning with the Duke of Buckingham. While there is both dialogue and feeling, these are not personal or individual, but generalized to support the main point, which is meditation upon representative events. The narrator stands apart, our interest not in him but in what he is observing and telling us. The structure is sequential: then . . . then . . . then. The sound-pattern is stanzaic, in the "rhyme royal" which Chaucer and others had earlier used to carry their stories forward. The substance of setting and action is carefully and minutely described, as in the appearance of Buckingham at the end of the passage. The poem is devoted to statement, to setting forth the facts and their significance, and therefore directs both sound and structure to this purpose.

Compare Marvell's "Definition of Love" of the seventeenth century with Cummings's three hundred years later to note how poetic observation and description has increased in sensory detail, decreased in reasoning structure. What was uncommon in Marvell's day, a descriptive impersonality, has become more common now. Marvell stands apart to analyze an abstraction. Step by step, he uses metaphor to tell us what love is: its origin in despair, its possibility in human desire but impossibility in the fate the stars have ordained, in the opposition of fate to love. Humorously, ruefully, he makes his "definition" sound like a scientific treatise, in sharp, neat sound and reasoning structure as they support the elaborate vocabulary of the definitional substance. This is like an essay in verse.

So is Cummings's, but with the humor now directed not so much toward concepts of astrology as toward concepts of quality and grammar, of qualification rather than relation. It moves not so much outward to the spheres as inward to human behavior, to "forget" and to "fail," as well as to sea and sky. And it is still supported by a regularized structure of sound and statement, as if the upset and intensive grammar should not upset the reasonableness and objectivity in the least.

Often this sort of poetry of statement is humorous or satiric, as if the poet were keeping a straight face with an effort in order to mock what he observes by setting it forth as accurately as possible. "MacFlecknoe" and Pope's "Rape of the Lock" are good examples, as are "The Deacon's Masterpiece" and "The Love-Song of J. Alfred Prufrock." Often, on the other hand, the poet's dedication to serious observation seems intense, and extremely focussed, as in the work of H. D., of Jeffers, of Williams, of Wallace Stevens. Compare, for example, the free-swinging intensity of Jeffers to the close scrutiny of H. D.; both adapt style, in line and phrase, to the special nature of the substance with which they are concerned.

To be considered: poems by Sackville, Shakespeare, Waller, Marvell, Wilmot, Dryden, Jonson, Cowper, Goldsmith, Dwight, Freneau, Wordsworth, Shelley, Bryant, Landor, Poe, Emerson, Longfellow, Holmes, Arnold, Swinburne, Bridges, Hopkins, de la Mare, Eliot, Stevens, H. D., Sandburg, Jeffers, Williams, Cummings, Patchen, Shapiro, Winters.

HISTORICAL PATTERN

Historically, English poetry has varied its emphases with some regularity. In the Renaissance, in the century from Wyatt to Cowley, most poets seemed to care about a closely argued structure for their substance and sound. They addressed their readers and other hearers directly and intensely; they took God, or a beloved lady, or a friend, straight into the line of thought, and often spoke as if in reply, in debate. They spoke on abstract ideas, on topics of faith and belief; they related themselves dramatically to the world and death; they were poets for whom the process of thought was exciting and dramatic. For them, sound was closely organized in measure, repetition, and refrain to follow the close organization of the ideas. Again, from Coleridge's day to our own, many poets—Browning, Meredith, Robinson, Eberhart—have delighted to write in this way, often calling it "metaphysical," in reference to Donne and his kind of poet, or "romantic," in reference to Coleridge, Byron, and the Pre-Raphaelites. Frost and Auden are such poets in our time; they speak directly, formally, and dramatically. Their tone is familiar, artful, speculative.

Milton in the seventeenth century most powerfully began another kind of speaking, in which sound was used for its powers to suggest as well as to organize; and words, sounds, and sentences all were used for their power to represent passions and cosmic forces. The senses led to passions, the passions to arts, the arts to the universe and God. This poetry, which often used irregular lines, gives the effect of striving and soaring to suggest the cumulative relationships between panorama and human soul. The odes of the eighteenth century, the myths of Thomson, Blake, and Keats, the sweeping cadences of Whitman and in modern times of Pound, Crane, and Dylan Thomas are of this kind. "Blank" and "free" verse suit it, the interior force of onomatopoeia, a language of connotation, and a structure of singular or plural exclamation. It is the high verse which Pindar wrote in his celebrations of Greek prowess, the verse of ceremonious Biblical passages, the verse of French Symbolists like Baudelaire and Mallarmé, portentous, subjective, and symbolic, in tones of awe, wonder, fear, and marvel.

At intervals throughout poetic history, and especially in the past century, certain poets have maintained a third emphasis, a more objective one, on observation, in the third person, with a tone of attentive and knowledgeable enjoyment. These are our narrators, describers, recorders, often our satirists, with some detachment of view and impersonality of reference. They like substance, event, and material; they like the normal human scene. Shakespeare and Spenser were such poets when they wrote sonnets, Dryden and Pope such satirists, Wordsworth and Arnold, Eliot and Stevens such philosophers. Value in what they refer to is important for these poets, along with regularity of sound and parallelism and balance of structure. The most sensitive recording of "Imagist" verse is often of this kind. Horace and Virgil wrote in this way, which is sometimes called classical for them and for the English poets who adopted their criteria of poise and objectivity. They may think of poetry as painting, whereas the more exclamatory poets think of it as music, and the more dramatic poets think of it as dialogue; these three common analogues for poetry suggest again the three usual emphases which our poets have historically chosen and still choose today.

The three interests are related not only to type and time but to philosophies of reality. The metaphysical poet is concerned with what is true and what is fictive, with what is literal and what is figurative, with what is earthly and what is heavenly, as aspects of divine truth. For him, man's life is a drama because he cannot know enough to be right, he must learn partially, and in relation to others, by metaphors and what Shakespeare called "assays of bias." His poetry is an argument with others and with himself. Aristotle and the rhetoric books of the Renaissance provide the critical theory for such poetry: the poet as fabricator of the truth as he can best discern it; this is a scientific or scholastic point of view.

For the aesthetic or sensory point of view, there is no double realm of reality; all is as we see and feel it and then vastly more, in a vastness we may reach by rapture and enthusiasm. Both the books of the Bible and the world of Nature are direct revelations of reality. The beauty of the universe which we can image and appreciate is the direct truth of the universe. For what we can sense, imagery; for what we feel beyond sense, the image as symbol of the indefinable; for wider truths, sensory qualities like *high* and *golden* as abstractions from the beauty of scene; and for the art of such extension and abstraction of quality, music. One early critic with such a point of view was Longinus, and he has been followed by many eighteenth-century critics like Bysshe and the Wartons, and the Symbolist "pure poetry" theorists of the present day. These are the Rousseaus, the Croces, the individualists among theorists.

For the moral point of view, the criteria are not so much those of truth or beauty as those of goodness, the ordering of emotions, the fidelity to human norms in general. Every century has its moral, its classical humanistic poets, as the seventeenth century had Dryden; the eighteenth, Pope and Jonson; the nineteenth, Arnold and Bridges; the twentieth, Yeats, Eliot, and Stevens.

The three preceding groups together give the historical pattern: first, metaphysical sixteenth and seventeenth centuries and, after a span of difference, the nineteenth and twentieth; second, the strong romantic change to the eighteenth-century aesthetic sublime, begun most strong with Milton, presently active in our younger poets; third, continuously through each century, some portion of the classical, coming to its present force in the late nineteenth century and the modern.

We may get a sense of this history in the work of five individual poets: John Donne, Alexander Pope, Samuel Taylor Coleridge, Walt Whitman, William Butler Yeats. Studying them may suggest a number of important variations in points of view, for their various poems suggest the complexities involved in the achievement of individuality in point of view. We may note that for some of these men style changed from poem to poem; there was little stability of tone. For others, there was constancy, as if the poet had stepped into a voice the way one might step into a suit which fitted exactly and need not be altered. All five were conscious of style; in a sense, all were in clear rebellion against their predecessors. But some knew how to rebel, and others chose to change by moderating and consolidating.

When John Donne began writing in his early youth at the end of the sixteenth century, nearly a full, solid century of "modern" English poetry lay behind him, a good deal of it seeming too smooth and substantial, too "feminine," as he called Spenser. He preferred the earlier efforts, those of Wyatt, for example, who had wrestled with the rough accents and monosyllables of English in order to get his thoughts on paper, and didn't mind letting the wrestling show. Donne liked thought, he liked to oppose his ideas to others', and he liked the opposition to be heard in all its force and difficulty. The arguments to be dealt with in his day were many: Roman Catholicism vs. Anglican or Church of England Catholicism—

Donne's family was oppressed for its Romanism and he himself after much troubled self-searching became an Anglican Dean; the old medieval rational scholasticism vs. the new observational science of Galileo and Harvey—Donne tried both to reason and to feel the one into the other; courtly convention vs. individual invention and skepticism—Donne could let neither go, and kept troubling the one with the other; love vs. doubt, immortality vs. mortality—the conflict could be within him, or between him and his wife, or between them both and God.

Others of his and the following generation avoided these conflicts either by treating them more lightly, as Sidney and Lovelace did, or by dividing them and separating them, as Herrick did in "Hesperides" and "Noble Numbers," or by challenging the validity of one force, as Vaughan and Crashaw did the secular, or by tempering the tone of conflict with a classical substantiality, as Marvell did. Donne was most pure, most extreme, in his dramatizing of the conflicts, making them personal, arguing them out from beginning to end.

A hundred years later, Alexander Pope, a poet highly sensitive to public taste, found himself and everyone else tired of the sort of wit which Donne had used so well and which later poets had abused. Because wit meant to Donne an intellectual perception of relationships, it involved argument, paradox, metaphor; but all these seemed too sharp in a world where reasoning from the pleasure of direct sense impression was the primary way to knowledge. With his predecessors, Marvell, Dryden, Addison, and others who consciously reacted from Donne's roughness, Pope suggested reviving the great Greek and Latin epics and satires as a way of getting poetry back to normal ground. By his translations of Homer especially, Pope was one of the first and few to make a living from poetry. The readers of the Augustan age, increasing rapidly in numbers because of the leisure available to mercantile city-dwellers and the improvement of light to read by, increased also their avidity for a stylish classicism, for what they felt to be its universality, so that translation became a profession by demand.

Close attention to the measured tones and lofty objectivity of Homer, Virgil, and Juvenal brought to the eighteenth-century English, early in Pope and late in Crabbe and Wordsworth, an ability to narrate objectively, to set forth sequentially and describe carefully, qualities which had long been lacking in the rather abrupt language of implicative and dramatic English. Latin helped smooth the way both in technique and in spirit. After their exile at the French court during the Commonwealth regime of mid-seventeenth century, many royalist poets had been inspired by the French to try epic narratives, secular or religious, on classical models, and most, like Cowley and Davenant, seemed to fail because of the very difficulties of English, its rough syllables and vocabulary. Milton managed to succeed by moving another way, up and around, rather than straightforward. It remained for Dryden particularly, and then for Pope, to learn through translation new ways for the language to speak.

Scientists helped effect this change, too, Hobbes, Boyle, Locke, members of the Royal Society, all encouraged a literal, concrete, specific, sequential language, more Latin than theretofore usual, and thus in many ways more accurate and dignified in dealing with general patterns of progression. Concrete imagery, near-literal simile, and abstract epithet took the place in poetry of fictive figures of speech. For example, Addison praised the phrase "a bosom white as snow" as true wit and condemned "a bosom cold as snow" as false, because the first was a literal analogy or simile, since the breast could be seen to be white as snow is white, while the second was fictive, a made-up metaphor which could not be proved by observation, since *cold* was meant as a metaphor for the lady's attitude. Along with this desire for a more literal and general terminology and forward-moving sentences came also reduction of stanza-unit to line-unit, the fine discriminations of measure and quality going on within the line or couplet and carrying progressively forward instead of returning back in the rounding forms of stanzas. Pope is one of the masters of all these: the literal and general language, the forward-moving structure, the carefully delineated line and couplet. Before him, there had been many less successful attempts at the combination; after him, there were many successful imitators for at least another century, but none so fine in his especial way.

His way was conditioned by the fact that he was sensitive to the future as well as to the past. He disliked what he knew was to come, as well as what had gone before. Milton's sublime was what he dreaded, and what he mocked in his *Peri Bathous* was the opposite of the sublime, that is, the "deep", in the sense of bathetic as well as pathetic. This sort of romantic style and attitude, the "going off the deep end," the Whiggish enthusiasm of such poets as Thomson and Shenstone, and what was to be characteristic of Blake, struck Pope as no more commendable than the metaphysics from which the Augustans were just escaping.

Therefore, between two poetic forces for what he considered ill, Pope turned in his own most inventive writing not to the sorts of description with which he began in his pastoral poems, and not toward the epics which he translated, that is, to the positive balances which classicism provided, but to a negative balance, a mocking acceptance of both the forces he felt to be dangerous. So we see, lightly in "The Rape of the Lock" and heavily in "The Dunciad," a poet's encompassing not only of past absurdities but also of future portents, not only of fantastic wit but also of orotund enthusiasm. These poems are called mock epics; they do not mock the epic form or spirit, but rather use these to mock two attitudes not suited to them: witty and capricious aggrandisement of trivia, and nonintellectual glorification of vast and dull emotions.

In our own day, Eliot's "Waste Land" is much the same sort of poem: irritated by the outworn quirks of nineteenth-century romantic conversations and confessions as well as by portents of Thomas-like soarings, the spectator Tiresias stands apart, observing a London foolish, sad, and grim, observing especially feminine trivia and mocking as he observes. The tone, like the tone of "The Rape of the Lock," is one of acceptance of the social frame with full realization of the discrepancies of meaning within the accepted frame: the distortion between wish and fact, the falsity of assumptions. Eliot's frame is the temporal layers of times past; Pope's, in the fashion of his day, was the spatial layers of human foolishnesses both "metaphysical" and "sublime." Most present-day satiric poets, Jeffers and Williams, for example, work within a more limited frame, stressing a few human values rather than a whole social complex of values.

One of the great narratives of English poetry, Coleridge's "Ancient Mariner," is written, like *Paradise Lost,* in a mode apart from the traditional narrative mode. As Milton overstated narrative, soaring into lyric, Coleridge understated it, turning back to the dramatic confrontations of the characters of the ballads. The Mariner is no observer and no mocker; he was there and he suffered; now he wants an audience for whom to dramatize the tale. The Wedding Guest becomes a character in his own right. Both relive, and we relive, the terrible and astonishing episodes, as if we too had been there.

We may see that Coleridge is another Donne, at the turn of a new century rebelling against the rich and lofty successes of his predecessors and calling a newly artful yet personal style into play, to involve his readers in his own concerns. In this turn away from the classically splendid, the romantic poet is like the metaphysical; he seeks something more immediately individual and difficult, more realistic yet with implications of spirit: again, a double view. Unlike Donne, Coleridge began by writing the way his predecessors wrote, elaborately, even at times sublimely, as in the lyrical invocations of "Dejection" and the musical incantations of "Kubla Khan." The pressures in this direction were much stronger in his day than in Donne's, who had a lot of young contemporaries and the whole practice of the current language in his favor. Coleridge had few colleagues; his friend Wordsworth, and later Shelley and Keats, moved not so far as he did from the old eighteenth century; but Coleridge had a theory of sound to aid him, a belief in the beauty of irregularity, much like Donne's belief in the power of roughness of speech.

Against the count of syllables of the classical couplet and blank verse, Coleridge set the count of stress, which we have been using strongly ever since, and which he drew from the native tradition of the ballad. According to such a count, the basic line-pattern is a regular number of stressed syllables, and the unstressed syllables may vary in number and placement. One may say "With the new," instead of the purer "with new": the ripple of the extra light syllable comes to be admired; for those who count feet, three-syllable anapestic and dactyllic feet, as well as two-syllable trochaic and iambic, come to be useful. From Coleridge on in the nineteenth century, we have a characteristic lightening of tone, an immediacy achieved by the simple, free increase of unstressed syllables, within the frame of measured stresses. In our own day, we have lost much of this lilt because we have given up much of the measure; our cadenced forms are closer to blank verse in that they produce an effect of onomatopoetic adaptability.

The interest of Pope was general man in the social order; he took up eccentricities and treated them in relation to norms or centers. The interest of Donne and Coleridge was individuality, even eccentricity, in relation to other individuals and the individuality of divine spirit. This was loss for Coleridge, as well as gain. His God was not so personal as Donne's, and could not be drawn into the poetry's action. We lose the intensity of that very double view which he and Wordsworth consciously agreed to strive for. On the other hand, we gain the scope and power of the natural world, which had been increasing all the way from Donne's day to his and which is his and our inheritance from the sublime poets like Milton and James Thomson. His rebellion against panorama was fortunately not complete; though he could not bring so close a scene with deity as could the Dean of St. Paul's, yet he could use in his spiritual drama the wider scenes of his predecessors, the force of the things of nature as characters. He helped to add to Donne's commitment of man to God, and to Pope's commitment of man to man, the modern commitment of man to the natural world.

Meanwhile, the most exclamatory poetry of this natural world, the sublime lyrical poetry of the eighteenth century, following Milton, had prospered with Thomson, Blake, and Keats, and had come to stability in Tennyson. Then, in America it achieved a new voice and vigor in Walt Whitman. It seems fitting that the individualist, Protestant mode first brought by Anne Bradstreet to these shores and fostered by the enthusiasts, the so-called wits, of Connecticut, should eventually find expression in the chief of our national poets.

His "Leaves of Grass" brings together earth, plant, and body, in the symbol of grass like leaf or hair; in this mode, entities fuse, outlines are unclear. The framework of story or drama, the frame of couplet or stanza, the frame of complex or periodic sentence structure, are dissolved to a hazier, boundary-less unity of lyrical exclamation and harmonic parallelism. Like blades of grass, the phrases, materials, and structures run parallel, in the tradition of the Psalms, and gather to as thoroughgoing a paean of praise as we know in our language.

Many have wondered how the young type-setter from Long

Island, working in the office of the *Brooklyn Eagle,* could create such a new synthesis for himself. Perhaps his very lack of formal literary study made him sensitive not to the congealing styles of his own literary day but to the freest and most prophetic in what he managed to read. Blake had much the same kinship with tradition, a seizing of some of its highest moments, Biblical and Miltonic; an alienation from the civil Roman spirit; he too was a craftsman with a sense of greater mission; a Whig; an individualist. For such poets, human relationships were not so much social and formal as natural and transcendental.

Modern Symbolism has its sources in such transcendence. What is ultimately inexpressible seeks at least tokens of expression, through images which stand for much more than they can show in themselves. A wordless lover sends flowers. Baudelaire's *l'azur* stands for eternity. The image is loaded with more than its own properties; it becomes a token or symbol for many more properties, as, in the original Greek use of the term *symbol,* the broken halves of a coin were put together to betoken a sealed friendship. Things become important for the whole of which they are part; so dream-symbols represent complexes of feeling, and ritual acts represent whole mythologies. Whitman's body is the world's body, and his Passage to India the passage of history and life.

We may see Whitman in Pound's poem to him, in Thomas's swinging line, in Marianne Moore's fidelity to the quality of things more than to their shape and relation. This is an adjectival mode of aesthetic discrimination, a poetry as "pure" as possible of comment or argument or objectivity, as personal as possible in improvisation and association. In Section III, "The Seasons" is a long poem, and perhaps difficult to read in its diction of two centuries ago; yet it is one of the basic poems behind the Whitman tradition, and a fine example of the kind. James Thomson drew on Biblical spirit and Protestant spirit and Scientific spirit to write it, all three revolutionary in his day, and "The Seasons" became the poetic handbook of revolutionary America: more free in sound, more rich in imagery, more lofty in exclamation than much that had gone before in English tradition. Now, blank verse, images, and seasons have all become conventional. Yet some of our youngest and most inventive present-day poetry is in this mode, not so much direct from Thomson or Whitman or even Pound, as from Dylan Thomas. It may carry us to new visions, new symbols.

A near contemporary of our own, born just after "Leaves of Grass" was published, and flourishing in poetry through the first third of the twentieth century, brings us back again to what is possibly the norm of our present style, the classical balance which has mediated between the extremes of Coleridge and Whitman, of Browning and Tennyson, of Auden and Thomas. As unlike Whitman as he could be, the Irishman William Butler Yeats grew up in an atmosphere intensely literary and critical; he therefore knew, technically and analytically, just what he was choosing between when he made his choices of style. His father was a painter in the Pre-Raphaelite tradition who night and day talked style, graphic and literary. Through him, Yeats met many of the leading poets in England, talked with them, and learned to trust or mistrust them. Further, his own first jobs were literary, editing such poets as Spenser and Blake along with collections of Irish tales. His next jobs were more characteristically his own: working with and writing plays for the Abbey Theatre in Dublin. After a late marriage, he sat back in his tower home at Ballylee to write, along with more plays and prose, more verse.

The selections in this book follow these three stages. First come the dreaming lyrical poems which made Yeats popular, the melodious and adjectival "Rose" poems. Then dramatic poems and a poetic drama. And finally, the "Tower" meditations. In all three ways, Yeats tells us something of ourselves in poetry: first, why we have liked Whitman and Thomas so much, in our sense of mystery and myth; second, the living power of drama in our poetry, even to its acting and staging; third, our hesitation between these two quite different forces, and our reconcilement, as Eliot and Stevens have it, in a balance between. A time of balance is a time of new thought, new substance, in which poetry can take new knowledge for its province, and give voice and shape to values hardly won.

II

Poems

FORGET NOT YET

SIR THOMAS WYATT

Forget not yet the tried intent
Of such a truth as I have meant:
My great travail so gladly spent
    Forget not yet.

Forget not yet when first began   5
The weary life ye know, since whan
The suit, the service none tell can.
    Forget not yet.

Forget not yet the great assays,
The cruel wrong, the scornful ways,   10
The painful patience in denays.
    Forget not yet.

Forget not O, forget not this,
How long ago hath been, and is,
The mind that never meant amiss.   15
    Forget not yet.

Forget not then thine own approved,
The which so long hath thee so loved,
Whose steadfast faith yet never moved:
    Forget not this.

denays—denials

THE GOLDEN GIFT

HENRY HOWARD, EARL OF SURREY

The golden gift that Nature did thee give,
To fasten friends and feed them at thy will
With form and favour, taught me to believe
How thou art made to show her greatest skill,
Whose hidden virtues are not so unknown   5
But lively dooms might gather at the first:
Where beauty so her perfect seed hath sown,
Of other graces follow needs there must.
Now certes, lady, since all this is true,
That from above thy gifts are thus elect,   10
Do not deface them then with fancies new,
Not change of minds, let not the mind infect:
But mercy him thy friend that doth thee serve,
Who seeks alway thine honour to preserve.

THE FIRST CHORUS
from
THE GLASS OF GOVERNMENT

GEORGE GASCOIGNE

When God ordained the restless life of man,
And made him thrall to sundry grievous cares:
The first born grief or sorrow that began,
To show it self, was this: to save from snares
The pleasant pledge, which God for us prepares.   5
I mean the seed, and offspring that he gives,
To any wight which in this world here lives.

Few see themselves, but each man seeth his child,
Such care for them, as care not for themself,
We care for them, in youth when wit is wild,   10
We care for them, in age to gather pelf:
We care for them, to keep them from the shelf
Of such quick sands, as we our selves first found,
When heady will, did set our ships on ground.

wight—person

61

The care which Christ did take to save his sheep,   15
Hath been compared, to father's care on child,
And as the hen, her harmless chicks can keep
From cruel kite: so must the father shield

His youthful Sons, that they be not beguiled,
By wicked world, by fleshly foul desire,   20
Which serve the devil, with fuel for his fire.

First parents care, to bring their children forth,
To breed them then, to bring them up in youth,
To match them eke, with wights of greatest worth,
To see them taught, the trusty tracks of truth: 25
To bar excess, from whence all sin ensueth.
And yet to give, enough for common need,
Lest lothsome lack make vice for virtue breed.

Let shame of sin, thy Children's bridle be,
And spur them forth, with bounty wisely used: 30
That difference, each man may plainly see,
Tween parents' care, and masters' bode abused:
So Terence taught, whose lore is not refused.
But yet where youth is prone to follow ill,
There spare the spur, and use the bridle still.   35

Thus infinite, the cares of Parents are.
Some care to save their children from mishap,
Some care for wealth, and some for honours care,
Whereby their Sons may sit in fortune's lap:
Yet they which cram them so with worldly pap,   40
And never care, to give them heavenly crumbs,
Shall see them starve, when hap of hunger comes.

Said Socrates: that man which careth more
To leave his child, much good and rich of rent:
Then he forseeth, to furnish him with store   45
Of virtue's wealth, which never can be spent:
Shall make him like, the steed that still is pent
In stable close: which may be fair in sight.
But seldom serves, such horse in field to fight.

So Xenophon, his friend Dan Tully told,   50
And so do here, Philopaes and his peer
Philocalus, that self same lesson hold:

bode—house
Dan Tully—Cicero

They rather love to leave their sons in fear
Of God above: than wealth to wallow here.
Which godly care, (O God) so deign to bliss,   55
That men may see how great thy glory is.

from INDUCTION
to The Mirrour for Magistrates

THOMAS SACKVILLE

The wrathful Winter, 'proaching on apace,
With blustering blasts had all ybar'd the treen,
And old Saturnus, with his frosty face,
With chilling cold had pierc'd the tender green;
The mantles rent, wherein enwrapped been   5
   The gladsome grove that now lay overthrown,
   The tapets torn, and every bloom down blown.

The soil, that erst so seemly was to seen,
Was all despiled of her beauty's hue;
And soote fresh flowers, wherewith the summer's queen   10
Had clad the earth, now Boreas' blasts down blew;
And small fowls flocking, in their song did rue
   The winter's wrath, wherewith each thing defac'd
   In woeful wise bewail'd the summer past.

Hawthorn had lost his motley livery,   15
The naked twigs were shivering all for cold,
And dropping down the tears abundantly;
Each thing, methought, with weeping eye me told
The cruel season, bidding me withhold
   Myself within; for I was gotten out   20
   Into the fields, whereas I walk'd about.

When lo, the night with misty mantles spread,
'Gan dark the day, and dim the azure skies;
And Venus in her message Hermes sped
To bloody Mars, to will him not to rise,   25
Which she herself approach'd in speedy wise;
   And Virgo hiding her disdainful breast,
   With Thetis now had laid her down to rest.

tapets—figured cloths, tapestries; here figurative for foliage

Whiles Scorpio dreading Sagittarius' dart,
Whose bow prest bent in fight, the string had slipp'd,   30
Down slid into the Ocean flood apart,
The Bear, that in the Irish seas had dipp'd
His grisly feet, with speed from thence he whipp'd:
    For Thetis, hasting from the Virgin's bed,
    Pursued the Bear, that ere she came was fled.   35

And Phaeton now, near reaching to his race
With glist'ring beams, gold streaming where they bent,
Was prest to enter in his resting place:
Erythius, that in the cart first went,
Had even now attain'd his journey's stent: 40
    And, fast declining, hid away his head,
    While Titan couch'd him in his purple bed.

And pale Cynthea, with her borrow'd light,
Beginning to supply her brother's place,
Was past the noonstead six degrees in sight,   45
When sparkling stars amid the heaven's face,
With twinkling light shone on the earth apace,
    That, while they brought about the nightes chare,
    The dark had dimm'd the day ere I was ware.

And sorrowing I to see the summer flowers,   50
The lively green, the lusty leas forlorn,
The sturdy trees so shatter'd with the showers,
The fields so fade that flourish'd so beforn,
It taught me well, all earthly things be born
    To die the death, for nought long time may last;   55
    The summer's beauty yields to winter's blast.

Then looking upward to the heaven's leams,
With nightes stars thick powder'd everywhere,
Which erst so glisten'd with the golden streams
That cheerful Phoebus spread down from his sphere,   60
Beholding dark oppressing day so near:
    The sudden sight reduced to my mind,
    The sundry changes that in earth we find.

That musing on this worldly wealth in thought,
Which comes, and goes, more faster than we see   65

prest—ready
Erythius—relating to the island Erythia,
one of the 'happy isles' in the west; perhaps a western star
leams—gleams, lights

The flickering flame that with the fire is wrought,
My busy mind presented unto me
Such fall of peers as in this realm had be;
    That oft I wish'd some would their woes descrive,
    To warn the rest whom fortune left alive.   70

• • •

THE WOOD, THE WEED, THE WAG

SIR WALTER RALEIGH

Three things there be that prosper all apace
And flourish, while they grow asunder far;
But on a day, they meet all in a place,
And when they meet they one another mar.

And they be these: the Wood, the Weed, the Wag.   5
The Wood is that that makes the gallows tree;
The Weed is that that strings the hangman's bag;
The Wag, my pretty knave, betokens thee.

Now mark, dear boy—while these assemble not,
Green springs the tree, hemp grows, the wag is wild;   10
But when they meet, it makes the timber rot,
It frets the halter, and it chokes the child.

Then bless thee, and beware, and let us pray
We part not with thee at this meeting-day.

THE NYMPH'S REPLY

SIR WALTER RALEIGH

If all the world and love were young,
And truth in every shepherd's tongue,
These pretty pleasures might me move
To live with thee and be thy love.

But Time drives flocks from field to fold,   5
When rivers rage and rocks grow cold;
And Philomel becometh dumb;
The rest complain of cares to come.

The flowers do fade, and wanton fields
To wayward Winter reckoning yields: 10
A honey tongue, a heart of gall,
Is fancy's spring, but sorrow's fall.

Thy gowns, thy shoes, thy beds of roses,
Thy cap, thy kirtle, and thy posies,
Soon break, soon wither, soon forgotten,   15
In folly ripe, in reason rotten.

Thy belt of straw and ivy buds,
Thy coral clasps and amber studs—
All those in me no means can move
To come to thee and be thy love.   20

But could youth last, and love still breed;
Had joys no date, nor age no need;
Then those delights my mind might move
To live with thee and be thy love.

AMORETTI: I

EDMUND SPENSER

Happy ye leaves! when as those lily hands,
Which hold my life in their dead-doing might,
Shall handle you, and hold in love's soft bands,
Like captives trembling at the victor's sight.
And happy lines! on which, with starry light,   5
Those lamping eyes will deign sometimes to look,
And read the sorrows of my dying spright,
Written with tears in heart's close-bleeding book.
And happy rhymes! bathed in the sacred brook
Of Helicon, whence she derivèd is,   10
When ye behold that angel's blessed look.
My soul's long-lackèd food, my heaven's bliss.
Leaves, lines, and rhymes, seek her to please alone,
Whom if ye please, I care for other none.

EPITHALAMION

EDMUND SPENSER

Ye learnéd sisters, which have oftentimes
Been to me aiding, others to adorn,
Whom ye thought worthy of your graceful rhymes,
That even the greatest did not greatly scorn
To hear their names sung in your simple lays,   5
But joyéd in their praise;
And when ye list your own mishaps to mourn,
Which death, or love, or fortune's wreck did raise,
Your string could soon to sadder tenor turn,
And teach the woods and waters to lament   10
Your doleful dreariment.
Now lay those sorrowful complaints aside;
And having all your heads with girlands crowned,
Help me mine own love's praises to resound;
Ne let the same of any be envide: 15
So Orpheus did for his own bride!
So I unto myself alone will sing;
The woods shall to me answer, and my echo ring.

Early, before the world's light-giving lamp
His golden beam upon the hills doth spread,   20
Having dispersed the night's uncheerful damp,
Do ye awake; and with fresh lustihead
Go to the bower of my belovéd love,
My truest turtle-dove,
Bid her awake; for Hymen is awake,   25
And long since ready forth his mask to move,
With his bright tead that flames with many a flake,
And many a bachelor to wait on him,
In their fresh garments trim.
Bid her awake therefore, and soon her dight,   30
For lo! the wishéd day is come at last,
That shall, for all the pains and sorrows past,
Pay to her usury of long delight:
And whilst she doth her dight,
Do ye to her of joy and solace sing,   35
That all the woods may answer, and your echo ring.

Bring with you all the nymphs that you can hear
Both of the rivers and the forests green,
And of the sea that neighbours to her near:
All with gay girlands goodly well beseen.   40

And let them also with them bring in hand
Another gay girland,
For my fair love, of lilies and of roses,
Bound true-love wise, with a blue silk riband.
And let them make great store of bridal posies,   45
And let them eke bring store of other flowers,
To deck the bridal bowers.
And let the ground whereas her foot shall tread,
For fear the stones her tender foot should wrong,
Be strewed with fragrant flowers all along,   50
And diap'red like the discoloured mead.
Which done, do at her chamber door await,
For she will waken straight;
The whiles do ye this song unto her sing,
The woods shall to you answer, and your echo ring.   55

Ye nymphs of Mulla, which with careful heed
The silver scaly trouts do tend full well,
And greedy pikes which use therein to feed
(Those trouts and pikes all others do excel);
And ye likewise, which keep the rushy lake,   60
Where none do fishes take:
Bind up the locks the which hang scattered light,
And in his waters, which your mirror make,
Behold your faces as the crystal bright,
That when you come whereas my love doth lie,   65
No blemish she may spy.
And eke, ye lightfoot maids, which keep the deer,
That on the hoary mountain used to tower;
And the wild wolves, which seek them to devour,
With your steel darts do chase from coming near;   70
Be also present here,
To help to deck her, and to help to sing,
That all the woods may answer, and your echo ring.

Wake now, my love, awake! for it is time;
The rosy Morn long since left Tithone's bed,   75
All ready to her silver coach to climb;
And Phœbus gins to shew his glorious head.
Hark! how the cheerful birds do chant their lays
And carol of Love's praise.
The merry lark her matins sings aloft;   80
The thrush replies; the mavis descant plays:
The ouzel shrills; the ruddock warbles soft;
So goodly all agree, with sweet consent,
To this day's merriment.

Ah! my dear love, why do ye sleep thus long,   85
When meeter were that ye should now awake,
T' await the coming of your joyous make,
And hearken to the birds' love-learnéd song,
The dewy leaves among!
For they of joy and pleasance to you sing,   90
That all the woods them answer, and their echo ring.

My love is now awake out of her dreams,
And her fair eyes, like stars that dimméd were
With darksome cloud, now shew their goodly beams
More bright than Hesperus his head doth rear.   95
Come now, ye damsels, daughters of delight,
Help quickly her to dight:
But first come, ye fair hours, which were begot
In Jove's sweet paradise of Day and Night;
Which do the seasons of the year allot,   100
And all, that ever in this world is fair,
Do make and still repair:
And ye three handmaids of the Cyprian Queen,
The which do still adorn her beauty's pride,
Help to adorn my beautifullest bride: 105
And, as ye her array, still throw between
Some graces to be seen;
And, as ye use to Venus, to her sing,
The whiles the woods shall answer, and your echo ring.

Now is my love all ready forth to come: 110
Let all the virgins therefore well await:
And ye fresh boys, that tend upon her groom,
Prepare yourselves, for he is coming straight.
Set all your things in seemly good array,
Fit for so joyful day: 115
The joyfull'st day that ever sun did see.
Fair sun! shew forth thy favourable ray,
And let thy lifeful heat not fervent be,
For fear of burning her sunshiny face,
Her beauty to disgrace.   120
O fairest Phœbus! father of the Muse!
If ever I did honour thee aright,
Or sing the thing that mote thy mind delight,
Do not thy servant's simple boon refuse;
But let this day, let this one day, be mine;   125
Let all the rest be thine.
Then I thy sovereign praises loud will sing,
That all the woods shall answer, and their echo ring.

Hark: how the minstrels gin to shrill aloud
Their merry music that resounds from far,   130
The pipe, the tabor, and the trembling croud,
That well agree withouten breach or jar.
But, most of all, the damsels do delight
When they their timbrels smite,
And thereunto do dance and carol sweet,   135
That all the senses they do ravish quite;
The whiles the boys run up and down the street,
Crying aloud with strong confuséd noise,
As if it were one voice,
Hymen, iö Hymen, Hymen, they do shout;   140
That even to the heavens their shouting shrill
Doth reach, and all the firmament doth fill;
To which the people standing all about,
As in approvance, do thereto applaud,
And loud advance her laud;   145
And evermore they Hymen, Hymen sing,
That all the woods them answer, and their echo ring.

Lo! where she comes along with portly pace,
Like Phœbe, from her chamber of the east,
Arising forth to run her mighty race,   150
Clad all in white, that 'seems a virgin best.
So well it her beseems, that ye would ween
Some angel she had been.
Her long loose yellow locks like golden wire,
Sprinkled with pearl, and purling flowers atween,   155
Do like a golden mantle her attire;
And, being crownéd with a girland green,
Seem like some maiden queen.
Her modest eyes, abashéd to behold
So many gazers as on her do stare,   160
Upon the lowly ground affixéd are;
Ne dare lift up her countenance too bold,
But blush to hear her praises sung so loud,
So far from being proud.
Nathless do ye still loud her praises sing,   165
That all the woods may answer, and your echo ring.

Tell me, ye merchants' daughters, did ye see
So fair a creature in your town before;
So sweet, so lovely, and so mild as she,
Adorned with beauty's grace and virtue's store?   170
Her goodly eyes like sapphires shining bright,
Her forehead ivory white,

Her cheeks like apples which the sun hath rudded,
Her lips like cherries charming men to bite,
Her breast like to a bowl of cream uncrudded,   175
Her paps like lilies budded,
Her snowy neck like to a marble tower;
And all her body like a palace fair,
Ascending up, with many a stately stair,
To honour's seat and chastity's sweet bower.   180
Why stand ye still, ye virgins, in amaze,
Upon her so to gaze,
Whiles ye forget your former lay to sing,
To which the woods did answer, and your echo ring?

But if ye saw that which no eyes can see,   185
The inward beauty of her lively sprite,
Garnisht with heavenly gifts of high degree,
Much more then would ye wonder at that sight,
And stand astonisht like to those which read
Medusa's mazeful head.   190
There dwells sweet love, and constant chastity,
Unspotted faith, and comely womanhood,
Regard of honour, and mild modesty;
There virtue reigns as queen in royal throne,
And giveth laws alone,   195
The which the base affections do obey,
And yield their services unto her will;
Ne thought of thing uncomely ever may
Thereto approach to tempt her mind to ill.
Had ye once seen these her celestial treasures,   200
And unrevealéd pleasures,
Then would ye wonder, and her praises sing,
That all the woods should answer, and your echo ring

Open the temple gates unto my love,
Open them wide that she may enter in,   205
And all the posts adorn as doth behove,
And all the pillars deck with girlands trim,
For to receive this saint with honour due,
That cometh in to you.
With trembling steps, and humble reverence,   210
She cometh in, before th' Almighty's view;
Of her ye virgins learn obedience,
Whenso ye come into those holy places,
To humble your proud faces:
Bring her up to th' high altar, that she may   215
The sacred ceremonies there partake,

The which do endless matrimony make;
And let the roaring organs loudly play
The praises of the Lord in lively notes;
The whiles, with hollow throats,   220
The choristers the joyous anthem sing,
That all the woods may answer, and their echo ring.

Behold, whiles she before the altar stands,
Hearing the holy priest that to her speaks,
And blesseth her with his two happy hands,   225
How the red roses flush up in her cheeks,
And the pure snow, with goodly vermeil stain
Like crimson dyed in grain:
That even th' angels, which continually
About the sacred altar do remain,   230
Forget their service and about her fly,
Oft peeping in her face, that seems more fair
The more they on it stare.
But her sad eyes, still fastened on the ground,
Are governéd with goodly modesty,   235
That suffers not one look to glance awry,
Which may let in a little thought unsound.
Why blush ye, love, to give to me your hand,
The pledge of all our band!
Sing, ye sweet angels, Alleluia sing,   240
That all the woods may answer, and your echo ring.

Now all is done: bring home the bride again;
Bring home the triumph of our victory:
Bring home with you the glory of her gain,
With joyance bring her and with jollity.   245
Never had man more joyful day than this,
Whom heaven would heap with bliss.
Make feast therefore now all this livelong day;
This day for ever to me holy is.
Pour out the wine without restraint or stay,   250
Pour not by cups, but by the bellyful,
Pour out to all that wull,
And sprinkle all the posts and walls with wine,
That they may sweat, and drunken be withal.
Crown ye God Bacchus with a coronal,   255
And Hymen also crown with wreaths of vine;
And let the Graces dance unto the rest,
For they can do it best:
The whiles the maidens do their carol sing,
To which the woods shall answer, and their echo ring.   260

Ring ye the bells, ye young men of the town,
And leave your wonted labours for this day:
This day is holy; do ye write it down,
That ye for ever it remember may.
This day the sun is in his chiefest height,   265
With Barnaby the bright,
From whence declining daily by degrees,
He somewhat loseth of his heat and light,
When once the Crab behind his back he sees.
But for this time it ill ordainéd was,   270
To choose the longest day in all the year,
And shortest night, when longest fitter were:
Yet never day so long, but late would pass.
Ring ye the bells, to make it wear away,
And bonfires make all day;   275
And dance about them, and about them sing,
That all the woods may answer, and your echo ring.

Ah! when will this long weary day have end,
And lend me leave to come unto my love?
How slowly do the hours their numbers spend!   280
How slowly does sad Time his feathers move!
Haste thee, O fairest planet, to thy home,
Within the western foam:
Thy tired steeds long since have need of rest.
Long though it be, at last I see it gloom,   285
And the bright evening-star with golden crest
Appear out of the east.
Fair child of beauty! glorious lamp of love!
That all the host of heaven in ranks dost lead,
And guidest lovers through the night's sad dread,   290
How cheerfully thou lookest from above,
And seem'st to laugh atween thy twinkling light,
As joying in the sight
Of these glad many, which for joy do sing,
That all the woods them answer, and their echo ring!   295

Now cease, ye damsels, your delights forepast;
Enough it is that all the day was yours:
Now day is done, and night is nighing fast,
Now bring the bride into the bridal bowers.
The night is come, now soon her disarray,   300
And in her bed her lay;
Lay her in lilies and in violets,
And silken curtains over her display,

And odoured sheets, and arras coverlets.
Behold how goodly my fair love does lie,   305
In proud humility!
Like unto Maia, whenas Jove her took
In Tempe, lying on the flow'ry grass,
'Twixt sleep and wake, after she weary was,
With bathing in the Acidalian brook.   310
Now it is night, ye damsels may be gone,
And leave my love alone,
And leave likewise your former lay to sing:
The woods no more shall answer, nor your echo ring.

Now welcome, night! thou night so long expected,   315
That long day's labour dost at last defray,
And all my cares, which cruel Love collected,
Hast summed in one, and cancelléd for aye:
Spread thy broad wing over my love and me,
That no man may us see;   320
And in thy sable mantle us enwrap,
From fear of peril and foul horror free.
Let no false treason seek us to entrap,
Nor any dread disquiet once annoy
The safety of our joy;   325
But let the night be calm, and quietsome,
Without tempestuous storms or sad affray:
Like as when Jove with fair Alcmena lay,
When he begot the great Tirynthian groom:
Or like as when he with thyself did lie   330
And begot Majesty.
And let the maids and young men cease to sing,
Ne let the woods them answer, nor their echo ring.

Let no lamenting cries, nor doleful tears,
Be heard all night within, nor yet without: 335
Ne let false whispers, breeding hidden fears,
Break gentle sleep with misconceivéd doubt.
Let no deluding dreams, nor dreadful sights,
Make sudden sad affrights;
Ne let house-fires, nor lightning's helpless harms,   340
Ne let the Pouke, nor other evil sprites,
Ne let mischievous witches with their charms,
Ne let hobgoblins, names whose sense we see not,
Fray us with things that be not:
Let not the shriek-owl nor the stork be heard,   345
Nor the night-raven, that still deadly yells;
Nor damnéd ghosts, called up with mighty spells,
Nor grisly vultures, make us once afeard:

Ne let th' unpleasant quire of frogs still croaking
Make us to wish their choking.   350
Let none of these their dreary accents sing;
Ne let the woods them answer, nor their echo ring.

But let still silence true night-watches keep,
That sacred peace may in assurance reign,
And timely sleep, when it is time to sleep,   355
May pour his limbs forth on your pleasant plain;
The whiles an hundred little wingéd loves,
Like divers-feathered doves,
Shall fly and flutter round about your bed,
And in the secret dark, that none reproves,   360
Their pretty stealths shall work, and snares shall spread
To filch away sweet snatches of delight,
Concealed through covert night.
Ye sons of Venus, play your sports at will!
For greedy pleasure, careless of your toys,   365
Thinks more upon her paradise of joys,
Than what ye do, albeit good or ill.
All night therefore attend your merry play,
For it will soon be day:
Now none doth hinder you, that say or sing;   370
Ne will the woods now answer, nor your echo ring.

Who is the same, which at my window peeps?
Or whose is that fair face that shines so bright?
Is it not Cynthia, she that never sleeps,
But walks about high heaven all the night?   375
O! fairest goddess, do thou not envý
My love with me to spy:
For thou likewise didst love, though now unthought,
And for a fleece of wool, which privily
The Latmian shepherd once unto thee brought,   380
His pleasures with thee wrought.
Therefore to us be favourable now;
And sith of women's labours thou hast charge,
And generation goodly dost enlarge,
Incline thy will t' effect our wishful vow,   385
And the chaste womb inform with timely seed,
That may our comfort breed:
Till which we cease our hopeful hap to sing;
Ne let the woods us answer, nor our echo ring.

And thou, great Juno! which with awful might   390
The laws of wedlock still dost patronize;

And the religion of the faith first plight
With sacred rites hast taught to solemnize;
And eke for comfort often calléd art
Of women in their smart;   395
Eternally bind thou this lovely band,
And all thy blessings unto us impart.
And thou, glad Genius! in whose gentle hand
The bridal bower and genial bed remain,
Without blemish or stain: 400
And the sweet pleasures of their love's delight
With secret aid dost succour and supply,
Till they bring forth the fruitful progeny;
Send us the timely fruit of this same night.
And thou, fair Hebe! and thou, Hymen free!   405
Grant that it may so be.
Till which we cease your further praise to sing;
Ne any woods shall answer, nor your echo ring.

And ye high heavens, the temple of the gods,
In which a thousand torches flaming bright   410
Do burn, that to us wretched earthly clods
In dreadful darkness lend desiréd light;
And all ye powers which in the same remain,
More than we men can feign,
Pour out your blessing on us plenteously,   415
And happy influence upon us rain.
That we may raise a large posterity,
Which from the earth, which they may long possess
With lasting happiness,
Up to your haughty palaces may mount;   420
And, for the guerdon of their glorious merit,
May heavenly tabernacles there inherit,
Of blessed saints for to increase the count.
So let us rest, sweet love, in hope of this,
And cease till then our timely joys to sing;   425
The woods no more us answer, nor our echo ring!

Song! made in lieu of many ornaments,
With which my love should duly have been deckt,
Which cutting off through hasty accidents,
Ye would not stay your due time to expect,   430
But promised both to recompense;
Be unto her a goodly ornament,
And for short time an endless monument.

ASTROPHEL AND STELLA

SIR PHILIP SIDNEY

I

Loving in truth, and fain in verse my love to show,
That She, dear She, might take some pleasure of my pain,
Pleasure might cause her read, reading might make her know,
Knowledge might pity win, and pity grace obtain,
I sought fit words to paint the blackest face of woe;   5
Studying inventions fine, her wits to entertain,
Oft turning others' leaves, to see if thence would flow
Some fresh and fruitful showers upon my sun-burn'd brain.
But words came halting out, wanting Invention's stay;
Invention, Nature's child, fled stepdame Study's blows;   10
And others' feet still seem'd but strangers in my way.
Thus, great with child to speak, and helpless in my throes,
Biting my truant pen, beating myself for spite,
'Fool,' said my Muse to me, 'look in thy heart and write.'

from DU BARTAS HIS FIRST WEEK:
or *Birth of the World* ~ *The First Day of the First Week*

JOSHUA SYLVESTER

• • •

CLEAR FIRE forever hath not Air embraced,
Nor Air for aye environed Waters vast,
Nor Waters always wrapped the Earth therein;
But all this All did once of nought begin.   40
Once *All* was made; not by the hand of *Fortune*
(As fond *Democritus* did first importune)
With jarring Concords making Motes to meet,
Invisible, immortal, infinite.
Th' immutable divine Decree, which shall   45
Cause the World's End caused his Original:
Neither in Time, nor yet before the same,
But in the instant when Time first became.
I mean a Time confusèd: for, the course
Of years, of months, of weeks, of days, of hours,   50
Of Ages, Times, and Seasons is confined
By th' ordered Dance unto the Stars assigned.
Before all Time, all Matter, Form, and Place,

God all in all, and all in God it was:
Immutable, immortal, infinite,   55
Incomprehensible, all spirit, all light,
All Majesty, all-self-Omnipotent,
Invisible, impassive, excellent,
Pure, wise, just, good, God reigned alone (at rest)
Himself alone, self's Palace, Host, and Guest.

THE PASSIONATE SHEPHERD
TO HIS LOVE

CHRISTOPHER MARLOWE

Come live with me, and be my love,
And we will all the pleasures prove
That valleys, groves, hills and fields,
Woods, or steepy mountain yields.

And we will sit upon the rocks,   5
Seeing the shepherds feed their flocks
By shallow rivers, to whose falls
Melodious birds sing madrigals.

And I will make thee beds of roses,
And a thousand fragrant posies;   10
A cap of flowers, and a kirtle,
Embroider'd all with leaves of myrtle.

A gown made of the finest wool,
Which from our pretty lambs we pull;
Fair lined slippers for the cold,   15
With buckles of the purest gold.

A belt of straw and ivy buds,
With coral clasps and amber studs,
An if these pleasures may thee move,
Come live with me, and be my love.   20

The shepherd swains shall dance and sing
For thy delight each May-morning:
If these delights thy mind may move,
Then live with me, and be my love.

SONNETS

WILLIAM SHAKESPEARE

XII

When I do count the clock that tells the time,
And see the brave day sunk in hideous night;
When I behold the violet past prime,
And sable curls all silver'd o'er with white;
When lofty trees I see barren of leaves,   5
Which erst from heat did canopy the herd,
And summer's green all girded up in sheaves,
Borne on the bier with white and bristly beard,
Then of thy beauty do I question make,
That thou among the wastes of time must go,   10
Since sweets and beauties do themselves forsake
And die as fast as they see others grow;
    And nothing 'gainst Time's scythe can make defence
    Save breed, to brave him when he takes thee hence.

XXIX

When, in disgrace with fortune and men's eyes,
I all alone beweep my outcast state,
And trouble deaf heaven with my bootless cries,
And look upon myself, and curse my fate,
Wishing me like to one more rich in hope,   5
Featured like him, like him with friends possess'd,
Desiring this man's art and that man's scope,
With what I most enjoy contented least;
Yet in these thoughts myself almost despising,
Haply I think on thee, and then my state,   10
Like to the larke at break of day arising
From sullen earth, sings hymns at heaven's gate;
    For thy sweet love remember'd such wealth brings
    That then I scorn to change my state with kings.

LX

Like as the waves make towards the pebbled shore,
So do our minutes hasten to their end;
Each changing place with that which goes before,
In sequent toil all forwards do contend.
Nativity, once in the main of light,   5
Crawls to maturity, wherewith being crown'd,
Crooked eclipses 'gainst his glory fight,
And Time that gave doth now his gift confound.

Time doth transfix the flourish set on youth
And delves the parallels in beauty's brow,   10
Feeds on the rarities of nature's truth,
And nothing stands but for his scythe to mow:
    And yet to times in hope my verse shall stand,
    Praising thy worth, despite his cruel hand.

CVI

When in the chronicle of wasted time
I see descriptions of the fairest wights,
And beauty making beautiful old rhyme
In praise of ladies dead and lovely knights,
Then, in the blazon of sweet beauty's best,   5
Of hand, of foot, of lip, of eye, of brow,
I see their antique pen would have express'd
Even such a beauty as you master now.
So all their praises are but prophecies
Of this our time, all you prefiguring;   10
And, for they look'd but with divining eyes,
They had not skill enough your worth to sing:
    For we, which now behold these present days,
    Have eyes to wonder, but lack tongues to praise.

CXVI

Let me not to the marriage of true minds
Admit impediment. Love is not love
Which alters when it alteration finds,
Or bends with the remover to remove:
O, no! it is an ever-fixèd mark,   5
That looks on tempests and is never shaken;
It is the star to every wandering bark,
Whose worth's unknown, although his height be taken.
Love's not Time's fool, though rosy lips and cheeks
Within his bending sickle's compass come;   10
Love alters not with his brief hours and weeks,
But bears it out even to the edge of doom.
    If this be error and upon me proved,
    I never writ, nor no man ever loved.

THE GOOD-MORROW

JOHN DONNE

I wonder by my troth, what thou and I
Did, till we loved? Were we not weaned till then,
But sucked on country pleasures, childishly?

Or snorted we in the seven sleepers' den?
'Twas so; but this, all pleasures fancies be.   5
If ever any beauty I did see,
Which I desired, and got, 'twas but a dream of thee.

And now good morrow to our waking souls,
Which watch not one another out of fear;
For love all love of other sights controls,   10
And makes one little room an everywhere.
Let sea-discoverers to new worlds have gone,
Let maps to other, worlds on worlds have shown;
Let us possess one world, each hath one, and is one.

My face in thine eye, thine in mine appears,   15
And true plain hearts do in the faces rest;
Where can we find two better hemispheres
Without sharp north, without declining west?
Whatever dies was not mixed equally;
If our two loves be one, or thou and I   20
Love so alike that none do slacken, none can die.

COMMUNITY

JOHN DONNE

Good we must love, and must hate ill,
For ill is ill, and good good still,
    But there are things indifferent,
Which we may neither hate, nor love,
But one, and then another prove,   5
    As we shall find our fancy bent.

If then at first wise Nature had
Made women either good or bad,
    Then some we might hate, and some chose,
But since she did them so create,   10
That we may neither love, nor hate,
    Only this rests, All, all may use.

seven sleepers—seven Christian youths,
fleeing to escape martyrdom, found refuge
in a cave, where they woke after a sleep
of 230 years

If they were good it would be seen,
Good is as visible as green,
   And to all eyes it self betrays: 15
If they were bad, they could not last,
Bad doth it self, and others wast,
   So, they deserve nor blame, nor praise.

But they are ours as fruits are ours,
He that but tastes, he that devours,   20
   And he that leaves all, doth as well:
Changed loves are but changed sorts of meat,
And when he hath the kernel eat,
   Who doth not fling away the shell?

THE CANONIZATION

JOHN DONNE

For God's sake hold your tongue, and let me love,
   Or chide my palsy, or my gout,
My five gray hairs, or ruined fortune flout;
   With wealth your state, your mind with arts improve,
     Take you a course, get you a place,   5
     Observe his honor, or his grace,
Or the king's real, or his stampèd face
   Contemplate, what you will, approve,
   So you will let me love.

Alas, alas, who's injured by my love?   10
   What merchant's ships have my sighs drowned?
Who says my tears have overflowed his ground?
   When did my colds a forward spring remove?
     When did the heats which my veins fill
     Add one more to the plaguy bill?   15
Soldiers find wars, and lawyers find out still
   Litigious men, which quarrels move,
   Though she and I do love.

Call us what you will, we are made such by love;
   Call her one, me another fly,   20
We're tapers too, and at our own cost die,
   And we in us find the 'eagle and the dove.

a real—a coin

The phoenix riddle hath more wit
By us; we two being one, are it.
So to one neutral thing both sexes fit,   25
    We die and rise the same, and prove
    Mysterious by this love.

We can die by it, if not live by love,
    And if unfit for tombs and hearse
Our legend be, it will be fit for verse;   30
    And if no piece of chronicle we prove,
        We'll build in sonnets pretty rooms;
        As well a well-wrought urn becomes
The greatest ashes, as half-acre tombs,
    And by these hymns, all shall approve   35
    Us canonized for love;

And thus invoke us: You whom reverend love
    Made one another's hermitage;
You, to whom love was peace, that now is rage;
    Who did the whole world's soul contract, and drove   40
        Into the glasses of your eyes—
        So made such mirrors and such spies
That they did all to you epitomize,—
    Countries, towns, courts; beg from above
    A pattern of your love!   45

THE TRIPLE FOOL

JOHN DONNE

I am two fools, I know,
For loving, and for saying so
    In whining poetry.
But where's that wise man that would not be I
    If she would not deny?   5
Then as th' earth's inward, narrow, crooked lanes
Do purge sea water's fretful salt away,
    I thought if I could draw my pains
Through rhyme's vexation, I should them allay.
Grief brought to numbers cannot be so fierce,   10
For he tames it that fetters it in verse.

    But when I have done so,
Some man, his art and voice to show,
    Doth set and sing my pain,

And by delighting many, frees again 15
    Grief, which verse did restrain.
To love and grief tribute of verse belongs,
But not of such as pleases when 'tis read,
    Both are increased by such songs,
For both their triumphs so are publishèd, 20
And I, which was two fools, do so grow three.
Who are a little wise, the best fools be.

THE FLEA

JOHN DONNE

Mark but this flea, and mark in this,
How little that which thou deny'st me is;
It sucked me first, and now sucks thee,
And in this flea our two bloods mingled be;
Thou know'st that this cannot be said 5
A sin, nor shame, nor loss of maidenhead;
    Yet this enjoys before it woo,
    And pampered swells with one blood made of two,
    And this, alas, is more than we would do.

Oh stay, three lives in one flea spare, 10
Where we almost, yea, more than married are.
This flea is you and I, and this
Our marriage bed, and marriage temple is;
Though parents grudge, and you, w' are met,
And cloistered in these living walls of jet. 15
    Though use make you apt to kill me,
    Let not to that, self-murder added be,
    And sacrilege, three sins in killing three.

Cruel and sudden, hast thou since
Purpled thy nail in blood of innocence? 20
Wherein could this flea guilty be,
Except in that drop which it sucked from thee?
Yet thou triumph'st and say'st that thou
Find'st not thyself, nor me the weaker now;
'Tis true, then learn how false fears be: 25
    Just so much honor, when thou yield'st to me,
    Will waste, as this flea's death took life from thee.

A VALEDICTION FORBIDDING MOURNING

JOHN DONNE

As virtuous men pass mildly away,
 And whisper to their souls to go,
Whilst some of their sad friends do say,
 The breath goes now, and some say, No;

So let us melt, and make no noise,   5
 No tear-floods, nor sigh-tempests move;
'Twere profanation of our joys
 To tell the laity our love.

Moving of th' earth brings harms and fears,
 Men reckon what it did and meant;   10
But trepidation of the spheres,
 Though greater far, is innocent.

Dull sublunary lovers' love,
 Whose soul is sense, cannot admit
Absence, because it doth remove   15
 Those things which elemented it.

But we by a love so much refined
 That ourselves know not what it is,
Inter-assurèd of the mind,
 Care less eyes, lips, hands to miss.   20

Our two souls therefore, which are one,
 Though I must go, endure not yet
A breach, but an expansìon,
 Like gold to airy thinness beat.

If they be two, they are two so   25
 As stiff twin compasses are two;
Thy soul, the fixed foot, makes no show
 To move, but doth if th' other do.

And though it in the center sit,
 Yet when the other far doth roam,   30
It leans, and hearkens after it,
 And grows erect as that comes home.

Such wilt thou be to me who must,
 Like th' other foot, obliquely run;
Thy firmness makes my circle just,   35
 And makes me end where I begun.

A LECTURE UPON THE SHADOW

JOHN DONNE

Stand still, and I will read to thee
A lecture, love, in love's philosophy.
   These three hours that we have spent
   Walking here, two shadows went
Along with us, which we ourselves produced;   5
   But, now the sun is just above our head,
   We do those shadows tread,
And to brave clearness all things are reduced.
   So whilst our infant loves did grow,
   Disguises did, and shadows, flow   10
   From us and our cares, but now 'tis not so.

That love hath not attained the high'st degree,
Which is still diligent lest others see.

Except our loves at this noon stay,
We shall new shadows make the other way.   20
   As the first were made to blind
   Others, these which come behind
Will work upon ourselves, and blind our eyes.
   If our loves faint, and westwardly decline,
   To me thou falsely thine,   25
And I to thee, mine actions shall disguise.
   The morning shadows wear away,
   But these grow longer all the day;
   But oh, love's day is short, if love decay.

Love is a growing, or full constant light,   30
And his short minute after noon, is night.

from HOLY SONNETS

JOHN DONNE

I

Thou hast made me, and shall thy work decay?
Repair me now, for now mine end doth haste;
I run to death, and death meets me as fast,
And all my pleasures are like yesterday.
I dare not move my dim eyes any way,   5

Despair behind, and death before doth cast
Such terror, and my feeble flesh doth waste
By sin in it, which it towards hell doth weigh.
Only thou art above, and when towards thee
By thy leave I can look, I rise again;   10
But our old subtle foe so tempteth me
That not one hour myself I can sustain.
Thy grace may wing me to prevent his art,
And thou like adamant draw mine iron heart.

VII

At the round earth's imagined corners, blow
Your trumpets, angels; and arise, arise
From death, you numberless infinities
Of souls, and to your scattered bodies go;
All whom the flood did, and fire shall o'erthrow,   5
All whom war, dearth, age, agues, tyrannies,
Despair, law, chance hath slain, and you whose eyes
Shall behold God and never taste death's woe.
But let them sleep, Lord, and me mourn a space,
For if above all these my sins abound,   10
'Tis late to ask abundance of thy grace
When we are there; here on this lowly ground
Teach me how to repent; for that's as good
As if thou'dst sealed my pardon with thy blood.

X

Death, be not proud, though some have callèd thee
Mighty and dreadful, for thou art not so;
For those whom thou think'st thou dost overthrow
Die not, poor Death, nor yet canst thou kill me.
From rest and sleep, which but thy pictures be,   5
Much pleasure; then from thee much more must flow,
And soonest our best men with thee do go,
Rest of their bones, and soul's delivery.
Thou art slave to fate, chance, kings, and desperate men,
And dost with poison, war, and sickness dwell,   10
And poppy or charms can make us sleep as well
And better than thy stroke; why swell'st thou then?
One short sleep past, we wake eternally,
And death shall be no more; Death, thou shalt die.

XIV

Batter my heart, three-personed God, for you
As yet but knock, breathe, shine, and seek to mend;
That I may rise and stand, o'erthrow me; and bend
Your force to break, blow, burn, and make me new.
I, like an usurped tower t'another due,   5
Labor to admit you, but oh, to no end.
Reason, your viceroy in me, me should defend,
But is captived, and proves weak or untrue.
Yet dearly I love you, and would be lovèd fain,
But am betrothed unto your enemy;   10
Divorce me, untie or break that knot again;
Take me to you, imprison me, for I,
Except you enthrall me, never shall be free,
Nor ever chaste, except you ravish me.

GOOD FRIDAY, 1613. RIDING WESTWARD

JOHN DONNE

Let man's soul be a sphere, and then in this
The intelligence that moves, devotion is;
And as the other spheres, by being grown
Subject to foreign motion, lose their own,
And being by others hurried every day   5
Scarce in a year their natural form obey,
Pleasure or business, so, our souls admit
For their first mover, and are whirled by it.
Hence is 't that I am carried towards the west
This day, when my soul's form bends towards the east.   10
There I should see a sun, by rising set,
And by that setting, endless day beget;
But that Christ on this cross did rise and fall,
Sin had eternally benighted all.
Yet dare I almost be glad I do not see   15
That spectacle of too much weight for me.
Who sees God's face, that is self life, must die;
What a death were it then to see God die!
It made his own lieutenant, nature, shrink;
It made his footstool crack, and the sun wink.   20
Could I behold those hands which span the poles
And tune all spheres at once, pierced with those holes?
Could I behold that endless height, which is
Zenith to us and our antipodes,

Humbled below us? or that blood which is 25
The seat of all our souls, if not of his,
Made dirt of dust, or that flesh which was worn
By God for his apparel, ragg'd and torn?
If on these things I durst not look, durst I
Upon his miserable mother cast mine eye, 30
Who was God's partner here, and furnished thus
Half of that sacrifice which ransomed us?
Though these things, as I ride, be from mine eye,
They are present yet unto my memory,
For that looks towards them; and thou look'st towards me, 35
O Savior, as thou hang'st upon the tree;
I turn my back to thee but to receive
Corrections, till thy mercies bid thee leave.
Oh, think me worth thine anger, punish me,
Burn off my rusts, and my deformity; 40
Restore thine image, so much, by thy grace,
That thou mayst know me, and I'll turn my face.

A HYMN TO CHRIST, AT THE AUTHOR'S LAST GOING INTO GERMANY

JOHN DONNE

In what torn ship soever I embark,
That ship shall be my emblem of thy ark;
What sea soever swallow me, that flood
Shall be to me an emblem of thy blood;
Though thou with clouds of anger do disguise 5
Thy face, yet through that mask I know those eyes,
 Which, though they turn away sometimes,
  They never will despise.

I sacrifice this island unto thee,
And all whom I loved there, and who loved me; 10
When I have put our seas 'twixt them and me,
Put thou thy seas betwixt my sins and thee.
As the tree's sap doth seek the root below
In winter, in my winter now I go
 Where none but thee, th' eternal root 15
  Of true love, I may know.

Nor thou nor thy religion dost control
The amorousness of an harmonious soul,

But thou wouldst have that love thyself; as thou
Art jealous, Lord, so I am jealous now;   20
Thou lov'st not, till from loving more thou free
My soul; whoever gives, takes liberty;
    Oh, if thou car'st not whom I love,
        Alas, thou lov'st not me.

Seal then this bill of my divorce to all   25
On whom those fainter beams of love did fall;
Marry those loves, which in youth scattered be
On fame, wit, hopes (false mistresses), to thee.
Churches are best for prayer that have least light:
To see God only, I go out of sight;   30
    And to scape stormy days, I choose
        An everlasting night.

A HYMN TO GOD THE FATHER

JOHN DONNE

Wilt thou forgive that sin where I begun,
    Which was my sin, though it were done before?
Wilt thou forgive that sin through which I run,
    And do run still, though still I do deplore?
        When thou hast done, thou hast not done,   5
            For I have more.

Wilt thou forgive that sin which I have won
    Others to sin, and made my sin their door?
Wilt thou forgive that sin which I did shun
    A year or two, but wallowed in a score?   10
        When thou hast done, thou hast not done,
            For I have more.

I have a sin of fear, that when I have spun
    My last thread, I shall perish on the shore;
But swear by thyself, that at my death thy Son   15
    Shall shine as he shines now, and heretofore;
        And having done that, thou hast done;
            I fear no more.

TO MY BOOK

BEN JONSON

It will be looked for, book, when some but see
Thy title, 'Epigrams,' and named of me,
Thou should'st be bold, licentious, full of gall,
Wormwood, and sulphur, sharp and toothed withal;
Become a petulant thing, hurl ink and wit,   5
As madmen stones, not caring whom they hit.
Deceive their malice, who could wish it so.
And by thy wiser temper, let men know
Thou art not covetous of least self-fame,
Made from the hazard of another's shame;   10
Much less with lewd, profane, and beastly phrase,
To catch the world's loose laughter or vain gaze.
He that departs with his own honesty
For vulgar praise, doth it too dearly buy.

A CELEBRATION OF CHARIS
4. Her Triumph

BEN JONSON

See the chariot at hand here of Love,
   Wherein my lady rideth!
Each that draws is a swan or a dove,
   And well the car Love guideth.
As she goes, all hearts do duty   5
   Unto her beauty;
And enamoured, do wish, so they might
   But enjoy such a sight,
That they still were to run by her side,
Through swords, through seas, whither she would ride.   10

Do but look on her eyes; they do light
   All that Love's world compriseth!
Do but look on her hair; it is bright
   As Love's star when it riseth!
Do but mark, her forehead's smoother   15
   Than words that soothe her!
And from her archèd brows, such a grace
   Sheds itself through the face,
As alone there triumphs to the life
All the gain, all the good of the elements' strife.   20

Have you seen but a bright lily grow,
   Before rude hands have touched it?
Ha' you marked but the fall o' the snow,
   Before the soil hath smutched it?
Ha' you felt the wool of bever,   25
     Or swan's-down ever?
Or have smelt o' the bud o' the briar,
     Or the nard in the fire?
Or have tasted the bag of the bee?
O so white! O so soft! O so sweet is she!

INVITING A FRIEND TO SUPPER

BEN JONSON

Tonight, grave sir, both my poor house and I
Do equally desire your company;
Not that we think us worthy such a guest,
But that your worth will dignify our feast
With those that come, whose grace may make that seem   5
Something, which else could hope for no esteem.
It is the fair acceptance, sir, creates
The entertainment perfect; not the cates.
Yet you shall have, to rectify your palate,
An olive, capers, or some better salad   10
Ush'ring the mutton; with a short-legged hen,
If we can get her, full of eggs, and then
Lemons and wine for sauce; to these a coney
Is not to be despaired of, for our money;
And though fowl now be scarce, yet there are clerks,   15
The sky not falling, think we may have larks.
I'll tell you of more, and lie, so you will come:
Of partridge, pheasant, woodcock, of which some
May yet be there; and godwit, if we can;
Knat, rail, and ruff too. Howsoe'er, my man   20
Shall read a piece of Virgil, Tacitus,
Livy, or of some better book to us,
Of which we'll speak our minds, amidst our meat.
And I'll profess no verses to repeat;
To this, if aught appear which I not know of,   25
That will the pastry, not my paper, show of.
Digestive cheese and fruit there sure will be;
But that which most doth take my Muse and me
Is a pure cup of rich Canary wine,

cates—supplies
godwit etc.—edible birds

Which is the Mermaid's now, but shall be mine;   30
Of which had Horace or Anacreon tasted,
Their lives, as do their lines, till now had lasted.
Tobacco, nectar, or the Thespian spring
Are all but Luther's beer to this I sing.
Of this we will sup free, but moderately,   35
And we will have no Polly or Parrot by;
Nor shall our cups make any guilty men,
But at our parting we will be as when
We innocently met. No simple word
That shall be uttered at our mirthful board,   40
Shall make us sad next morning, or affright
The liberty that we'll enjoy tonight.

DEAN-BOURN, A RUDE RIVER IN DEVON, BY WHICH SOMETIMES HE LIVED

ROBERT HERRICK

Dean-bourn, farewell; I never look to see
Dean, or thy warty incivility.
Thy rocky bottom that doth tear thy streams
And makes them frantic, ev'n to all extremes,
To my content I never should behold,   5
Were thy streams silver, or thy rocks all gold.
Rocky thou art, and rocky we discover
Thy men, and rocky are thy ways all over.
O men, O manners, now and ever known
To be a rocky generation!   10
A people currish, churlish as the seas,
And rude, almost, as rudest savages,
With whom I did, and may re-sojourn, when
Rocks turn to rivers, rivers turn to men.

UPON LOVE, BY WAY OF QUESTION AND ANSWER

ROBERT HERRICK

I bring ye love, *Quest.* What will love do?
Ans. Like, and dislike ye:

Polly or Parrot—Poley, Parrot, two known
informers

I bring ye love: *Quest*. What will love do?
  Ans. Stroke ye to strike ye.
I bring ye love: *Quest*. What will love do? 5
  Ans. Love will be-fool ye:
I bring ye love: *Quest*. What will love do?
  Ans. Heat ye to cool ye:
I bring ye love: *Quest*. What will love do?
  Ans. Love gifts will send ye: 10
I bring ye love: *Quest*. What will love do?
  Ans. Stock ye to spend ye:
I bring ye love: *Quest*. What will love do?
  Ans. Love will fulfill ye:
I bring ye love: *Quest*. What will love do? 15
  Ans. Kiss ye, to kill ye.

CORINNA'S GOING A-MAYING

ROBERT HERRICK

Get up, get up for shame, the blooming morn
Upon her wings presents the god unshorn.
  See how Aurora throws her fair
  Fresh-quilted colors through the air;
  Get up, sweet slug-a-bed, and see 5
  The dew bespangling herb and tree.
Each flower has wept and bowèd toward the east
Above an hour since, yet you not dressed;
  Nay, not so much as out of bed.
  When all the birds have matins said, 10
  And sung their thankful hymns, 'tis sin,
  Nay, profanation to keep in,
Whenas a thousand virgins on this day
Spring, sooner than the lark, to fetch in May.

Rise and put on your foliage, and be seen 15
To come forth like the springtime, fresh and green,
  And sweet as Flora. Take no care
  For jewels for your gown or hair;
  Fear not, the leaves will strew
  Gems in abundance upon you; 20
Besides, the childhood of the day has kept,
Against you come, some orient pearls unwept;
  Come and receive them while the light
  Hangs on the dew-locks of the night,
  And Titan on the eastern hill 25

Retires himself, or else stands still
Till you come forth. Wash, dress, be brief in praying:
Few beads are best when once we go a-maying.
Come, my Corinna, come; and coming, mark
How each field turns a street, each street a park   30
   Made green and trimmed with trees; see how
   Devotion gives each house a bough
   Or branch; each porch, each door, ere this,
     An ark, a tabernacle is,
Made up of white-thorn neatly interwove,   35
As if here were those cooler shades of love.
   Can such delights be in the street
   And open fields, and we not see't?
   Come, we'll abroad, and let's obey
   The proclamation made for May,   40
And sin no more, as we have done, by staying;
But, my Corinna, come, let's go a-maying.

There's not a budding boy or girl this day
But is got up, and gone to bring in May.
   A deal of youth, ere this, is come   45
   Back, and with white-thorn laden, home.
   Some have despatched their cakes and cream
   Before that we have left to dream;
And some have wept, and wooed, and plighted troth,
And chose their priest, ere we can cast off sloth;   50
   Many a green-gown has been given,
   Many a kiss, both odd and even,
Many a glance too has been sent
   From out the eye, love's firmament,
Many a jest told of the keys betraying   55
This night, and locks picked, yet we're not a-maying.

Come, let us go while we are in our prime,
And take the harmless folly of the time.
   We shall grow old apace, and die
   Before we know our liberty.   60
   Our life is short, and our days run
   As fast away as does the sun;
And as a vapor, or a drop of rain
Once lost, can ne'er be found again,
   So when or you or I are made   65
   A fable, song, or fleeting shade,
   All love, all liking, all delight
   Lies drowned with us in endless night.
Then while time serves, and we are but decaying,
Come, my Corinna, come, let's go a-maying.

JORDAN [1]

GEORGE HERBERT

Who says that fictions only and false hair
Become a verse? Is there in truth no beauty?
Is all good structure in a winding stair?
May no lines pass except they do their duty
    Not to a true, but painted chair?   5

Is it no verse except enchanted groves
And sudden arbors shadow coarse-spun lines?
Must purling streams refresh a lover's loves?
Must all be veiled, while he that reads, divines,
    Catching the sense at two removes?   10

Shepherds are honest people; let them sing.
Riddle who list for me, and pull for prime;
I envy no man's nightingale or spring,
Nor let them punish me with loss of rhyme,
    Who plainly say, My God, my King.   15

VIRTUE

GEORGE HERBERT

Sweet day, so cool, so calm, so bright,
  The bridal of the earth and sky;
The dew shall weep thy fall to-night,
    For thou must die.

Sweet rose, whose hue angry and brave   5
  Bids the rash gazer wipe his eye;
Thy root is ever in its grave,
    And thou must die.

Sweet spring, full of sweet days and roses,
  A box where sweets compacted lie;   10
My music shows ye have your closes,
    And all must die.

Only a sweet and virtuous soul,
  Like seasoned timber, never gives;

pull for prime—draw for a winning hand
in a card game

But though the whole world turn to coal,   15
  Then chiefly lives.

LOVE

GEORGE HERBERT

Love bade me welcome, yet my soul drew back,
  Guilty of dust and sin.
But quick-eyed Love, observing me grow slack
  From my first entrance in,
Drew nearer to me, sweetly questioning   5
  If I lacked anything.

A guest, I answered, worthy to be here.
  Love said, You shall be he.
I, the unkind, the ungrateful? ah, my dear,
  I cannot look on thee.   10
Love took my hand and smiling did reply,
  Who made the eyes but I?

Truth, Lord, but I have marred them; let my shame
  Go where it doth deserve.
And know you not, says Love, who bore the blame?   15
  My dear, then I will serve.
You must sit down, says Love, and taste my meat.
  So I did sit and eat.

Stanzas from
CONTEMPLATIONS

ANNE BRADSTREET

Some time now past in the autumnal tide,
  When Phoebus wanted but one hour to bed,
The trees all richly clad, yet void of pride,
  Were gilded o'er by his rich golden head;
Their leaves and fruits seemed painted, but were true,   5
Of green, of red, of yellow, mixéd hue.
Rapt were my senses at this delectable view.

I wist not what to wish, yet sure, thought I,
  If so much excellence abide below

How excellent is He that dwells on high,   10
    Whose power and beauty by his works we know!
Sure He is wisdom, goodness, glory, light,
That hath this under world so richly dight.
More heaven than earth was here, no winter and no night.

Then on a stately oak I cast mine eye,   15
    Whose ruffling top the clouds seemed to aspire.
How long since thou wast in thine infancy?
    Thy strength and stature more thy years admire.
Hath hundred winters passed since thou wast born,
Or thousand since thou break'st thy shell of horn?   20
If so, all these as naught eternity doth scorn.

Then higher on the glistering sun I gazed,
    Whose beams were shaded by the leafy tree;
The more I looked the more I grew amazed,
    And softly said, What glory's like to thee?   25
Soul of this world, this universe's eye,
No wonder some made thee a deity.
Had I not better known, alas, the same had I.

Thou as a bridegroom from thy chamber rushes,
    And as a strong man joys to run a race;   30
The morn doth usher thee with smiles and blushes,
    The earth reflects her glances in thy face.
Birds, insects, animals, with vegetive,
Thy heart from death and dulness doth revive,
And in the darksome womb of fruitful nature dive.   35

Thy swift annual and diurnal course,
    Thy daily straight and yearly oblique path,
Thy pleasing fervor, and thy scorching force,
    All mortals here the feeling knowledge hath.
Thy presence makes it day, thy absence night.   40
Quaternal seasons caoséd by thy might.
Hail, creature full of sweetness, beauty, and delight!

Art thou so full of glory that no eye
    Hath strength thy shining rays once to behold?
And is thy splendid throne erect so high   45
    As to approach it can no earthly mould?
How full of glory then must thy Creator be
Who gave this bright light luster unto thee?
Admired, adored, forever be that Majesty.
Silent, alone, where none or saw or heard,   50
    In pathless paths I led my wandering feet;

My humble eyes to lofty skies I reared,
    To sing some song my amazéd muse thought meet.
My great Creator I would magnify
That nature had thus decked liberally.   55
But ah, and ah again, my imbecility!

I heard the merry grasshopper then sing,
    The black-clad cricket bear a second part;
They kept one tune and played on the same string,
    Seeming to glory in their little art.   60
Shall creatures abject thus their voices raise,
And in their kind resound their maker's praise,
Whilst I as mute can warble forth no higher lays?

UPON OUR LATE LOSS OF
THE DUKE OF CAMBRIDGE

EDMUND WALLER

The failing blossoms, which a young plant bears,
Engage our hope for the succeeding years:
And hope is all which Art or Nature brings,
At the first trial, to accomplish things.
Mankind was first created an essay;   5
That ruder draught the deluge wash'd away.
How many ages pass'd, what blood and toil,
Before we made one kingdom of this isle!
How long in vain had Nature striv'd to frame
A perfect princess, ere her highness came?   10
For joys so great we must with patience wait,
'Tis the set price of happiness complete.
As a first-fruit, Heaven claim'd that lovely boy:
The next shall live, and be the nation's joy.

ON THE HEAD OF A STAG

EDMUND WALLER

So we some antique hero's strength
Learn by his lance's weight, and length;

As these vast beams express the beast,
Whose shady brows alive they drest.
Such game, while yet the world was new,   5
The mighty Nimrod did pursue.
What huntsman of our feeble race,
Or dogs, dare such a monster chase?
Resembling, with each blow he strikes,
The charge of a whole troop of pikes.   10
O fertile head! which every year
Could such a crop of wonder bear!
The teeming Earth did never bring,
So soon, so hard, so huge a thing:
Which might it never have been cast,   15
(Each year's growth added to the last)
These lofty branches had supply'd
The Earth's bold sons' prodigious pride:
Heaven with these engines had been scal'd,
When mountains heap'd on mountains fail'd.

SONNETS

JOHN MILTON

XV

On the Late Massacre in Piedmont

Avenge O Lord thy slaughtered saints, whose bones
 Lie scattered on the Alpine mountains cold,
 Ev'n them who kept thy truth so pure of old
 When all our fathers worshipped stocks and stones,
Forget not: in thy book record their groans   5
 Who were thy sheep and in their ancient fold
 Slain by the bloody Piemontese that rolled
 Mother with infant down the rocks. Their moans
The vales redoubled to the hills, and they
 To Heaven. Their martyred blood and ashes sow   10
 O'er all th'Italian fields where still doth sway
The triple tyrant: that from these may grow
 A hundredfold, who having learnt thy way
 Early may fly the Babylonian woe.

XVI

When I consider how my light is spent
 Ere half my days in this dark world and wide,
 And that one talent which is death to hide,
 Lodged with me useless, though my soul more bent

100

To serve therewith my Maker, and present   5
    My true account, lest he returning chide,
    Doth God exact day-labour, light denied?
    I fondly ask; but Patience to prevent
That murmur, soon replies, God doth not need
    Either man's work or his own gifts; who best   10
    Bear his mild yoke, they serve him best. His state
Is kingly. Thousands at his bidding speed
    And post o'er land and ocean without rest:
    They also serve who only stand and wait.

LYCIDAS

JOHN MILTON

In this monody the author bewails a
learned friend, unfortunately drowned in
his passage from Chester on the Irish seas,
1637. And by occasion foretells the ruin
of our corrupted clergy, then in their
height.

Yet once more, O ye laurels, and once more
Ye myrtles brown, with ivy never sere,
I come to pluck your berries harsh and crude,
And with forced fingers rude,
Shatter your leaves before the mellowing year.   5
Bitter constraint, and sad occasion dear,
Compels me to disturb your season due:
For Lycidas is dead, dead ere his prime
Young Lycidas, and hath not left his peer:
Who would not sing for Lycidas? He knew   10
Himself to sing, and build the lofty rhyme.
He must not float upon his watery bier
Unwept, and welter to the parching wind,
Without the meed of some melodious tear.
    Begin then, sisters of the sacred well   15
That from beneath the seat of Jove doth spring,
Begin, and somewhat loudly sweep the string.
Hence with denial vain, and coy excuse;
So may some gentle Muse
With lucky words favour my destined urn,   20
And as he passes turn,
And bid fair peace be to my sable shroud.
For we were nursed upon the self-same hill,

Fed the same flock, by fountain, shade, and rill.
   Together both, ere the high lawns appeared   25
Under the opening eyelids of the morn,
We drove afield, and both together heard
What time the gray-fly winds her sultry horn,
Battening our flocks with the fresh dews of night,
Oft till the star that rose at evening bright   30
Toward Heaven's descent had sloped his westering wheel.
Meanwhile the rural ditties were not mute,
Tempered to th'oaten flute;
Rough satyrs danced, and fauns with cloven heel,
From the glad sound would not be absent long,   35
And old Damoetas loved to hear our song.
   But O the heavy change, now thou art gone,
Now thou art gone, and never must return!
Thee shepherd, thee the woods, and desert caves,
With wild thyme and the gadding vine o'ergrown,   40
And all their echoes mourn.
The willows, and the hazel copses green,
Shall now no more be seen,
Fanning their joyous leaves to thy soft lays.
As killing as the canker to the rose,   45
Or taint-worm to the weanling herds that graze,
Or frost to flowers that their gay wardrobe wear,
When first the white thorn blows;
Such, Lycidas, thy loss to shepherds' ear.
   Where were ye nymphs when the remorseless deep   50
Closed o'er the head of your loved Lycidas?
For neither were ye playing on the steep,
Where your old Bards, the famous Druids lie,
Nor on the shaggy top of Mona high,
Nor yet where Deva spreads her wizard stream: 55
Ay me, I fondly dream!
Had ye been there—for what could that have done?
What could the Muse herself that Orpheus bore,
The Muse herself, for her inchanting son
Whom universal nature did lament,   60
When by the rout that made the hideous roar,
His gory visage down the stream was sent,
Down the swift Hebrus to the Lesbian shore.
   Alas! What boots it with uncessant care
To tend the homely slighted shepherd's trade,   65
And strictly meditate the thankless muse,
Were it not better done as others use,
To sport with Amaryllis in the shade,
Or with the tangles of Neaera's hair?
Fame is the spur that the clear spirit doth raise   70

(That last infirmity of noble mind)
To scorn delights, and live laborious days;
But the fair guerdon when we hope to find,
And think to burst out into sudden blaze,
Comes the blind Fury with th'abhorred shears,   75
And slits the thin spun life. But not the praise,
Phoebus replied, and touched my trembling ears:
Fame is no plant that grows on mortal soil,
Nor in the glistering foil
Set off to th'world, nor in broad rumour lies,   80
But lives and spreads aloft by those pure eyes,
And perfect witness of all-judging Jove;
As he pronounces lastly on each deed,
Of so much fame in Heaven expect thy meed.
    O fountain Arethuse, and thou honoured flood,   85
Smooth-sliding Mincius, crowned with vocal reeds,
That strain I heard was of a higher mood.
But now my oat proceeds,
And listens to the herald of the sea
That came in Neptune's plea;   90
He asked the waves, and asked the felon winds,
What hard mishap hath doomed this gentle swain?
And questioned every gust of rugged wings
That blows from off each beaked promontory;
They knew not of his story;   95
And sage Hippotades their answer brings,
That not a blast was from his dungeon strayed,
The air was calm, and on the level brine,
Sleek Panope with all her sisters played.
It was that fatal and perfidious bark   100
Built in th'eclipse, and rigged with curses dark,
That sunk so low that sacred head of thine.
    Next Camus, reverend sire, went footing slow,
His mantle hairy, and his bonnet sedge,
Inwrought with figures dim, and on the edge   105
Like to that sanguine flower inscribed with woe.
Ah! who hath reft (quoth he) my dearest pledge?
Last came and last did go,
The pilot of the Galilean lake,
Two massy keys he bore of metals twain,   110
(The golden opes, the iron shuts amain)
He shook his mitred locks, and stern bespake,
How well could I have spared for thee, young swain,
Enow of such as for their bellies' sake,
Creep and intrude, and climb into the fold?   115
Of other care they little reckoning make,
Than how to scramble at the shearers' feast,

And shove away the worthy bidden guest.
Blind mouths! That scarce themselves know how to hold
A sheep-hook, or have learned aught else the least   120
That to the faithful herdsman's art belongs!
What recks it them? What need they? They are sped;
And when they list, their lean and flashy songs
Grate on their scrannel pipes of wretched straw;
The hungry sheep look up, and are not fed,   125
But swoln with wind, and the rank mist they draw,
Rot inwardly, and foul contagion spread:
Besides what the grim wolf with privy paw
Daily devours apace, and nothing said.
But that two-handed engine at the door,   130
Stands ready to smite once, and smite no more.
    Return Alpheus, the dread voice is past,
That shrunk thy streams; return Sicilian muse,
And call the vales, and bid them hither cast
Their bells, and flowerets of a thousand hues.   135
Ye valleys low where the mild whispers use,
Of shades and wanton winds, and gushing brooks,
On whose fresh lap the swart star sparely looks,
Throw hither all your quaint enamelled eyes,
That on the green turf suck the honeyed showers,   140
And purple all the ground with vernal flowers.
Bring the rathe primrose that forsaken dies.
The tufted crow-toe, and pale jessamine,
The white pink, and the pansy freaked with jet,
The glowing violet.   145
The musk-rose, and the well attired woodbine.
With cowslips wan that hang the pensive head,
And every flower that sad embroidery wears:
Bid amaranthus all his beauty shed,
And daffadillies fill their cups with tears,   150
To strew the laureate hearse where Lycid lies.
For so to interpose a little ease,
Let our frail thoughts dally with false surmise.
Ay me! Whilst thee the shores, and sounding seas
Wash far away, where e'er thy bones are hurled,   155
Whether beyond the stormy Hebrides,
Where thou perhaps under the whelming tide
Visit'st the bottom of the monstrous world;
Or whether thou to our moist vows denied,
Sleepst by the fable of Bellerus old,   160
Where the great vision of the guarded mount
Looks toward Namancos and Bayona's hold;
Look homeward angel now, and melt with ruth.
And, O ye dolphins, waft the hapless youth.

Weep no more, woeful shepherds, weep no more,   165
For Lycidas your sorrow is not dead,
Sunk though he be beneath the watery floor,
So sinks the day-star in the ocean bed,
And yet anon repairs his drooping head,
And tricks his beams, and with new spangled ore,   170
Flames in the forehead of the morning sky:
So Lycidas sunk low, but mounted high,
Through the dear might of him that walked the waves,
Where other groves, and other streams along,
With nectar pure his oozy locks he laves,   175
And hears the unexpressive nuptial song,
In the blest kingdoms meek of joy and love.
There entertain him all the saints above,
In solemn troops and sweet societies
That sing, and singing in their glory move,   180
And wipe the tears for ever from his eyes.
Now Lycidas the shepherds weep no more;
Henceforth thou art the genius of the shore,
In thy large recompense, and shalt be good
To all that wander in that perilous flood.   185
   Thus sang the uncouth swain to th'oaks and rills,
While the still morn went out with sandals gray;
He touched the tender stops of various quills,
With eager thought warbling his Doric lay:
And now the sun had stretched out all the hills,   190
And now was dropt into the western bay;
At last he rose, and twitched his mantle blue:
To-morrow to fresh woods, and pastures new.

UPON THE BODY OF OUR BL. LORD, NAKED AND BLOODY

RICHARD CRASHAW

They have left thee naked, LORD, O that they had!
This garment too I would they had deny'd.

   Thee with thy self they have too richly clad;
Opening the purple wardrobe in thy side.

   O never could there be garment too good   5
For thee to wear, But this, of thine own Blood.

THE MUSE

ABRAHAM COWLEY

NOTE: Pindar in the 6. *Olymp.* has a *Fancy* somewhat of this kind;
where he says, 'Ω φίυτις ἀλλά ,ζεῦξον ἤδη μοι σθέυος ἡμιόνων ʼ
Αττάχος ὄφρα κελεύθψ τʼ ἐν καθαρᾳ βάσωμεν ὂχχον. sed, ô Phinty,
junge jam mihi robur Mularum quibus celeritas est, ut viâ purâ
ducamus currum. Where by the Name of *Phintis* he speaks to his
own Soul. O, my *Soul*, join me the strong and swift *Mules* together,
that I may drive the *Chariot* in this fair way.

1.

Go, the rich Chariot instantly prepare;
The Queen, my Muse, will take the air;
Unruly Fancy with strong Judgment trace,
   Put in nimble-footed Wit,
   Smooth-paced Eloquency join with it,   5
Sound Memory with young Invention place,
   Harness all the winged race.
Let the Postillion Nature mount, and let
   The Coachman Art be set.
And let the airy Footmen running all beside,   10
   Make a long row of goodly pride.
Figures, Conceits, Raptures, and Sentences
   In a well-worded dress.
And innocent Loves, and pleasant Truths, and useful Lies,
In all their gaudy Liveries.   15
   Mount, glorious Queen, thy travelling Throne,
     And bid it to put on;
   For long, though cheerful, is the way,
And Life, alas, allows but one ill winters Day.

2.

Where never Foot of Man, or Hoof of Beast,   20
     The passage prest,
   Where never Fish did fly,
And with short silver wings cut the low liquid Sky.
   Where Bird with painted Oars did near
Row through the trackless Ocean of the Air.   25
     Where never yet did pry
   The busy Mornings curious Eye:
The Wheels of thy bold Coach pass quick and free;
   And all's an open Road to Thee.
     Whatever God did Say,   30

Is all thy plain and smooth, uninterrupted way.
Nay even beyond his works thy Voyages are known,
　　Thou 'hast thousand worlds too of thine own.
Thou speakst, great Queen, in the same style as He,
And a New world leaps forth when Thou say'st, Let it Be.　35

3.

Thou fathom'st the deep Gulf of Ages past,
　　And canst pluck up with ease
The years which Thou dost please,
Like shipwrecked Treasures by rude Tempests cast
　　Long since into the Sea,　　　　　　　　　　40
Brought up again to light and public Use by Thee.
　　Nor dost thou only Dive so low,
　　　　But Fly
With an unwearied Wing the other way on high,
　　Where Fates among the Stars do grow;　　　45
There into the close Nests of Time dost peep,
　　And there with piercing Eye,
Through the firm shell, and the thick White dost spy,
　　Years to come a forming lie,
Close in their sacred Secondine asleep,　　　　50
　　Till hatched by the Suns vital heat
　　Which o're them yet does brooding set
　　They Life and Motion get,
　　And ripe at last with vigorous might
Break through the Shell, and take their everlasting Flight.　55

4.

　　And sure we may
　　The same too of the Present say,
If Past, and Future Times do thee obey.
　　Thou stopst this Current, and dost make
This running River settle like a Lake,　　　　60
Thy certain hand holds fast this slippery Snake.
　　The Fruit which does so quickly waste,
　　Men scarce can see it, much less taste,
Thou Comfitest in Sweets to make it last.
　　This shining piece of Ice　　　　　　　65
　　Which melts so soon away
　　　　With the Suns ray,
Thy Verse does solidate and Crystallize,
　　Till it a lasting Mirror be.
　　Nay thy Immortal Rhyme　　　　　　70
　　Makes this one short Point of Time,
To fill up half the Orb of Round Eternity.

TO LUCASTA, ON GOING TO THE WARS

RICHARD LOVELACE

Tell me not, sweet, I am unkind,
    That from the nunnery
Of thy chaste breast and quiet mind
    To war and arms I fly.

True, a new mistress now I chase,   5
    The first foe in the field;
And with a stronger faith embrace
    A sword, a horse, a shield.

Yet this inconstancy is such
    As thou too shalt adore: 10
I could not love thee, dear, so much,
    Loved I not honor more.

THE GRASSHOPPER

RICHARD LOVELACE

TO MY NOBLE FRIEND MR. CHARLES COTTON. ODE

O thou that swing'st upon the waving hair
    Of some well-filled oaten beard,
Drunk ev'ry night with a delicious tear
    Dropt thee from heav'n, where now th' art rear'd;

The joys of earth and air are thine entire,   5
    That with thy feet and wings dost hop and fly;
And when thy poppy works thou dost retire
    To thy carv'd acorn-bed to lie.

Up with the day, the sun thou welcom'st then,
    Sport'st in the gilt plats of his beams,   10
And all these merry days mak'st merry men,
    Thyself and melancholy streams.

But ah the sickle! golden ears are cropt;
    Ceres and Bacchus bid good night;
Sharp frosty fingers all your flow'rs have topt,   15
    And what scythes spar'd, winds shave off quite.

Poor verdant fool, and now green ice! thy joys,
    Large and as lasting as thy perch of grass,

Bid us lay in 'gainst winter rain, and poise
    Their floods with an o'erflowing glass.   20

Thou best of men and friends! we will create
    A genuine Summer in each other's breast;
And spite of this cold Time and frozen Fate,
    Thaw us a warm seat to our rest.

Our sacred hearths shall burn eternally   25
    As vestal flames; the North-wind, he
Shall strike his frost-stretch'd wings, dissolve, and fly
    This Etna in epitome.

Dropping December shall come weeping in,
    Bewail th' usurping of his reign;   30
But when in show'rs of old Greek we begin,
    Shall cry he hath his crown again.

Night as clear Hesper shall our tapers whip
    From the light casements where we play,
And the dark hag from her black mantle strip,   35
    And stick there everlasting day.

Thus richer than untempted kings are we,
    That asking nothing, nothing need:
Though lord of all what seas embrace, yet he
    That wants himself is poor indeed.

THE DEFINITION OF LOVE

ANDREW MARVELL

My love is of a birth as rare
    As 'tis for object strange and high;
It was begotten by despair
    Upon impossibility.

Magnanimous despair alone   5
    Could show me so divine a thing,
Where feeble hope could ne'er have flown,
    But vainly flapped its tinsel wing.

And yet I quickly might arrive
    Where my extended soul is fixed   10

But fate does iron wedges drive,
And always crowds itself betwixt.

For fate with jealous eye does see
Two perfect loves, nor lets them close;
Their union would her ruin be,   15
And her tyrannic power depose.

And therefore her decrees of steel
Us as the distant poles have placed,
Though love's whole world on us doth wheel,
Not by themselves to be embraced;   20

Unless the giddy heaven fall,
And earth some new convulsion tear,
And, us to join, the world should all
Be cramped into a planisphere.

As lines, so loves, oblique may well   25
Themselves in every angle greet;
But ours so truly parallel,
Though infinite, can never meet.

Therefore the love which doth us bind,
But fate so enviously debars,   30
Is the conjunction of the mind,
And opposition of the stars.

THE GARDEN

ANDREW MARVELL

How vainly men themselves amaze,
To win the palm, the oak or bays,
And their incessant labours see
Crown'd from some single herb or tree,
Whose short and narrow-verged shade   5
Does prudently their toils upbraid,
While all the flowers, and trees, do close,
To weave the garlands of repose!

palm, oak, bays: military, civilian, literary

Fair Quiet, have I found thee here,
And Innocence, thy sister dear? 10
Mistaken long, I sought you then
In busy companies of men;
Your sacred plants, if here below,
Only among the plants will grow;
Society is all but rude, 15
To this delicious solitude.

No white nor red was ever seen
So amorous as this lovely green.
Fond lovers, cruel as their flame,
Cut in these trees their mistress' name: 20
Little, alas! they know or heed,
How far these beauties hers exceed!
Fair trees! where'er your barks I wound,
No name shall but your own be found.

When we have run our passions' heat, 25
Love hither makes his best retreat.
The gods, who mortal beauty chase,
Still in a tree did end their race;
Apollo hunted Daphne so,
Only that she might laurel grow; 30
And Pan did after Syrinx speed,
Not as a nymph, but for a reed.

What wond'rous life is this I lead!
Ripe apples drop about my head;
The luscious clusters of the vine 35
Upon my mouth do crush their wine;
The nectarine, and curious peach,
Into my hands themselves do reach;
Stumbling on melons, as I pass,
Insnared with flowers, I fall on grass. 40

Meanwhile the mind, from pleasure less,
Withdraws into its happiness;—
The mind, that ocean where each kind
Does straight its own resemblance find;—
Yet it creates, transcending these, 45
Far other worlds, and other seas,
Annihilating all that's made
To a green thought in a green shade.

Here at the fountain's sliding foot,
Or at some fruit-tree's mossy root, 50
Casting the body's vest aside,
My soul into the boughs does glide:
There, like a bird, it sits and sings,
Then whets and claps its silver wings,
And, till prepar'd for longer flight, 55
Waves in its plumes the various light.

Such was that happy garden-state,
While man there walked without a mate:
After a place so pure and sweet,
What other help could yet be meet! 60
But 'twas beyond a mortal's share
To wander solitary there:
Two paradises 'twere in one,
To live in paradise alone.

How well the skilful gardener drew 65
Of flowers, and herbs, this dial new,
Where, from above, the milder sun
Does through a fragrant zodiac run,
And, as it works, the industrious bee
Computes its time as well as we! 70
How could such sweet and wholesome hours
Be reckoned but with herbs and flowers?

MOUNT OF OLIVES

HENRY VAUGHAN

1

Sweet, sacred hill! on whose fair brow
My Saviour sate, shall I allow
    Language to love,
And idolize some shade, or grove,
Neglecting thee? such ill-plac'd wit, 5
Conceit, or call it what you please,
    Is the brain's fit,
    And mere disease.

2

Cotswold and Cooper's both have met
With learnèd swains, and echo yet 10

Their pipes and wit;
But thou sleep'st in a deep neglect,
Untouch'd by any; and what need
The sheep bleat thee a silly lay,
That heard'st both reed 15
And sheepward play?

3

Yet if poets mind thee well,
They shall find thou art their hill,
And fountain too.
Their Lord with thee had most to do; 20
He wept once, walk'd whole nights on thee:
And from thence—His suff'rings ended—
Unto glory
Was attended.

4

Being there, this spacious ball 25
Is but His narrow footstool all;
And what we think
Unsearchable, now with one wink
He doth comprise; but in this air
When He did stay to bear our ill 30
And sin, this hill
Was then His chair.

PEACE

HENRY VAUGHAN

My soul, there is a country
Far beyond the stars,
Where stands a wingèd sentry
All skilful in the wars:
There, above noise and danger, 5
Sweet Peace sits crown'd with smiles,
And One born in a manger
Commands the beauteous files.
He is thy gracious Friend,
And—O my soul awake!— 10
Did in pure love descend,
To die here for thy sake.
If thou canst get but thither,

There grows the flower of Peace,
The Rose that cannot wither, 15
Thy fortress, and thy ease.
Leave then thy foolish ranges;
For none can thee secure,
But One, who never changes,
Thy God, thy life, thy cure.

THE WORLD

HENRY VAUGHAN

1

I saw Eternity the other night,
Like a great ring of pure and endless light,
All calm, as it was bright;
And round beneath it, Time in hours, days, years,
Driv'n by the spheres 5
Like a vast shadow mov'd; in which the world
And all her train were hurl'd.
The doting lover in his quaintest strain
Did there complain;
Near him, his lute, his fancy, and his flights, 10
Wit's sour delights;
With gloves, and knots, the silly snares of pleasure,
Yet his dear treasure,
All scatter'd lay, while he his eyes did pour
Upon a flow'r. 15

2

The darksome statesman, hung with weights and woe,
Like a thick midnight-fog, mov'd there so slow,
He did nor stay, nor go;
Condemning thoughts—like sad eclipses—scowl
Upon his soul,
And clouds of crying witnesses without 20
Pursued him with one shout.
Yet digg'd the mole, and lest his ways be found,
Work'd under ground,
Where he did clutch his prey; but one did see 25
That policy:
Churches and altars fed him; perjuries
Were gnats and flies;

It rain'd about him blood and tears, but he
　　Drank them as free.　　　　　　　　　　　　　30

3

The fearful miser on a heap of rust
Sate pining all his life there, did scarce trust
　　His own hands with the dust,
Yet would not place one piece above, but lives
　　In fear of thieves.　　　　　　　　　　　　　35
Thousands there were as frantic as himself,
　　And hugg'd each one his pelf;
The downright epicure plac'd heav'n in sense,
　　And scorn'd pretence;
While others, slipp'd into a wide excess,　　　40
　　Said little less;
The weaker sort slight, trivial wares enslave,
　　Who think them brave;
And poor, despisèd Truth sate counting by
　　Their victory.　　　　　　　　　　　　　　45

4

Yet some, who all this while did weep and sing,
And sing, and weep, soar'd up into the ring;
　　But most would use no wing.
O fools—said I—thus to prefer dark night
　　Before true light!　　　　　　　　　　　　50
To live in grots and caves, and hate the day
　　Because it shows the way;
The way, which from this dead and dark abode
　　Leads up to God;
A way where you might tread the sun, and be　　55
　　More bright than he!
But as I did their madness so discuss,
　　One whisper'd thus,
"This ring the Bridegroom did for none provide,
　　But for His bride."　　　　　　　　　　　　60

John, Chap. 2. ver. 16, 17

All that is in the world, the lust of the flesh, the lust of the eyes, and the pride of life, is not of the Father, but is of the world.

And the world passeth away, and the lusts thereof; but he that doeth the will of God abideth for ever.

A SONG FOR
ST. CECILIA'S DAY, 1687

JOHN DRYDEN

1

From harmony, from heav'nly harmony
   This universal frame began.
When nature underneath a heap
   Of jarring atoms lay,
And could not heave her head,   5
The tuneful voice was heard from high,
   'Arise ye more than dead.'
Then cold, and hot, and moist, and dry,
   In order to their stations leap,
     And music's pow'r obey.   10
From harmony, from heav'nly harmony
   This universal frame began;
   From harmony to harmony
Through all the compass of the notes it ran,
The diapason closing full in man.   15

2

What passion cannot music raise and quell!
   When Jubal struck the corded shell,
   His list'ning brethren stood around
   And wond'ring on their faces fell
   To worship that celestial sound.   20
Less than a god they thought there could not dwell
   Within the hollow of that shell,
   That spoke so sweetly and so well.
What passion cannot music raise and quell!

3

The trumpet's loud clangour   25
   Excites us to arms
With shrill notes of anger
   And mortal alarms.
The double double double beat
   Of the thund'ring drum   30
   Cries hark the foes come!
Charge, charge, 'tis too late to retreat.

The soft complaining flute
In dying notes discovers
The woes of hopeless lovers,   35
Whose dirge is whisper'd by the warbling lute.

5

Sharp violins proclaim
Their jealous pangs and desperation,
Fury, frantic indignation,
Depth of pains and height of passion,   40
  For the fair, disdainful dame.

6

But oh! what art can teach
  What human voice can reach
The sacred organ's praise?
Notes inspiring holy love,   45
Notes that wing their heav'nly ways
    To mend the choirs above.

7

Orpheus could lead the savage race,
And trees uprooted left their place,
  Sequacious of the lyre.   50
But bright Cecilia raised the wonder high'r;
  When to her organ vocal breath was giv'n,
An angel heard and straight appeared
  Mistaking earth for heav'n.

GRAND CHORUS

As from the pow'r of sacred lays   55
  The spheres began to move,
And sung the great creator's praise
  To all the blessed above;
So when the last and dreadful hour
This crumbling pageant shall devour,   60
The trumpet shall be heard on high,
The dead shall live, the living die,
And music shall untune the sky.

MAC FLECKNOE

OR A SATIRE UPON THE

TRUE-BLUE PROTESTANT POET
T.S.

JOHN DRYDEN

All human things are subject to decay,
And when Fate summons monarchs must obey.
This Flecknoe found, who, like Augustus, young
Was called to Empire and had governed long;
In prose and verse was owned, without dispute   5
Through all the realms of Nonsense, absolute.
This aged prince, now flourishing in peace
And blest with issue of a large increase,
Worn out with business, did at length debate
To settle the succession of the state;   10
And pond'ring which of all his sons was fit
To reign and wage immortal war with wit,
Cried: ' 'Tis resolved; for nature pleads that he
Should only rule who most resembles me.
Shadwell alone my perfect image bears,   15
Mature in dullness from his tender years.
Shadwell alone, of all my sons, is he
Who stands confirmed in full stupidity.
The rest to some faint meaning make pretence,
But Shadwell never deviates into sense.   20
Some beams of wit on other souls may fall,
Strike through and make a lucid interval,
But Shadwell's genuine night admits no ray,
His rising fogs prevail upon the day.
Besides his goodly fabric fills the eye,   25
And seems designed for thoughtless majesty:
Thoughtless as monarch oaks that shade the plain
And, spread in solemn state, supinely reign.
Heywood and Shirley were but types of thee,
Thou last great prophet of tautology.   30
Even I, a dunce of more renown than they,
Was sent before but to prepare thy way;
And coarsely clad in Norwich drugget came

Flecknoe—Richard Flecknoe (d. 1678),
Irish poet
Shadwell—Thomas Shadwell (1642-92),
the dramatist, a political as well as profes-
sional rival, supported Shaftesbury and the
Whigs

To teach the nations in thy greater name.
My warbling lute, the lute I whilom strung   35
When to King John of Portugal I sung,
Was but the prelude to that glorious day
When thou on silver Thames did'st cut thy way
With well-timed oars before the Royal Barge,
Swelled with the pride of thy celestial charge;   40
And big with hymn, commander of an host,
The like was ne'er in Epsom blankets tossed.
Methinks I see the new Arion sail,
The lute still trembling underneath thy nail,
At thy well-sharpened thumb from shore to shore   45
The treble squeaks for fear, the basses roar;
Echoes from Pissing-Alley Shadwell call,
And Shadwell they resound from Aston Hall.
About thy boat the little fishes throng
As at the morning toast that floats along.   50
Sometimes as prince of thy harmonious band
Thou wield'st thy papers in thy threshing hand.
St Andre's feet ne'er kept more equal time,
Not ev'n the feet of thy own Psyche's rhyme
Though they in number as in sense excel;   55
So just, so like tautology they fell,
That, pale with envy, Singleton forswore
The lute and sword which he in triumph bore
And vowed he ne'er would act Villerius more.'
Here stopped the good old sire, and wept for joy   60
In silent raptures of the hopeful boy.
All arguments, but most his plays, persuade
That for anointed dullness he was made.
    Close to the walls which fair Augusta bind
(The fair Augusta much to fears inclined),   65
An ancient fabric, raised t' inform the sight,
There stood of yore and Barbican it hight.
A watchtower once; but now, so Fate ordains,
Of all the pile an empty name remains.
From its old ruins brothel-houses rise,   70
Scenes of lewd loves and of polluted joys.
Where their vast courts the mother-strumpets keep,

Epsom blankets—Shadwell's *Epsom Wells*
(1673); the phrase occurs in Shadwell's
The Sudden Lovers
St. Andre—a dancing master
Psyche's rhyme—Shadwell's *Psyche*
(1676)
Villerius—Singleton played the part in
D'Avenant's *The Siege of Rhodes*
Barbican—in Aldersgate Street

And, undisturbed by watch, in silence sleep.
Near these a Nursery erects its head,
Where queens are formed and future heroes bred;   75
Where unfledged actors learn to laugh and cry,
Where infant punks their tender voices try,
And little Maximins the gods defy.
Great Fletcher never treads in buskins here,
Nor greater Jonson dares in socks appear;   80
But gentle Simkin just reception finds
Amidst this monument of vanished minds;
Pure clinches the suburban muse affords,
And Panton waging harmless war with words.
Here Flecknoe, as a place to fame well-known,   85
Ambitiously designed his Shadwell's throne.
For ancient Decker prophesied long since
That in this pile should reign a mighty prince,
Born for a scourge of wit and flail of sense;
To whom true dullness should some Psyches owe,   90
But worlds of Misers from his pen should flow;
Humorists and hypocrites it should produce,
Whole Raymond families and tribes of Bruce.
    Now Empress Fame had published the renown
Of Shadwell's coronation through the town.   95
Roused by report of fame the nations meet
From near Bunhill and distant Watling Street.
No Persian carpets spread th' imperial way,
But scattered limbs of mangled poets lay;
From dusty shops neglected authors come,   100
Martyrs of pies and relics of the bum.
Much Heywood, Shirley, Ogleby there lay,
But loads of Shadwell almost choked the way.
Bilked stationers for Yoemen stood prepared,
And Herringman was captain of the guard.   105
The hoary Prince in majesty appeared,
High on a throne of his own labours reared.
At his right hand our young Ascanius sat,

Nursery—a theatrical school, training chil-
dren for the stage, established 1662
Panton—a celebrated punster
Decker—Thomas Dekker (1570?-1632),
dramatist
Misers . . . Humorists—The Miser and
The Humorists, two of Shadwell's plays.
Raymond is a character in The Humorists,
and Bruce, in The Virtuoso
Ogleby—John Ogilby (1600-76), trans-
lated Virgil
Herringman—Henry Herringman had been
Dryden's publisher

Rome's other hope and pillar of the State.
His brows thick fogs, instead of glories, grace,   110
And lambent dullness played around his face.
As Hannibal did to the altars come,
Sworn by his sire a mortal foe to Rome;
So Shadwell swore, nor should his vow be vain,
That he till death true dullness would maintain,   115
And in his father's right and realm's defence
Ne'er to have peace with wit nor truce with sense.
The King himself the sacred unction made,
As King by office, and as priest by trade.
In his sinister hand instead of ball   120
He placed a mighty mug of potent ale;
Love's Kingdom to his right he did convey,
At once his sceptre and his rule of sway,
Whose righteous lore the Prince had practised young
And from whose loins recorded Psyche sprung.   125
His Temples last with poppies were o'erspread,
That nodding seemed to consecrate his head.
Just at that point of time, if fame not lie,
On his left hand twelve reverend owls did fly:
So Romulus, 'tis sung, by Tiber's brook   130
Presage of sway from twice six vultures took.
Th' admiring throng loud acclamations make,
And omens of his future empire take.
The sire then shook the honours of his head,
And from his brows damps of oblivion shed   135
Full on the filial dullness. Long he stood
Repelling from his breast the raging god;
At length burst out in this prophetic mood:
    'Heavens bless my son, from Ireland let him reign
To far Barbadoes on the western main;   140
Of his dominion may no end be known,
And greater than his father's be his throne.
Beyond Love's Kingdom let him stretch his pen.'
He paused and all the people cried 'Amen.'
'Then thus,' continued he, 'my son, advance   145
Still in new impudence, new ignorance.
Success let others teach, learn thou from me
Pangs without birth and fruitless industry.
Let Virtuoso's in five years be writ;
Yet not one thought accuse thy toil of wit.   150
Let gentle George in triumph tread the stage,

Love's Kingdom—Flecknoe's pastoral tragi-
comedy
gentle George—Sir George Etherege
(1634?-91?), the dramatist, and characters
in his comedies

Make Dorimant betray, and Loveit rage;
Let Cully, Cockwood, Fopling, charm the pit,
And in their folly show the writer's wit.
Yet still thy fools shall stand in thy defence,   155
And justify their author's want of sense.
Let 'em be all by thy own model made
Of dullness and desire no foreign aid,
That they to future ages may be known
Not copies drawn but issue of thy own.   160
Nay, let thy men of wit, too, be the same,
All full of thee and differing but in name;
But let no alien Sedley interpose
To lard with wit thy hungry Epsom prose.
And when false flowers of rhetoric thou would'st cull,   165
Trust nature, do not labour to be dull
But write thy best and top; and in each line
Sir Formal's oratory will be thine.
Sir Formal, though unsought, attends thy quill
And does thy northern dedications fill.   170
Nor let false friends seduce thy mind to fame
By arrogating Jonson's hostile name.
Let father Flecknoe fire thy mind with praise,
And uncle Ogleby thy envy raise.
Thou art my blood, where Jonson has no part;   175
What share have we in nature or in art?
Where did his wit on learning fix a brand
And rail at arts he did not understand?
Where made he love in Prince Nicander's vein,
Or swept the dust in Psyche's humble strain?   180
Where sold he bargains, whip-stitch, kiss my arse,
Promised a play and dwindled to a farce?
When did his muse from Fletcher scenes purloin,
As thou whole Eth'rege dost transfuse to thine?
But so transfused as oil on waters flow,   185
His always floats above, thine sinks below.
This is thy province, this thy wondrous way,
New humours to invent for each new play;
This is that boasted bias of thy mind
By which one way, to dullness, 'tis inclined,   190
Which makes thy writings lean on one side still,
And in all changes that way bends thy will.
Nor let thy mountain belly make pretence

Epsom prose—Sir Charles Sedley (1639?-
1701), who may have helped Shadwell
with *Epsom Wells*
Sir Formal—an oratorical character in *The
Virtuoso*

Of likeness; thine's a tympany of sense.
A tun of man in thy large bulk is writ,   195
But sure thou 'rt but a kilderkin of wit.
Like mine thy gentle numbers feebly creep,
Thy tragic muse gives smiles, thy comic sleep.
With whate'er gall thou sett'st thyself to write,
Thy inoffensive satires never bite.   200
In thy felonious heart though venom lies,
It does but touch thy Irish pen and dies.
Thy genius calls thee not to purchase fame
In keen iambics but mild anagram;
Leave writing plays and choose for thy command   205
Some peaceful province in acrostic land.
There thou may'st wings display and altars raise,
And torture one poor word ten thousand ways.
Or, if thou would'st thy diff'rent talents suit,
Set thy own songs and sing them to thy lute.'   210
He said, but his last words were scarcely heard,
For Bruce and Longville had a trap prepared,
And down they sent the yet declaiming bard.
Sinking, he left his drugget robe behind;
Born upwards by a subterranean wind   215
The mantle fell to the young prophet's part,
With double portion of his father's art.

AN ADDRESS TO THE SOUL
OCCASIONED BY A RAIN

EDWARD TAYLOR

Ye Flippering Soul,
    Why dost between the Nippers dwell?
Not stay, nor go. Not yea, nor yet Control.
    Doth this do well?
        Rise journy'ng when the skies fall weeping Showers,   5
        Not o're nor under th' Clouds and Cloudy Powers.

Not yea, nor no:
    On tiptoes thus? Why sit on thorns?
Resolve the matter: Stay thyself or go:

altars raise—shapes of poems in the earlier
years of the seventeenth century
declaiming bard—through a trap-door, as
in Shadwell's *The Virtuoso*

Ben't both ways born. 10
   Wager thyself against thy surplic'd see,
   And win thy Coat, or let thy Coat win thee.

Is this th' Effect
   To leaven thus my Spirits all?
To make my heart a Crabtree Cask direct? 15
   A Verjuc'te Hall?
      As Bottle Ale, whose Spirits prison'd must
      When jogg'd, the bung with Violence doth burst?

Shall I be made
   A sparkling Wildfire Shop, 20
Where my dull Spirits at the Fireball trade
   Do frisk and hop?
      And while the Hammer doth the Anvil pay,
      The fire ball matter sparkles e'ry way.

One sorry fret, 25
   An anvil Spark, rose higher,
And in thy Temple falling, almost set
   The house on fire.
      Such fireballs dropping in the Temple Flame
      Burns up the building: Lord, forbid the same.

SATIRES

LI: UPON NOTHING

JOHN WILMOT, EARL OF ROCHESTER

1.

Nothing! thou Elder Brother ev'n to Shade,
That hadst a Being e're the World was made,
And (well fixt) art alone, of ending not afraid.

2.

E're time and place were, time and place were not,
When Primitive Nothing something strait begot, 5
Then all proceeded from the great united—What.

3.

Something, the Gen'ral Attribute of all,
Sever'd from thee, it's sole Original,
Into thy boundless self must undistinguish'd fall.

4

Yet something did thy mighty Pow'r command,   10
And from thy fruitful emptiness's hand,
Snatch'd Men, Beasts, Birds, Fire, Air and Land.

5.

Matter, the wicked'st off-spring of thy Race,
By Form assisted, flew from thy Embrace,
And Rebel Light obscur'd thy revernd dusky Face.   15

6.

With Form, and Matter, Time and Place did joyn,
Body, thy Foe, with thee did Leagues combine,
To spoil thy peaceful Realm, and ruine all thy Line.

7.

But turn-Coat Time assists the Foe in vain,
And, brib'd by thee, assists thy short-liv'd Reign,   20
And to thy hungry Womb drives back thy Slaves again.

8.

Tho' Mysteries are barr'd from Laick Eyes,
And the Divine alone, with Warrant, pryes
Into thy Bosom, where the truth in private lies,

9.

Yet this of thee the wise may freely say,   25
Thou from the virtuous nothing tak'st away,
And to be part with thee the Wicked wisely pray.

10.

Great Negative, how vainly would the Wise,
Enquire, define, distinguish, teach, devise?
Didst thou not stand to point their dull Philosophies.   30

11.

Is, or *is not*, the two great Ends of Fate,
And, true or false, the subject of debate,
That perfect, or destroy, the vast designs of Fate,

12.

When they have rack'd the *Politician*'s Breast,
Within thy Bosom most securely rest,   35
And, when reduc'd to thee, are least unsafe and best.

13.

But, *Nothing*, why does *Something* still permit,
That Sacred Monarchs should at Council sit,
With Persons highly thought at best for nothing fit,

14.

Whilst weighty *Something* modestly abstains, 40
From Princes Coffers, and from States-Men's Brains,
And Nothing there like stately *Nothing* reigns,

15.

Nothing who dwell'st with Fools in grave Disguise,
For whom they rev'rend Shapes, and Forms devise,
Lawn Sleeves, and Furs, and Gowns, when they like thee look wise.

16.

French Truth, *Dutch* Prowess, *British* Policy, 46
Hibernian Learning, *Scotch* Civility,
Spaniards Dispatch, *Danes* Wit, are mainly seen in thee.

17.

The great Man's Gratitude to his best Friend,
Kings Promises, Whores Vows, tow'rds thee they bend, 50
Flow swiftly into thee, and in thee ever end.

ADAM POSED

ANNE, COUNTESS OF WINCHILSEA

Could our first father, at his toilsome plough,
Thorns in his path and labour on his brow,
Cloth'd only in a rude, unpolish'd skin,
　　Could he a vain fantastic nymph have seen,
In all her airs, in all her antic graces, 5
Her various fashions, and more various faces,
How had it pos'd that skill, which late assign'd

Just appellations to each several kind,
A right idea of the sight to frame!
T' have guessed from what new element she came,   10
To have hit the wav'ring form, or giv'n this thing a name!

TO STELLA
March 13, M DCC XXIII-IV

JONATHAN SWIFT

[Written on the Day of her Birth, but not on the Subject, when
I was sick in bed.]

Tormented with incessant pains,
Can I devise poetic strains?
Time was, when I could yearly pay
My verse on Stella's native day:
But now, unable grown to write,   5
I grieve she ever saw the light.
Ungrateful; since to her I owe
That I these pains can undergo.
She tends me, like an humble slave;
And, when indecently I rave,   10
When out my brutish passions break,
With gall in ev'ry word I speak,
She, with soft speech, my anguish chears,
Or melts my passions down with tears:
Although 'tis easy to descry   15
She wants assistance more than I;
Yet seems to feel my pains alone,
And is a Stoic in her own.
When, among scholars, can we find
So soft, and yet so firm a mind?   20
All accidents of life conspire
To raise up Stella's virtue higher;
Or else, to introduce the rest
Which had been latent in her breast.
Her firmness who could e'er have known,   25
Had she not evils of her own?
Her kindness who could ever guess,
Had not her friends been in distress?
Whatever base returns you find
From me, Dear Stella, still be kind.   30
In your own heart you'll reap the fruit,

Tho' I continue still a brute.
But when I once am out of pain,
I promise to be good again:
Meantime your other juster friends   35
Shall for my follies make amends:
So may we long continue thus,
Admiring you, you pitying us.

A RECEIPT
to
Restore Stella's Youth

JONATHAN SWIFT

The *Scottish* Hinds too poor to house
In frosty Nights their starving Cows,
While not a Blade of Grass, or Hay,
Appears from *Michaelmas* to *May*;
Must let their Cattle range in vain   5
For Food, along the barren Plain;
Meager and lank with fasting grown,
And nothing left but Skin and Bone;
Expos'd to Want, and Wind, and Weather,
They just keep Life and Soul together,   10
'Till Summer Show'rs and Ev'ning Dew,
Again the verdant Glebe renew;
And as the Vegetables rise,
The famish't Cow her Want supplies;
Without an Ounce of last Year's Flesh,   15
Whate'er she gains is young and fresh;
Grows plump and round, and full of Mettle,
As rising from *Medea's* Kettle;
With Youth and Beauty to enchant
Europa's counterfeit Gallant.   20
   Why, *Stella*, should you knit your Brow,
If I compare you to the Cow?
'Tis just the Case: For you have fasted
So long till all your Flesh is wasted,
And must against the warmer Days   25

Michaelmas—September 27

Be sent to *Quilca* down to graze;
Where Mirth, and Exercise, and Air,
Will soon your Appetite repair.
The Nutriment will from within
Round all your Body plump your Skin;   30
Will agitate the lazy Flood,
And fill your Veins with sprightly Blood:
Nor Flesh nor Blood will be the same,
Nor ought to *Stella*, but the Name;
For, what was ever understood   35
By human Kind, but Flesh and Blood?
And if your Flesh and Blood be new,
You'll be no more your former *You;*
But for a blooming Nymph will pass,
Just Fifteen, coming Summer's Grass: 40
Your jetty Locks with Garlands crown'd,
While all the Squires from nine Miles round,
Attended by a Brace of Curs,
With Jocky Boots, and Silver Spurs;
No less than Justices o' *Quorum*,   45
Their Cow-boys bearing Cloaks before 'um,
Shall leave deciding broken Pates,
To kiss your Steps at *Quilca* Gates;
But, lest you should my Skill disgrace,
Come back before you're out of Case;   50
For if to *Michaelmas* you stay,
The new-born Flesh will melt away;
The Squires in Scorn will fly the House
For better Game, and look for Grouse:
But here, before the Frost can marr it,   55
We'll make it firm with Beef and Claret.

VERSES ON THE PROSPECT OF PLANTING
ARTS AND LEARNING IN AMERICA

BISHOP GEORGE BERKELEY

The Muse, disgusted at an age and clime,
    Barren of every glorious theme,
In distant lands now waits a better time,
    Producing subjects worthy fame:

In happy climes, where from the genial sun $\qquad$ 5
   And virgin earth such scenes ensue,
The force of art by nature seems out done,
   And fancied beauties by the true:

In happy climes, the seat of innocence,
   Where nature guides and virtue rules, $\qquad$ 10
Where men shall not impose for truth and sense
   The pedantry of courts and schools:

There shall be sung another golden age,
   The rise of empire and of arts,
The good and great inspiring epic rage, $\qquad$ 15
   The wisest heads and noblest hearts.

Not such as Europe breeds in her decay;
   Such as she bred when fresh and young,
When heav'nly flame did animate her clay,
   By future poets shall be sung. $\qquad$ 20

Westward the course of empire takes its way;
   The four first acts already past,
A fifth shall close the drama with the day;
   Time's noblest offspring is the last.

THE RAPE OF THE LOCK

AN HEROI-COMICAL POEM
TO MRS. ARABELLA FERMOR

ALEXANDER POPE

MADAM,

IT will be in vain to deny that I have some regard for this piece,
since I dedicate it to You. Yet you may bear me witness, it was in-
tended only to divert a few young Ladies, who have good sense
and good humour enough to laugh not only at their sex's little un-
guarded follies, but at their own. But as it was communicated with
the air of a Secret, it soon found its way into the world. An imperfect copy having been offer'd to a Bookseller, you had the good-

---

The Rape of the Lock—Lord Petre, the
Baron of the poem, cut off a lock of Miss
Arabella Fermor's hair, which occasioned a
quarrel between their two families and this
mock-epic treatment

nature for my sake to consent to the publication of one or more correct: This I was forc'd to, before I had executed half my design, for the Machinery was entirely wanting to complete it.

The Machinery, Madam, is a term invented by the Critics, to signify that part which the Deities, Angels, or Demons, are made to act in a Poem: For the ancient Poets are in one respect like many modern Ladies: let an action be never so trivial in itself, they always make it appear of the utmost importance. These Machines I determin'd to raise on a very new and odd foundation, the Rosicrucian doctrine of Spirits.

I know how disagreeable it is to make use of hard words before a Lady; but 'tis so much concern of a Poet to have his works understood, and particularly by your Sex, that you must give me leave to explain two or three difficult terms.

The Rosicrucians are a people I must bring you acquainted with. The best account I know of them is in a French book call'd *Le Comte de Gabalis,* which both in its title and size is so like a Novel, that many of the Fair Sex have read it for one by mistake. According, to these Gentlemen, the four Elements are inhabited by Spirits which they call Sylphs, Gnomes, Nymphs, and Salamanders. The Gnomes or Demons of Earth delight in mischief; but the Sylphs, whose habitation is in the Air, are the best condition'd creatures imaginable. For they say, any mortals may enjoy the most intimate familiarities with these gentle Spirits, upon a condition very easy to all true Adepts, an inviolate preservation of Chastity.

As to the following Cantos, all the passages of them are as fabulous, as the Vision at the beginning, or the Transformation at the end; (except the loss of your Hair, which I always mention with reverence.) The Human persons are as fictitious as the Airy ones; and the character of Belinda, as it is now manag'd, resembles you in nothing but in Beauty.

If this Poem had as many Graces as there are in your Person, or in your Mind, yet I could never hope it should pass through the world half so Uncensur'd as You have done. But let its fortune be what it will, mine is happy enough, to have given me this occasion of assuring you that I am, with the truest esteem,

MADAM,

Your most obedient, humble servant,

A. POPE.

CANTO I

What dire offence from am'rous causes springs,
What mighty contests rise from trivial things,
I sing—This verse to CARYL, Muse! is due:
This, ev'n Belinda may vouchsafe to view:
Slight is the subject, but not so the praise,   5
If She inspire, and He approve my lays.

Say what strange motive, Goddess! could compel
A well-bred Lord t' assault a gentle Belle?
O say what stranger cause, yet unexplor'd,
Could make a gentle Belle reject a Lord?   10
In tasks so bold, can little men engage,
And in soft bosoms, dwells such mighty Rage?
    Sol, through white curtains shot a tim'rous ray,
And ope'd those eyes that must eclipse the day:
Now lap-dogs give themselves the rousing shake.   15
And sleepless lovers, just at twelve, awake:
Thrice rung the bell, the slipper knock'd the ground,
And the press'd watch return'd a silver sound.
Belinda still her downy pillow prest,
Her guardian SYLPH prolong'd the balmy rest: 20
'Twas He had summon'd to her silent bed
The morning-dream that hover'd o'er her head,
A Youth more glitt'ring than a Birth-night Beau,
(That ev'n in slumber caus'd her cheek to glow)
Seem'd to her ear his winning lips to lay,   25
And thus in whispers said, or seem'd to say.
    'Fairest of mortals, thou distinguish'd care
Of thousand bright Inhabitants of Air!
If e'er one Vision touch thy infant thought,
Of all the Nurse and all the Priest have taught;   30
Of airy Elves by moonlight shadows seen,
The silver token, and the circled green,
Or virgins visited by Angel-pow'rs
With golden crowns and wreaths of heav'nly flow'rs;
Hear and believe! thy own importance know,   35
Nor bound thy narrow views to things below.
Some secret truths, from learned pride conceal'd,
To Maids alone and Children are reveal'd:
What tho' no credit doubting Wits may give?
The Fair and Innocent shall still believe.   40
Know then, unnumber'd Spirits round thee fly,
The light Militia of the lower sky:
These, tho' unseen, are ever on the wing,
Hang o'er the Box, and hover round the Ring.
Think what an equipage thou hast in Air,   45
And view with scorn two Pages and a Chair.
As now your own, our beings were of old,
And once inclos'd in Woman's beauteous mould;
Thence, by a soft transition, we repair
From earthly Vehicles to these of air.   50
Think not, when Woman's transient breath is fled,

the Ring—a fashionable public walk in
Hyde Park

That all her vanities at once are dead;
Succeeding vanities she still regards,
And tho' she plays no more, o'erlooks the cards.
Her joy in gilded Chariots, when alive,   55
And love of Ombre, after death survive.
For when the Fair in all their pride expire,
To their first Elements their Souls retire:
The Sprites of fiery Termagants in Flame
Mount up, and take a Salamander's name.   60
Soft yielding minds to Water glide away,
And sip, with Nymphs, their elemental Tea.
The graver Prude sinks downward to a Gnome,
In search of mischief still on Earth to roam.
The light coquettes in Sylphs aloft repair,   65
And sport and flutter in the fields of air.
      'Know farther yet; whoever fair and chaste
Rejects mankind, is by some Sylph embrac'd:
For Spirits, freed from mortal laws, with ease
Assume what sexes and what shapes they please.   70
What guards the purity of melting Maids,
In courtly balls, and midnight masquerades,
Safe from the treach'rous friend, the daring spark,
The glance by day, the whisper in the dark,
When kind occasion prompts their warm desires,   75
When music softens, and when dancing fires?
'Tis but their Sylph, the wise Celestials know,
Though Honour is the word with Men below.
      'Some nymphs there are, too conscious of their face,
For life predestin'd to the Gnomes embrace.   80
These swell their prospects and exalt their pride,
When offers are disdain'd, and love deny'd;
Then gay Ideas crowd the vacant brain,
While Peers, and Dukes, and all their sweeping train,
And Garters, Stars, and Coronets appear,   85
And in soft sounds, 'YOUR GRACE' salutes their ear.
'Tis these that early taint the female soul,
Instruct the eyes of young Coquettes to roll,
Teach Infant-cheeks a bidden blush to know,
And little hearts to flutter at a Beau.   90
      'Oft, when the world imagine women stray,
The Sylphs through mystic mazes guide their way,
Through all the giddy circle they pursue,
And old impertinence expell by new.
What tender maid but must a victim fall   95
To one man's treat, but for another's ball?
When Florio speaks, what virgin could withstand,
If gentle Damon did not squeeze her hand?

With varying vanities, from ev'ry part,
They shift the moving Toyshop of their heart;   100
Where wigs with wigs, with sword-knots sword-knots strive,
Beaux banish beaux, and coaches coaches drive.
This erring mortals Levity may call,
Oh, blind to truth! the Sylphs contrive it all.
   'Of these am I, who thy protection claim,   105
A watchful sprite, and Ariel is my name.
Late, as I rang'd the crystal wilds of air,
In the clear Mirror of thy ruling Star
I saw, alas! some dread event impend,
Ere to the main this morning sun descend,   110
But heav'n reveals not what, or how, or where:
Warn'd by the Sylph, oh pious maid, beware!
This to disclose is all thy guardian can:
Beware of all, but most beware of Man!'
   He said; when Shock, who thought she slept too long, 115
Leap'd up, and wak'd his mistress with his tongue.
'Twas then, Belinda, if report say true,
Thy eyes first open'd on a Billet-doux;
Wounds, Charms, and Ardours, were no sooner read,
But all the Vision vanish'd from thy head.   120
   And now, unveil'd, the Toilet stands display'd,
Each silver Vase in mystic order laid.
First, rob'd in white, the Nymph intent adores,
With head uncover'd, the Cosmetic pow'rs.
A heav'nly Image in the glass appears,   125
To that she bends, to that her eyes she rears;
Th' inferior Priestess, at her altar's side,
Trembling begins the sacred rites of Pride.
Unnumber'd treasures ope at once, and here
The various off'rings of the world appear;   130
From each she nicely culls with curious toil,
And decks the Goddess with the glitt'ring spoil.
This casket India's glowing gems unlocks,
And all Arabia breathes from yonder box.
The Tortoise here and Elephant unite,   135
Transform'd to combs, the speckled, and the white.
Here files of pins extend their shining rows,
Puffs, Powders, Patches, Bibles, Billet-doux.
Now awful Beauty puts on all its arms;
The fair each moment rises in her charms,   140
Repairs her smiles, awakens ev'ry grace,
And calls forth all the wonders of her face;
Sees by degrees a purer blush arise,
And keener lightnings quicken in her eyes.
The busy Sylphs surround their darling care,   145

These set the head, and those divide the hair,
Some fold the sleeve, whilst others plait the gown;
And Betty's prais'd for labours not her own.

Not with more glories, in th' ethereal plain,
The Sun first rises o'er the purpled main, 150
Than, issuing forth, the rival of his beams
Launch'd on the bosom of the silver Thames.
Fair Nymphs, and well-drest Youths around her shone,
But ev'ry eye was fix'd on her alone.
On her white breast a sparkling Cross she wore, 155
Which Jews might kiss, and Infidels adore.
Her lively looks a sprightly mind disclose,
Quick as her eyes, and as unfix'd as those:
Favours to none, to all she smiles extends;
Oft she rejects, but never once offends. 160
Bright as the sun, her eyes the gazers strike,
And, like the sun, they shine on all alike.
Yet graceful ease, and sweetness void of pride,
Might hide her faults, if Belles had faults to hide:
If to her share some female errors fall, 165
Look on her face, and you'll forget 'em all.
      This Nymph, to the destruction of mankind,
Nourish'd two Locks, which graceful hung behind
In equal curls, and well conspir'd to deck
With shining ringlets the smooth iv'ry neck. 170
Love in these labyrinths his slaves detains,
And mighty hearts are held in slender chains.
With hairy springes we the birds betray,
Slight lines of hair surprise the finny prey,
Fair tresses man's imperial race insnare, 175
And beauty draws us with a single hair.
      Th' advent'rous Baron the bright locks admir'd;
He saw, he wish'd, and to the prize aspir'd.
Resolv'd to win, he meditates the way,
By force to ravish, or by fraud betray; 180
For when success a Lover's toil attends,
Few ask, if fraud or force attain'd his ends.
      For this, ere Phoebus rose, he had implor'd
Propitious Heav'n, and ev'ry pow'r ador'd,
But chiefly Love—to Love an Altar built, 185
Of twelve vast French Romances, neatly gilt.
There lay three garters, half a pair of gloves,
And all the trophies of his former loves;
With tender Billet-doux he lights the pyre,
And breathes three am'rous sighs to raise the fire. 190

Then prostrate falls, and begs with ardent eyes
Soon to obtain, and long possess the prize:
The pow'rs gave ear, and granted half his pray'r,
The rest, the winds dispers'd in empty air.
    But now secure the painted vessel glides,   195
The sun-beams trembling on the floating tides:
While melting music steals upon the sky,
And soften'd sounds along the waters die;
Smooth flow the waves, the Zephyrs gently play,
Belinda smil'd, and all the world was gay.   200
All but the Sylph—with careful thoughts opprest,
Th' impending woe sat heavy on his breast.
He summons straight his Denizens of air;
The lucid squadrons round the sails repair;
Soft o'er the shrouds aërial whispers breathe,   205
That seem'd but Zephyrs to the train beneath.
Some to the sun their insect-wings unfold,
Waft on the breeze, or sink in clouds of gold:
Transparent forms, too fine for mortal sight,
Their fluid bodies half dissolv'd in light.   210
Loose to the wind their airy garments flew,
Thin glitt'ring textures of the filmy dew,
Dipt in the richest tincture of the skies,
Where light disports in ever-mingling dyes;
While ev'ry beam new transient colours flings,   215
Colours that change whene'er they wave their wings
Amid the circle, on the gilded mast,
Superior by the head, was Ariel plac'd;
His purple pinions op'ning to the sun,
He rais'd his azure wand, and thus begun.   220
    'Ye Sylphs and Sylphids, to your chief give ear,
Fays, Fairies, Genii, Elves, and Demons hear!
Ye know the spheres and various tasks assign'd
By laws eternal to th' aerial kind.
Some in the fields of purest Ether play,   225
And bask and whiten in the blaze of day.
Some guide the course of wand'ring orbs on high,
Or roll the planets through the boundless sky.
Some less refin'd, beneath the moon's pale light
Pursue the stars that shoot athwart the night,   230
Or suck the mists in grosser air below,
Or dip their pinions in the painted bow,
Or brew fierce tempests on the wintry main,
Or o'er the glebe distil the kindly rain.
Others on earth o'er human race preside,   235
Watch all their ways, and all their actions guide:
Of these the chief the care of Nations own,

And guard with Arms divine the British Throne.
   'Our humbler province is to tend the Fair,
Not a less pleasing, tho' less glorious care;   240
To save the powder from too rude a gale,
Nor let th' imprison'd essences exhale;
To draw fresh colours from the vernal flow'rs;
To steal from rainbows, e'er they drop in show'rs
A brighter wash; to curl their waving hairs,   245
Assist their blushes, and inspire their airs;
Nay oft, in dreams, invention we bestow,
To change a Flounce, or add a Furbelow.
   'This day, black Omens threat the brightest Fair
That e'er deserv'd a watchful spirit's care;   250
Some dire disaster, or by force, or sight;
But what, or where, the fates have wrapt in night.
Whether the nymph shall break Diana's law,
Or some frail China jar receive a flaw;
Or stain her honour, or her new brocade;   255
Forget her pray'rs, or miss a masquerade;
Or lose her heart, or necklace, at a ball;
Or whether Heav'n has doom'd that Shock must fall.
Haste then, ye spirits! to your charge repair:
The flutt'ring fan be Zephyretta's care;   260
The drops to thee, Brillante, we consign;
And, Momentilla, let the watch be thine;
Do thou, Crispissa, tend her fav'rite Lock;
Ariel himself shall be the guard of Shock.
   'To fifty chosen Sylphs, of special note,   265
We trust th' important charge, the Petticoat:
Oft have we known that seven-fold fence to fail,
Tho' stiff with hoops, and arm'd with ribs of whale;
Form a strong line about the silver bound,
And guard the wide circumference around.   270
   'Whatever spirit, careless of his charge,
His post neglects, or leaves the fair at large,
Shall feel sharp vengeance soon o'ertake his sins,
Be stop'd in vials, or transfix'd with pins;
Or plung'd in lakes of bitter washes lie,   275
Or wedg'd whole ages in a bodkin's eye:
Gums and Pomatums shall his flight restrain,
While, clog'd, he beats his silken wings in vain;
Or Alum styptics with contracting pow'r
Shrink his thin essence like a rivel'd flow'r: 280
Or, as Ixion fix'd, the wretch shall feel
The giddy motion of the whirling Mill,
In fumes of burning Chocolate shall glow,
And tremble at the sea that froths below!'

He spoke; the spirits from the sails descend;   285
Some, orb in orb, around the nymph extend;
Some thrid the mazy ringlets of her hair;
Some hang upon the pendants of her ear;
With beating hearts the dire event they wait,
Anxious, and trembling for the birth of Fate.   290

Close by those meads, for ever crown'd with flow'rs,
Where Thames with pride surveys his rising tow'rs,
There stands a structure of majestic frame,
Which from the neighb'ring Hampton takes its name.
Here Britain's statesmen oft the fall foredoom   295
Of foreign Tyrants, and of Nymphs at home;
Here thou, great ANNA! whom three realms obey,
Dost sometimes counsel take—and sometimes Tea.
    Hither the Heroes and the Nymphs resort,
To taste awhile the pleasures of a Court;   300
In various talk th' instructive hours they past,
Who gave the ball, or paid the visit last;
One speaks the glory of the British Queen,
And one describes a charming Indian screen;
A third interprets motions, looks, and eyes;   305
At ev'ry word a reputation dies.
Snuff, or the fan, supply each pause of chat,
With singing, laughing, ogling, *and all that*.
    Mean while declining from the noon of day,
The sun obliquely shoots his burning ray;   310
The hungry Judges soon the sentence sign,
And wretches hang that Jury-men may dine;
The merchant from th' Exchange returns in peace,
And the long labours of the Toilet cease.
Belinda now, whom thirst of fame invites,   315
Burns to encounter two advent'rous Knights,
At Ombre singly to decide their doom;
And swells her breast with conquests yet to come.
Straight the three bands prepare in arms to join,
Each band the number of the sacred Nine.   320
Soon as she spreads her hand, th' aërial guard
Descend, and sit on each important card:
First Ariel perch'd upon a Matadore,
Then each according to the rank they bore;
For Sylphs, yet mindful of their ancient race,   325
Are, as when women, wond'rous fond of place.
    Behold, four Kings in majesty rever'd,

Ombre—a card game played by three
players with a pack of forty cards

With hoary whiskers and a forky beard;
And four fair Queens whose hands sustain a flow'r,
Th' expressive emblem of their softer pow'r;   330
Four Knaves in garbs succinct, a trusty band,
Caps on their heads, and halberts in their hand;
And particolour'd troops, a shining train,
Draw forth to combat on the velvet plain.
　　The skilful Nymph reviews her force with care: 335
'Let Spades be trumps!' she said, and trumps they were.
　　Now move to war her sable Matadores,
In show like leaders of the swarthy Moors.
Spadillio first, unconquerable Lord!
Led off two captive trumps, and swept the board.   340
As many more Manillio forc'd to yield,
And march'd a victor from the verdant field.
Him Basto follow'd, but his fate more hard
Gain'd but one trump and one Plebeian card.
With his broad sabre next, a chief in years,   345
The hoary Majesty of Spades appears,
Puts forth one manly leg, to sight reveal'd,
The rest, his many-colour'd robe conceal'd.
The rebel Knave, who dares his prince engage,
Proves the just victim of his royal rage.   350
Ev'n mighty Pam, that Kings and Queens o'er-threw
And mow'd down armies in the fights of Loo,
Sad chance of war! now destitute of aid,
Falls undistinguish'd by the victor Spade!
　　Thus far both armies to Belinda yield;   355
Now to the Baron fate inclines the field.
His warlike Amazon her host invades,
Th' imperial consort of the crown of Spades.
The Club's black Tyrant first her victim dy'd,
Spite of his haughty mien, and barb'rous pride: 360
What boots the regal circle on his head,
His giant limbs, in state unwieldy spread;
That long behind he trails his pompous robe,
And, of all monarchs, only grasps the globe?
　　The Baron now his Diamonds pours apace;   365
Th' embroider'd King who shows but half his face,
And his refulgent Queen, with pow'rs combin'd,
Of broken troops an easy conquest find.
Clubs, Diamonds, Hearts, in wild disorder seen,

Spadillio—Ace of Spades
Manillio—Two of Spades
Bast—Ace of Clubs
Pam—Knave of Clubs

With throngs promiscuous strow the level green. 370
Thus when dispers'd a routed army runs,
Of Asia's troops, and Afric's sable sons,
With like confusion different nations fly,
Of various habit and of various dye;
The pierc'd battalions disunited fall, 375
In heaps on heaps; one fate o'erwhelms them all.
    The Knave of Diamonds tries his wily arts,
And wins (oh shameful chance!) the Queen of Hearts.
At this, the blood the virgin's cheek forsook,
A livid paleness spreads o'er all her look; 380
She sees, and trembles at th' approaching ill,
Just in the jaws of ruin, and Codille.
And now, (as oft in some distemper'd State)
On one nice Trick depends the gen'ral fate:
An Ace of Hearts steps forth: the King unseen 385
Lurk'd in her hand, and mourn'd his captive Queen:
He springs to vengeance with an eager pace,
And falls like thunder on the prostrate Ace.
The nymph, exulting, fills with shouts the sky;
The walls, the woods, and long canals reply. 390
    O thoughtless mortals! ever blind to fate,
Too soon dejected, and too soon elate.
Sudden these honours shall be snatch'd away,
And curs'd for ever this victorious day.
    For lo! the board with cups and spoons is crown'd, 395
The berries crackle, and the mill turns round;
On shining altars of Japan they raise
The silver lamp; the fiery spirits blaze:
From silver spouts the grateful liquors glide,
While China's earth receives the smoking tide: 400
At once they gratify their sense and taste,
And frequent cups prolong the rich repast.
Straight hover round the Fair her airy band;
Some, as she sipp'd, the fuming liquor fann'd,
Some o'er her lap their careful plumes display'd, 405
Trembling, and conscious of the rich brocade.
Coffee (which makes the politician wise,
And see through all things with his half-shut eyes)
Sent up in vapours to the Baron's brain
New stratagems, the radiant Lock to gain. 410
Ah cease, rash youth! desist ere 'tis too late,
Fear the just Gods, and think of Scylla's Fate!
Chang'd to a bird, and sent to flit in air,
She dearly pays for Nisus' injur'd hair!

Codille—the loss of the game

But when to mischief mortals bend their will,   415
How soon they find fit instruments of ill?
Just then, Clarissa drew with tempting grace
A two-edg'd weapon from her shining case:
So Ladies in Romance assist their Knight,
Present the spear, and arm him for the fight.   420
He takes the gift with rev'rence, and extends
The little engine on his fingers' ends;
This just behind Belinda's neck he spread,
As o'er the fragrant steams she bends her head.
Swift to the Lock a thousand Sprites repair,   425
A thousand wings, by turns, blow back the hair;
And thrice they twitch'd the diamond in her ear;
Thrice she look'd back, and thrice the foe drew near.
Just in that instant, anxious Ariel sought
The close recesses of the Virgin's thought;   430
As on the nosegay in her breast reclin'd,
He watch'd th' ideas rising in her mind,
Sudden he view'd, in spite of all her art,
An earthly Lover lurking at her heart.
Amaz'd, confus'd, he found his pow'r expir'd,   435
Resign'd to fate, and with a sigh retir'd.
    The Peer now spreads the glitt'ring Forfex wide,
T' inclose the Lock; now joins it, to divide.
Ev'n then, before the fatal engine clos'd,
A wretched Sylph too fondly interpos'd;   440
Fate urg'd the sheers, and cut the Sylph in twain,
(But airy substance soon unites again)
The meeting points the sacred hair dissever
From the fair head, for ever, and for ever!
    Then flash'd the living lightning from her eyes,   445
And screams of horror rend th' affrighted skies.
Not louder shrieks to pitying heav'n are cast,
When husbands, or when lap-dogs breathe their last;
Or when rich China vessels, fall'n from high,
In glitt'ring dust and painted fragments lie!   450
    'Let wreaths of triumph now my temples twine,
(The Victor cry'd) the glorious Prize is mine!
While fish in streams, or birds delight in air,
Or in a coach-and-six the British Fair,
As long as Atalantis shall be read,   455
Or the small pillow grace a Lady's bed,
While visits shall be paid on solemn days,
When num'rous wax-lights in bright order blaze,
While nymphs take treats, or assignations give,

Atalantis—a scandalous romance of the
period

141

So long my honour, name, and praise shall live!' 460
    What Time would spare, from Steel receives its date,
And monuments, like men, submit to fate!
Steel could the labour of the Gods destroy,
And strike to dust th' imperial tow'rs of Troy;
Steel could the works of mortal pride confound, 465
And hew triumphal arches to the ground.
What **wonder then**, fair nymph! thy hairs should feel
The conqu'ring force of unresisted Steel?

But anxious cares the pensive nymph oppress'd,
And secret passions labour'd in her breast. 470
Not youthful kings in battle seiz'd alive,
Not scornful virgins who their charms survive,
Not ardent lovers robb'd of all their bliss,
Not ancient ladies when refus'd a kiss,
Not tyrants fierce that unrepenting die, 475
Not Cynthia when her manteau's pinn'd awry,
E'er felt such rage, resentment, and despair,
As thou, sad Virgin! for thy ravish'd Hair.
    For, that sad moment, when the Sylphs withdrew,
And Ariel weeping from Belinda flew, 480
Umbriel, a dusky, melanchoiy sprite,
As ever sully'd the fair face of light,
Down to the central earth, his proper scene,
Repair'd to search the gloomy Cave of Spleen.
    Swift on his sooty pinions flits the Gnome, 485
And in a vapour reach'd the dismal dome.
No cheerful breeze this sullen region knows,
The dreaded East is all the wind that blows.
Here in a grotto, shelter'd close from air,
And screen'd in shades from day's detested glare, 490
She sighs for ever on her pensive bed,
Pain at her side, and Megrim at her head.
    Two handmaids wait the throne: alike in place,
But diff'ring far in figure and in face.
Here stood Ill-nature like an ancient maid, 495
Her wrinkled form in black and white array'd!
With store of pray'rs, for mornings, nights, and noons
Her hand is fill'd; her bosom with lampoons.
    There Affectation, with a sickly mien,
Shows in her cheek the roses of eighteen, 500
Practis'd to lisp, and hang the head aside,
Faints into airs, and languishes with pride,
On the rich quilt sinks with becoming woe,
Wrapt in a gown, for sickness, and for show.

The fair-ones feel such maladies as these, 505
When each new night-dress gives a new disease.
    A constant Vapour o'er the palace flies,
Strange phantoms rising as the mists arise;
Dreadful, as hermits dreams in haunted shades,
Or bright, as visions of expiring maids. 510
Now glaring fiends, and snakes on rolling spires,
Pale spectres, gaping tombs, and purple fires:
Now lakes of liquid gold, Elysian scenes,
And crystal domes, and Angels in machines.
    Unnumber'd throngs, on ev'ry side are seen, 515
Of bodies chang'd to various forms by Spleen.
Here living Tea-pots stand, one arm held out,
One bent; the handle this, and that the spout:
A pipkin there, like Homer's Tripod walks;
Here sighs a Jar, and there a Goose-pye talks; 520
Men prove with child, as pow'rful fancy works,
And maids turn'd bottles, call aloud for corks.
    Safe past the Gnome through this fantastic band,
A branch of healing Spleenwort in his hand.
Then thus address'd the pow'r—'Hail, wayward Queen! 525
Who rule the sex to fifty from fifteen:
Parent of vapours and of female wit,
Who give th' hysteric, or poetic fit,
On various tempers act by various ways,
Make some take physic, others scribble plays; 530
Who cause the proud their visits to delay,
And send the godly in a pet to pray;
A nymph there is, that all thy pow'r disdains,
And thousands more in equal mirth maintains.
But oh! if e'er thy Gnome could spoil a grace, 535
Or raise a pimple on a beauteous face,
Like Citron-waters matrons' cheeks inflame,
Or change complexions at a losing game;
If e'er with airy horns I planted heads,
Or rumpled petticoats, or tumbled beds, 540
Or caus'd suspicion when no soul was rude,
Or discompos'd the head-dress of a Prude,
Or e'er to costive lap dog gave disease,
Which not the tears of brightest eyes could ease:
Hear me, and touch Belinda with chagrin, 545
That single act gives half the world the spleen.'
    The Goddess with a discontented air
Seems to reject him, tho' she grants his pray'r.
A wond'rous Bag with both her hands she binds,
Like that where once Ulysses held the winds; 550
There she collects the force of female lungs,

Sighs, sobs, and passions, and the war of tongues.
A Vial next she fills with fainting fears,
Soft sorrows, melting griefs, and flowing tears.
The Gnome rejoicing bears her gifts away,   555
Spreads his black wings, and slowly mounts to day.
 Sunk in Thalestris' arms the nymph he found,
Her eyes dejected, and her hair unbound.
Full o'er their heads the swelling bag he rent,
And all the Furies issu'd at the vent.   560
Belinda burns with more than mortal ire,
And fierce Thalestris fans the rising fire.
'O wretched maid!' she spread her hands, and cry'd,
(While Hampton's echoes 'Wretched maid!' reply'd)
'Was it for this you took such constant care   565
The bodkin, comb, and essence to prepare?
For this your locks in paper durance bound?
For this with tort'ring irons wreath'd around?
For this with fillets strain'd your tender head?
And bravely bore the double loads of lead?   570
Gods! shall the ravisher display your hair,
While the Fops envy, and the Ladies stare?
Honour forbid! at whose unrival'd shrine
Ease, pleasure, virtue, all our sex resign.
Methinks already I your tears survey,   575
Already hear the horrid things they say,
Already see you a degraded toast,
And all your honour in a whisper lost!
How shall I, then, your helpless fame defend?
'Twill then be infamy to seem your friend!   580
And shall this prize, th' inestimable prize,
Expos'd through crystal to the gazing eyes,
And heighten'd by the diamond's circling rays,
On that rapacious hand for ever blaze?
Sooner shall grass in Hyde-park Circus grow,   585
And wits take lodging in the sound of Bow;
Sooner let earth, air, sea, to Chaos fall,
Men, monkeys, lap-dogs, parrots, perish all!'
 She said; then raging to Sir Plume repairs,
And bids her Beau demand the precious hairs: 590
(Sir Plume of amber snuff-box justly vain,
And the nice conduct of a clouded cane)
With earnest eyes, and round unthinking face,
He first the snuff-box open'd, then the case,
And thus broke out—'My Lord, why, what the devil!   595
Z—ds! damn the Lock! 'fore Gad, you must be civil!
Plague on 't! 'tis past a jest—nay, prithee, pox!
Give her the hair'—he spoke, and rapp'd his box.
 'It grieves me much' (reply'd the Peer again)

'Who speaks so well should ever speak in vain.   600
But by this Lock, this sacred Lock I swear,
(Which never more shall join its parted hair;
Which never more its honours shall renew,
Clip'd from the lovely head where late it grew)
That while my nostrils draw the vital air,   605
This hand, which won it, shall for ever wear.'
He spoke, and speaking, in proud triumph spread
The long-contended honours of her head.
    But Umbriel, hateful Gnome! forbears not so,
He breaks the Vial whence the sorrows flow.   610
Then see! the nymph in beauteous grief appears,
Her eyes half-languishing, half-drown'd in tears;
On her heav'd bosom hung her drooping head,
Which, with a sigh, she rais'd; and thus she said.
    'For ever curs'd be this detested day,   615
Which snatch'd my best, my fav'rite curl away!
Happy! ah ten times happy had I been,
If Hampton-Court these eyes had never seen!
Yet am not I the first mistaken maid,
By love of Courts to num'rous ill betray'd.   620
Oh had I rather un-admir'd remain'd
In some lone isle, or distant Northern land;
Where the gilt Chariot never marks the way,
Where none learn Ombre, none e'er taste Bohea!
There kept my charms conceal'd from mortal eye,   625
Like roses, that in deserts bloom and die.
What mov'd my mind with youthful Lords to roam?
O had I stay'd, and said my pray'rs at home!
'Twas this, the morning omens seem'd to tell:
Thrice from my trembling hand the patch-box fell;   630
The tott'ring China shook without a wind,
Nay Poll sat mute, and Shock was most unkind!
A Sylph too warn'd me of the threats of fate,
In mystic visions, now believ'd too late!
See the poor remnants of these slighted hairs!   635
My hands shall rend what ev'n thy rapine spares:
These in two sable ringlets taught to break,
Once gave new beauties to the snowy neck;
The sister-lock now sits uncouth, alone,
And in its fellow's fate foresees its own;   640
Uncurl'd it hangs, the fatal sheers demands,
And tempts, once more, thy sacrilegious hands.
Oh hadst thou, cruel! been content to seize
Hairs less in sight, or any hairs but these!'

CANTO V

She said: the pitying audience melt in tears,   645

145

But Fate and Jove had stopp'd the Baron's ears.
In vain Thalestris with reproach assails,
For who can move when fair Belinda fails?
Not half so fix'd the Trojan could remain,
While Anna begg'd and Dido rag'd in vain.   650
Then grave Clarissa graceful wav'd her fan;
Silence ensu'd, and thus the nymph began.
    'Say, why are Beauties prais'd and honour'd most,
The wise man's passion, and the vain man's toast?
Why deck'd with all that land and sea afford   655
Why Angels call'd, and Angel-like adored?
Why round our coaches crowd the white-glov'd Beaus,
Why bows the side-box from its inmost rows?
How vain are all these glories, all our pains,
Unless good sense preserve what beauty gains: 660
That men may say, when we the front-box grace,
Behold the first in virtue as in face!
Oh! if to dance all night, and dress all day,
Charm'd the small-pox, or chas'd old-age away;
Who would not scorn what housewife's cares produce,   665
Or who would learn one earthly thing of use?
To patch, nay ogle, might become a Saint,
Nor could it sure be such a sin to paint.
But since, alas! frail beauty must decay,
Curl'd or uncurl'd, since Locks will turn to grey;   670
Since painted, or not painted, all shall fade,
And she who scorns a man, must die a maid;
What then remains, but well our pow'r to use,
And keep good-humour still, whate'er we lose?
And trust me, dear! good-humour can prevail,   675
When airs, and flights, and screams, and scolding fail.
Beauties in vain their pretty eyes may roll;
Charms strike the sight, but merit wins the soul.'
    So spoke the Dame, but no applause ensu'd;
Belinda frown'd, Thalestris call'd her Prude.   680
'To arms, to arms!' the fierce Virago cries,
And swift as lightning to the combat flies.
All side in parties, and begin th' attack;
Fans clap, silks russle, and tough whalebones crack;
Heroes' and Heroines' shouts counfus'dly rise,   685
And base and treble voices strike the skies.
No common weapons in their hands are found,
Like Gods they fight, nor dread a mortal wound.
    So when bold Homer makes the Gods engage,
And heav'nly breasts with human passions rage;   690
'Gainst Pallas, Mars; Latona, Hermes arms,
And all Olympus rings with loud alarms:
Jove's thunder roars, heav'n trembles all around,

146

Blue Neptune storms, the bellowing deeps resound:
Earth shakes her nodding tow'rs, the ground gives way,   695
And the pale ghosts start at the flash of day!
　　Triumphant Umbriel on a sconce's height
Clap'd his glad wings, and sat to view the fight:
Prop'd on their bodkin spears, the Sprites survey
The growing combat, or assist the fray.   700
　　While through the press enrag'd Thalestris flies,
And scatters death around from both her eyes,
A Beau and Witling perish'd in the throng,
One dy'd in metaphor, and one in song.
'O cruel nymph! a living death I bear,'   705
Cry'd Dapperwit, and sunk beside his chair.
A mournful glance Sir Fopling upwards cast,
'Those eyes are made so killing'—was his last.
Thus on Maeander's flow'ry margin lies
Th' expiring Swan, and as he sings he dies.   710
　　When bold Sir Plume had drawn Clarissa down,
Chloe stepp'd in, and kill'd him with a frown;
She smil'd to see the doughty hero slain,
But, at her smile, the Beau reviv'd again.
　　Now Jove suspends his golden scales in air,   715
Weighs the Men's wits against the Lady's hair;
The doubtful beam long nods from side to side;
At length with wits mount up, the hairs subside.
　　See fierce Belinda on the Baron flies,
With more than usual lightning in her eyes: 720
Nor fear'd the chief th' unequal fight to try,
Who sought no more than on his foe to die.
But this bold Lord, with manly strength endu'd,
She with one finger and a thumb subdu'd:
Just where the breath of life his nostrils drew,   725
A charge of snuff the wily virgin threw;
The Gnomes direct, to ev'ry atom just,
The pungent grains of titillating dust
Sudden, with starting tears each eye o'erflows,
And the high dome re-echoes to his nose.   730
　　'Now meet thy fate!' incens'd Belinda cry'd,
And drew a deadly bodkin from her side,
(The same, his ancient personage to deck,
Her great great grandsire wore about his neck,
In three seal-rings; which after, melted down,   735
Form'd a vast buckle for his widow's gown:
Her infant grandame's whistle next it grew,
The bells she jingled, and the whistle blew;
Then in a bodkin grac'd her mother's hairs,
Which long she wore, and now Belinda wears.)   740
　　'Boast not my fall,' (he cry'd) 'insulting foe!

Thou by some other shalt be laid as low.
Nor think, to die dejects my lofty mind;
All that I dread is leaving you behind!
Rather than so, ah let me still survive,   745
And burn in Cupid's flames—but burn alive.'
    'Restore the Lock!' she cries; and all around
'Restore the Lock!' the vaulted roofs rebound.
Not fierce Othello in so loud a strain
Roar'd for the handkerchief that caus'd his pain.   750
But see how oft ambitious aims are cross'd,
And chiefs contend 'till all the prize is lost!
The Lock, obtain'd with guilt, and kept with pain,
In ev'ry place is sought, but sought in vain:
With such a prize no mortal must be blest,   755
So Heav'n decrees! with Heav'n who can contest?
    Some thought it mounted to the Lunar sphere,
Since all things lost on earth are treasur'd there.
There Heroe's wits are kept in pond'rous vases,
And Beaux' in snuff-boxes and tweezer-cases.   760
There broken vows, and death-bed alms are found,
And lovers hearts with ends of ribband bound,
The courtier's promises, and sick man's pray'rs,
The smiles of harlots, and the tears of heirs,
Cages for gnats, and chains to yoak a flea,   765
Dry'd butterflies, and tomes of casuistry.
    But trust the Muse—she saw it upward rise,
Tho' mark'd by none but quick, poetic eyes:
(So Rome's great founder to the heav'ns withdrew,
To Proculus alone confess'd in view)   770
A sudden Star, it shot through liquid air,
And drew behind a radiant trail of hair.
Not Berenice's Locks first rose so bright,
The heav'ns bespangling with dishevel'd light.
The Sylphs behold it kindling as it flies,   775
And pleas'd pursue its progress through the skies.
    This the Beau monde shall from the Mall survey,
And hail with music its propitious ray;
This the bless'd Lover shall for Venus take,
And send up vows from Rosamonda's lake;   780
This Partridge soon shall view in cloudless skies,
When next he looks through Galileo's eyes;

Rosamonda's lake—a pond once in St.
James's Park
Partridge—*John Partridge was a ridiculous
star-gazer, who in his Almanacks every
year, never fail'd to predict the downfall of
the Pope, and the King of France, then at
war with the English* (Pope's note)

And hence th' egregious wizard shall foredoom
The fate of Louis, and the fall of Rome.
    Then cease, bright Nymph! to mourn thy ravish'd hair,   785
Which adds new glory to the shining sphere!
Not all the tresses that fair head can boast,
Shall draw such envy as the Lock you lost.
For, after all the murders of your eye,
When, after millions slain, yourself shall die;   790
When those fair suns shall set, as set they must,
And all those tresses shall be laid in dust,
This Lock, the Muse shall consecrate to fame,
And 'midst the stars inscribe Belinda's name.

from WINTER

JAMES THOMSON

The Argument

The subject proposed. Address to the Earl of Wilmington. First
approach of Winter. According to the natural course of the season,
various storms described. Rain. Wind. Snow. The driving of the
snows: a man perishing among them; whence reflections on the
wants and miseries of human life. The wolves descending from
the Alps and Apennines. A winter evening described: as spent
by philosophers; by the country people; in the city. Frost. A view
of Winter within the polar circle. A thaw. The whole concluding
with moral reflections on a future state.

    See, Winter comes to rule the varied year,
Sullen and sad, with all his rising train—
Vapours, and clouds, and storms. Be these my theme;
These, that exalt the soul to solemn thought
And heavenly musing. Welcome, kindred glooms!   5
Congenial horrors, hail! With frequent foot,
Pleased have I, in my cheerful morn of life,
When nursed by careless solitude I lived
And sung of Nature with unceasing joy,
Pleased have I wandered through your rough domain;   10
Trod the pure virgin-snows, myself as pure;
Heard the winds roar, and the big torrent burst;
Or seen the deep-fermenting tempest brewed
In the grim evening-sky. Thus passed the time,
Till through the lucid chambers of the south   15
Looked out the joyous Spring—looked out and smiled.

To thee, the patron of this first essay,
The Muse, O Wilmington! renews her song.
Since has she rounded the revolving year:
Skimm'd the gay Spring; on eagle-pinions borne,   20
Attempted through the Summer-blaze to rise;
Then swept o'er Autumn with the shadowy gale.
And now among the Wintry clouds again,
Rolled in the doubling storm, she tries to soar,
To swell her note with all the rushing winds,   25
To suit her sounding cadence to the floods;
As is her theme, her numbers wildly great.
Thrice happy, could she fill thy judging ear
With bold description and with manly thought!
Nor art thou skilled in awful schemes alone,   30
And how to make a mighty people thrive;
But equal goodness, sound integrity,
A firm, unshaken, uncorrupted soul
Amid a sliding age, and burning strong,
Not vainly blazing, for thy country's weal,   35
A steady spirit, regularly free—
These, each exalting each, the statesman light
Into the patriot; these, the public hope
And eye to thee converting, bid the Muse
Record what envy dares not flattery call.   40

Now, when the cheerless empire of the sky
To Capricorn the Centaur-Archer yields,
And fierce Aquarius stains the inverted year—
Hung o'er the farthest verge of heaven, the sun
Scarce spreads o'er ether the dejected day.   45
Faint are his gleams, and ineffectual shoot
His struggling rays in horizontal lines
Through the thick air; as clothed in cloudy storm,
Weak, wan, and broad, he skirts the southern sky;
And, soon descending, to the long dark night,   50
Wide-shading all, the prostrate world resigns.
Nor is the night unwished; while vital heat,
Light, life, and joy the dubious day forsake.
Meantime, in sable cincture, shadows vast,
Deep-tinged and damp, and congregated clouds,   55
And all the vapoury turbulence of heaven
Involve the face of things. Thus Winter falls,
A heavy gloom oppressive o'er the world,
Through Nature shedding influence malign,
And rouses up the seeds of dark disease.   60
The soul of man dies in him, loathing life,
And black with more than melancholy views.

The cattle droop; and o'er the furrowed land,
Fresh from the plough, the dun discoloured flocks,
Untended spreading, crop the wholesome root.   65
Along the woods, along the moorish fens,
Sighs the sad genius of the coming storm;
And up among the loose disjointed cliffs
And fractured mountains wild, the brawling brook
And cave, presageful, send a hollow moan,   70
Resounding long in listening fancy's ear.
    Then comes the father of the tempest forth,
Wrapt in black glooms. First, joyless rains obscure
Drive through the mingling skies with vapour foul,
Dash on the mountain's brow, and shake the woods   75
That grumbling wave below. The unsightly plain
Lies a brown deluge; as the low-bent clouds
Pour flood on flood, yet unexhausted still
Combine, and, deepening into night, shut up
The day's fair face. The wanderers of heaven,   80
Each to his home, retire; save those that love
To take their pastime in the troubled air,
Or skimming flutter round the dimply pool.
The cattle from the untasted fields return
And ask, with meaning low, their wonted stalls,   85
Or ruminate in the contiguous shade.
Thither the household feathery people crowd,
The crested cock, with all his female train,
Pensive and dripping; while the cottage-hind
Hangs o'er the enlivening blaze, and taleful there   90
Recounts his simple frolic: much he talks,
And much he laughs, nor recks the storm that blows
Without, and rattles on his humble roof.
    Wide o'er the brim, with many a torrent swelled,
And the mixed ruin of its banks o'erspread,   95
At last the roused-up river pours along:
Resistless, roaring, dreadful, down it comes,
From the rude mountain and the mossy wild,
Tumbling through rocks abrupt, and sounding far;
Then o'er the sanded valley floating spreads,   100
Calm, sluggish, silent; till again, constrained
Between two meeting hills, it bursts a way
Where rocks and woods o'erhang the turbid stream;
There, gathering triple force, rapid and deep,
It boils, and wheels, and foams, and thunders through.   105

    Nature! great parent! whose unceasing hand
Rolls round the Seasons of the changeful year,
How mighty, how majestic are thy works!

With what a pleasing dread they swell the soul,
That sees astonished, and astonished sings! 110
Ye too, ye winds! that now begin to blow
With boisterous sweep, I raise my voice to you.
Where are your stores, ye powerful beings! say,
Where your aerial magazines reserved
To swell the brooding terrors of the storm? 115
In what far-distant region of the sky,
Hushed in deep silence, sleep you when 'tis calm?...

...

'Tis done! Dread Winter spreads his latest glooms,
And reigns tremendous o'er the conquered year. 1025
How dead the vegetable kingdom lies!
How dumb the tuneful! Horror wide extends
His desolate domain. Behold, fond man!
See here thy pictured life; pass some few years,
Thy flowering Spring, thy Summer's ardent strength, 1030
Thy sober Autumn fading into age,
And pale concluding Winter comes at last
And shuts the scene. Ah! whither now are fled
Those dreams of greatness? those unsolid hopes
Of happiness? those longings after fame? 1035
Those restless cares? those busy bustling days?
Those gay-spent festive nights? those veering thoughts,
Lost between good and ill, that shared thy life?
All now are vanished! Virtue sole survives—
Immortal, never-failing friend of man, 1040
His guide to happiness on high. And see!
'Tis come, the glorious morn! the second birth
Of heaven and earth! awakening nature hears
The new-creating word, and starts to life
In every heightened form, from pain and death 1045
For ever free. The great eternal scheme,
Involving all, and in a perfect whole
Uniting, as the prospect wider spreads,
To reason's eye refined clears up apace.
Ye vainly wise! ye blind presumptuous! now, 1050
Confounded in the dust, adore that Power
And Wisdom—oft arraigned: see now the cause
Why unassuming worth in secret lived
And died neglected: why the good man's share
In life was gall and bitterness of soul: 1055
Why the lone widow and her orphans pined
In starving solitude; while luxury
In palaces lay straining her low thought

To form unreal wants: why heaven-born truth
And moderation fair wore the red marks   1060
Of superstition's scourge; why licensed pain,
That cruel spoiler, that embosomed foe,
Embittered all our bliss. Ye good distressed!
Ye noble few! who here unbending stand
Beneath life's pressure, yet bear up a while,   1065
And what your bounded view, which only saw
A little part, deemed evil is no more:
The storms of wintry time will quickly pass,
And one unbounded Spring encircle all.

from THE VANITY OF HUMAN WISHES

THE TENTH SATIRE OF JUVENAL IMITATED

SAMUEL JOHNSON

Let observation with extensive view,
Survey mankind, from China to Peru;
Remark each anxious toil, each eager strife,
And watch the busy scenes of crouded life;
Then say how hope and fear, desire and hate,   5
O'erspread with snares the clouded maze of fate,
Where wav'ring man, betray'd by vent'rous pride,
To tread the dreary paths without a guide,
As treach'rous phantoms in the mist delude,
Shuns fancied ills, or chases airy good;   10
How rarely reason guides the stubborn choice,
Rules the bold hand, or prompts the suppliant voice;
How nations sink, by darling schemes oppress'd,
When vengeance listens to the fool's request.
Fate wings with ev'ry wish th' afflictive dart,   15
Each gift of nature, and each grace of art,
With fatal heat impetuous courage glows,
With fatal sweetness elocution flows,
Impeachment stops the speaker's pow'rful breath,
And restless fire precipitates on death.   20
    But scarce observ'd, the knowing and the bold
Fall in the gen'ral massacre of gold;
Wide-wasting pest! that rages unconfin'd,
And crouds with crimes the records of mankind;
For gold his sword the hireling ruffian draws,   25
For gold the hireling judge distorts the laws;
Wealth heap'd on wealth, nor truth nor safety buys,

The dangers gather as the treasures rise.
   Let hist'ry tell where rival kings command,
And dubious title shakes the madded land,   30
When statutes glean the refuse of the sword,
How much more safe the vassal than the lord;
Low skulks the hind beneath the rage of pow'r,
And leaves the wealthy traytor in the Tow'r,
Untouch'd his cottage, and his slumbers sound,   35
Tho' confiscation's vulturs hover round.
   The needy traveller, serene and gay,
Walks the wild heath, and sings his toil away.
Does envy seize thee? crush th' upbraiding joy,
Increase his riches and his peace destroy;   40
Now fears in dire vicissitude invade,
The rustling brake alarms, and quiv'ring shade,
Nor light nor darkness bring his pain relief,
One shews the plunder, and one hides the thief.
   Yet still one gen'ral cry the skies assails,   45
And gain and grandeur load the tainted gales;
Few know the toiling statesman's fear or care,
Th' insidious rival and the gaping heir.
   Once more, Democritus, arise on earth,
With cheerful wisdom and instructive mirth,   50
See motley life in modern trappings dress'd,
And feed with varied fools th' eternal jest:
Thou who couldst laugh where want enchain'd caprice,
Toil crush'd conceit, and man was of a piece;
Where wealth unlov'd without a mourner dy'd,   55
And scarce a sycophant was fed by pride;
Where ne'er was known the form of mock debate,
Or seen a new-made mayor's unwieldy state;
Where change of fav'rites made no change of laws,
And senates heard before they judg'd a cause;   60
How wouldst thou shake at Britain's modish tribe,
Dart the quick taunt, and edge the piercing gibe?
Attentive truth and nature to descry,
And pierce each scene with philosophic eye.
To thee were solemn toys or empty shew,   65
The robes of pleasure and the veils of woe:
All aid the farce, and all thy mirth maintain,
Whose joys are causeless, or whose griefs are vain.
   Such was the scorn that fill'd the sage's mind,
Renew'd at ev'ry glance on humankind;   70
How just that scorn ere yet thy voice declare,
Search every state, and canvass ev'ry pray'r.
   Unnumber'd suppliants croud Preferment's gate,
Athirst for wealth, and burning to be great;

Delusive Fortune hears th' incessant call,   75
They mount, they shine, evaporate, and fall.
On ev'ry stage the foes of peace attend,
Hate dogs their flight, and insult mocks their end.
Love ends with hope, the sinking statesman's door
Pours in the morning worshiper no more;   80
For growing names the weekly scribbler lies,
To growing wealth the dedicator flies,
From every room descends the painted face,
That hung the bright Palladium of the place,
And smok'd in kitchens, or in auctions sold,   85
To better features yields the frame of gold;
For now no more we trace in ev'ry line
Heroic worth, benevolence divine:
The form distorted justifies the fall,
And detestation rids th' indignant wall.   90
    But will not Britain hear the last appeal,
Sign her foes doom, or guard her fav'rites zeal?
Through Freedom's sons no more remonstrance rings,
Degrading nobles and controuling kings;
Our supple tribes repress their patriot throats,   95
And ask no questions but the price of votes;
With weekly libels and septennial ale,
Their wish is full to riot and to rail.

• • •

ELEGY WRITTEN IN A COUNTRY
CHURCH YARD

THOMAS GRAY

The curfew tolls the knell of parting day;
    The lowing herd winds slowly o'er the lea;
The ploughman homeward plods his weary way,
    And leaves the world to darkness and to me.

Now fades the glimmering landscape on the sight,   5
    And all the air a solemn stillness holds,
Save where the beetle wheels his droning flight,
    And drowsy tinklings lull the distant folds;

Save that from yonder ivy-mantled tow'r,
    The moping owl does to the moon complain   10
Of such as, wand'ring near her secret bow'r,
    Molest her ancient solitary reign.

Beneath those rugged elms, that yew-tree's shade,
    Where heaves the turf in many a mould'ring heap,
Each in his narrow cell forever laid,   15
    The rude forefathers of the hamlet sleep.

The breezy call of incense-breathing Morn,
    The swallow twitt'ring from the strawbuilt shed,
The cock's shrill clarion, or the echoing horn,
    No more shall rouse them from their lowly bed.   20

For them no more the blazing hearth shall burn,
    Or busy housewife ply her evening care;
No children run to lisp their sire's return,
    Or climb his knees the envied kiss to share.

Oft did the harvest to their sickle yield,   25
    Their furrow oft the stubborn glebe has broke:
How jocund did they drive their team afield!
    How bow'd the woods beneath their sturdy stroke!

Let not Ambition mock their useful toil,
    Their homely joys, and destiny obscure;   30
Nor Grandeur hear with a disdainful smile
    The short and simple annals of the poor.

The boast of heraldry, the pomp of pow'r,
    And all that beauty, all that wealth e'er gave,
Awaits alike th' inevitable hour: 35
    The paths of glory lead but to the grave.

Nor you, ye proud, impute to these the fault,
    If Memory o'er their tomb no trophies raise,
Where through the long-drawn aisle and fretted vault
    The pealing anthem swells the note of praise.   40

Can storied urn, or animated bust,
    Back to its mansion call the fleeting breath?
Can Honor's voice provoke the silent dust,
    Or Flatt'ry soothe the dull cold ear of Death?

Perhaps in this neglected spot is laid   45
    Some heart once pregnant with celestial fire;
Hands that the rod of empire might have sway'd,
    Or wak'd to extasy the living lyre.

But Knowledge to their eyes her ample page,
    Rich with the spoils of time, did ne'er unroll;   50

glebe—sod

Chill Penury repress'd their noble rage,
    And froze the genial current of the soul.

Full many a gem of purest ray serene
    The dark unfathom'd caves of ocean bear;
Full many a flower is born to blush unseen,   55
    And waste its sweetness on the desert air.

Some village Hampden that with dauntless breast,
    The little tyrant of his fields withstood,
Some mute inglorious Milton here may rest,
    Some Cromwell guiltless of his country's blood.   60

Th' applause of list'ning senates to command,
    The threats of pain and ruin to despise,
To scatter plenty o'er a smiling land,
    And read their history in a nation's eyes,

Their lot forbad: nor circumscrib'd alone   65
    Their growing virtues, but their crimes confined
Forbad to wade thro' slaughter to a throne,
    And shut the gates of mercy on mankind,

The struggling pangs of conscious truth to hide,
    To quench the blushes of ingenuous shame,   70
Or heap the shrine of Luxury and Pride
    With incense kindled at the Muse's flame.

Far from the madding crowd's ignoble strife,
    Their sober wishes never learn'd to stray;
Along the cool sequester'd vale of life   75
    They kept the noiseless tenor of their way.

Yet ev'n these bones from insult to protect,
    Some frail memorial still erected nigh,
With uncouth rhymes and shapeless sculpture deck'd,
    Implores the passing tribute of a sigh.   80

Their name, their years, spelt by th' unletter'd Muse,
    The place of fame and elegy supply;
And many a holy text around she strews,
    That teach the rustic moralist to die.

For who, to dumb Forgetfulness a prey,   85
    This pleasing anxious being e'er resign'd,
Left the warm precincts of the cheerful day,
    Nor cast one longing, ling'ring look behind?

On some fond breast the parting soul relies,
    Some pious drops the closing eye requires;   90
E'en from the tomb the voice of Nature cries,
    E'en in our ashes live their wonted fires.

For thee, who, mindful of th' unhonor'd dead,
    Dost in these lines their artless tale relate,
If chance, by lonely Contemplation led,   95
    Some kindred spirit shall enquire thy fate,—

Haply some hoary-headed swain may say,
    "Oft have we seen him at the peep of dawn
Brushing with hasty steps the dews away,
    To meet the sun upon the upland lawn.   100

"There, at the foot of yonder nodding beech,
    That wreathes its old fantastic roots so high,
His listless length at noontide would he stretch,
    And pore upon the brook that babbles by.

"Hard by yon wood, now smiling as in scorn,   105
    Mutt'ring his wayward fancies, he would rove,
Now drooping, woful-wan, like one forlorn,
    Or craz'd with care, or cross'd in hopeless love.

"One morn I miss'd him on the custom'd hill,
    Along the heath, and near his fav'rite tree;   110
Another came; nor yet beside the rill,
    Nor up the lawn, nor at the wood was he;

"The next, with dirges due, in sad array
    Slow through the church-way path we saw him borne:—
Approach and read (for thou can'st read) the lay   115
    Grav'd on the stone beneath yon aged thorn."

THE EPITAPH

Here rests his head upon the lap of Earth
    A youth, to Fortune and to Fame unknown:
Fair Science frown'd not on his humble birth,
    And Melancholy mark'd him for her own.   120

Large was his bounty, and his soul sincere;
    Heaven did a recompense as largely send:
He gave to Mis'ry all he had, a tear,
    He gain'd from Heav'n ('twas all he wish'd) a friend.
No farther seek his merits to disclose,   125

Or draw his frailties from their dread abode
(There they alike in trembling hope repose),
The bosom of his Father and his God.

THE BARD

THOMAS GRAY

I. 1

"Ruin seize thee, ruthless King!
 Confusion on thy banners wait;
Tho' fann'd by Conquest's crimson wing,
 They mock the air with idle state.
Helm, nor hauberk's twisted mail,   5
Nor e'en thy virtues, tyrant, shall avail
To save thy secret soul from nightly fears,
From Cambria's curse, from Cambria's tears!"
Such were the sounds that o'er the crested pride
 Of the first Edward scatter'd wild dismay,   10
As down the steep of Snowdon's shaggy side
 He wound with toilsome march his long array.
Stout Glo'ster stood aghast in speechless trance;
"To arms!" cried Mortimer, and couch'd his quiv'ring lance.

I. 2

On a rock, whose haughty brow   15
Frowns o'er cold Conway's foaming flood,
 Robed in the sable garb of woe,
With haggard eyes the poet stood
(Loose his beard, and hoary hair
Stream'd, like a meteor, to the troubled air)   20
And with a master's hand, and prophet's fire,
Struck the deep sorrows of his lyre:
 "Hark, how each giant-oak and desert cave
Sighs to the torrent's awful voice beneath!
 O'er thee, oh King! their hundred arms they wave,   25
 Revenge on thee in hoarser murmurs breathe,
Vocal no more, since Cambria's fatal day,
To high-born Hoel's harp, or soft Llewellyn's lay.

ruthless King—Edward I said to have condemned Welsh bards to death. A survi-
vor speaks.
confusion—destruction

"Cold is Cadwallo's tongue,
   That hush'd the stormy main;   30
Brave Urien sleeps upon his craggy bed;
     Mountains, ye mourn in vain
     Modred, whose magic song
Made huge Plinlimmon bow his cloud-topt head.
   On dreary Arvon's shore they lie,   35
Smear'd with gore, and ghastly pale;
Far, far aloof th' affrighted ravens sail;
   The famish'd eagle screams, and passes by.
Dear lost companions of my tuneful art,
   Dear as the light that visits these sad eyes,   40
Dear as the ruddy drops that warm my heart,
   Ye died amidst your dying country's cries—
No more I weep. They do not sleep!
   On yonder cliffs, a griesly band,
I see them sit; they linger yet,   45
   Avengers of their native land:
With me in dreadful harmony they join,
And weave with bloody hands the tissue of thy line.

II. 1

"Weave the warp, and weave the woof,
The winding-sheet of Edward's race;   50
   Give ample room, and verge enough
The characters of hell to trace.
Mark the year, and mark the night,
When Severn shall re-echo with affright
The shrieks of death, thro' Berkley's roofs that ring,   55
Shrieks of an agonizing king!
   She-wolf of France, with unrelenting fangs,
That tear'st the bowels of thy mangled mate,
   From thee be born, who o'er thy country hangs
The scourge of Heav'n. What Terrors round him wait!   60
Amazement in his van, with Flight combin'd,
And Sorrow's faded form, and Solitude behind.

II. 2

"Mighty victor, mighty lord!
Low on his funeral couch he lies!
   No pitying heart, no eye, afford   65
A tear to grace his obsequies.
   Is the Sable Warrior fled?
Thy son is gone; he rests among the dead.
The swarm, that in thy noontide beam were born?
Gone to salute the rising morn.   70

Fair laughs the morn, and soft the zephyr blows,
　　While proudly riding o'er the azure realm,
　In gallant trim the gilded vessel goes;
　　Youth on the prow, and Pleasure at the helm;
Regardless of the sweeping Whirlwind's sway,　　　　75
That, hush'd in grim repose, expects his ev'ning prey.

II. 3

"Fill high the sparkling bowl;
The rich repast prepare;
　Reft of a crown, he yet may share the feast:
Close by the regal chair　　　　　　　　　　　　　80
　　Fell Thirst and Famine scowl
　　A baleful smile upon their baffled guest.
Heard ye the din of battle bray,
　　Lance to lance, and horse to horse?
　　Long years of havoc urge their destined course,　85
And thro' the kindred squadrons mow their way.
　Ye towers of Julius, London's lasting shame,
With many a foul and midnight murther fed,
　Revere his consort's faith, his father's fame,
And spare the meek usurper's holy head!　　　　　90
Above, below, the rose of snow,
　　Twin'd with her blushing foe, we spread:
The bristled Boar in infant-gore
　　Wallows beneath the thorny shade.
Now, brothers, bending o'er th' accursed loom,　　95
Stamp we our vengeance deep, and ratify his doom!

III. 1

"Edward, lo! to sudden fate
(Weave we the woof: the thread is spun.)
　Half of thy heart we consecrate.
(The web is wove. The work is done.)　　　　　　100
Stay, oh stay! nor thus forlorn
Leave me unbless'd, unpitied, here to mourn!
In yon bright track, that fires the western skies,
They melt, they vanish from my eyes.
But oh! what solemn scenes on Snowdon's height,　105
　　Descending slow, their glittering skirts unroll?
Visions of glory, spare my aching sight!
　　Ye unborn ages, crowd not on my soul!
No more our long-lost Arthur we bewail.
　All hail, ye genuine kings, Britannia's issue, hail!　110
long-lost Arthur—it was commonly be-
lieved that King Arthur would return from
fairyland to reign over Britain
ye genuine kings—the house of Tudor
which was of Welsh blood

"Girt with many a baron bold
Sublime their starry fronts they rear;
　And gorgeous dames, and statesmen old
In bearded majesty, appear.
In the midst a form divine!　　　　　　　　　　115
Her eye proclaims her of the Briton line;
Her lion-port, her awe-commanding face,
Attemper'd sweet to virgin-grace.
What strings symphonious tremble in the air,
　What strains of vocal transport round her play!　120
Hear from the grave, great Taliessin, hear;
　They breathe a soul to animate thy clay.
Bright Rapture calls, and soaring as she sings,
Waves in the eye of Heav'n her many-color'd wings.

III. 3

"The verse adorn again　　　　　　　　　　　125
　Fierce War, and faithful Love,
And Truth severe, by fairy Fiction drest.
　In buskin'd measures move
Pale Grief, and pleasing Pain,
With Horror, tyrant of the throbbing breast.　　130
　A voice, as of the cherub-choir,
Gales from blooming Eden bear;
And distant warblings lessen on my ear,
　That, lost in long futurity, expire.
Fond impious man, think'st thou yon sanguine cloud,　135
　Rais'd by thy breath, has quench'd the orb of day?
Tomorrow he repairs the golden flood,
　And warms the nations with redoubled ray.
Enough for me; with joy I see
　The diff'rent doom our Fates assign.　　　　140
Be thine Despair, and scept'red Care,
　To triumph, and to die, are mine."
He spoke, and headlong from the mountain's height
Deep in the roaring tide he plunged to endless night.

a form divine—Queen Elizabeth
fairy Fiction—an allusion to *The Faerie
Queene* of Spenser

A SONG TO DAVID

CHRISTOPHER SMART

LXXII

Sweet is the dew that falls betimes,
And drops upon the leafy lines;
   Sweet Hermon's fragrant air:
Sweet is the lily's silver bell,
And sweet the wakeful tapers' smell   5
   That watch for early pray'r.

LXXIII

Sweet the young nurse with love intense,
Which smiles o'er sleeping innocence;
   Sweet when the lost arrive:
Sweet the musician's ardour beats,   10
While his vague mind's in quest of sweets,
   The choicest flow'rs to hive.

LXXIV

Sweeter in all the Strains of love,
The language of thy turtle dove,
   Pair'd to thy swelling chord;   15
Sweeter with ev'ry grace endu'd,
The glory of thy gratitude,
   Respir'd unto the Lord.

LXXV

Strong is the horse upon his speed;
Strong in pursuit the rapid glede,   20
   Which makes at once his game:
Strong the tall ostrich on the ground;
Strong through the turbulent profound
   Shoots xiphias to his aim.

LXXVI

Strong is the lion—like a coal   25
His eye-ball—like a bastion's mole
   His chest against the foes:
Strong the gier-eagle on his sail,
Strong against tide, th' enormous whale
   Emerges, as he goes.   30

LXXVII

But stronger still, in earth and air,
And in the sea, the man of pray'r;
   And far beneath the tide;
And in the seat to faith assign'd,
Where ask is have, where seek is find,   35
   Where knock is open wide.

LXXVIII

Beauteous the fleet before the gale;
Beauteous the multitudes in mail,
   Rank'd arms and crested heads:
Beauteous the garden's umbrage mild,   40
Walk, water, meditated wild,
   And all the bloomy beds.

LXXIX

Beauteous the moon full on the lawn;
And beauteous, when the veil's withdrawn,
   The virgin to her spouse: 45
Beauteous the temple deck'd and fill'd,
When to the heav'n of heav'ns they build
   Their heart-directed vows.

LXXX

Beauteous, yea beauteous more than these,
The shepherd king upon his knees,   50
   For his momentous trust;
With wish of infinite conceit,
For man, beast, mute, the small and great,
   And prostrate dust to dust.

LXXXI

Precious the bounteous widow's mite;   55
And precious, for extreme delight,
   The largess from the churl:
Precious the ruby's blushing blaze,
And alba's blest imperial rays,
   And pure cerulean pearl.   60

LXXXII

Precious the penitential tear;
And precious is the sigh sincere,
   Acceptable to God:
And precious are the winning flow'rs,
In gladsome Israel's feast of bow'rs,   65
   Bound on the hallow'd sod.

LXXXIII

More precious that diviner part
Of David, ev'n the Lord's own heart,
   Great, beautiful, and new:
In all things where it was intent,   70
In all extreams, in each event,
   Proof—answ'ring true to true.

LXXXIV

Glorious the sun in mid career;
Glorious th' assembled fires appear;
   Glorious the comet's train: 75
Glorious the trumpet and alarm;
Glorious th' almighty stretch'd-out arm;
   Glorious th' enraptur'd main:

LXXXV

Glorious the northern lights astream;
Glorious the song, when God's the theme;   80
   Glorious the thunder's roar:
Glorious hosanna from the den;
Glorious the catholic amen;
   Glorious the martyr's gore:

LXXXVI

Glorious—more glorious is the crown   85
Of Him, that brought salvation down
   By meekness, call'd thy Son;
Thou that stupendous truth believ'd,
And now the matchless deed's atchiev'd,
   DETERMIN'D, DAR'D, and DONE.

THE ENTHUSIAST
or the
LOVER OF NATURE

JOSEPH WARTON

Rure vero barbaroque laetatur.   Martial

Ut mihi devio
Rupes et vacuum nemus
Mirari libet!   Horace

Ye green-rob'd Dryads, oft at dusky eve
By wondering shepherds seen, to forests brown,
To unfrequented meads, and pathless wilds,
Lead me from gardens deck'd with art's vain pomps.
Can gilt alcoves, can marble-mimic gods, 5
Parterres embroider'd, obelisks, and urns,
Of high relief; can the long, spreading lake
Or vista lessening to the sight; can Stow,
With all her Attic fanes, such raptures raise,
As the thrush-haunted copse, where lightly leaps 10
The fearful fawn the rustling leaves along,
And the brisk squirrel sports from bough to bough,
While from an hollow oak, whose naked roots
O'erhang a pensive rill, the busy bees
Hum drowsy lullabies? The bards of old, 15
Fair Nature's friends, sought such retreats, to charm
Sweet Echo with their songs; oft too they met
In summer evenings, near sequester'd bowers,
Or mountain-nymph, or muse, and eager learnt
The moral strains she taught to mend mankind. 20
As to a secret grot Aegeria stole
With patriot Numa, and in silent night
Whisper'd him sacred laws, he list'ning sat,
Rapt with her virtuous voice, old Tyber lean'd
Attentive on his urn, and hush'd his waves. 25
      Rich in her weeping country's spoils, Versailles
May boast a thousand fountains, that can cast
The tortur'd waters to the distant heav'ns;
Yet let me choose some pine-topt precipice
Abrupt and shaggy, whence a foamy stream, 30
Like Anio, tumbling roars; or some black heath,
Where straggling stands the mournful juniper,
Or yew-tree scath'd; while in clear prospect round,
From the grove's bosom spires emerge, and smoke
In bluish wreaths ascends, ripe harvests wave, 35
Low, lonely cottages, and ruin'd tops
Of Gothic battlements appear, and streams
Beneath the sun-beams twinkle. —The shrill lark,
That wakes the wood-man to his early task,
Or love-sick Philomel, whose luscious lays 40
Soothe lone night-wanderers, the moaning dove
Pitied by list'ning milk-maid, far excel
The deep-mouth'd viol, the soul-lulling lute,

Stowe—the most famous garden in 18th-
century England, Viscount Cobham's estate
fanes—temples

And battle-breathing trumpet. Artful sounds!
That please not like the choristers of air,   45
When first they hail th' approach of laughing May.

. . .

ODE TO FEAR

WILLIAM COLLINS

Thou, to whom the world unknown
With all its shadowy shapes is shown;
Who see'st appall'd th' unreal scene,
While Fancy lifts the veil between:
    Ah Fear! Ah frantic Fear!   5
    I see, I see thee near.
I know thy hurried step, thy haggard eye!
Like thee I start, like thee disorder'd fly,
    For lo what Monsters in thy train appear!
    Danger, whose limbs of giant mold   10
    What mortal eye can fix'd behold?
    Who stalks his round, an hideous form,
    Howling amidst the midnight storm,
    Or throws him on the ridgy steep
    Of some loose hanging rock to sleep: 15
    And with him thousand phantoms join'd,
    Who prompt to deeds accurs'd the mind:
    And those, the fiends, who near allied,
    O'er Nature's wounds, and wrecks preside;
    Whilst Vengeance, in the lurid air,   20
    Lifts her red arm, expos'd and bare:
    On whom that rav'ning brood of fate,
      Who lap the blood of sorrow, wait;
    Who, Fear, this ghastly train can see,
    And look not madly wild, like thee?   25

EPODE

In earliest Greece to thee with partial choice,
    The grief-full Muse addrest her infant tongue;
The maids and matrons, on her awful voice,
    Silent and pale in wild amazement hung.

Yet he, the bard who first invok'd thy name,   30
    Disdain'd in Marathon its pow'r to feel:

brood of fate—see Sophocles, the *Electra*
the bard—Aeschylus

For not alone he nurs'd the poet's flame,
    But reach'd from Virtue's hand the patriot's steel.

But who is he whom later garlands grace,
    Who left a-while o'er Hybla's dews to rove,   35
With trembling eyes thy dreary steps to trace,
    Where thou and Furies shar'd the baleful grove?

Wrapt in thy cloudy veil th' incestuous queen
    Sigh'd the sad call her son and husband hear'd,
When once alone it broke the silent scene,   40
    And he the wretch of Thebes no more appear'd.

O Fear, I know thee by my throbbing heart,
    Thy with'ring pow'r inspir'd each mournful line,
Tho' gentle Pity claim her mingled part,
    Yet all the thunders of the scene are thine!   45

ANTISTROPHE

Thou who such weary lengths hast past,
Where wilt thou rest, mad nymph, at last?
Say, wilt thou shroud in haunted cell,
Where gloomy Rape and Murder dwell?
Or, in some hollow'd seat,   50
'Gainst which the big waves beat,
Hear drowning sea-men's cries in tempests brought!
Dark pow'r, with shudd'ring meek submitted thought
Be mine, to read the visions old,
Which thy awak'ning bards have told: 55
And lest thou meet my blasted view,
Hold each strange tale devoutly true;
Ne'er be I found, by thee o'eraw'd,
In that thrice-hallow'd eve abroad,
When ghosts, as cottage-maids believe,   60
Their pebbled beds permitted leave,
And Gobblins haunt from fire, or fen,
Or mine, or flood, the walks of men!
    O thou whose spirit most possest
The sacred seat of Shakespear's breast!   65
By all that from thy prophet broke,
In thy divine emotions spoke:
Hither again thy fury deal,
Teach me but once like him to feel:
His cypress wreath my meed decree,   70
And I, O Fear, will dwell with thee!

th' incestuous queen—Jocasta

ODE TO EVENING

WILLIAM COLLINS

If ought of oaten stop, or pastoral song,
May hope, O pensive Eve, to soothe thine ear,
    Like thy own brawling springs,
    Thy springs, and dying gales,
O Nymph reserv'd, while now the bright-hair'd sun   5
Sits in yon western tent, whose cloudy skirts,
    With brede ethereal wove,
    O'erhang his wavy bed:
Now air is hush'd, save where the weak-ey'd bat,
With short shrill shriek flits by on leathern wing,   10
    Or where the beetle winds
    His small but sullen horn,
As oft he rises 'midst the twilight path,
Against the pilgrim born in heedless hum:
    Now teach me, maid compos'd,   15
    To breathe some soften'd strain,
Whose numbers stealing thro' thy darkening vale,
May not unseemly with its stillness suit,
    As musing slow, I hail
    Thy genial lov'd return!   20
For when thy folding star arising shews
His paly circlet, at his warning lamp
    The fragrant Hours, and Elves
    Who slept in buds the day,
And many a Nymph who wreaths her brows with sedge,   25
And sheds the fresh'ning dew, and lovlier still,
    The pensive Pleasures sweet
    Prepare thy shadowy ear.
Then lead, calm votaress where some sheety lake
Cheers the lone heath or some time-hallowed pile,   30
    Or upland fallows grey
    Reflect its last cool gleam.
Then let me rove some wild and healthy scene,
Or find some ruin 'midst its dreary dells,
    Whose walls more awful nod   35
    By thy religious gleams.
Or if chill blustering winds, or driving rain,
Prevent my willing feet, be mine the hut,
    That from the mountain's side,
    Views wilds, and swelling floods,   40
And hamlets brown, and dim-discover'd spires,
And hears their simple bell, and marks o'er all
    Thy dewy fingers draw

The gradual dusky veil.
While Spring shall pour his show'rs, as oft he wont,   45
And bathe thy breathing tresses, meekest Eve!
    While Summer loves to sport,
    Beneath thy ling'ring light:
While sallow autumn fills thy lap with leaves,
Or Winter yelling thro' the troublous air,   50
    Affrights thy shrinking train,
    And rudely rends thy robes.
So long regardful of thy quiet rule,
Shall Fancy, Friendship, Science, smiling Peace,
    Thy gentlest influence own,   55
    And love thy fav'rite name!

from THE DESERTED VILLAGE

OLIVER GOLDSMITH

Sweet Auburn! loveliest village of the plain;
Where health and plenty cheered the labouring swain,
Where smiling spring its earliest visit paid,
And parting summer's lingering blooms delayed:
Dear lovely bowers of innocence and ease,   5
Seats of my youth, when every sport could please,
How often have I loitered o'er thy green,
Where humble happiness endeared each scene!
How often have I paused on every charm,
The sheltered cot, the cultivated farm,   10
The never-failing brook, the busy mill,
The decent church that topped the neighbouring hill.
The hawthorn bush, with seats beneath the shade,
For talking age and whispering lovers made!
How often have I blest the coming day,   15
When toil remitting lent its turn to play,
And all the village train, from labour free,
Led up their sports beneath the spreading tree,
While many a pastime circled in the shade,
The young contending as the old surveyed;   20
And many a gambol frolicked o'er the ground,
And sleights of art and feats of strength went round.
And still, as each repeated pleasure tired,
Succeeding sports the mirthful band inspired;
The dancing pair that simply sought renown,   25
By holding out to tire each other down;

The swain mistrustless of his smutted face,
While secret laughter tittered round the place;
The bashful virgin's side-long looks of love,
The matron's glance that would those looks reprove: 30
These were thy charms, sweet village! sports like these,
With sweet succession, taught even toil to please:
These round thy bowers their cheerful influence shed;
These were thy charms—but all these charms are fled.

    Sweet smiling village, loveliest of the lawn,   35
Thy sports are fled, and all thy charms withdrawn;
Amidst thy bowers the tyrant's hand is seen,
And desolation saddens all the green:
One only master grasps the whole domain,
And half a tillage stints thy smiling plain.   40
No more thy glassy brook reflects the day,
But, choked with sedges, works its weedy way;
Along thy glades, a solitary guest,
The hollow sounding bittern guards its nest:
Amidst thy desert walks the lapwing flies,   45
And tires their echoes with unvaried cries;
Sunk are thy bowers in shapeless ruin all,
And the long grass o'ertops the mouldering wall;
And trembling, shrinking from the spoiler's hand,
Far, far away thy children leave the land.   50

    Ill fares the land, to hastening ills a prey,
Where wealth accumulates, and men decay:
Princes and lords may flourish, or may fade;
A breath can make them, as a breath has made;
But a bold peasantry, their country's pride,   55
When once destroyed, can never be supplied.

• • •

THE POPLAR-FIELD

WILLIAM COWPER

The poplars are fell'd; farewell to the shade
And the whispering sound of the cool colonnade;
The winds play no longer and sing in the leaves,
Nor Ouse on his bosom their image receives.

Twelve years have elaps'd since I first took a view   5
Of my favorite field and the bank where they grew;

171

And now in the grass behold they are laid,
And the tree is my seat that once lent me a shade.

The blackbird has fled to another retreat,
Where the hazels afford him a screen from the heat,   10
And the scene where his melody charm'd me before,
Resounds with his sweet-flowing ditty no more.

My fugitive years are all hasting away,
And I must ere long lie as lowly as they,
With a turf on my breast, and a stone at my head,   15
Ere another such grove shall arise in its stead.

'Tis a sight to engage me, if anything can,
To muse on the perishing pleasures of man;
Though his life be a dream, his enjoyments, I see,
Have a being less durable even than he.

from GREENFIELD HILL

TIMOTHY DWIGHT

And when new regions prompt their feet to roam,
And fix, in untrod fields, another home,
No dreary realms our happy race explore,
Nor mourn their exile from their native shore.
For there no endless frosts the glebe deform,   5
Nor blows, with icy breath, perpetual storm:
No wrathful suns, with sickly splendour glare,
Nor moors, impoison'd, taint the balmy air,
But medial climates change the healthful year;
Pure streamlets wind, and gales of Eden cheer;   10
In misty pomp the sky-topp'd mountains stand,
And with green bosom humbler hills expand:
With flowery brilliance smiles the woodland glade;
Full teems the soil, and fragrant twines the shade.
There cheaper fields the numerous household charm,   15
And the glad sire gives every son a farm;
In falling forests, Labour's axe resounds;
Opes the new field; and winds the fence's bounds;
The green wheat sparkles; nods the towering corn;
And meads, and pastures, lessening wastes adorn.   20
Where howl'd the forest, herds unnumber'd low;
The fleecy wanderers fear no prowling foe;
The village springs; the humble school aspires;

And the church brightens in the morning fires!
Young Freedom wantons; Art exalts her head;   25
And infant Science prattles through the shade.
There changing neighbours learn their manners mild;
And toil and prudence dress th'improving wild:
The savage shrinks, nor dares the bliss annoy;
And the glad traveller wonders at the joy.   30
    All hail, thou western world! by heaven design'd
Th'example bright, to renovate mankind.
Soon shall thy sons across the mainland roam;
And claim, on far Pacific shores, their home;
Their rule, religion, manners, arts, convey   35
And spread their freedom to the Asian sea.
Where erst six thousand suns have roll'd the year
O'er plains of slaughter, and o'er wilds of fear,
Towns, cities, fanes, shall lift their towery pride;
The village bloom, on every streamlet's side;   40
Proud Commerce' mole the western surges lave;
The long, white spire lie imag'd on the wave;
O'er morn's pellucid main expand their sails,
And the star'd ensign court Korean gales.
Then nobler thoughts shall savage trains inform;   45
Then barbarous passions cease the heart to storm;
No more the captive circling flames devour;
Through the war path the Indian creep no more;
No midnight scout the slumbering village fire;
Nor the scalp'd infant stain his gasping sire;   50
But peace, and truth, illume the twilight mind,
The gospel's sunshine, and the purpose kind.
Where marshes teem'd with death, shall meads unfold;
Untrodden cliffs resign their stores of gold;
The dance refin'd on Albion's margin move,   55
And her lone bowers rehearse the tale of love.
Where slept perennial night, shall science rise,
And new-born Oxfords cheer the evening skies;
Miltonic strains the Mexic hills prolong,
And Louis murmurs to Sicilian song.   60

    Then to new climes the bliss shall trace its way,
And Tartar desarts hail the rising day;
From the long torpor startled China wake;
Her chains of misery rous'd Peruvia break;
Man link to man; with bosom bosom twine;   65
And one great bond the house of Adam join:
The sacred promise full completion know,
And peace, and piety, the world o'erflow.

THE INDIAN BURYING GROUND

PHILIP FRENEAU

In spite of all the learned have said,
I still my old opinion keep;
The posture, that we give the dead,
Points out the soul's eternal sleep.

Not so the ancients of these lands—   5
The Indian, when from life released,
Again is seated with his friends,
And shares again the joyous feast.

His imaged birds, and painted bowl,
And venison, for a journey dressed,   10
Bespeak the nature of the soul,
Activity, that knows no rest.

His bow, for action ready bent,
And arrows, with a head of stone,
Can only mean that life is spent,   15
And not the old ideas gone.

Thou, stranger, that shalt come this way,
No fraud upon the dead commit—
Observe the swelling turf, and say
They do not lie, but here they sit.   20

Here still a lofty rock remains,
On which the curious eye may trace
(Now wasted, half, by wearing rains)
The fancies of a ruder race.

Here still an aged elm aspires,   25
Beneath whose far-projecting shade
(And which the shepherd still admires)
The children of the forest played!

There oft a restless Indian queen
(Pale Shebah, with her braided hair)   30

And many a barbarous form is seen
To chide the man that lingers there.

By midnight moons, o'er moistening dews,
In habit for the chase arrayed,
The hunter still the deer pursues,   35
The hunter and the deer, a shade!

And long shall timorous fancy see
The painted chief, and pointed spear,
And Reason's self shall bow the knee
To shadows and delusions here.

ON THE RELIGION OF NATURE

PHILIP FRENEAU

The power, that gives with liberal hand
   The blessings man enjoys, while here,
And scatters through a smiling land
   The abundant products of the year;
      That power of nature, ever bless'd,   5
      Bestow'd religion with the rest.

Born with ourselves, her early sway
   Inclines the tender mind to take
The path of right, fair virtue's way
   Its own felicity to make.   10
      This universally extends
      And leads to no mysterious ends.

Religion, such as nature taught,
   With all divine perfection suits;
Had all mankind this system sought   15
   Sophists would cease their vain disputes,
      And from this source would nations know
      All that can make their heaven below.

This deals not curses on mankind,
   Or dooms them to perpetual grief,   20
If from its aid no joys they find,
   It damns them not for unbelief;
      Upon a more exalted plan
      Creatress nature dealt with man—

Joy to the day, when all agree
On such grand systems to proceed,
From fraud, design, and error free,
And which to truth and goodness lead:
Then persecution will retreat
And man's religion be complete.

INTRODUCTION TO SONGS
OF INNOCENCE

WILLIAM BLAKE

Piping down the valleys wild,
Piping songs of pleasant glee,
On a cloud I saw a child,
And he, laughing, said to me:

"Pipe a song about a Lamb!"   5
So I piped with merry cheer.
"Piper, pipe that song again;"
So I piped: he wept to hear.

"Drop thy pipe, thy happy pipe;
Sing thy songs of happy cheer!"   10
So I sang the same again,
While he wept with joy to hear.

"Piper, sit thee down, and write
In a book, that all may read."
So he vanished from my sight;   15
And I plucked a hollow reed,

And I made a rural pen,
And I stained the water clear,
And I wrote my happy songs
Every child may joy to hear.   20

THE TIGER

WILLIAM BLAKE

Tiger, tiger, burning bright
In the forests of the night,

What immortal hand or eye
Could frame thy fearful symmetry?

In what distant deeps or skies   5
Burnt the fire of thine eyes?
On what wings dare he aspire?
What the hand dare seize the fire?

And what shoulder and what art
Could twist the sinews of thy heart?   10
And, when thy heart began to beat,
What dread hand and what dread feet?

What the hammer? what the chain?
In what furnace was thy brain?
What the anvil? what dread grasp   15
Dare its deadly terrors clasp?

When the stars threw down their spears,
And watered heaven with their tears,
Did He smile His work to see?
Did He who made the lamb make thee?   20

Tiger, tiger, burning bright
In the forests of the night,
What immortal hand or eye
Dare frame thy fearful symmetry?

AUGURIES OF INNOCENCE

WILLIAM BLAKE

To see a World in a Grain of Sand
And a Heaven in a Wild Flower,
Hold Infinity in the palm of your hand
And Eternity in an hour.
A Robin Red breast in a Cage   5
Puts all Heaven in a Rage.
A dove house fill'd with doves & Pigeons
Shudders Hell thro' all its regions.
A dog starv'd at his Master's Gate
Predicts the ruin of the State.   10
A Horse misus'd upon the Road
Calls to Heaven for Human blood.
Each outcry of the hunted Hare

A fibre from the Brain does tear.
A Skylark wounded in the wing,   15
A Cherubim does cease to sing.
The Game Cock clip'd & arm'd for fight
Does the Rising Sun affright.
Every Wolf's & Lion's howl
Raises from Hell a Human Soul.   20
The wild deer, wand'ring here & there,
Keeps the Human Soul from Care.
The Lamb misus'd breeds Public strife
And yet forgives the Butcher's Knife.
The Bat that flits at close of Eve   25
Has left the Brain that won't Believe.
The Owl that calls upon the Night
Speaks the Unbeliever's fright.
He who shall hurt the little Wren
Shall never be belov'd by Men.   30
He who the Ox to wrath has mov'd
Shall never be by Woman lov'd.
The wanton Boy that kills the Fly
Shall feel the Spider's enmity.
He who torments the Chafer's sprite   35
Weaves a Bower in endless Night.
The Catterpiller on the Leaf
Repeats to thee thy Mother's grief.
Kill not the Moth nor Butterfly,
For the Last Judgment draweth nigh.   40
He who shall train the Horse to War
Shall never pass the Polar Bar.
The Beggar's Dog & Widow's Cat,
Feed them & thou wilt grow fat.
The Gnat that sings his Summer's song   45
Poison gets from Slander's tongue.
The poison of the Snake & Newt
Is the sweat of Envy's Foot.
The Poison of the Honey Bee
Is the Artist's Jealousy.   50
The Prince's Robes & Beggar's Rags
Are Toadstools on the Miser's Bags.
A truth that's told with bad intent
Beats all the Lies you can invent.
It is right it should be so;   55
Man was made for Joy & Woe;
And when this we rightly know
Thro' the World we safely go.
Joy & Woe are woven fine,
A Clothing for the Soul divine;   60

Under every grief & pine
Runs a joy with silken twine.
The Babe is more than swadling Bands;
Throughout all these Human Lands
Tools were made, & Born were hands, 65
Every Farmer Understands.
Every Tear from Every Eye
Becomes a Babe in Eternity;
This is caught by Females bright
And return'd to its own delight. 70
The Bleat, the Bark, Bellow & Roar
Are Waves that Beat on Heaven's Shore.
The Babe that weeps the Rod beneath
Writes Revenge in realms of death.
The Beggar's Rags, fluttering in Air, 75
Does to Rags the Heavens tear.
The Soldier, arm'd with Sword & Gun,
Palsied strikes the Summer's Sun.
The poor Man's Farthing is worth more
Than all the Gold on Afric's Shore. 80
One Mite wrung from the Labrer's hands
Shall buy & sell the Miser's Lands:
Or, if protected from on high,
Does that whole Nation see & buy.
He who mocks the Infant's Faith 85
Shall be mock'd in Age & Death.
He who shall teach the Child to Doubt
The rotting Grave shall ne'er get out.
He who respects the Infant's faith
Triumphs over Hell & Death. 90
The Child's Toys & the Old Man's Reasons
Are the Fruits of the Two seasons.
The Questioner, who sits so sly,
Shall never know how to Reply.
He who replies to words of Doubt 95
Doth put the Light of Knowledge out.
The Strongest Poison ever known
Came from Caesar's Laurel Crown.
Nought can deform the Human Race
Like to the Armour's iron brace. 100
When Gold & Gems adorn the Plow
To peaceful Arts shall Envy Bow.
A Riddle or the Cricket's Cry
Is to Doubt a fit Reply.
The Emmet's Inch & Eagle's Mile 105

Make Lame Philosophy to smile.
He who Doubts from what he sees
Will ne'er Believe, do what you Please.
If the Sun & Moon should doubt,
They'd immediately Go out.   110
To be in a Passion you Good may do,
But no Good if a Passion is in you.
The Whore & Gambler, by the State
Licenc'd, build that Nation's Fate.
The Harlot's cry from Street to Street   115
Shall weave Old England's winding Sheet.
The Winner's Shout, the Loser's Curse,
Dance before dead England's Hearse.
Every Night & every Morn
Some to Misery are Born.   120
Every Morn & every Night
Some are Born to sweet delight.
Some are Born to sweet delight,
Some are Born to Endless Night.
We are led to Believe a Lie   125
When we see not Thro' the Eye
Which was Born in a Night to perish in a Night
When the Soul Slept in Beams of Light.
God Appears & God is Light
To those poor Souls who dwell in Night,   130
But does a Human Form Display
To those who Dwell in Realms of day.

THE BOOK OF THEL

WILLIAM BLAKE

THEL'S MOTTO

Does the Eagle know what is in the pit,
Or wilt thou go ask the Mole?
Can Wisdom be put in a silver rod?
Or Love in a golden bowl?

I

The Daughters of the Seraphim led round their sunny flocks,   5
All but the youngest: she in paleness sought the secret air,

To fade away like morning beauty from her mortal day:
Down by the river of Adona her soft voice is heard,
And thus her gentle lamentation falls like morning dew:

"O life of this our spring! why fades the lotus of the water,   10
Why fade these children of the spring, born but to smile & fall?
Ah! Thel is like a wat'ry bow, and like a parting cloud;
Like a reflection in a glass; like shadows in the water;
Like dreams of infants, like a smile upon an infant's face;
Like the dove's voice; like transient day; like music in the air.   15
Ah! gentle may I lay me down, and gentle rest my head,
And gentle sleep the sleep of death, and gentle hear the voice
Of him that walketh in the garden in the evening time."

The Lilly of the valley, breathing in the humble grass,
Answer'd the lovely maid and said: "I am a wat'ry weed,   20
And I am very small and love to dwell in lowly vales;
So weak, the gilded butterfly scarce perches on my head.
Yet I am visited from heaven, and he that smiles on all
Walks in the valley and each morn over me spreads his hand,
Saying, 'Rejoice, thou humble grass, thou new-born lilly flower,   25
Thou gentle maid of silent valleys and of modest brooks;
For thou shalt be clothed in light, and fed with morning manna,
Till summer's heat melts thee beside the fountains and the springs
To flourish in eternal vales.' Then why should Thel complain?
Why should the mistress of the vales of Har utter a sigh?"   30

She ceas'd & smil'd in tears, then sat down in her silver shrine.

Thel answer'd: "O thou little virgin of the peaceful valley,
Giving to those that cannot crave, the voiceless, the o'ertired;
Thy breath doth nourish the innocent lamb, he smells thy milky
    garments,
He crops thy flowers while thou sittest smiling in his face,   35
Wiping his mild and meekin mouth from all contagious taints.
Thy wine doth purify the golden honey; thy perfume,
Which thou dost scatter on every little blade of grass that springs,
Revives the milked cow, & tames the fire-breathing steed.
But Thel is like a faint cloud kindled at the rising sun: 40
I vanish from my pearly throne, and who shall find my place?"

"Queen of the vales," the Lilly answer'd, "ask the tender cloud,
And it shall tell thee why it glitters in the morning sky,
And why it scatters its bright beauty thro' the humid air.
Descend, O little Cloud, & hover before the eyes of Thel."   45

meekin—gentle

The Cloud descended, and the Lilly bow'd her modest head ·
And went to mind her numerous charge among the verdant grass.

II

"O little Cloud," the virgin said, "I charge thee tell to me
Why thou complainest not when in one hour thou fade away:
Then we shall seek thee, but not find. Ah! Thel is like to thee: 50
I pass away: yet I complain, and no one hears my voice."
The Cloud then showed his golden head, and his bright form
    emerged,
Hovering and glittering on the air, before the face of Thel.
"O virgin, know'st thou not our steeds drink of the golden springs
Where Luvah doth renew his horses? Look'st thou on my youth,
And fearest thou because I vanish and am seen no more?   56
Nothing remains. O maid, I tell thee, when I pass away,
It is to tenfold life, to love, to peace, and raptures holy.
Unseen, descending, weigh my light wings upon balmy flowers,
And court the fair-eyed Dew to take me to her shining tent: 60
The weeping virgin, trembling, kneels before the risen sun,
Till we arise, linked in a golden band, and never part,
But walk united, bearing food to all our tender flowers."

"Dost thou, O little Cloud? I fear that I am not like thee;   64
For I walk through the vales of Har, and smell the sweetest flowers,
But I feed not the little flowers; I hear the warbling birds,
But I feed not the warbling birds—they fly and seek their food.
But Thel delights in these no more, because I fade away,
And all shall say, 'Without a use this shining woman lived;
Or did she only live to be at death the food of worms?' "   70
The Cloud reclined upon his airy throne, and answered thus:

"Then if thou art the food of worms, O virgin of the skies,
How great thy use, how great thy blessing! Everything that lives
Lives not alone nor for itself. Fear not, and I will call   74
The weak Worm from its lowly bed, and thou shalt hear its voice.
Come forth, Worm of the silent valley, to thy pensive queen."

The helpless Worm arose, and sat upon the Lily's leaf,
And the bright Cloud sailed on to find his partner in the vale.

III

Then Thel, astonished, viewed the Worm upon its dewy bed.
"Art thou a worm, image of weakness? art thou but a worm?   80
I see thee, like an infant, wrapped in the Lily's leaf.
Ah! weep not, little voice; thou canst not speak, but thou canst
    weep.

Is this a worm? I see thee lie helpless and naked, weeping,
And none to answer, none to cherish thee with mother's smiles."

The Clod of Clay heard the Worm's voice, and raised her pitying
    head: 85
She bowed over the weeping infant, and her life exhaled
In milky fondness; then on Thel she fixed her humble eyes.

"O beauty of the vales of Har! we live not for ourselves.
Thou seest me, the meanest thing, and so I am indeed.
My bosom of itself is cold, and of itself is dark;   90
But He that loves the lowly pours His oil upon my head,
And kisses me, and binds His nuptial bands around my breast,
And says: 'Thou mother of my children, I have loved thee,
And I have given thee a crown that none can take away.'
But how this is, sweet maid, I know not, and I cannot know;   95
I ponder, and I cannot ponder; yet I live and love!"

The Daughter of Beauty wiped her pitying tears with her white
    veil,
And said: "Alas! I knew not this, and therefore did I weep.
That God would love a worm I knew, and punish the evil foot
That wilful bruised its helpless form; but that He cherished it   100
With milk and oil, I never knew, and therefore did I weep.
And I complained in the mild air, because I fade away,
And lay me down in thy cold bed, and leave my shining lot."

"Queen of the vales," the matron Clay answer'd, "I heard thy sighs,
And all thy moans flew o'er my roof, but I have call'd them down.
Wilt thou, O Queen, enter my house? 'Tis given thee to enter   106
And to return: fear nothing, enter with thy virgin feet."

IV

The eternal gates' terrific porter lifted the northern bar:
Thel enter'd in & saw the secrets of the land unknown.
She saw the couches of the dead, & where the fibrous roots   110
Of every heart on earth infixes deep its restless twists:
A land of sorrows & of tears where never smile was seen.
She wander'd in the land of clouds thro' valleys dark, list'ning
Dolours & lamentations; waiting oft beside a dewy grave
She stood in silence, list'ning to the voices of the ground,   115
Till to her own grave plot she came, & there she sat down,
And heard this voice of sorrow breathed from the hollow pit.

"Why cannot the Ear be closed to its own destruction?
Or the glist'ning Eye to the poison of a smile?

Why are Eyelids stor'd with arrows ready drawn,   120
Where a thousand fighting men in ambush lie?
Or an Eye of gifts & graces show'ring fruits & coined gold?
Why a Tongue impress'd with honey from every wind?
Why an Ear, a whirlpool fierce to draw creations in?
Why a Nostril wide inhaling terror, trembling, & affright?   125
Why a tender curb upon the youthful burning boy?
Why a little curtain of flesh on the bed of our desire?"

The Virgin started from her seat, & with a shriek
Fled back unhinder'd till she came into the vales of Har.

JOHN ANDERSON MY JO

ROBERT BURNS

1

John Anderson, my jo, John,
    When we were first acquent,
Your locks were like the raven,
    Your bonie brow was brent;
But now your brow is beld, John,   5
    Your locks are like the snow,
But blessings on your frosty pow,
    John Anderson, my jo!

2

John Anderson, my jo, John,
    We clamb the hill thegither,   10
And monei a canty day, John,
    We've had wi' ane anither;
Now we maun totter down, John:
    And hand in hand we'll go,
And sleep thegither at the foot,   15
    John Anderson, my jo!

jo—sweetheart
brent—straight
beld—bald
pow—head
canty—cheerful, merry

TO A LOUSE

On Seeing one on a Lady's Bonnet at Church

1

Ha! whare ye gaun, ye crowlin ferlie?
Your impudence protects you sairly,
I canna say but ye strunt rarely
      Owre gauze and lace,
Tho' faith, I fear ye dine but sparely   5
      On sic a place.

2

Ye ugly, creepin, blastit wonner,
Detested, shunn'd by saunt an' sinner,
How daur ye set your fit upon her—
      Sae fine a lady!   10
Gae somewhere else and seek your dinner
      On some poor body.

3

Swith! in some beggar's haffet squattle:
There ye may creep, and sprawl, and sprattle,
Wi' ither kindred, jumping cattle,   15
      In shoals and nations;
Whare horn nor bane ne'er daur unsettle
      Your thick plantations.

4

Now haud you there, ye're out o' sight,
Below the fatt'rils, snug an' tight;   20
Na, faith ye yet! ye'll no be right,
      Till ye've got on it—
The vera tapmost, tow'ring height
      O' Miss's bonnet.

---

ferlie—wonder
wonner—blasted marvel
haffet—side of the head
sprattle—struggle
horn—horn-comb
bane—bone-comb
fatt'rils—ribbon-ends

5

My sooth! right bauld ye set your nose out,   25
As plump and grey as onie grozet:
O for some rank, mercurial rozet,
      Or fell, red smeddum,
I'd gie ye sic a hearty dose o't,
      Wad dress your droddum!   30

6

I was na been surpris'd to spy
You on an auld wife's flainen toy;
Or aiblins some bit duddie boy,
      On's wyliecoat;
But Miss's fine *Lunardi!* fye!   35
      How daur ye do't?

7

O Jenny, dinna toss your head,
An' set your beauties a' abread!
Ye little ken what cursèd speed
      The blastie's makin!   40
Thae winks an' finger-ends, I dread,
      Are notice takin!

8

O wad some Power the giftie gie us
To see oursels as ithers see us!
It wad frae monie a blunder free us,   45
      An' foolish notion:
What airs in dress an' gait wad lea'e us,
      An' ev'n Devotion!

grozet—gooseberry
rozet—rosin
smeddum—powder
droddum—breech
flainen toy—flannel cap
aiblins—perhaps
duddie—small ragged
Lunardi—balloon-bonnet

A SLUMBER DID MY SPIRIT SEAL

WILLIAM WORDSWORTH

A slumber did my spirit seal;
   I had no human fears:
She seemed a thing that could not feel
   The touch of earthly years.

No mótion has she now, no force;   5
   She neither hears nor sees;
Rolled round in earth's diurnal course,
   With rocks, and stones, and trees.

STRANGE FITS OF PASSION
HAVE I KNOWN

WILLIAM WORDSWORTH

Strange fits of passion have I known:
And I will dare to tell,
But in the lover's ear alone,
What once to me befell.

When she I loved looked every day   5
Fresh as a rose in June,
I to her cottage bent my way,
Beneath an evening moon.

Upon the moon I fixed my eye,
All over the wide lea;   10
With quickening pace my horse drew nigh
Those paths so dear to me.

And now we reached the orchard-plot;
And, as we climbed the hill,
The sinking moon to Lucy's cot   15
Came near, and nearer still.

In one of those sweet dreams I slept,
Kind Nature's gentlest boon!
And all the while my eyes I kept
On the descending moon.   20

My horse moved on; hoof after hoof
He raised, and never stopped:
When down behind the cottage roof,
At once, the bright moon dropped.

What fond and wayward thoughts will slide   25
Into a lover's head!
"O mercy!" to myself I cried,
"If Lucy should be dead!"

I GRIEVED FOR BUONAPARTÉ

WILLIAM WORDSWORTH

I grieved for Buonaparté, with a vain
And an unthinking grief! The tenderest mood
Of that Man's mind—what can it be? what food
Fed his first hopes? what knowledge could *he* gain?
'Tis not in battles that from youth we train   5
The Governor who must be wise and good,
And temper with the sternness of the brain
Thoughts motherly, and meek as womanhood.
Wisdom doth live with children round her knees:
Books, leisure, perfect freedom, and the talk   10
Man holds with week-day man in the hourly walk
Of the mind's business: these are the degrees
By which true Sway doth mount; this is the stalk
True Power doth grow on; and her rights are these.

KUBLA KHAN

SAMUEL TAYLOR COLERIDGE

In Xanadu did Kubla Khan
A stately pleasure-dome decree:
Where Alph, the sacred river, ran
Through caverns measureless to man
    Down to a sunless sea.   5
So twice five miles of fertile ground
With walls and towers were girdled round:
And there were gardens bright with sinuous rills,
Where blossomed many an incense-bearing tree;

And here were forests ancient as the hills,   10
Enfolding sunny spots of greenery.
But oh! that deep romantic chasm which slanted
Down the green hill athwart a cedarn cover!
A savage place! as holy and enchanted
As e'er beneath a waning moon was haunted   15
By woman wailing for her demon-lover!
And from this chasm, with ceaseless turmoil seething,
As if this earth in fast thick pants were breathing,
A mighty fountain momently was forced:
Amid whose swift half-intermitted burst   20
Huge fragments vaulted like rebounding hail,
Or chaffy grain beneath the thresher's flail:
And 'mid these dancing rocks at once and ever
It flung up momently the sacred river.
Five miles meandering with a mazy motion   25
Through wood and dale the sacred river ran,
Then reached the caverns measureless to man,
And sank in tumult to a lifeless ocean:
And 'mid this tumult Kubla heard from far
Ancestral voices prophesying war!   30

    The shadow of the dome of pleasure
    Floated midway on the waves;
    Where was heard the mingled measure
    From the fountain and the caves.
It was a miracle of rare device,   35
A sunny pleasure-dome with caves of ice!

    A damsel with a dulcimer
    In a vision once I saw:
    It was an Abyssinian maid,
    And on her dulcimer she played,   40
    Singing of Mount Abora.
    Could I revive within me
    Her symphony and song,
    To such a deep delight 'twould win me,
That with music loud and long,   45
I would build that dome in air,
That sunny dome! those caves of ice!
And all who heard should see them there,
And all should cry, Beware! Beware!
His flashing eyes, his floating hair!   50
Weave a circle round him thrice,
And close your eyes with holy dread,
For he on honey-dew hath fed,
And drunk the milk of Paradise.

THE RIME OF THE ANCIENT MARINER
IN SEVEN PARTS

SAMUEL TAYLOR COLERIDGE

ARGUMENT

How a Ship having passed the Line was driven by storms to the cold
Country towards the South Pole; and how from thence she made her
course to the tropical Latitude of the Great Pacific Ocean; and of the
strange things that befell; and in what manner the Ancyent Marinere
came back to his own Country.

PART I

It is an ancient Mariner,
And he stoppeth one of three.
"By thy long gray beard and glittering eye,
Now wherefore stopp'st thou me?

An ancient Mariner
meeteth three Gal-
lants bidden to a
wedding-feast, and
detaineth one.

The Bridegroom's doors are opened wide,   5
And I am next of kin;
The guests are met, the feast is set:
May'st hear the merry din."

He holds him with his skinny hand,
"There was a ship," quoth he.   10
"Hold off! unhand me, gray-beard loon!"
Eftsoons his hand dropt he.

He holds him with his glittering eye—
The Wedding-Guest stood still,
And listens like a three years' child: 15
The Mariner hath his will.

The Wedding-
Guest is spell-
bound by the eye
of the old sea-
faring man, and
constrained to hear
his tale.

The Wedding-Guest sat on a stone:
He cannot choose but hear;
And thus spake on that ancient man,
The bright-eyed Mariner.   20

"The ship was cheered, the harbor cleared,
Merrily did we drop
Below the kirk, below the hill,
Below the lighthouse top.

The Mariner tells
how the ship sailed
southward with a
good wind and fair
weather, till it
reached the Line.

The Sun came up upon the left,   25
Out of the sea came he!
And he shone bright, and on the right
Went down into the sea.

190

Higher and higher every day,
Till over the mast at noon—"   30
The Wedding-Guest here beat his breast,
For he heard the loud bassoon.

The bride hath paced into the hall,
Red as a rose is she;
Nodding their heads before her goes   35
The merry minstrelsy.

The Wedding-Guest he beat his breast,
Yet he cannot choose but hear;
And thus spake on that ancient man,
The bright-eyed Mariner.   40

"And now the Storm-blast came, and he
Was tyrannous and strong:
He struck with his o'ertaking wings,
And chased us south along.

With sloping masts and dipping prow,   45
As who pursued with yell and blow
Still treads the shadow of his foe,
And forward bends his head,
The ship drove fast, loud roared the blast,
And southward aye we fled.   50

And now there came both mist and snow,
And it grew wondrous cold:
And ice, mast-high, came floating by,
As green as emerald.

And through the drifts the snowy clifts   55
Did send a dismal sheen:
Nor shapes of men nor beasts we ken—
The ice was all between.

The ice was here, the ice was there,
The ice was all around: 60
It cracked and growled, and roared and
      howled,
Like noises in a swound!

At length did cross an Albatross,
Through the fog it came;
As if it had been a Christian soul,   65
We hailed it in God's name.

191

The Wedding-Guest heareth the bridal music; but the Mariner continueth his tale.

The ship driven by a storm toward the south pole.

The land of ice, and of fearful sounds, where no living thing was to be seen.

Till a great sea-bird, called the Albatross, came through the snow-fog, and was received with great joy and hospitality.

It ate the food it ne'er had eat,
And round and round it flew.
The ice did split with a thunder-fit;
The helmsman steered us through!　　　　70

And a good south wind sprung up behind;
The Albatross did follow,
And every day, for food or play,
Came to the mariners' hollo!

In mist or cloud, on mast or shroud,
It perched for vespers nine;
Whiles all the night, through fog-smoke white,
Glimmered the white moon-shine."

And lo! the Albatross proveth a bird of good omen, and followeth the ship as it returned northward through fog and floating ice.

"God save thee, ancient Mariner!
From the fiends, that plague thee thus!—　　　80
Why look'st thou so?"—"With my crossbow
I shot the Albatross!"

The ancient Mariner inhospitably killeth the pious bird of good omen.

PART II

"The Sun now rose upon the right:
Out of the sea came he,
Still hid in mist, and on the left　　　　85
Went down into the sea.

His shipmates cry out against the ancient Mariner, for killing the bird of good luck.

And the good south wind still blew behind,
But no sweet bird did follow,
Nor any day for food or play
Came to the mariners' hollo!　　　　90

And I had done a hellish thing,
And it would work 'em woe:
For all averred, I had killed the bird
That made the breeze to blow.
'Ah wretch!' said they, 'the bird to slay,　　　95
That made the breeze to blow!'

Nor dim nor red, like God's own head,
The glorious Sun uprist:
Then all averred, I had killed the bird
That brought the fog and mist.　　　　100
' 'Twas right,' said they, 'such birds to slay,
That bring the fog and mist.'

But when the fog cleared off, they justify the same, and thus make themselves accomplices in the crime.

192

The fair breeze blew, the white foam flew,
The furrow followed free;
We were the first that ever burst   105
Into that silent sea.

The fair breeze continues; the ship enters the Pacific Ocean, and sails northward, even till it reaches the Line.

Down dropt the breeze, the sails dropt down,
'Twas sad as sad could be;
And we did speak only to break
The silence of the sea!   110

The ship hath been suddenly becalmed.

All in a hot and copper sky,
The bloody Sun, at noon,
Right up above the mast did stand,
No bigger than the Moon.

Day after day, day after day,   115
We stuck, nor breath nor motion;
As idle as a painted ship
Upon a painted ocean.

Water, water, everywhere,
And all the boards did shrink;   120
Water, water, everywhere,
Nor any drop to drink.

And the Albatross begins to be avenged.

The very deep did rot: O Christ!
That ever this should be!
Yea, slimy things did crawl with legs   125
Upon the slimy sea.

About, about, in reel and rout
The death-fires danced at night;
The water, like a witch's oils,
Burnt green, and blue, and white.   130

And some in dreams assuréd were
Of the Spirit that plagued us so;
Nine fathom deep he had followed us
From the land of mist and snow.

A Spirit had followed them; one of the invisible inhabitants of this planet, neither departed souls nor angels; concerning whom the learned Jew, Josephus, and the Platonic Constantinopolitan, Michael Psellus, may be consulted. They are very numerous, and there is no climate or element without one or more.

And every tongue, through utter drought,   135
Was withered at the root;

death-fires—phosphorescent lights (supposed to forebode death)

We could not speak, no more than if
We had been choked with soot.

Ah! well-a-day! what evil looks
Had I from old and young!   140
Instead of the cross, the Albatross
About my neck was hung.

The shipmates, in
their sore distress,
would fain throw
the whole guilt on
the ancient Mari-
ner; in sign
whereof they hang
the dead sea-bird
round his neck.

PART III

"There passed a weary time. Each throat
Was parched, and glazed each eye.
A weary time! a weary time!   145
How glazed each weary eye,
When looking westward, I beheld
A something in the sky.

The ancient Mari-
ner beholdeth a
sign in the element
afar off.

At first it seemed a little speck,
And then it seemed a mist;   150
It moved and moved, and took at last
A certain shape, I wist.

A speck, a mist, a shape, I wist!
And still it neared and neared:
As if it dodged a water-sprite,   155
It plunged and tacked and veered.

With throats unslaked, with black lips baked,
We could nor laugh nor wail;
Through utter drought all dumb we stood!
I bit my arm, I sucked the blood,   160
And cried, A sail! a sail!

At its nearer ap-
proach, it seemeth
him to be a ship;
and at a dear ran-
som he freeth his
speech from the
bonds of thirst.

With throats unslaked, with black lips baked,
Agape they heard me call:
Gramercy! They for joy did grin,
And all at once their breath drew in,
As they were drinking all.

A flash of joy.

See! see! (I cried) she tacks no more!
Hither to work us weal;
Without a breeze, without a tide,
She steadies with upright keel!   170

And horror fol-
lows. For can it
be a ship that
comes onward
without wind or
tide?

The western wave was all a-flame.
The day was well nigh done!
Almost upon the western wave
Rested the broad bright Sun;

When that strange shape drove suddenly 175
Betwixt us and the Sun.

And straight the Sun was flecked with bars,
(Heaven's Mother send us grace!)
As if through a dungeon-grate he peered
With broad and burning face.   180

It seemeth him but
the skeleton of a
ship. And its ribs
are seen as bars on
the face of the set-
ting Sun.

Alas! (thought I, and my heart beat loud)
How fast she nears and nears!
Are those her sails that glance in the Sun,
Like restless gossameres?

Are those her ribs through which the Sun 185
Did peer, as through a grate?
And is that Woman all her crew?
Is that a Death? and are there two?
Is Death that woman's mate?

The Spectre-
Woman and her
Deathmate, and no
other on board the
skeleton-ship. Like
vessel, like crew!

Her lips were red, her looks were free,   190
Her locks were yellow as gold:
Her skin was white as leprosy,
The Nightmare Life-in-Death was she,
Who thicks man's blood with cold.

The naked hulk alongside came,   195
And the twain were casting dice;
'The game is done! I've won! I've won!'
Quoth she, and whistles thrice.

Death and Life-in-
Death have diced
for the ship's crew,
and she (the
latter) winneth the
ancient Mariner.

The Sun's rim dips; the stars rush out:
At one stride comes the dark;   200
With far-heard whisper, o'er the sea,
Off shot the spectre-bark.

No twilight within
the courts of the
Sun.

We listened and looked sideways up!
Fear at my heart, as at a cup,
My life-blood seemed to sip!   205
The stars were dim, and thick the night,

At the rising of
the Moon, one
after another his
shipmates drop
down dead. But

The steersman's face by his lamp gleamed
    white;
From the sails the dew did drip—
Till clomb above the eastern bar
The hornéd Moon, with one bright star   210
Within the nether tip.

Life-in-Death
begins her work on
the ancient Mari-
ner.

195

One after one, by the star-dogged Moon,
Too quick for groan or sigh,
Each turned his face with a ghastly pang,
And cursed me with his eye.   215

Four times fifty living men,
(And I heard nor sigh nor groan)
With heavy thump, a lifeless lump,
They dropped down one by one.

The souls did from their bodies fly,—   220
They fled to bliss or woe!
And every soul, it passed me by,
Like the whizz of my cross-bow!"

PART IV

"I fear thee, ancient Mariner!
I fear thy skinny hand!   225
And thou are long, and lank, and brown,
As is the ribbed sea-sand.

I fear thee and thy glittering eye,
And thy skinny hand, so brown."—
"Fear not, fear not, thou Wedding-Guest!   230
This body dropt not down.

Alone, alone, all, all alone,
Alone on a wide, wide sea!
And never a saint took pity on
My soul in agony.   235

The many men, so beautiful!
And they all dead did lie:
And a thousand thousand slimy things
Lived on; and so did I.

I looked upon the rotting sea,   240
And drew my eyes away;
I looked upon the rotting deck,
And there the dead men lay.

I looked to heaven, and tried to pray;
But or ever a prayer had gusht,   245
A wicked whisper came, and made
My heart as dry as dust.

I closed my lids, and kept them close,

The Wedding-Guest feareth that a Spirit is talking to him; but the ancient Mariner assureth him of his bodily life, and proceedeth to relate his horrible penance.

He despiseth the creatures of the calm, and envieth that they should live, and so many lie dead.

And the balls like pulses beat;
For the sky and the sea, and the sea and the
    sky   250
Lay like a load on my weary eye,
And the dead were at my feet.

The cold sweat melted from their limbs,   *But the curse liveth*
Nor rot nor reek did they: *for him in the eye*
The look with which they looked on me   255 *of the dead men.*
Had never passed away.

An orphan's curse would drag to hell
A spirit from on high;
But oh! more horrible than that
Is the curse in a dead man's eye!   260 *In his loneliness*
Seven days, seven nights, I saw that curse, *and fixedness he*
And yet I could not die.   *yearneth towards*
                                      the journeying
The moving moon went up the sky,   *Moon, and the*
And nowhere did abide: *stars that still*
Softly she was going up,   265 *sojourn, yet still*
And a star or two beside—   *move onward; and*
                                      everywhere the
Her beams bemocked the sultry main,   *blue sky belongs*
Like April hoar-frost spread;   *to them, and is*
But where the ship's huge shadow lay,   *their apppointed*
The charméd water burnt alway   270 *rest, and their*
A still and awful red.   *native country and*
                                      their own natural
Beyond the shadow of the ship,   *homes, which they*
I watched the water-snakes: *enter unannounced*
They moved in tracks of shining white,   *as lords that are*
And when they reared, the elfish light 275 *certainly expected,*
Fell off in hoary flakes.   *and yet there is a*
                                    silent joy at their
Within the shadow of the ship   *arrival.*
I watched their rich attire:
Blue, glossy green, and velvet black   *By the light of the*
They coiled and swam; and every track 280 *Moon he beholdeth*
Was a flash of golden fire.   *God's creatures of*
                                    the great calm.
O happy living things! no tongue
Their beauty might declare:
A spring of love gushed from my heart,
And I blessed them unaware: 285 *Their beauty and*
Sure my kind saint took pity on me,   *their happiness.*
And I blessed them unaware.

                                      He blesseth them
                                      in his heart.

The self-same moment I could pray;
And from my neck so free
The Albatross fell off, and sank   290
Like lead into the sea.

The spell begins to break.

PART V

"Oh sleep! it is a gentle thing,
Beloved from pole to pole!
To Mary Queen the praise be given!
She sent the gentle sleep from Heaven,   295
That slid into my soul.

By grace of the holy Mother, the ancient Mariner is refreshed with rain.

The silly buckets on the deck,
That had so long remained,
I dreamt that they were filled with dew;
And when I awoke, it rained.   300

My lips were wet, my throat was cold,
My garments all were dank;
Sure I had drunken in my dreams,
And still my body drank.

I moved, and could not feel my limbs: 305
I was so light—almost
I thought that I had died in sleep,
And was a blesséd ghost.

And soon I heard a roaring wind:
It did not come anear;   310
But with its sound it shooks the sails,
That were so thin and sere.

He heareth sounds and seeth strange sights and commotions in the sky and the element.

The upper air burst into life!
And a hundred fire-flags sheen,
To and fro they were hurried about!   315
And to and fro, and in and out,
The wan stars danced between.

And the coming wind did roar more loud,
And the sails did sigh like sedge;
And the rain poured down from one black
        cloud;   320
The Moon was at its edge.

silly—innocent, or useless
sheen—bright

The thick black cloud was cleft, and still
The Moon was at its side:
Like water shot from some high crag,
The lightning fell with never a jag,   325
A river steep and wide.

The loud wind never reached the ship,
Yet now the ship moved on!
Beneath the lightning and the Moon
The dead men gave a groan.   330

The bodies of the ship's crew are inspired, and the ship moves on; but not by the souls of the men, nor by demons of earth or middle air, but by a blessed troop of angelic spirits, sent down by the invocation of the guardian saint.

They groaned, they stirred, they all uprose,
Nor spake, nor moved their eyes;
It had been strange, even in a dream,
To have seen those dead men rise.

The helmsman steered, the ship moved on;
Yet never a breeze up-blew;   336
The mariners all 'gan work the ropes,
Where they were wont to do;
They raised their limbs like lifeless tools—
We were a ghastly crew.   340

The body of my brother's son
Stood by me, knee to knee:
The body and I pulled at one rope,
But he said nought to me."—

"I fear thee, ancient Mariner!"   345
"Be calm, thou Wedding-Guest!
'Twas not those souls that fled in pain,
Which to their corses came again,
But a troop of spirits blest:

For when it dawned—they dropped their arms,
And clustered round the mast;   351
Sweet sounds rose slowly through their mouths,
And from their bodies passed.

Around, around, flew each sweet sound,
Then darted to the Sun;   355
Slowly the sounds came back again,
Now mixed, now one by one.

Sometimes a-dropping from the sky
I heard the skylark sing;

Sometimes all little birds that are,   360
How they seemed to fill the sea and air
With their sweet jargoning!

And now 'twas like all instruments,
Now like a lonely flute;
And now it is an angel's song,   365
That makes the heavens be mute.

It ceased; yet still the sails made on
A pleasant noise till noon,
A noise like of a hidden brook
In the leafy month of June,   370
That to the sleeping woods all night
Singeth a quiet tune.

Till noon we quietly sailed on,
Yet never a breeze did breathe:
Slowly and smoothly went the ship,   375
Moved onward from beneath.

Under the keel nine fathom deep,
From the land of mist and snow,
The spirit slid: and it was he
That made the ship to go.
The sails at noon left off their tune,
And the ship stood still also.

The lonesome Spirit from the south-pole carries on the ship as far as the Line, in obedience to the angelic troop, but still requireth vengeance.

The Sun, right up above the mast,
Had fixed her to the ocean:
But in a minute she 'gan stir,   385
With a short uneasy motion—
Backwards and forwards half her length
With a short uneasy motion.

Then like a pawing horse let go,
She made a sudden bound: 390
It flung the blood into my head,
And I fell down in a swound.

How long in that same fit I lay,
I have not to declare;
But ere my living life returned,   395
I heard and in my soul discerned
Two voices in the air.

The Polar Spirit's fellow-demons, the invisible inhabitants of the element, take part in his wrong; and two of them relate one to the other, that

'Is it he?' quoth one, 'Is this the man?
By him who died on cross,
With his cruel bow he laid full low   400
The harmless Albatross.

The spirit who bideth by himself
In the land of mist and snow,
He loved the bird that loved the man
Who shot him with his bow.'   405

The other was a softer voice,
As soft as honey-dew:
Quoth he, 'The man hath penance done,
And penance more will do.'

penance long and
heavy for the an-
cient Mariner hath
been accorded to
the Polar Spirit,
who returneth
southward.

PART VI

FIRST VOICE

" 'But tell me, tell me! speak again,   410
Thy soft response renewing—
What makes that ship drive on so fast?
What is the ocean doing?'

SECOND VOICE

'Still as a slave before his lord,
The ocean hath no blast;   415
His great bright eye most silently
Up to the Moon is cast—

If he may know which way to go;
For she guides him smooth or grim.
See, brother, see! how graciously   420
She looketh down on him.'

The Mariner hath
been cast into a
trance; for the
angelic power
causeth the vessel
to drive northward
faster than human
life could endure.

FIRST VOICE

'But why drives on that ship so fast,
Without or wave or wind?'

SECOND VOICE

'The air is cut away before,
And closes from behind.   425

Fly, brother, fly! more high, more high!
Or we shall be belated:
For slow and slow that ship will go,
When the Mariner's trance is abated.'

I woke, and we were sailing on 430
As in a gentle weather:
'Twas night, calm night, the moon was high;
The dead men stood together.

All stood together on the deck,
For a charnel-dungeon fitter: 435
All fixed on me their stony eyes,
That in the Moon did glitter

The pang, the curse, with which they died,
Had never passed away:
I could not draw my eyes from theirs, 440
Nor turn them up to pray.

And now this spell was snapt: once more
I viewed the ocean green,
And looked far forth, yet little saw
Of what had else been seen— 445

Like one, that on a lonesome road
Doth walk in fear and dread,
And having once turned round walks on,
And turns no more his head;
Because he knows, a frightful fiend 450
Doth close behind him tread.

But soon there breathed a wind on me,
Nor sound nor motion made:
Its path was not upon the sea,
In ripple or in shade. 455

It raised my hair, it fanned my cheek
Like a meadow-gale of spring—
It mingled strangely with my fears,
Yet it felt like a welcoming.

Swiftly, swiftly flew the ship, 460
Yet she sailed softly too:
Sweetly, sweetly blew the breeze—
On me alone it blew.
•

Oh! dream of joy! is this indeed
The light-house top I see? 465
Is this the hill? is this the kirk?
Is this mine own countree?

The supernatural
motion is retarded;
the Mariner
awakes, and his
penance begins
anew.

The curse is finally
expiated.

And the ancient
Mariner beholdeth
his native country.

We drifted o'er the harbor-bar,
And I with sobs did pray—
O let me be awake, my God!   470
Or let me sleep alway.

The harbor-bay was clear as glass,
So smoothly it was strewn!
And on the bay the moonlight lay,
And the shadow of the Moon.   475

The rock shone bright, the kirk no less,
That stands above the rock:
The moonlight steeped in silentness
The steady weathercock.

And the bay was white with silent light,   480   The angelic spirits
Till rising from the same,   leave the dead
Full many shapes, that shadows were,   bodies and appear
In crimson colors came.   in their own forms
                                                       of light.

A little distance from the prow
Those crimson shadows were: 485
I turned my eyes upon the deck—
Oh, Christ! what saw I there!

Each corse lay flat, lifeless and flat,
And, by the holy rood!
A man all light, a seraph-man,   490
On every corse there stood.

This seraph-band, each waved his hand:
It was a heavenly sight!
They stood as signals to the land,
Each one a lovely light;   495

This seraph-band, each waved his hand,
No voice did they impart—
No voice; but oh! the silence sank
Like music on my heart.

But soon I heard the dash of oars,   500
I heard the Pilot's cheer;
My head was turned perforce away
And I saw a boat appear.

rood—cross

The Pilot and the Pilot's boy,
I heard them coming fast: 505
Dear Lord in Heaven! it was a joy
The dead men could not blast.

I saw a third—I heard his voice:
It is the Hermit good!
He singeth loud his godly hymns   510
That he makes in the wood.
He'll shrieve my soul, he'll wash away
The Albatross's blood.

PART VII

The Hermit of the
Wood approacheth
the ship with
wonder.

"This Hermit good lives in that wood
Which slopes down to the sea.   515
How loudly his sweet voice he rears!
He loves to talk with marineres
That come from a far countree.

He kneels at morn, and noon, and eve—
He hath a cushion plump: 520
It is the moss that wholly hides
The rotted old oak-stump.

The skiff-boat neared: I heard them talk,
'Why this is strange, I trow!
Where are those lights so many and fair, 525
That signal made but now?'

'Strange, by my faith!' the Hermit said—
'And they answered not our cheer!
The planks look warped! and see those sails,
How thin they are and sere!   530
I never saw aught like to them,
Unless perchance it were

Brown skeletons of leaves that lag
My forest-brook along;
When the ivy-tod is heavy with snow, 535
And the owlet whoops to the wolf below,
That eats the she-wolf's young.'

'Dear Lord! it hath a fiendish look'—
(The Pilot made reply)
'I am a-feared'—'Push on, push on!'   540
Said the Hermit cheerily.

ivy-tod—ivy-bush

The boat came closer to the ship,
But I nor spake nor stirred;
The boat came close beneath the ship,
And straight a sound was heard.   545

Under the water it rumbled on,   The ship suddenly
Still louder and more dread: sinketh.
It reached the ship, it split the bay;
The ship went down like lead.

Stunned by that loud and dreadful sound,   The ancient
Which sky and ocean smote,   551   Mariner is saved in
Like one that hath been seven days drowned   the Pilot's boat.
My body lay afloat;
But swift as dreams, myself I found
Within the Pilot's boat.   555

Upon the whirl, where sank the ship,
The boat spun round and round;
And all was still, save that the hill
Was telling of the sound.

I moved my lips—the Pilot shrieked   560
And fell down in a fit;
The holy Hermit raised his eyes,
And prayed where he did sit.

I took the oars: the Pilot's boy,
Who now doth crazy go,   565
Laughed loud and long, and all the while
His eyes went to and fro.
'Ha! ha!' quoth he, 'full plain I see,
The Devil knows how to row.'

And now, all in my own countree,   570
I stood on the firm land!
The Hermit stepped forth from the boat,
And scarcely he could stand.

'Oh shrieve me, shrieve me, holy man!'
The Hermit crossed his brow.   575
'Say quick,' quoth he, 'I bid thee say—   The ancient
What manner of man art thou?'   Mariner earnestly
                                                   entreateth the
                                                   Hermit to shrieve
Forthwith this frame of mine was wrenched   him; and the pen-
With a woful agony,   ance of life falls on
                                                   him.

Which forced me to begin my tale;   580
And then it left me free.

Since then, at an uncertain hour,
That agony returns:
And till my ghastly tale is told,
This heart within me burns.   585

And ever and anon throughout his future life an agony constraineth him to travel from land to land and to teach, by his own example, love and reverence to all things that God made and loveth.

I pass, like night, from land to land;
I have strange power of speech;
That moment that his face I see,
I know the man that must hear me:
To him my tale I teach.   590

What loud uproar bursts from that door!
The wedding-guests are there:
But in the garden-bower the bride
And bride-maids singing are:
And hark the little vesper bell,   595
Which biddeth me to prayer!

O Wedding-Guest! this soul hath been
Alone on a wide, wide sea:
So lonely 'twas, that God himself
Scarce seeméd there to be.   600

O sweeter than the marriage-feast,
'Tis sweeter far to me,
To walk together to the kirk
With a goodly company!—

To walk together to the kirk,   605
And all together pray,
While each to his great Father bends,
Old men, and babes, and loving friends
And youths and maidens gay!

Farewell, farewell! but this I tell   610
To thee, thou Wedding-Guest!
He prayeth well, who loveth well
Both man and bird and beast.

He prayeth best, who loveth best
All things both great and small;   615
For the dear God who loveth us,
He made and loveth all."

The Mariner, whose eye is bright,
Whose beard with age is hoar,
Is gone: and now the Wedding-Guest 620
Turned from the bridegroom's door.

He went like one that hath been stunned,
And is of sense forlorn:
A sadder and a wiser man,
He rose the morrow morn.   625

PAST RUIN'D ILION HELEN LIVES

WALTER SAVAGE LANDOR

Past ruin'd Ilion Helen lives,
 Alcestis rises from the shades;
Verse calls them forth; 'tis verse that gives
 Immortal youth to mortal maids.

Soon shall Oblivion's deepening veil 5
 Hide all the peopled hills you see,
The gay, the proud, while lovers hail
 These many summers you and me.

SO WE'LL GO NO MORE A-ROVING

GEORGE GORDON, LORD BYRON

1

So we'll go no more a-roving
 So late into the night,
Though the heart be still as loving,
 And the moon be still as bright.

2

For the sword outwears its sheath, 5
 And the soul wears out the breast,
And the heart must pause to breathe,
 And Love itself have rest.

Though the night was made for loving,
  And the day returns too soon,
Yet we'll go no more a-roving   10
  By the light of the moon.

DON JUAN

GEORGE GORDON, LORD BYRON

From
Canto the First

I

I want a hero: an uncommon want,
  When every year and month sends forth a new one,
Till, after cloying the gazettes with cant,
  The age discovers he is not the true one:
Of such as these I should not care to vaunt,   5
  I'll therefore take our ancient friend Don Juan—
We all have seen him, in the pantomime,
Sent to the devil somewhat ere his time.

• • •

VI

Most epic poets plunge *"in medias res"*
  (Horace makes this the heroic turnpike road),
And then your hero tells, whene'er you please,
  What went before—by way of episode,
While seated after dinner at his ease,   45
  Beside his mistress in some soft abode,
Palace, or garden, paradise, or cavern,
Which serves the happy couple for a tavern.

VII

That is the usual method, but not mine—
  My way is to begin with the beginning;   50
The regularity of my design
  Forbids all wandering as the worst of sinning,
And therefore I shall open with a line
  (Although it cost me half an hour in spinning)

Narrating somewhat of Don Juan's father,
And also of his mother, if you'd rather.   55

VIII

In Seville was he born, a pleasant city,
   Famous for oranges and women—he
Who has not seen it will be much to pity,
   So says the proverb—and I quite agree;   60
Of all the Spanish towns is none more pretty,
   Cadiz perhaps—but that you soon may see;—
Don Juan's parents lived beside the river,
A noble stream, and call'd the Guadalquivir.

IX

His father's name was José—*Don*, of course,   65
   A true Hidalgo, free from every stain
Of Moor or Hebrew blood, he traced his source
   Through the most Gothic gentlemen of Spain;
A better cavalier ne'er mounted horse,
   Or, being mounted, e'er got down again,   70
Than José, who begot our hero, who
Begot—but that's to come—Well, to renew:

X

His mother was a learnéd lady, famed
For every branch of every science known—
In every Christian language ever named,   75
   With virtues equalled by her wit alone:
She made the cleverest people quite ashamed,
   And even the good with inward envy groan,
Finding themselves so very much exceeded,
In their own way, by all the things that she did.   80

•••

XVIII

Perfect she was, but as perfection is
   Insipid in this naughty world of ours,
Where our first parents never learn'd to kiss
   Till they were exiled from their earlier bowers,   140
Where all was peace, and innocence, and bliss

209

(I wonder how they got through the twelve hours),
Don José, like a lineal son of Eve,
Went plucking various fruit without her leave.

XIX

He was a mortal of the careless kind,   145
    With no great love for learning, or the learned,
Who chose to go where'er he had a mind,
    And never dream'd his lady was concerned;
The world, as usual, wickedly inclined
    To see a kingdom or a house o'erturned,   150
Whisper'd he had a mistress, some said *two,*
But for domestic quarrels *one* will do.

XX

Now Donna Inez had, with all her merit,
    A great opinion of her own good qualities;
Neglect, indeed, requires a saint to bear it,   155
    And such, indeed, she was in her moralities;
But then she had a devil of a spirit,
    And sometimes mix'd up fancies with realities,
And let few opportunities escape
Of getting her liege lord into a scrape.   160

XXI

This was an easy matter with a man
    Oft in the wrong, and never on his guard;
And even the wisest, do the best they can,
    Have moments, hours, and days, so unprepared,
That you might "brain them with their lady's fan;"   165
    And sometimes ladies hit exceeding hard,
And fans turn into falchions in fair hands,
And why and wherefore no one understands.

XXII

'Tis pity learnèd virgins ever wed
    With persons of no sort of education,   170
Or gentlemen, who, though well born and bred,
    Grow tired of scientific conversation;
I don't choose to say much upon this head,
    I'm a plain man, and in a single station,
But—Oh! ye lords of ladies intellectual,   175
Inform us truly, have they not hen-pecked you all?

falchions—swords

XXIII

Don José and his lady quarrell'd—*why,*
   Not any of the many could divine,
Though several thousand people chose to try,
   'Twas surely no concern of theirs nor mine;   180
I loathe that low vice—curiosity;
   But if there's anything in which I shine,
'Tis in arranging all my friends' affairs,
Not having, of my own, domestic cares.

XXIV

And so I interfered, and with the best   185
   Intentions, but their treatment was not kind;
I think the foolish people were possessed,
   For neither of them could I ever find,
Although their porter afterwards confessed—
   But that's no matter, and the worst's behind,   190
For little Juan o'er me threw, down stairs,
A pail of housemaid's water unawares.

XXV

A little curly-headed, good-for-nothing,
   And mischief-making monkey from his birth;
His parents ne'er agreed except in doting   195
   Upon the most unquiet imp on earth;
Instead of quarrelling, had they been but both in
   Their senses, they'd have sent young master forth
To school, or had him soundly whipped at home,
To teach him manners for the time to come.

HYMN TO INTELLECTUAL BEAUTY

PERCY BYSSHE SHELLEY

The awful shadow of some unseen Power
   Floats though unseen among us, visiting
   This various world with as inconstant wing
As summer winds that creep from flower to flower;
Like moonbeams that behind some piny mountain shower,   5
     It visits with inconstant glance
     Each human heart and countenance;

Like hues and harmonies of evening,—
    Like clouds in starlight widely spread,—
    Like memory of music fled,—   10
    Like aught that for its grace may be
Dear, and yet dearer for its mystery.

Spirit of Beauty, that dost consecrate
    With thine own hues all thou dost shine upon
    Of human thought or form, where art thou gone?   15
Why dost thou pass away and leave our state,
This dim vast vale of tears, vacant and desolate?
    Ask why the sunlight not forever
    Weaves rainbows o'er yon mountain-river;
Why aught should fail and fade that once is shown;   20
    Why fear and dream and death and birth
    Cast on the daylight of this earth
    Such gloom; why man has such a scope
For love and hate, despondency and hope?

No voice from some sublimer world hath ever   25
    To sage or poet these responses given;
    Therefore the names of Demon, Ghost, and Heaven,
Remain the records of their vain endeavor—
Frail spells, whose uttered charm might not avail to sever,
    From all we hear and all we see,   30
    Doubt, chance, and mutability.
Thy light alone, like mist o'er mountains driven,
    Or music by the night wind sent
    Through strings of some still instrument,
    Or moonlight on a midnight stream,   35
Gives grace and truth to life's unquiet dream.

Love, Hope, and Self-esteem, like clouds depart
    And come, for some uncertain moments lent.
    Man were immortal, and omnipotent,
Didst thou, unknown and awful as thou art,   40
Keep with thy glorious train firm state within his heart.
    Thou messenger of sympathies
    That wax and wane in lovers' eyes—
Thou, that to human thought art nourishment,
    Like darkness to a dying flame,   45
    Depart not as thy shadow came!
    Depart not, lest the grave should be,
Like life and fear, a dark reality.

While yet a boy I sought for ghosts, and sped
    Through many a listening chamber, cave and ruin,   50

And starlight wood, with fearful steps pursuing
Hopes of high talk with the departed dead.
I called on poisonous names with which our youth is fed;
    I was not heard—I saw them not—
    When, musing deeply on the lot   55
Of life, at that sweet time when winds are wooing
    All vital things that wake to bring
    News of birds and blossoming,—
    Sudden, thy shadow fell on me;
I shrieked, and clasped my hands in ecstasy!   60

I vowed that I would dedicate my powers
    To thee and thine—have I not kept the vow?
    With beating heart and streaming eyes, even now
I call the phantoms or a thousand hours
Each from his voiceless grave: they have in visioned bowers
    Of studious zeal of love's delight   66
    Outwatched with me the envious night—
They know that never joy illumed my brow
    Unlinked with hope that thou wouldst free
    This world from its dark slavery,—   70
    That thou, O awful Loveliness,
Wouldst give whate'er these words cannot express.

The day becomes more solemn and serene
    When noon is past; there is a harmony
    In autumn, and a lustre in its sky,   75
Which through the summer is not heard or seen,
As if it could not be, as if it had not been!
    Thus let thy power, which like the truth
    Of nature on my passive youth
Descended, to my onward life supply   80
    Its calm—to one who worships thee,
    And every form containing thee,
    Whom, Spirit fair, thy spells did bind
To fear himself, and love all human kind.

OZYMANDIAS

PERCY BYSSHE SHELLEY

I met a traveller from an antique land
Who said: "Two vast and trunkless legs of stone
Stand in the desert. Near them, on the sand,
Half sunk, a shattered visage lies, whose frown,

And wrinkled lip, and sneer of cold command,   5
Tell that its sculptor well those passions read
Which yet survive, stamped on these lifeless things,
The hand that mocked them, and the heart that fed:
And on the pedestal these words appear:
'My name is Ozymandias, king of kings: 10
Look on my works, ye Mighty, and despair!'
Nothing beside remains. Round the decay
Of that colossal wreck, boundless and bare
The lone and level sands stretch far away."

TO A WATERFOWL

WILLIAM CULLEN BRYANT

Whither, midst falling dew,
While glow the heavens with the last steps of day,
Far, through their rosy depths, dost thou pursue
    Thy solitary way?

Vainly the fowler's eye   5
Might mark thy distant flight to do thee wrong,
As, darkly seen against the crimson sky,
    Thy figure floats along.

Seek'st thou the plashy brink
Of weedy lake, or marge of river wide,   10
Or where the rocking billows rise and sink
    On the chafed ocean-side?

There is a Power whose care
Teaches thy way along that pathless coast—
The desert and illimitable air—   15
    Lone wandering, but not lost.

All day thy wings have fanned,
At that far height, the cold, thin atmosphere,
Yet stoop not, weary, to the welcome land,
    Though the dark night is near.   20

And soon that toil shall end;
Soon shalt thou find a summer home, and rest,
And scream among thy fellows; reeds shall bend,
    Soon, o'er thy sheltered nest.

Thou'rt gone, the abyss of heaven   25
Hath swallowed up thy form; yet, on my heart
Deeply has sunk the lesson thou hast given,
    And shall not soon depart.

He who, from zone to zone,
Guides through the boundless sky thy certain flight,   30
In the long way that I must tread alone,
    Will lead my steps aright.

THE PRAIRIES

WILLIAM CULLEN BRYANT

These are the gardens of the Desert, these
The unshorn fields, boundless and beautiful,
For which the speech of England has no name—
The Prairies. I behold them for the first,
And my heart swells, while the dilated sight   5
Takes in the encircling vastness. Lo! they stretch
In airy undulations, far away,
As if the Ocean, in his gentlest swell,
Stood still, with all his rounded billows fixed
And motionless forever.—Motionless?—   10
No—they are all unchained again. The clouds
Sweep over with their shadows, and, beneath,
The surface rolls and fluctuates to the eye;
Dark hollows seem to glide along and chase
The sunny ridges. Breezes of the South!   15
Who toss the golden and the flame-like flowers,
And pass the prairie-hawk that, poised on high,
Flaps his broad wings, yet moves not—ye have played
Among the palms of Mexico and vines
Of Texas, and have crisped the limpid brooks   20
That from the fountains of Sonora glide
Into the calm Pacific—have ye fanned
A nobler or a lovelier scene than this?
Man hath no part in all this glorious work:

The hand that built the firmament hath heaved   25
And smoothed these verdant swells, and sown their slopes
With herbage, planted them with island-groves,
And hedged them round with forests. Fitting floor
For this magnificent temple of the sky—
With flowers whose glory and whose multitude   30
Rival the constellations! The great heavens
Seem to stoop down upon the scene in love,—
A nearer vault, and of a tenderer blue,
Than that which bends above our eastern hills.

    As o'er the verdant waste I guide my steed,   35
Among the high rank grass that sweeps his sides,
The hollow beating of his footstep seems
A sacrilegious sound. I think of those
Upon whose rest he tramples. Are they here—
The dead of other days?—and did the dust   40
Of these fair solitudes once stir with life
And burn with passion? Let the mighty mounds
That overlook the rivers, or that rise
In the dim forest crowded with old oaks,
Answer. A race, that long has passed away,   45
Built them; a discipline and populous race
Heaped, with long toil, the earth, while yet the Greek
Was hewing the Pentelicus to forms
Of symmetry, and rearing on its rock
The glittering Parthenon. These ample fields   50
Nourished their harvests, here their herds were fed,
When haply by their stalls the bison lowed,
And bowed his manèd shoulder to the yoke.
All day this desert murmured with their toils,
Till twilight blushed, and lovers walked, and wooed   55
In a forgotten language, and old tunes,
From instruments of unremembered form,
Gave the soft winds a voice. The red-man came—
The roaming hunter-tribes, warlike and fierce,
And the mound-builders vanished from the earth.   60
The solitude of centuries untold
Has settled where they dwelt. The prairie-wolf
Hunts in their meadows, and his fresh-dug den
Yawns by my path. The gopher mines the ground
Where stood their swarming cities. All is gone;   65
All—save the piles of earth that hold their bones,
The platforms where they worshipped unknown gods,
The barriers which they builded from the soil
To keep the foe at bay—till o'er the walls
The wild beleaguerers broke, and, one by one,   70

The strongholds of the plain were forced, and heaped
With corpses. The brown vultures of the wood
Flocked to those vast uncovered sepulchres,
And sat, unscared and silent, at their feast.
Haply some solitary fugitive,   75
Lurking in marsh and forest, till the sense
Of desolation and of fear became
Bitterer than death, yielded himself to die.
Man's better nature triumphed then. Kind words
Welcomed and soothed him; the rude conquerors   80
Seated the captive with their chiefs; he chose
A bride among their maidens, and at length
Seemed to forget—yet ne'er forgot—the wife
Of his first love, and her sweet little ones
Butchered, amid their shrieks, with all his race.   85

      Thus change the forms of being. Thus arise
Races of living things, glorious in strength,
And perish, as the quickening breath of God
Fills them, or is withdrawn. The red-man, too,
Has left the blooming wilds he ranged so long,   90
And, nearer to the Rocky Mountains, sought
A wilder hunting-ground. The beaver builds
No longer by these streams, but far away,
On waters whose blue surface ne'er gave back
The white man's face—among Missouri's springs,   95
And pools whose issues swell the Oregon—
He rears his little Venice. In these plains
The bison feeds no more. Twice twenty leagues
Beyond remotest smoke of hunter's camp,
Roams the majestic brute, in herds that shake   100
The earth with thundering steps—yet here I meet
His ancient footprints stamped beside the pool.

      Still this great solitude is quick with life.
Myriads of insects, gaudy as the flowers
They flutter over, gentle quadrupeds,   105
And birds, that scarce have learned the fear of man,
Are here, and sliding reptiles of the ground,
Startlingly beautiful. The graceful deer
Bounds to the wood at my approach. The bee,
A more adventurous colonist than man,   110
With whom he came across the eastern deep,
Fills the savannas with his murmurings,
And hides his sweets, as in the golden age,
Within the hollow oak. I listen long
To his domestic hum, and think I hear   115

The sound of that advancing multitude
Which soon shall fill these deserts. From the ground
Comes up the laugh of children, the soft voice
Of maidens, and the sweet and solemn hymn
Of Sabbath worshippers. The low of herds   120
Blends with the rustling of the heavy grain
Over the dark brown furrows. All at once
A fresher wind sweeps by, and breaks my dream,
And I am in the wilderness alone.

ON SEEING THE ELGIN MARBLES

JOHN KEATS

My spirit is too weak—mortality
Weighs heavily on me like unwilling sleep,
And each imagin'd pinnacle and steep
Of godlike hardship, tells me I must die
Like a sick eagle looking at the sky.   5
Yet 'tis a gentle luxury to weep
That I have not the cloudy winds to keep
Fresh for the opening of the morning's eye.
Such dim-conceived glories of the brain
Bring round the heart an undescribable feud;   10
So do these wonders a most dizzy pain,
That mingles Grecian grandeur with the rude
Wasting of old Time—with a billowy main—
A sun—a shadow of a magnitude.

WHEN I HAVE FEARS THAT I MAY
CEASE TO BE

JOHN KEATS

When I have fears that I may cease to be
Before my pen has glean'd my teeming brain,
Before high-piled books, in charactry,
Hold like rich garners the full ripen'd grain;
When I behold, upon the night's starr'd face,   5
Huge cloudy symbols of a high romance,
And think that I may never live to trace
Their shadows, with the magic hand of chance;

And when I feel, fair creature of an hour,
That I shall never look upon thee more,   10
Never have relish in the faery power
Of unreflecting love;—then on the shore
Of the wide world I stand alone, and think
Till love and fame to nothingness do sink.

ODE TO A NIGHTINGALE

JOHN KEATS

1

My heart aches, and a drowsy numbness pains
  My sense, as though of hemlock I had drunk,
Or emptied some dull opiate to the drains
  One minute past, and Lethe-wards had sunk:
'Tis not through envy of thy happy lot,   5
  But being too happy in thine happiness,—
    That thou, light-winged Dryad of the trees,
      In some melodious plot
  Of beechen green, and shadows numberless,
    Singest of summer in full-throated ease.   10

2

O for a draught of vintage! that hath been
  Cooled a long age in the deep-delved earth,
Tasting of Flora and the country green,
  Dance, and Provençal song, and sunburnt mirth!
O for a beaker full of the warm South,   15
  Full of the true, the blushful Hippocrene,
    With beaded bubbles winking at the brim,
      And purple-stained mouth;
  That I might drink, and leave the world unseen,
    And with thee fade away into the forest dim: 20

3

Fade far away, dissolve, and quite forget
  What thou among the leaves hast never known,
The weariness, the fever, and the fret
  Here, where men sit and hear each other groan;
Where palsy shakes a few, sad, last gray hairs,   25
  Where youth grows pale, and spectre-thin, and dies;
    Where but to think is to be full of sorrow

And leaden-eyed despairs,
 Where Beauty cannot keep her lustrous eyes,
  Or new Love pine at them beyond tomorrow.   30

4

Away! away! for I will fly to thee,
 Not charioted by Bacchus and his pards,
But on the viewless wings of Poesy,
 Though the dull brain perplexes and retards:
Already with thee! tender is the night,   35
 And haply the Queen-Moon is on her throne,
  Clustered around by all her starry Fays;
   But here there is no light,
 Save what from heaven is with the breezes blown
  Through verdurous glooms and winding mossy ways. 40

5

I cannot see what flowers are at my feet,
 Nor what soft incense hangs upon the boughs,
But, in embalmed darkness, guess each sweet
 Wherewith the seasonable month endows
The grass, the thicket, and the fruit-tree wild; 45
 White hawthorn, and the pastoral eglantine;
  Fast-fading violets covered up in leaves;
   And mid-May's eldest child,
 The coming musk-rose, full of dewy wine,
  The murmurous haunt of flies on summer eves. 50

6

Darkling I listen; and for many a time
 I have been half in love with easeful Death,
Called him soft names in many a mused rhyme,
 To take into the air my quiet breath;
Now more than ever seems it rich to die,   55
 To cease upon the midnight with no pain,
  While thou art pouring forth thy soul abroad
   In such an ecstasy!
 Still wouldst thou sing, and I have ears in vain—
  To thy high requiem become a sod.   60

7

Thou wast not born for death, immortal Bird!
 No hungry generations tread thee down;
The voice I hear this passing night was heard
 In ancient days by emperor and clown:

Perhaps the self-same song that found a path   65
   Through the sad heart of Ruth, when, sick for home,
      She stood in tears amid the alien corn,
         The same that oft-times hath
   Charmed magic casements, opening on the foam
      Of perilous seas, in faery lands forlorn.   70

8

Forlorn! the very word is like a bell
   To toll me back from thee to my sole self!
Adieu! the fancy cannot cheat so well
   As she is famed to do, deceiving elf.
Adieu! adieu! thy plaintive anthem fades   75
   Past the near meadows, over the still stream,
      Up the hill-side; and now 'tis buried deep
         In the next valley-glades:
   Was it a vision, or a waking dream?
      Fled is that music:—Do I wake or sleep?   80

ODE ON A GRECIAN URN

JOHN KEATS

Thou still unravish'd bride of quietness,
   Thou foster-child of silence and slow time,
Sylvan historian, who canst thus express
   A flowery tale more sweetly than our rhyme:
What leaf-fring'd legend haunts about thy shape   5
   Of deities or mortals, or of both,
      In Tempe or the dales of Arcady?
   What men or gods are these? What maidens loth?
What mad pursuit? What struggle to escape?
   What pipes and timbrels? What wild ecstasy?   10

Heard melodies are sweet, but those unheard
   Are sweeter; therefore, ye soft pipes, play on;
Not to the sensual ear, but, more endear'd,
   Pipe to the spirit ditties of no tone:
Fair youth, beneath the trees, thou canst not leave   15
   Thy song, nor ever can those trees be bare;
      Bold lover, never, never canst thou kiss,
Though winning near the goal—yet, do not grieve;
      She cannot fade, though thou hast not thy bliss,
   Forever wilt thou love, and she be fair!   20

Ah, happy, happy boughs! that cannot shed
  Your leaves, nor ever bid the spring adieu;
And, happy melodist, unwearied,
  Forever piping songs forever new;
More happy love! more happy, happy love!   25
  Forever warm and still to be enjoy'd,
    Forever panting, and forever young;
All breathing human passion far above,
  That leaves a heart high-sorrowful and cloy'd,
    A burning forehead, and a parching tongue.   30

Who are these coming to the sacrifice?
  To what green altar, O mysterious priest,
Lead'st thou that heifer lowing at the skies,
  And all her silken flanks with garlands drest?
What little town by river or sea shore,   35
  Or mountain-built with peaceful citadel,
    Is emptied of this folk, this pious morn?
And, little town, thy streets forevermore
  Will silent be; and not a soul to tell
    Why thou art desolate, can e'er return.   40

O Attic shape! Fair attitude! with brede
  Of marble men and maidens overwrought,
With forest branches and the trodden weed;
  Thou, silent form, dost tease us out of thought
As doth eternity. Cold pastoral!   45
  When old age shall this generation waste,
    Thou shalt remain, in midst of other woe
Than ours, a friend to man, to whom thou say'st,
"Beauty is truth, truth beauty," that is all
  Ye know on earth, and all ye need to know.

TO AUTUMN

JOHN KEATS

Season of mists and mellow fruitfulness,
  Close bosom-friend of the maturing sun;
Conspiring with him how to load and bless
  With fruit the vines that round the thatch-eaves run;

brede—embroidery

To bend with apples the moss'd cottage-trees, 5
    And fill all fruit with ripeness to the core;
      To swell the gourd, and plump the hazel shells
    With a sweet kernel; to set budding more,
And still more, later flowers for the bees,
Until they think warm days will never cease, 10
      For Summer has o'er-brimm'd their clammy cells.

Who hath not seen thee oft amid thy store?
    Sometimes whoever seeks abroad may find
Thee sitting careless on a granary floor,
    Thy hair soft-lifted by the winnowing wind; 15
Or on a half-reap'd furrow sound asleep,
    Drows'd with the fume of poppies, while thy hook
      Spares the next swath and all its twined flowers:
And sometimes like a gleaner thou dost keep
    Steady thy laden head across a brook; 20
    Or by a cider-press, with patient look,
      Thou watchest the last oozings hours by hours.

Where are the songs of Spring? Ay, where are they?
    Think not of them, thou hast thy music too,—
While barred clouds bloom the soft-dying day, 25
    And touch the stubble-plains with rosy hue;
Then in a wailful choir the small gnats mourn
    Among the river sallows, borne aloft
      Or sinking as the light wind lives or dies;
And full-grown lambs loud bleat from hilly bourn; 30
    Hedge-crickets sing; and now with treble soft
    The redbreast whistles from a gardencroft;
      And gathering swallows twitter in the skies.

CONCORD HYMN

RALPH WALDO EMERSON

SUNG AT THE COMPLETION OF THE
BATTLE MONUMENT, JULY 4, 1837

By the rude bridge that arched the flood,
    Their flag to April's breeze unfurled,
Here once the embattled farmers stood
    And fired the shot heard round the world.

sallows—willows

The foe long since in silence slept;   5
   Alike the conqueror silent sleeps;
And time for the ruined bridge has swept
   Down the dark stream which seaward creeps.

On this green bank, by this soft stream,
   We set to-day a votive stone;   10
That memory may their deed redeem,
   When, like our sires, our sons are gone.

Spirit, that made those heroes dare
   To die, and leave their children free,
Bid Time and Nature gently spare   15
   The shaft we raise to them and thee.

BRAHMA

RALPH WALDO EMERSON

If the red slayer think he slays,
   Or if the slain think he is slain,
They know not well the subtle ways
   I keep, and pass, and turn again.

Far or forgot to me is near;   5
   Shadow and sunlight are the same;
The vanished gods to me appear;
   And one to me are shame and fame.

They reckon ill who leave me out;
   When me they fly, I am the wings;   10
I am the doubter and the doubt,
   And I the hymn the Brahmin sings.

The strong gods pine for my abode,
   And pine in vain the sacred Seven;
But thou, meek lover of the good!   15
   Find me, and turn thy back on heaven.

HOW DO I LOVE THEE?

ELIZABETH BARRETT BROWNING

43

How do I love thee? Let me count the ways.
I love thee to the depth and breadth and height
My soul can reach, when feeling out of sight
For the ends of Being and ideal Grace.
I love thee to the level of everyday's   5
Most quiet need, by sun and candle-light.
I love thee freely, as men strive for Right;
I love thee purely, as they turn from Praise.
I love thee with the passion put to use
In my old griefs, and with my childhood's faith.   10
I love thee with a love I seemed to lose
With my lost saints—I love thee with the breath,
Smiles, tears, of all my life!—and, if God choose,
I shall but love thee better after death.

MY LOST YOUTH

HENRY WADSWORTH LONGFELLOW

Often I think of the beautiful town
  That is seated by the sea;
Often in thought go up and down
The pleasant streets of that dear old town,
  And my youth comes back to me.   5
    And a verse of a Lapland song
    Is haunting my memory still:
    "A boy's will is the wind's will,
And the thoughts of youth are long, long thoughts."

I can see the shadowy lines of its trees,   10
  And catch, in sudden gleams,
The sheen of the far-surrounding seas,
And islands that were the Hesperides
  Of all my boyish dreams.
    And the burden of that old song,   15

225

It murmurs and whispers still:
"A boy's will is the wind's will,
And the thoughts of youth are long, long thoughts."

I remember the black wharves and the slips,
   And the sea-tides tossing free;   20
And Spanish sailors with bearded lips,
And the beauty and mystery of the ships,
   And the magic of the sea.
      And the voice of that wayward song
      Is singing and saying still: 25
      "A boy's will is the wind's will,
And the thoughts of youth are long, long thoughts."

I remember the bulwarks by the shore,
   And the fort upon the hill;
The sunrise gun, with its hollow roar,   30
The drum-beat repeated o'er and o'er,
   And the bugle wild and shrill.
      And the music of that old song
      Throbs in my memory still:
      "A boy's will is the wind's will,   35
And the thoughts of youth are long, long thoughts."

I remember the sea-fight far away,
   How it thundered o'er the tide!
And the dead captains, as they lay
In their graves, o'erlooking the tranquil bay   40
   Where they in battle died.
      And the sound of that mournful song
      Goes through me with a thrill:
      "A boy's will is the wind's will,
And the thoughts of youth are long, long thoughts."   45

I can see the breezy dome of groves,
   The shadows of Deering's Woods;
And the friendships old and the early loves
Come back with a Sabbath sound, as of doves
   In quiet neighborhoods.   50
      And the verse of that sweet old song,
      It flutters and murmurs still:
      "A boy's will is the wind's will,
And the thoughts of youth are long, long thoughts."

I remember the gleams and glooms that dart   55
   Across the school-boy's brain;

The song and the silence in the heart,
That in part are prophecies, and in part
 Are longings wild and vain.
  And the voice of that fitful song   60
  Sings on, and is never still:
  "A boy's will is the wind's will,
And the thoughts of youth are long, long thoughts."

There are things of which I may not speak;
 There are dreams that cannot die;   65
There are thoughts that make the strong heart weak,
And bring a pallor into the cheek,
 And a mist before the eye.
  And the words of that fatal song
  Come over me like a chill: 70
  "A boy's will is the wind's will,
And the thoughts of youth are long, long thoughts."

Strange to me now are the forms I meet
 When I visit the dear old town;
But the native air is pure and sweet,   75
And the trees that o'ershadow each well-known street,
 As they balance up and down,
  Are singing the beautiful song,
  Are sighing and whispering still:
  "A boy's will is the wind's will,   80
And the thoughts of youth are long, long thoughts."

And Deering's Woods are fresh and fair,
 And with joy that is almost pain
My heart goes back to wander there,
And among the dreams of the days that were,   85
 I find my lost youth again.
  And the strange and beautiful song,
  The groves are repeating it still:
  "A boy's will is the wind's will,
And the thoughts of youth are long, long thoughts."

THE SOUND OF THE SEA

HENRY WADSWORTH LONGFELLOW

The sea awoke at midnight from its sleep,
 And round the pebbly beaches far and wide

I heard the first wave of the rising tide
Rush onward with uninterrupted sweep;
A voice out of the silence of the deep,   5
  A sound mysteriously multiplied
  As of a cataract from the mountain's side,
Or roar of winds upon a wooded steep.
So comes to us at times, from the unknown
  And inaccessible solitudes of being,   10
  The rushing of the sea-tides of the soul;
And inspirations, that we deem our own,
  Are some divine foreshadowing and foreseeing
  Of things beyond our reason or control.

ICHABOD

JOHN GREENLEAF WHITTIER

So fallen! so lost! the light withdrawn
  Which once he wore!
The glory from his gray hairs gone
  Forevermore!

Revile him not, the Tempter hath   5
  A snare for all;
And pitying tears, not scorn and wrath,
  Befit his fall!

Oh, dumb be passion's stormy rage,
  When he who might   10
Have lighted up and led his age,
  Falls back in night.

Scorn! would the angels laugh, to mark
  A bright soul driven,
Fiend-goaded, down the endless dark,   15
  From hope and heaven!

Let not the land once proud of him
  Insult him now,
Nor brand with deeper shame his dim,
  Dishonored brow.   20

Ichabod—Daniel Webster after he had
accepted the notorious "Compromise"
which included the Fugitive Slave Law

But let its humbled sons, instead,
  From sea to lake,
A long lament, as for the dead,
  In sadness make.

Of all we loved and honored, naught   25
  Save power remains;
A fallen angel's pride of thought,
  Still strong in chains.

All else is gone; from those great eyes
  The soul has fled: 30
When faith is lost, when honor dies,
  The man is dead!

Then pay the reverence of old days
  To his dead fame;
Walk backward, with averted gaze,   35
  And hide the shame!

THE DEACON'S MASTERPIECE
OR, THE WONDERFUL "ONE-HOSS SHAY": A LOGICAL STORY

OLIVER WENDELL HOLMES

Have you heard of the wonderful one-hoss shay,
That was built in such a logical way
It ran a hundred years to a day,
And then, of a sudden, it—ah, but stay,
I'll tell you what happened without delay,   5
Scaring the parson into fits,
Frightening people out of their wits,—
Have you ever heard of that, I say?

Seventeen hundred and fifty-five.
Georgius Secundus was then alive,—   10
Snuffy old drone from the German hive.
That was the year when Lisbon-town
Saw the earth open and gulp her down,
And Braddock's army was done so brown,
Left without a scalp to its crown.   15
It was on the terrible Earthquake-day
That the Deacon finished the one-hoss shay.

Now in building of chaises, I tell you what
There is always *somewhere* a weakest spot,—
In hub, tire, felloe, in spring or thill,   20
In panel, or crossbar, or floor, or sill,
In screw, bolt, thoroughbrace,—lurking still,
Find it somewhere you must and will,—
Above or below, or within or without,—
And that's the reason, beyond a doubt,   25
That a chaise *breaks down,* but doesn't *wear out.*

But the Deacon swore (as Deacons do,
With an "I dew vum," or an "I tell *yeou,*")
He would build one shay to beat the taown
'N' the keounty 'n' all the kentry raoun';   30
It should be so built that it *couldn'* break daown:
"Fur," said the Deacon, " 't's mighty plain
Thut the weakes' place mus' stan' the strain;
'N' the way t' fix it, uz I maintain,
Is only jest   35
T' make that place uz strong uz the rest."

So the Deacon inquired of the village folk
Where he could find the strongest oak,
That couldn't be split nor bent nor broke,—
That was for spokes and floor and sills;   40
He sent for lancewood to make the thills;
The crossbars were ash, from the straightest trees;

The panels of white-wood, that cuts like cheese,
But last like iron for things like these;
The hubs of logs from the "Settler's ellum,"—   45
Last of its timber,—they couldn't sell 'em,
Never an axe had seen their chips,
And the wedges flew from between their lips,
Their blunt ends frizzled like celery-tips;
Step and prop-iron, bolt and screw,   50
Spring, tire, axle, and linchpin too,
Steel of the finest, bright and blue;
Thoroughbrace bison-skin, thick and wide;
Boot, top, dasher, from tough old hide
Found in the pit when the tanner died.   55
That was the way he "put her through."
"There!" said the Deacon, "naow she'll dew!"

Do! I tell you, I rather guess
She was a wonder, and nothing less!
Colts grew horses, beards turned gray,   60

230

Deacon and deaconess dropped away,
Children and grandchildren—where were they?
But there stood the stout old one-hoss shay
As fresh as on Lisbon-earthquake-day!

EIGHTEEN HUNDRED;—it came and found   65
The Deacon's masterpiece strong and sound.
Eighteen hundred increased by ten;—
"Hahnsum kerridge" they called it then.
Eighteen hundred and twenty came;—
Running as usual; much the same.   70
Thirty and forty at last arrive,
And then come fifty, and FIFTY-FIVE.

Little of all we value here
Wakes on the morn of its hundredth year
Without both feeling and looking queer.   75
In fact, there's nothing that keeps its youth,
So far as I know, but a tree and truth.
(This is a moral that runs at large;
Take it.—You're welcome.—No extra charge.)

FIRST OF NOVEMBER,—the Earthquake-day.—   80
There are traces of age in the one-hoss shay,
A general flavor of mild decay,
But nothing local, as one may say.
There couldn't be,—for the Deacon's art
Had made it so like in every part   85
That there wasn't a chance for one to start.
For the wheels were just as strong as the thills,
And the floor was just as strong as the sills,
And the panels just as strong as the floor,
And the whipple-tree neither less nor more,   90
And the back crossbar as strong as the fore,
And spring and axle and hub *encore*.
And yet, *as a whole*, it is past a doubt
In another hour it will be *worn out!*

First of November, 'Fifty-five!   95
This morning the parson takes a drive.
Now, small boys, get out of the way!
Here comes the wonderful one-horse shay,
Drawn by a rat-tailed, ewe-necked bay.
"Huddup!" said the parson.—Off went they.   100
The parson was working his Sunday's text,—
Had got to *fifthly*, and stopped perplexed
At what the—Moses—was coming next.

All at once the horse stood still,
Close by the meet'n-house on the hill. 105
First a shiver, and then a thrill,
Then something decidedly like a spill,—

And the parson was sitting upon a rock,
At half-past nine by the meet'n-house clock,—
Just the hour of the Earthquake shock! 110
What do you think the parson found,
When he got up and stared around?
The poor old chaise in a heap or mound,
As if it had been to the mill and ground!
You see, of course, if you're not a dunce, 115
How it went to pieces all at once,—
All at once and nothing first,—
Just as bubbles do when they burst.
End of the wonderful one-hoss shay.
Logic is logic. That's all I say.

TO HELEN

EDGAR ALLAN POE

Helen, thy beauty is to me
  Like those Nicean barks of yore,
That gently, o'er a perfumed sea,
  The weary, way-worn wanderer bore
  To his own native shore. 5

On desperate seas long wont to roam,
  Thy hyacinth hair, thy classic face,
Thy Naiad airs have brought me home
  To the glory that was Greece
And the grandeur that was Rome. 10

Lo! in yon brilliant window-niche
  How statue-like I see thee stand!
  The agate lamp within thy hand,
Ah, Psyche, from the regions which
  Are Holy Land!

232

THE HAUNTED PALACE

EDGAR ALLAN POE

In the greenest of our valleys
 By good angels tenanted,
Once a fair and stately palace—
 Radiant palace—reared its head.
In the monarch Thought's dominion—   5
 It stood there!
Never seraph spread a pinion
 Over fabric half so fair!

Banners yellow, glorious, golden,
 On its roof did float and flow,   10
(This—all this—was in the olden
 Time long ago,)
And every gentle air that dallied,
 In that sweet day,
Along the ramparts plumed and pallid,   15
 A wingèd odor went away.

Wanderers in that happy valley,
 Through two luminous windows, saw
Spirits moving musically,
 To a lute's well-tunèd law,   20
Round about a throne where, sitting
 (Porphyrogene!)
In state his glory well befitting,
 The ruler of the realm was seen.

And all with pearl and ruby glowing   25
 Was the fair palace-door,
Through which came flowing, flowing, flowing,
 And sparkling evermore,
A troop of Echoes, whose sweet duty
 Was but to sing,   30
In voices of surpassing beauty,
 The wit and wisdom of their king.

But evil things, in robes of sorrow,
 Assailed the monarch's high estate.
(Ah, let us mourn!—for never morrow   35
 Shall dawn upon him desolate!)
And round about his home, the glory
 That blushed and bloomed

Is but a dim-remembered story
    Of the old time entombed.   40

And travellers now, within that valley,
    Through the red-litten windows see
Vast forms, that move fantastically
    To a discordant melody,
While, like a ghastly rapid river,   45
    Through the pale door
A hideous throng rush out forever
    And laugh—but smile no more.

THE KRAKEN

ALFRED, LORD TENNYSON

Below the thunders of the upper deep,
Far, far beneath in the abysmal sea,
His ancient, dreamless, uninvaded sleep
The Kraken sleepeth: faintest sunlights flee
About his shadowy sides; above him swell   5
Huge sponges of millennial growth and height;
And far away into the sickly light,
From many a wondrous grot and secret cell
Unnumbered and enormous polypi
Winnow with giant arms the slumbering green.   10
There hath he lain for ages, and will lie
Battening upon huge sea-worms in his sleep,
Until the latter fire shall heat the deep;
Then once by man and angels to be seen,
In roaring he shall rise and on the surface die.

MARIANA

ALFRED, LORD TENNYSON

With blackest moss the flower-plots
    Were thickly crusted, one and all;

the Kraken—a fabulous Scandinavian sea
monster
Mariana—in Shakespeare's *Measure for
Measure,* is deserted by her lover. She is
described as waiting for him "at the
moated grange" (III, i, 277), a large
country house surrounded by a moat
trance—traverse

The rusted nails fell from the knots
    That held the pear to the gable-wall.
The broken sheds looked sad and strange: 5
    Unlifted was the clinking latch;
    Weeded and worn the ancient thatch
Upon the lonely moated grange.
      She only said, "My life is dreary,
        He cometh not," she said;   10
      She said, "I am aweary, aweary,
        I would that I were dead!"

Her tears fell with the dews at even;
    Her tears fell ere the dews were dried;
She could not look on the sweet heaven,   15
    Either at morn or eventide.
After the flitting of the bats,
    When thickest dark did trance the sky,
    She drew her casement-curtain by,
And glanced athwart the glooming flats.   20
      She only said, "The night is dreary,
        He cometh not," she said;
      She said, "I am aweary, aweary,
        I would that I were dead!"

Upon the middle of the night,   25
    Waking she heard the night-fowl crow;
The cock sung out an hour ere light;
    From the dark fen the oxen's low
Came to her; without hope of change,
    In sleep she seemed to walk forlorn,   30
    Till cold winds woke the gray-eyed morn
About the lonely moated grange.
      She only said, "The day is dreary,
        He cometh not," she said;
      She said, "I am aweary, aweary,   35
        I would that I were dead!"

About a stone-cast from the wall
    A sluice with blackened waters slept,
And o'er it many, round and small,
    The clustered marish-mosses crept.   40
Hard by a poplar shook alway,
    All silver-green with gnarléd bark;
    For leagues no other tree did mark
The level waste, the rounding gray.

marish-mosses—mosses that grow in a
marsh

She only said, "My life is dreary,
   He cometh not," she said;
She said, "I am aweary, aweary,
   I would that I were dead!"

And ever when the moon was low,
   And the shrill winds were up and away,
In the white curtain, to and fro,
   She saw the gusty shadow sway.
But when the moon was very low,
   And wild winds bound within their cell,
The shadow of the poplar fell
Upon her bed, across her brow.
   She only said, "The night is dreary,
      He cometh not," she said;
   She said, "I am aweary, aweary,
      I would that I were dead!"

All day within the dreamy house,
   The doors upon their hinges creaked;
The blue fly sung in the pane; the mouse
   Behind the moldering wainscot shrieked,
Or from the crevice peered about.
   Old faces glimmered through the doors,
   Old footsteps trod the upper floors,
Old voices called her from without.
   She only said, "My life is dreary,
      He cometh not," she said;
   She said, "I am aweary, aweary,
      I would that I were dead!"

The sparrow's chirrup on the roof,
   The slow clock ticking, and the sound
Which to the wooing wind aloof
   The poplar made, did all confound
Her sense; but most she loathed the hour
   When the thick-moted sunbeam lay
   Athwart the chambers, and the day
Was sloping toward his western bower.
   Then said she, "I am very dreary,
      He will not come," she said;
   She wept, "I am aweary, aweary,
      O God, that I were dead!"

BREAK, BREAK, BREAK *

ALFRED, LORD TENNYSON

Break, break, break,
  On thy cold gray stones, O Sea!
And I would that my tongue could utter
  The thoughts that arise in me.

O well for the fisherman's boy,   5
  That he shouts with his sister at play!
O well for the sailor lad,
  That he sings in his boat on the bay!

And the stately ships go on
  To their haven under the hill;   10
But O for the touch of a vanished hand,
  And the sound of a voice that is still!

Break, break, break,
  At the foot of thy crags, O Sea!
But the tender grace of a day that is dead   15
  Will never come back to me.

ULYSSES

ALFRED, LORD TENNYSON

It little profits that an idle king,
By this still hearth, among these barren crags,
Matched with an aged wife, I mete and dole
Unequal laws unto a savage race,
That hoard, and sleep, and feed, and know not me.   5
I cannot rest from travel; I will drink
Life to the lees. All times I have enjoyed
Greatly, have suffered greatly, both with those
That loved me; and alone; on shore, and when
Through scudding drifts the rainy Hyades   10

---

* This is one of the poems on the death of
Tennyson's friend, Arthur Hallam
an aged wife—Penelope
Hyades—a group of seven stars in the
constellation Taurus, associated with the
rainy season

Vexed the dim sea. I am become a name;
For always roaming with a hungry heart
Much have I seen and known—cities of men
And manners, climates, councils, governments,
Myself not least, but honoured of them all—   15
And drunk delight of battle with my peers,
Far on the ringing plains of windy Troy.
I am a part of all that I have met;
Yet all experience is an arch wherethrough
Gleams that untraveled world whose margin fades   20
Forever and forever when I move.
How dull it is to pause, to make an end,
To rust unburnished, not to shine in use!
As though to breathe were life! Life piled on life
Were all too little, and of one to me   25
Little remains; but every hour is saved
From that eternal silence, something more,
A bringer of new things; and vile it were
For some three suns to store and hoard myself,
And this gray spirit yearning in desire   30
To follow knowledge like a sinking star,
Beyond the utmost bound of human thought.
    This is my son, mine own Telemachus,
To whom I leave the scepter and the isle—
Well-loved of me, discerning to fulfill   35
This labor, by slow prudence to make mild
A rugged people, and through soft degrees
Subdue them to the useful and the good.
Most blameless is he, centered in the sphere
Of common duties, decent not to fail   40
In offices of tenderness, and pay
Meet adoration to my household gods,
When I am gone. He works his work, I mine.
    There lies the port; the vessel puffs her sail;
There gloom the dark, broad seas. My mariners,   45
Souls that have toiled, and wrought, and thought with me—
That ever with a frolic welcome took
The thunder and the sunshine, and opposed
Free hearts, free foreheads—you and I are old;
Old age hath yet his honor and his toil.   50
Death closes all; but something ere the end,
Some work of noble note, may yet be done,
Not unbecoming men that strove with gods.
The lights begin to twinkle from the rocks;
The long day wanes; the slow moon climbs; the deep   55
Moans round with many voices. Come, my friends.
'Tis not too late to seek a newer world.

Push off, and sitting well in order smite
The sounding furrows; for my purpose holds
To sail beyond the sunset, and the baths   60
Of all the western stars, until I die.
It may be that the gulfs will wash us down;
It may be we shall touch the Happy Isles,
And see the great Achilles, whom we knew.
Though much is taken, much abides; and though   65
We are not now that strength which in old days
Moved earth and heaven, that which we are, we are—
One equal temper of heroic hearts,
Made weak by time and fate, but strong in will
To strive, to seek, to find, and not to yield.   70

THE BISHOP ORDERS HIS TOMB AT
SAINT PRAXED'S CHURCH

ROBERT BROWNING

ROME, 15—

Vanity, saith the preacher, vanity!
Draw round my bed; is Anselm keeping back?
Nephews—sons mine . . . ah, God, I know not! Well—
She, men would have to be your mother once,
Old Gandolf envied me, so fair she was!   5
What's done is done, and she is dead beside,
Dead long ago, and I am Bishop since,
And as she died so must we die ourselves,
And thence ye may perceive the world's a dream.
Life, how and what is it? As here I lie   10
In this state-chamber, dying by degrees,
Hours and long hours in the dead night, I ask
"Do I live, am I dead?" Peace, peace seems all.
Saint Praxed's ever was the church for peace;
And so, about this tomb of mine. I fought   15
With tooth and nail to save my niche, ye know—
Old Gandolf cozened me, despite my care;
Shrewd was that snatch from out the corner South
He graced his carrion with, God curse the same!
Yet still my niche is not so cramped but thence   20
One sees the pulpit o' the epistle-side,
And somewhat of the choir, those silent seats,

the epistle-side—the right-hand side of the
altar

And up into the aery dome where live
The angels, and a sunbeam's sure to lurk;
And I shall fill my slab of basalt there,   25
And 'neath my tabernacle take my rest,
With those nine columns round me, two and two,
The odd one at my feet where Anselm stands:
Peach-blossom marble all, the rare, the ripe
As fresh-poured red wine of a mighty pulse.   30
—Old Gandolf with his paltry onion-stone,
Put me where I may look at him! True peach,
Rosy and flawless; how I earned the prize!
Draw close; that conflagration of my church—
What then? So much was saved if aught were missed! 35
My sons, ye would not be my death? Go dig
The white-grape vineyard where the oil-press stood,
Drop water gently till the surface sink,
And if ye find . . . Ah, God, I know not, I! . . .
Bedded in store of rotten fig-leaves soft,   40
And corded up in a tight olive-frail,
Some lump, ah God, of *lapis lazuli*,
Big as a Jew's head cut off at the nape,
Blue as a vein o'er the Madonna's breast . . .
Sons, all have I bequeathed you, villas, all,   45
That brave Frascati villa with its bath,
So, let the blue lump poise between my knees,
Like God the Father's globe on both his hands
Ye worship in the Jesu Church so gay,
For Gandolf shall not choose but see and burst!   50
Swift as a weaver's shuttle fleet our years;
Man goeth to the grave, and where is he?
Did I say basalt for my slab, sons? Black—
'Twas ever antique-black I meant! How else
Shall ye contrast my frieze to come beneath?   55
The bas-relief in bronze ye promised me,
Those Pans and Nymphs ye wot of, and perchance
Some tripod, thyrsus, with a vase or so,
The Savior at his sermon on the mount,
Saint Praxed in a glory, and one Pan   60
Ready to twitch the Nymph's last garment off,

basalt—a hard rock of dark color
pulse—a fruit mash
lapis lazuli—a valuable blue stone
tripod—the three-legged stool on which the
priestess of Apollo sat when giving responses
to persons consulting the oracle at Delphi
thyrsus—the staff used by followers of Bacchus, god of wine

And Moses with the tables . . . but I know
Ye mark me not! What do they whisper thee,
Child of my bowels, Anselm? Ah, ye hope
To revel down my villas while I gasp 65
Bricked o'er with beggar's moldy travertine
Which Gandolf from his tomb-top chuckles at!
Nay, boys, ye love me—all of jasper, then!
'Tis jasper ye stand pledged to, lest I grieve
My bath must needs be left behind, alas! 70
One block, pure green as a pistachio-nut,
There's plenty jasper somewhere in the world—
And have I not Saint Praxed's ear to pray
Horses for ye, and brown Greek manuscripts,
And mistresses with great smooth marbly limbs? 75
—That's if ye carve my epitaph aright,
Choice Latin, picked phrase, Tully's every word,
No gaudy ware like Gandolf's second line—
Tully, my masters? Ulpian serves his need!
And then how I shall lie through centuries, 80
And hear the blessed mutter of the Mass,
And see God made and eaten all day long,
And feel the steady candle-flame, and taste
Good strong thick stupefying incense-smoke!
For as I lie here, hours of the dead night, 85
Dying in state and by such slow degrees,
I fold my arms as if they clasped a crook,
And stretch my feet forth straight as stone can **point,**
And let the bedclothes, for a mortcloth, drop
Into great laps and folds of sculptor's-work; 90
And as yon tapers dwindle, and strange **thoughts**
Grow, with a certain humming in my ears,
About the life before I lived this life,
And this life too, popes, cardinals, and priests,
Saint Praxed at his sermon on the mount, 95
Your tall pale mother with her talking eyes,
And new-found agate urns as fresh as day,
And marble's language, Latin pure, discreet—
Aha, ELUCESCEBAT quoth our friend?
No Tully, said I, Ulpian at the best! 100
Evil and brief hath been my pilgrimage.
All *lapis,* all, sons! Else I give the Pope
My villas! Will ye ever eat my heart?
Ever your eyes were as a lizard's quick,
They glitter like your mother's for my soul. 105

travertine—a kind of white limestone
jasper—a dark green stone of smooth surface

Or ye would heighten my impoverished frieze,
Piece out its starved design, and fill my vase
With grapes, and add a visor and a term,
And to the tripod ye would tie a lynx
That in his struggle throws the thyrsus down,   110
To comfort me on my entablature
Whereon I am to lie till I must ask,
"Do I live, am I dead?" There, leave me, there!
For ye have stabbed me with ingratitude
To death—ye wish it—God, ye wish it! Stone—   115
Gritstone, a-crumble! Clammy squares which sweat
As if the corpse they keep were oozing through—
And no more *lapis* to delight the world!
Well, go! I bless ye. Fewer tapers there,
But in a row; and, going, turn your backs—   120
Aye, like departing altar-ministrants,
And leave me in my church, the church for peace,
That I may watch at leisure if he leers—
Old Gandolf—at me, from his onion-stone,
As still he envied me, so fair she was!

"CHILDE ROLAND TO THE DARK TOWER CAME"

ROBERT BROWNING

My first thought was, he lied in every word,
 That hoary cripple, with malicious eye
 Askance to watch the working of his lie
On mine, and mouth scarce able to afford
Suppression of the glee, that pursed and scored   5
 Its edge, at one more victim gained thereby.

What else should he be set for, with his staff?
 What, save to waylay with his lies, ensnare
 All travelers who might find him posted there,
And ask the road? I guessed what skull-like laugh   10
Would break, what crutch 'gin write my epitaph
 For pastime in the dusty thoroughfare,

Childe—a title given to a young knight
who had not yet distinguished himself;
for Roland, see Shakespeare's *King Lear*
III, 4

If at his counsel I should turn aside
   Into that ominous tract which, all agree,
   Hides the Dark Tower. Yet acquiescingly   15
I did turn as he pointed—neither pride
Nor hope rekindling at the end described,
   So much as gladness that some end might be.

For, what with my whole world-wide wandering,
   What with my search drawn out through years, my hope   20
   Dwindled into a ghost not fit to cope
With that obstreperous joy success would bring—
I hardly tried now to rebuke the spring
   My heart made, finding failure in its scope.

As when a sick man very near to death   25
   Seems dead indeed, and feels begin and end
   The tears, and takes the farewell of each friend,
And hears one bid the other go, draw breath
Freelier outside ("since all is o'er," he saith,
   "And the blow fallen no grieving can amend"),   30

While some discuss if near the other graves
   Be room enough for this, and when a day
   Suits best for carrying the corpse away,
With care about the banners, scarves and staves;
And still the man hears all, and only craves   35
   He may not shame such tender love and stay.

Thus, I had so long suffered in this quest,
   Heard failure prophesied so oft, been writ
   So many times among "The Band"—to wit,
The knights who to the Dark Tower's search addressed   40
Their steps—that just to fail as they, seemed best,
   And all the doubt was now—should I be fit?

So, quiet as despair, I turned from him,
   That hateful cripple, out of his highway
   Into the path he pointed. All the day   45
Had been a dreary one at best, and dim
Was settling to its close, yet shot one grim
   Red leer to see the plain catch its estray.

For mark! no sooner was I fairly found
   Pledged to the plain, after a pace or two,   50

Than, pausing to throw backward a last view
O'er the safe road, 'twas gone; gray plain all round—
Nothing but plain to the horizon's bound.
　　I might go on; naught else remained to do.

So, on I went. I think I never saw　　　　　　　　　　55
　　Such starved ignoble nature; nothing throve,
　　For flowers—as well expect a cedar grove!
But cockle, spurge, according to their law
Might propagate their kind, with none to awe,
　　You'd think; a burr had been a treasure trove.　　60

No! penury, inertness, and grimace,
　　In some strange sort, were the land's portion. "See
　　Or shut your eyes," said Nature peevishly,
"It nothing skills—I cannot help my case;
'Tis the Last Judgment's fire must cure this place,　　65
　　Calcine its clods, and set my prisoners free."

If there pushed any ragged thistle-stalk
　　Above its mates, the head was chopped; the bents
　　Were jealous else. What made those holes and rents
In the dock's harsh swarth leaves, bruised as to balk　　70
All hope of greenness? 'Tis a brute must walk
　　Pashing their life out, with a brute's intents.

As for the grass, it grew as scant as hair
　　In leprosy; thin dry blades pricked the mud,
　　Which underneath looked kneaded up with blood.　　75
One stiff blind horse, his every bone a-stare,
Stood stupefied, however he came there—
　　Thrust out past service from the devil's stud!

Alive? he might be dead for aught I know,
　　With that red gaunt and colloped neck a-strain,　　80
　　And shut eyes underneath the rusty mane;
Seldom went such grotesqueness with such woe;
I never saw a brute I hated so;
　　He must be wicked to deserve such pain.

I shut my eyes and turned them on my heart.　　　　85
　　As a man calls for wine before he fights,
　　I asked one draft of earlier, happier sights,
Ere fitly I could hope to play my part.

bents—coarse grasses
colloped—marked with ridges

Think first, fight afterwards—the soldier's art;
  One taste of the old time sets all to rights.   90

Not it! I fancied Cuthbert's reddening face
  Beneath its garniture of curly gold,
  Dear fellow, till I almost felt him fold
  An arm in mine to fix me to the place,
That way he used. Alas, one night's disgrace!   95
  Out went my heart's new fire and left it cold.

Giles then, the soul of honor—there he stands
  Frank as ten years ago when knighted first.
  What honest man should dare (he said) he durst.
Good—but the scene shifts—faugh! what hangman hands   100
Pin to his breast a parchment? His own bands
  Read it. Poor traitor, spit upon and curst!

Better this present than a past like that;
  Back therefore to my darkening path again!
  No sound, no sight as far as eye could strain.   105
Will the night send a howlet or a bat?
I asked—when something on the dismal flat
  Came to arrest my thoughts and change their train.

A sudden little river crossed my path
  As unexpected as a serpent comes.   110
  No sluggish tide congenial to the glooms;
This, as it frothed by, might have been a bath
For the fiend's glowing hoof—to see the wrath
  Of its black eddy bespate with flakes and spumes.

So petty yet so spiteful! All along,   115
  Low scrubby alders kneeled down over it;
  Drenched willows flung them headlong in a fit
Of mute despair, a suicidal throng;
The river which had done them all the wrong,
  Whate'er that was, rolled by, deterred no whit.   120

Which, while I forded—good saints, how I feared
  To set my foot upon a dead man's cheek,
  Each step, or feel the spear I thrust to seek
For hollows, tangled in his hair or beard!
—It may have been a water-rat I speared,   125
  But, ugh! it sounded like a baby's shriek.

Glad was I when I reached the other bank.
  Now for a better country. Vain presage!

Who were the strugglers, what war did they wage,
Whose savage trample thus could pad the dank   130
Soil to a plash? Toads in a poisoned tank,
    Or wild cats in a red-hot iron cage—

The fight must so have seemed in that fell cirque.
    What penned them there, with all the plain to choose?
    No footprint leading to that horrid mews,   135
None out of it. Mad brewage set to work
Their brains, no doubt, like galley-slaves the Turk
    Pits for his pastime, Christians against Jews.

And more than that—a furlong on—why, there!
    What bad use was that engine for, that wheel,   140
    Or brake, not wheel—that harrow fit to reel
Men's bodies out like silk? with all the air
Of Tophet's tool, on earth left unaware,
    Or brought to sharpen its rusty teeth of steel.

Then came a bit of stubbed ground, once a wood,   145
    Next a marsh, it would seem, and now mere earth
    Desperate and done with—so a fool finds mirth,
Makes a thing and then mars it, till his mood
Changes and off he goes!—within a rood,
    Bog, clay and rubble, sand and stark black dearth.   150

Now blotches rankling, colored gay and grim,
    Now patches where some leanness of the soil's
    Broke into moss or substances like boils;
Then came some palsied oak, a cleft in him
Like a distorted mouth that splits its rim   155
    Gaping at death, and dies while it recoils.

And just as far as ever from the end!
    Naught in the distance but the evening, naught
    To point my footstep further! At the thought,
A great black bird, Apollyon's bosom-friend,   160
Sailed past, nor beat his wide wing dragon-penned
    That brushed my cap—perchance the guide I sought.

For, looking up, aware I somehow grew,
    'Spite of the dusk, the plain had given place

mews—enclosure, pen
Tophet—an Old Testament name for hell
Apollyon's—the devil's
dragon-penned—furnished with feathers
like those in a dragon's wing

All round to mountains—with such name to grace   165
Mere ugly heights and heaps now stolen in view.
How thus they had surprised me—solve it, you!
   How to get from them was no clearer case.

Yet half I seemed to recognize some trick
   Of mischief happened to me, God knows when—   170
   In a bad dream perhaps. Here ended, then,
Progress this way. When, in the very nick
Of giving up, one time more, came a click
   As when a trap shuts—you're inside the den!

Burningly it came on me all at once,   175
   This was the place! those two hills on the right,
   Crouched like two bulls locked horn in horn in fight;
While to the left, a tall scalped mountain . . . Dunce,
Dotard, a-dozing at the very nonce,
   After a life spent training for the sight!   180

What in the midst lay but the Tower itself?
   The round squat turret, blind as the fool's heart,
   Built of brown stone, without a counterpart
In the whole world. The tempest's mocking elf
Points to the shipman thus the unseen shelf   185
   He strikes on, only when the timbers start.

Not see? because of night perhaps?—why, day
   Came back again for that! before it left,
   The dying sunset kindled through a cleft;
The hills, like giants at a hunting, lay,   190
Chin upon hand, to see the game at bay—
   "Now stab and end the creature—to the heft!"

Not hear? when noise was everywhere! it tolled
   Increasing like a bell. Names in my ears,
   Of all the lost adventurers my peers—   195
How such a one was strong, and such was bold,
And such was fortunate, yet each of old
   Lost, lost! one moment knelled the woe of years.

There they stood, ranged along the hillsides, met
   To view the last of me, a living frame   200
   For one more picture! in a sheet of flame
I saw them and I knew them all. And yet
Dauntless the slug-horn to my lips I set,
   And blew. *"Childe Roland to the Dark Tower came."*

CAVALRY CROSSING A FORD

WALT WHITMAN

A line in long array where they wind betwixt green islands,
They take a serpentine course, their arms flash in the sun—hark to
    the musical clank,
Behold the silvery river, in it the splashing horses loitering stop to
    drink,
Behold the brown-faced men, each group, each person a picture,
    the negligent rest on the saddles,
Some emerge on the opposite bank, others are just entering the
    ford—while,   5
Scarlet and blue and snowy white,
The guidon flags flutter gayly in the wind.

BIVOUAC ON A MOUNTAIN SIDE

WALT WHITMAN

I see before me now a traveling army halting,
Below a fertile valley spread, with barns and the orchards of
    summer,
Behind, the terraced sides of a mountain, abrupt, in places rising
    high,
Broken, with rocks, with clinging cedars, with tall shapes dingily
    seen,
The numerous camp-fires scatter'd near and far, some away up on
    the mountain,   5
The shadowy forms of men and horses, looming, large-sized, flicker-
    ing,
And over all the sky—the sky! far, far out of reach, studded,
    breaking out, the eternal stars.

BY THE BIVOUAC'S FITFUL FLAME

WALT WHITMAN

By the bivouac's fitful flame,
A procession winding around me, solemn and sweet and slow—but
    first I note,
The tents of the sleeping army, the fields' and woods' dim outline,

The darkness lit by spots of kindled fire, the silence,
Like a phantom far or near an occasional figure moving,   5
The shrubs and trees, (as I lift my eyes they seem to be stealthily
    watching me,)
While wind in procession thoughts, O tender and wondrous
    thoughts,
Of life and death, of home and the past and loved, and of those
    that are far away;
A solemn and slow procession there as I sit on the ground,
By the bivouac's fitful flame.   10

FACES

WALT WHITMAN

1

Sauntering the pavement or riding the country by-road, lo, such
    faces!
Faces of friendship, precision, caution, suavity, ideality,
The spiritual-prescient face, the always welcome common benevo-
    lent face,
The face of the singing of music, the grand faces of natural lawyers
    and judges broad at the back-top,
The faces of hunters and fishers bulged at the brows, the shaved
    blanch'd faces of orthodox citizens,   5
The pure, extravagant, yearning, questioning artist's face,
The ugly face of some beautiful soul, the handsome detested or
    despised face,
The sacred faces of infants, the illuminated face of the mother of
    many children,
The face of an amour, the face of veneration,
The face as of a dream, the face of an immobile rock,   10
The face withdrawn of its good and bad, a castrated face,
A wild hawk, his wings clipp'd by the clipper,
A stallion that yielded at last to the thongs and knife of the gelder.
Sauntering the pavement thus, or crossing the ceaseless ferry, faces
    and faces and faces,
I see them and complain not, and am content with all.   15

2

Do you suppose I could be content with all if I thought them their
    own finalè?
This now is too lamentable a face for a man,

Some abject louse asking leave to be, cringing for it,
Some milk-nosed maggot blessing what lets it wrig to its hole.

This face is a dog's snout sniffing for garbage,   20
Snakes nest in that mouth, I hear the sibilant threat.

This face is a haze more chill than the arctic sea,
Its sleepy and wabbling icebergs crunch as they go.
This is a face of bitter herbs, this an emetic, they need no label,
And more of the drug-shelf, laudanum, caoutchouc, or hog's-lard.

This face is an epilepsy, its wordless tongue gives out the un-
        earthly cry,   26
Its veins down the neck distend, its eyes roll till they show nothing
        but their whites,
Its teeth grit, the palms of the hands are cut by the turn'd-in nails,
The man falls struggling and foaming to the ground, while he
        speculates well.

This face is bitten by vermin and worms,   30
And this is some murderer's knife with a half-pull'd scabbard.

This face owes to the sexton his dismalest fee,
An unceasing death-bell tolls there.

3

Features of my equals would you trick me with your creas'd and
        cadaverous march?
Well, you cannot trick me.   35

I see your rounded never-erased flow,
I see 'neath the rims of your haggard and mean disguises.

Splay and twist as you like, poke with the tangling fores of fishes
        or rats,
You'll be unmuzzled, you certainly will.
I saw the face of the most smear'd and slobbering idiot they had
        at the asylum,   40
And I knew for my consolation what they knew not,
I knew of the agents that emptied and broke my brother,
The same wait to clear the rubbish from the fallen tenement,
And I shall look again in a score or two of ages,
And I shall meet the real landlord perfect and unharm'd, every inch
        as good as myself.   45

4

The Lord advances, and yet advances,

Always the shadow in front, always the reach'd hand bringing up
the laggards.

Out of this face emerge banners and horses—O superb! I see what
is coming,
I see the high pioneer-caps, see staves of runners clearing the way,
I hear victorious drums.   50

This face is a life-boat,
This is the face commanding and bearded, it asks no odds of the
rest,
This face is flavor'd fruit ready for eating,
This face of a healthy honest boy is the programme of all good.

These faces bear testimony slumbering or awake,   55
They show their descent from the Master himself.

Of the word I have spoken I except not one—red, white, black, are
all deific,
In each house is the ovum, it comes forth after a thousand years.

Spots or cracks at the windows do not disturb me,
Tall and sufficient stand behind and make signs to me,   60
I read the promise and patiently wait.

This is a full-grown lily's face,
She speaks to the limber-hipp'd man near the garden pickets,
Come here she blushingly cries, *Come night to me limber-hipp'd
man,*
Stand at my side till I lean as high as I can upon you,   65
Fill me with albescent honey, bend down to me,
Rub to me with your chafing beard, rub to my breast and shoulders.

5

The old face of the mother of many children,
Whist! I am fully content.

Lull'd and late is the smoke of the First-day morning,   70
It hangs low over the rows of trees by the fences,
It hangs thin by the sassafras and wild-cherry and cat-brier under
them.

I saw the rich ladies in full dress at the soiree,
I heard what the singers were singing so long,
Heard who sprang in crimson youth from the white froth and the
water-blue.   75

Behold a woman!
She looks out from her quaker cap, her face is clearer and more
    beautiful than the sky.

She sits in an armchair under the shaded porch of the farmhouse,
The sun just shines on her old white head.

Her ample gown is of cream-hued linen,   80
Her grandsons raised the flax, and her grand-daughters spin it with
    the distaff and the wheel.

The melodious character of the earth,
The finish beyond which philosophy cannot go and does not wish
    to go,
The justified mother of men.

O CAPTAIN! MY CAPTAIN!

WALT WHITMAN

O Captain! my Captain! our fearful trip is done,
The ship has weather'd every rack, the prize we sought is won,
The port is near, the bells I hear, the people all exulting,
While follow eyes the steady keel, the vessel grim and daring;
        But O heart! heart! heart!   5
            O the bleeding drops of red,
                Where on the deck my Captain lies,
                    Fallen cold and dead.

O Captain! my Captain! rise up and hear the bells;
Rise up—for you the flag is flung—for you the bugle trills,   10
For you bouquets and ribbon'd wreaths—for you the shores
            a-crowding,
For you they call, the swaying mass, their eager faces turning;
        Here Captain! dear father!
            The arm beneath your head!
                It is some dream that on the deck,   15
                    You've fallen cold and dead.

My Captain does not answer, his lips are pale and still,
My father does not feel my arm, he has no pulse nor will,
The ship is anchor'd safe and sound, its voyage closed and done,
From fearful trip the victor ship comes in with object won: 20
        Exult O shores, and ring O bells!
            But I with mournful tread,

Walk the deck my Captain lies,
Fallen cold and dead.

WHEN LILACS LAST IN THE DOORYARD BLOOM'D

WALT WHITMAN

1

When lilacs last in the dooryard bloom'd,
And the great star early droop'd in the western sky in the night,
I mourn'd, and yet shall mourn with ever-returning spring.

Ever-returning spring, trinity sure to me you bring,
Lilac blooming perennial and drooping star in the west.   5
And thought of him I love.

2

O powerful western fallen star!
O shades of night—O moody, tearful night!
O great star disappear'd—O the black murk that hides the star!
O cruel hands that hold me powerless—O helpless soul of me!   10
O harsh surrounding cloud that will not free my soul.

3

In the dooryard fronting an old farm-house near the white-wash'd
          palings,
Stands the lilac-bush tall-growing with heart-shaped leaves of rich
          green,
With many a pointed blossom rising delicate, with the perfume
          strong I love,
With every leaf a miracle—and from this bush in the dooryard,
With delicate-color'd blossoms and heart-shaped leaves of rich
          green,   16
A sprig with its flower I break.

4

In the swamp in secluded recesses,
A shy and hidden bird is warbling a song.

Solitary the thrush,   20

The hermit withdrawn to himself, avoiding the settlements,
Sings by himself a song.

Song of the bleeding throat,
Death's outlet song of life, (for well dear brother I know,
If thou wast not granted to sing thou would'st surely die.)

5

Over the breast of the spring, the land, amid cities,   25
Amid lanes and through old woods, where lately the violets peep'd
    from the ground, spotting the gray debris,
Amid the grass in the fields each side of the lanes, passing the end-
    less grass,
Passing the yellow-spear'd wheat, every grain from its shroud in
    the dark-brown fields uprisen,
Passing the apple-tree blows of white and pink in the orchards,
Carrying a corpse to where it shall rest in the grave,   30
Night and day journeys a coffin.

6

Coffin that passes through lanes and streets,
Through day and night with the great cloud darkening the land,
With the pomp of the inloop'd flags with the cities draped in
    black,
With the show of the States themselves as of crape-veil'd women
    standing,   35
With processions long and winding and the flambeaus of the night,
With the countless torches lit, with the silent sea of faces and the
    unbared heads,
With the waiting depot, the arriving coffin, and the sombre faces,
With dirges through the night, with the thousand voices rising
    strong and solemn,
With all the mournful voices of the dirges pour'd around the
    coffin,   40
The dim-lit churches and the shuddering organs—where amid
    these you journey,
With the tolling tolling bells' perpetual clang,
Here, coffin that slowly passes,
I give you my sprig of lilac.

7

(Nor for you, for one alone,   45
Blossoms and branches green to coffins all I bring,
For fresh as the morning, thus would I chant a song for you O
    sane and sacred death.

All over bouquets of roses,
O death, I cover you over with roses and early lilies,

But mostly and now the lilac that blooms the first,   50
Copious I break, I break the sprigs from the bushes,
With loaded arms I come, pouring for you,
For you and the coffins all of you O death.)

8

O western orb sailing the heaven,
Now I know what you must have meant as a month since I walk'd,
As I walk'd in silence the transparent shadowy night,   56
As I saw you had something to tell as you bent to me night after
    night,
As you droop'd from the sky low down as if to my side, (while the
    other stars all look'd on,)
As we wander'd together the solemn night, (for something I know
    not what kept me from sleep,)
As the night advanced, and I saw on the rim of the west how full
    you were of woe,   60
As I stood on the rising ground in the breeze in the cool transparent
    night,
As I watch'd where you pass'd and was lost in the netherward
    black of the night,
As my soul in its trouble dissatisfied sank, as where you sad orb,
Concluded, dropt in the night, and was gone.

9

Sing on there in the swamp,   65
O singer bashful and tender, I hear your notes, I hear your call,
I hear, I come presently, I understand you,
But a moment I linger, for the lustrous star has detain'd me,
The star my departing comrade holds and detains me.

10

O how shall I warble myself for the dead one there I loved?   70
And how shall I deck my song for the large sweet soul that has
    gone?
And what shall my perfume be for the grave of him I love?

Sea-winds blown from east and west,
Blown from the Eastern sea and blown from the Western sea, till
    there on the prairies meeting,
These and with these and the breath of my chant,   75
I'll perfume the grave of him I love.

11

O what shall I hang on the chamber walls?
And what shall the pictures be that I hang on the walls,
To adorn the burial-house of him I love?

Pictures of growing spring and farms and homes,   80
With the Fourth-month eve at sundown, and the gray smoke lucid
    and bright,
With floods of the yellow gold of the gorgeous, indolent, sinking
    sun, burning, expanding the air,
With the fresh sweet herbage under foot, and the pale green leaves
    of the trees prolific,
In the distance the flowing glaze, the breast of the river, with a
    wind-dapple here and there,
With ranging hills on the banks, with many a line against the sky,
    and shadows,   85
And the city at hand with dwellings so dense, and stacks of
    chimneys,
And all the scenes of life and the workshops, and the workmen
    homeward returning.

12

Lo, body and soul—this land,
My own Manhattan with spires, and the sparkling and hurrying
    tides, and the ships,
The varied and ample land, the South and the North in the light,
    Ohio's shores and flashing Missouri,   90
And ever the far-spreading prairies cover'd with grass and corn.

Lo, the most excellent sun so calm and haughty,
The violet and purple morn with just-felt breezes,
The gentle soft-born measureless light,
The miracle spreading bathing all, the fulfill'd noon,   95
The coming eve delicious, the welcome night and the stars,
Over my cities shining all, enveloping man and land.

13

Sing on, sing on you gray-brown bird,
Sing from the swamps, the recesses, pour your chant from the
    bushes,
Limitless out of the dusk, out of the cedars and pines.   100

Sing on dearest brother, warble your reedy song,
Loud human song, with voice of uttermost woe.

O liquid and free and tender!
O wild and loose to my soul—O wondrous singer!
You only I hear—yet the star holds me, (but will soon depart,)
Yet the lilac with mastering odor holds me.   106

14

Now while I sat in the day and look'd forth,

In the close of the day with its light and the fields of spring, and
    the farmers preparing their crops,

In the large unconscious scenery of my land with its lakes and
    forests,

In the heavenly aerial beauty, (after the perturb'd winds and the
    storms,)   110

Under the arching heavens of the afternoon swift passing, and the
    voices of children and women,

The many-moving sea-tides, and I saw the ships how they sail'd,

And the summer approaching with richness, and the fields all busy
    with labor,

And the infinite separate houses, how they all went on, each with
    its meals and minutia of daily usages,

And the streets how their throbbings throbb'd, and the cities pent
    —lo, then and there,   115

Falling upon them all and among them all, enveloping me with
    the rest,

Appear'd the cloud, appear'd the long black trail,

And I knew death, its thought, and the sacred knowledge of death.

Then with the knowledge of death as walking one side of me,

And the thought of death close-walking the other side of me,   120

And I in the middle as with companions, and as holding the hands
    of companions,

I fled forth to the hiding receiving night that talks not,

Down to the shores of the water, the path by the swamp in the
    dimness,

To the solemn shadowy cedars and ghostly pines so still.

And the singer so shy to the rest receiv'd me,   125

The gray-brown bird I know receiv'd us comrades three,

And he sang the carol of death, and a verse for him I love.

From deep secluded recesses,

From the fragrant cedars and the ghostly pines so still,

Came the carol of the bird.   130

And the charm of the carol rapt me,

As I held as if by their hands my comrades in the night,

And the voice of my spirit tallied the song of the bird.

Come lovely and soothing death,

Undulate round the world, serenely arriving, arriving,   135

In the day, in the night, to all, to each,

Sooner or later delicate death.

Prais'd be the fathomless universe,
For life and joy, and for objects and knowledge curious,
And for love, sweet love—but praise! praise! praise!   140
For the sure-enwinding arms of cool-enfolding death.

Dark mother always gliding near with soft feet,
Have none chanted for thee a chant of fullest welcome?
Then I chant it for thee, I glorify thee above all,
I bring thee a song that when thou must indeed come, come un-
        falteringly.   145

Approach strong deliveress,
When it is so, when thou hast taken them I joyously sing the dead,
Lost in the loving floating ocean of thee,
Laved in the flood of thy bliss O death.

From me to thee glad serenades,   150
Dances for thee I propose saluting thee, adornments and feastings
        for thee,
And the sights of the open landscape and the high-spread sky are
        fitting,
And life and the fields, and the huge and thoughtful night.

The night in silence under many a star,
The ocean shore and the husky whispering wave whose voice I
        know,   155
And the soul turning to thee O vast and well-veil'd death,
And the body gratefully nestling close to thee.

Over the tree-tops I float thee a song,
Over the rising and sinking waves, over the myriad fields and the
        prairies wide,
Over the dense-pack'd cities all and the teeming wharves and ways,
I float this carol with joy, with joy to thee O death.   161

15

To the tally of my soul,
Loud and strong kept up the gray-brown bird,
With pure deliberate notes spreading filling the night.

Loud in the pines and cedars dim,   165
Clear in the freshness moist and the swamp-perfume,
And I with my comrades there in the night.

While my sight that was bound in my eyes unclosed,
As to long panoramas of visions.

And I saw askant the armies, 170
I saw as in noiseless dreams hundreds of battle-flags,
Borne through the smoke of the battles and pierc'd with missiles
    I saw them,
And carried hither and yon through the smoke, and torn and
    bloody,
And at last but a few shreds left on the staffs, (and all in silence,)
And the staffs all splinter'd and broken. 175

I saw battle-corpses, myriads of them,
And the white skeletons of young men, I saw them,
I saw the debris and debris of all the slain soldiers of the war,
But I saw they were not as was thought,
They themselves were fully at rest, they suffer'd not, 180
The living remain'd and suffer'd, the mother suffer'd,
And the wife and the child and the musing comrade suffer'd,
And the armies that remain'd suffer'd.

16

Passing the visions, passing the night,
Passing, unloosing the hold of my comrades' hands, 185
Passing the song of the hermit bird and the tallying song of my
    soul,
Victorious song, death's outlet song, yet varying ever-altering song,
As low and wailing, yet clear the notes, rising and falling, flood-
    ing the night,
Sadly sinking and fainting, as warning and warning, and yet again
    bursting with joy,
Covering the earth and filling the spread of the heaven, 190
As that powerful psalm in the night I heard from recesses,
Passing, I leave thee lilac with heart-shaped leaves,
I leave thee there in the dooryard, blooming, returning with spring.

I cease from my song for thee,
From my gaze on thee in the west, fronting the west, communing
    with thee, 195
O comrade lustrous with silver face in the night.

Yet each to keep and all, retrievements out of the night,
The song, the wondrous chant of the gray-brown bird,
And the tallying chant, the echo arous'd in my soul,
With the lustrous and drooping star with the countenance full of
    woe, 200
With the holders holding my hand nearing the call of the bird,
Comrades mine and I in the midst, and their memory ever to keep,
    for the dead I loved so well,

For the sweetest, wisest soul of all my days and lands—and this
    for his dear sake,
Lilac and star and bird twined with the chant of my soul,
There in the fragrant pines and the cedars dusk and dim.   205

DOVER BEACH

MATTHEW ARNOLD

The sea is calm tonight,
The tide is full, the moon lies fair
Upon the straits;—on the French coast the light
Gleams and is gone; the cliffs of England stand,
Glimmering and vast, out in the tranquil bay.   5
Come to the window, sweet is the night-air!
Only, from the long line of spray
Where the sea meets the moon-blanched land,
Listen! you hear the grating roar
Of pebbles which the waves draw back, and fling,   10
At their return, up the high strand,
Begin, and cease, and then again begin,
With tremulous cadence slow, and bring
The eternal note of sadness in.

Sophocles long ago   15
Heard it on the Aegean, and it brought
Into his mind the turbid ebb and flow
Of human misery; we
Find also in the sound a thought,
Hearing it by this distant northern sea.   20

The Sea of Faith
Was once, too, at the full, and round earth's shore
Lay like the folds of a bright girdle furled.
But now I only hear
Its melancholy, long, withdrawing roar,   25
Retreating, to the breath
Of the night-wind, down the vast edges drear
And naked shingles of the world.

Ah, love, let us be true
To one another! for the world, which seems   30

Sophocles—Antigone
shingles—beaches covered with shingles or
large stones

To lie before us like a land of dreams,
So various, so beautiful, so new,
Hath really neither joy, nor love, nor light,
Nor certitude, nor peace, nor help for pain;
And we are here as on a darkling plain   35
Swept with confused alarms of struggle and flight,
Where ignorant armies clash by night.

WINTER HEAVENS

GEORGE MEREDITH

Sharp is the night, but stars with frost alive
Leap off the rim of earth across the dome.
It is a night to make the heavens our home
More than the nest whereto apace we strive.
Lengths down our road each fir-tree seems a hive,   5
In swarms outrushing from the golden comb.
They waken waves of thoughts that burst to foam:
The living throb in me, the dead revive.
Yon mantle clothes us: there, past mortal breath,
Life glistens on the river of the death.   10
It folds us, flesh and dust; and have we knelt,
Or never knelt, or eyed as kine the springs
Of radiance, the radiance enrings:
And this is the soul's haven to have felt.

NATURE AND LIFE

GEORGE MEREDITH

Leave the uproar! At a leap
Thou shalt strike a woodland path,
Enter silence, not of sleep,
Under shadows, not of wrath;
Breath which is the spirit's bath,   5
In the old Beginnings find,
And endow them with a mind,
Seed for seedling, swathe for swathe.
That gives Nature to us, this
Give we her, and so we kiss.   10

Fruitful is it so—but hear
How within the shell thou art,
Music sounds; nor other near
Can to such a tremor start.
Of the waves our life is part;   15
They our running harvests bear—
Back to them for manful air,
Laden with the woodland's heart!
That gives Battle to us, this
Give we it, and good the kiss.

SUDDEN LIGHT

D. G. ROSSETTI

I have been here before,
But when or how I cannot tell:
I know the grass beyond the door,
The sweet keen smell,
The sighing sound, the lights around the shore.   5

You have been mine before,—
How long ago I may not know:
But just when at that swallow's soar
Your neck turned so,
Some veil did fall,—I knew it all of yore.   10

Has this been thus before?
And shall not thus time's eddying flight
Still with our lives our loves restore
In death's despite,
And day and night yield one delight once more?

THE HOUSE OF LIFE

D. G. ROSSETTI

27. HEART'S COMPASS

Sometimes thou seem'st not as thyself alone,
But as the meaning of all things that are;
A breathless wonder, shadowing forth afar
Some heavenly solstice hushed and halcyon;

Whose unstirred lips are music's visible tone;   5
    Whose eyes the sun-gate of the soul unbar,
    Being of its furthest fires oracular;—
The evident heart of all life sown and mown,
Even such love is; and is not thy name Love?
    Yea, by thy hand the Love-god rends apart   10
    All gathering clouds of Night's ambiguous art;
Flings them far down, and sets thine eyes above;
And simply, as some gage of flower or glove,
    Stakes with a smile the world against thy heart.

AFTER GREAT PAIN

EMILY DICKINSON

After great pain, a formal feeling comes—
The Nerves sit ceremonious, like Tombs—
The stiff Heart questions was it He, that bore,
And Yesterday, or Centuries before?

The Feet, mechanical, go round—   5
Of Ground, or Air, or Ought—
A Wooden way
Regardless grown,
A Quartz contentment, like a stone—

This is the Hour of Lead—   10
Remembered, if outlived,
As Freezing persons, recollect the Snow—
First—Chill—then Stupor—then the letting go—

UNDER THE LIGHT

EMILY DICKINSON

Under the Light, yet under,
Under the Grass and the Dirt,
Under the Beetle's Cellar
Under the Clover's Root,

Further than Arm could stretch   5
Were it Giant long,
Further than Sunshine could
Were the Day Year long,

Over the Light, yet over,
Over the Arc of the Bird—   10
Over the Comet's chimney—
Over the Cubit's Head,

Further than Guess can gallop
Further than Riddle ride—
Oh for a Disc to the Distance   15
Between Ourselves and the Dead!

TO FLEE FROM MEMORY

EMILY DICKINSON

To flee from memory
Had we the Wings
Many would fly
Inured to slower things
Birds with dismay
Would scan the mighty van
Of men escaping
From the mind of man

TO MAKE A PRAIRIE

EMILY DICKINSON

To make a prairie it takes a clover and one bee,
One clover, and a bee,
And revery.
The revery alone will do,
If bees are few.

See also Bryant's "Prairies"

UPHILL

CHRISTINA ROSSETTI

Does the road wind uphill all the way?
   Yes, to the very end.
Will the day's journey take the whole long day?
   From morn to night, my friend.

But is there for the night a resting-place?   5
   A roof for when the slow dark hours begin.
May not the darkness hide it from my face?
   You cannot miss that inn.

Shall I meet other wayfarers at night?
   Those who have gone before.   10
Then must I knock, or call when just in sight?
   They will not keep you standing at that door.

Shall I find comfort, travel-sore and weak?
   Of labour you shall find the sum.
Will there be beds for me and all who seek?   15
   Yea, beds for all who come.

Chorus from "ATALANTA IN CALYDON"

ALGERNON CHARLES SWINBURNE

When the hounds of spring are on winter's traces,
   The mother of months in meadow or plain
Fills the shadows and windy places
   With lisp of leaves and ripple of rain;
And the brown bright nightingale amorous   5
Is half assuaged for Itylus,
For the Thracian ships and the foreign faces,
   The tongueless vigil, and all the pain.

Come with bows bent and with emptying of quivers,
   Maiden most perfect, lady of light,   10
With a noise of winds and many rivers,
   With a clamor of waters, and with might;
Bind on thy sandals, O thou most fleet,

Over the splendor and speed of thy feet;
For the faint east quickens, the wan west shivers,   15
    Round the feet of the day and the feet of the night.

Where shall we find her, how shall we sing to her,
    Fold our hands round her knees, and cling?
Oh, that man's heart were as fire and could spring to her,
    Fire, or the strength of the streams that spring!   20
For the stars and the winds are unto her
As raiment, as songs of the harp-player;
For the risen stars and the fallen cling to her,
    And the southwest-wind and the west-wind sing.

For winter's rains and ruins are over,   25
    And all the season of snows and sins;
The days dividing lover and lover,
    The light that loses, the night that wins;
And time remembered is grief forgotten,
And frosts are slain and flowers begotten,   30
And in green underwood and cover
    Blossom by blossom the spring begins.

The full streams feed on flower of rushes,
    Ripe grasses trammel a traveling foot,
The faint fresh flame of the young year flushes   35
    From leaf to flower and flower to fruit;
And fruit and leaf are as gold and fire,
And the oat is heard above the lyre,
And the hooféd heel of a satyr crushes
    The chestnut-husk at the chestnut-root.   40

And Pan by noon and Bacchus by night,
    Fleeter of foot than the fleet-foot kid,
Follows with dancing and fills with delight
    The Mænad and the Bassarid;

And soft as lips that laugh and hide   45
The laughing leaves of the trees divide,
And screen from seeing and leave in sight
    The god pursuing, the maiden hid.

The ivy falls with the Bacchanal's hair
    Over her eyebrows hiding her eyes;   50
The wild vine slipping down leaves bare
    Her bright breast shortening into sighs;

oat—the shepherd's pipe of oaten straw
Maenad, Bassarid—followers of Bacchus

The wild vine slips with the weight of its leaves,
But the berried ivy catches and cleaves
To the limbs that glitter, the feet that scare   55
    The wolf that follows, the fawn that flies.

SAPPHICS

ALGERNON CHARLES SWINBURNE

All the night sleep came not upon my eyelids,
Shed not dew, nor shook nor unclosed a feather,
Yet with lips shut close and with eyes of iron
    Stood and beheld me.

Then to me so lying awake a vision   5
Came without sleep over the seas and touched me,
Softly touched mine eyelids and lips; and I, too,
    Full of the vision

Saw the white implacable Aphrodite,
Saw the hair unbound and the feet unsandaled   10
Shine as fire of sunset on western waters;
    Saw the reluctant

Feet, the straining plumes of the doves that drew her,
Looking always, looking with necks reverted,
Back to Lesbos, back to the hills whereunder   15
    Shone Mitylene;

Heard the flying feet of the Loves behind her
Make a sudden thunder upon the waters,
As the thunder flung from the strong unclosing
    Wings of a great wind.   20

So the goddess fled from her place, with awful
Sound of feet and thunder of wings around her;
While behind a clamor of singing women
    Severed the twilight.

Sapphics—A verse form employed by
Sappho (c. 600 B. C.), a Greek poet of
Mitylene, on the island of Lesbos. Each
stanza consists of three lines five feet each
and a fourth line of two feet, trochaic and
dactylic.

Ah, the singing, ah, the delight, the passion!   25
All the Loves wept, listening; sick with anguish,
Stood the crowned nine Muses about Apollo;
    Fear was upon them,

While the tenth sang wonderful things they knew not.
Ah, the tenth, the Lesbian! the nine were silent,   30
None endured the sound of her song for weeping;
    Laurel by laurel,

Faded all their crowns; but about her forehead.
Round her woven tresses and ashen temples
White as dead snow, paler than grass in summer,   35
    Ravaged with kisses,

Shone a light of fire as a crown forever.
Yea, almost the implacable Aphrodite
Paused, and almost wept; such a song was that song.
    Yea, by her name, too,   40

Called her, saying, "Turn to me, O my Sappho";
Yet she turned her face from the Loves, she saw not
Tears for laughter darken immortal eyelids.
    Heard not about her

Fearful fitful wings of the doves departing,   45
Saw not how the bosom of Aphrodite
Shook with weeping, saw not her shaken raiment,
    Saw not her hands wrung;

Saw the Lesbians kissing across their smitten
Lutes with lips more sweet than the sound of lute-strings,   50
Mouth to mouth and hand upon hand, her chosen,
    Fairer than all men;

Only saw the beautiful lips and fingers,
Full of songs and kisses and little whispers,
Full of music; only beheld among them   55
    Soar, as a bird soars

Newly fledged, her visible song, a marvel,
Made of perfect sound and exceeding passion,
Sweetly shapen, terrible, full of thunders,
    Cloth'd with the wind's wings.   60

Then rejoiced she, laughing with love, and scattered
Roses, awful roses of holy blossom;

Then the Loves thronged sadly with hidden faces
    Round Aphrodite,

Then the Muses, stricken at heart, were silent;   65
Yea, the gods waxed pale; such a song was that song.
All reluctant, all with a fresh repulsion,
    Fled from before her.

All withdrew long since, and the land was barren,
Full of fruitless women and music only.   70
Now perchance, when winds are assuaged at sunset,
    Lulled at the dewfall,

By the gray seaside, unassuaged, unheard of,
Unbeloved, unseen in the ebb of twilight,
Ghosts of outcast women return lamenting,   75
    Purged not in Lethe,

Clothed about with flame and with tears, and singing
Songs that move the heart of the shaken heaven,
Songs that break the heart of the earth with pity,
    Hearing, to hear them.

HER DILEMMA
(In —— Church)

THOMAS HARDY

The two were silent in a sunless church,
Whose mildewed walls, uneven paving-stones,
And wasted carvings passed antique research;
And nothing broke the clock's dull monotones.

Leaning against a wormy poppy-head,   5
So wan and worn that he could scarcely stand,
—For he was soon to die,—he softly said,
"Tell me you love me!"—holding long her hand.

She would have given a world to breathe "yes" truly,
So much his life seemed hanging on her mind,   10
And hence she lied, her heart persuaded throughly
'Twas worth her soul to be a moment kind.

But the sad need thereof, his nearing death,
So mocked humanity that she shamed to prize
A world conditioned thus, or care for breath   15
Where Nature such dilemmas could devise.

THE OXEN

THOMAS HARDY

Christmas Eve, and twelve of the clock.
    "Now they are all on their knees,"
An elder said as we sat in a flock
    By the embers in hearthside ease.

We pictured the meek mild creatures where   5
    They dwelt in their strawy pen,
Nor did it occur to one of us there
    To doubt they were kneeling then.

So fair a fancy few would weave
    In these years! Yet, I feel,   10
If someone said on Christmas Eve,
    "Come; see the oxen kneel,

"In the lonely barton by yonder coomb
    Our childhood used to know,"
I should go with him in the gloom,   15
    Hoping it might be so.

GOD'S GRANDEUR

GERARD MANLEY HOPKINS

The world is charged with the grandeur of **God**.
It will flame out, like shining from shook foil;
It gathers to a greatness, like the ooze of oil
Crushed. Why do men then now not reck his rod?
Generations have trod, have trod, have trod;   5

barton—farmyard
coomb—deep, narrow valley

And all is seared with trade; bleared, smeared with toil;
And wears man's smudge and shares man's smell—the soil
Is bare now, nor can foot feel, being shod.
And for all this, nature is never spent;
There lives the dearest freshness deep down things;   10
And though the last lights off the black West went
Oh, morning, at the brown brink eastward, springs—
Because the Holy Ghost over the bent
World broods with warm breast and with ah! bright wings.

THE WINDHOVER

(To Christ Our Lord)

GERARD MANLEY HOPKINS

I caught this morning morning's minion, king-
   dom of daylight's dauphin, dapple-dawn-drawn Falcon in his
      riding
Of the rolling level underneath him steady air, and striding
High there, how he rung upon the rein of a wimpling wing
In his ecstasy! then off, off forth on swing,
   As a skate's heel sweeps smooth on a bow-bend; the hurl and
      gliding   5
   Rebuffed the big wind. My heart in hiding
Stirred for a bird—the achieve of, the mastery of the thing!

Brute beauty and valor and act, oh, air, pride, plume, here
   Buckle! AND the fire that breaks from thee then, a billion
Times told lovelier, more dangerous, O my chevalier!   10
   No wonder of it: shéer plód makes plow down sillion
Shine, and blue-beak embers, ah, my dear,
   Fall, gall themselves, and gash gold-vermilion.

LONDON VOLUNTARIES

WILLIAM ERNEST HENLEY

1. Grave

   St. Margaret's bells,
   Quiring their innocent, old-world canticles,
Voluntary—music preceding church service

Sing in the storied air,
All rosy-and-golden, as with memories
Of woods at evensong, and sands and seas   5
Disconsolate for that the night is nigh.
O the low, lingering lights! The large last gleam
(Hark! how those brazen choristers cry and call!)
Touching these solemn ancientries, and there,
The silent River ranging tide-mark high   10
And the callow, gray-faced Hospital,
With the strange glimmer and glamour of a dream!
The Sabbath peace is in the slumbrous trees,
And from the wistful, the fast-widowing sky
(Hark! how those plangent comforters call and cry!)   15
Falls as in August plots late roseleaves fall.
The sober Sabbath stir—
Leisurely voices, desultory feet!—
Comes from the dry, dust-colored street,
Where in their summer frocks the girls go by,   20
And sweethearts lean and loiter and confer,
Just as they did an hundred years ago,
Just as an hundred years to come they will—
When you and I, dear Love, lie lost and low,
And sweet-throats none our welkin shall fulfill,   25
Nor any sunset fade serene and slow;
But, being dead, we shall not grieve to die.

2. Andante con moto

Forth from the dust and din,
The crush, the heat, the many-spotted glare,
The odor and sense of life and lust aflare,   30
The wrangle and jangle of unrests,
Let us take horse, dear heart, take horse and win—
As from swart August to the green lap of May—
To quietness and the fresh and fragrant breasts
Of the still, delicious night, not yet aware   35
In any of her innumerable nests
Of that first sudden plash of dawn,
Clear, sapphirine, luminous, large,
Which tells that soon the flowing springs of day

In deep and ever deeper eddies drawn   40
Forward and up, in wider and wider way,
Shall float the sands, and brim the shores,
On this our lith of the world, as round it roars
And spins into the outlook of the sun
(The Lord's first gift, the Lord's especial charge),   45
With light, with living light, from marge to marge
Until the course He set and staked be run.

Through street and square, through square and street,
Each with his home-grown quality of dark
And violated silence, loud and fleet,   50
Waylaid by a merry ghost at every lamp,
The hansom wheels and plunges. Hark, O hark,
Sweet, how the old mare's bit and chain
Ring back a rough refrain
Upon the marked and cheerful tramp   55
Of her four shoes! Here is the Park,
And, oh, the languid midsummer wafts adust,
The tired midsummer blooms!
O the mysterious distances, the glooms
Romantic, the august   60
And solemn shapes! At night this City of Trees
Turns to a tryst of vague and strange
And monstrous Majesties,
Let loose from some dim underworld to range
These terrene vistas till their twilight sets;   65
When, dispossessed of wonderfulness, they stand
Beggared and common, plain to all the land
For stooks of leaves! And lo! the Wizard Hour,
His silent, shining sorcery winged with power!
Still, still the streets, between the carcanets   70
Of linking gold, are avenues of sleep.
But see how gable ends and parapets
In gradual beauty and significance

lith—limb, section
terrene—earthly
stooks—bundles
carcanets—golden collars set with jewels

Emerge! And did you hear
That little twitter-and-acheep,   75
Breaking inordinately loud and clear
On this still, spectral, exquisite atmosphere?
'Tis a first nest at matins! And behold
A rakehell cat—how furtive and acold!
A spent witch homing from some infamous dance—   80
Obscene, quick-trotting, see her tip and fade
Through shadowy railing into a pit of shade!
And now! A little wind and shy,
The smell of ships (that earnest of romance),
A sense of space and water, and thereby   85
A lamplit bridge touching the troubled sky,
And look, O look! a tangle of silver gleams
And dusky lights, our River and all his dreams,
His dreams that never save in our deaths can die.

matins—morning songs

IN HOSPITAL

WILLIAM ERNEST HENLEY

XXII: PASTORAL

It's the Spring.
Earth has conceived, and her bosom,
Teeming with summer, is glad.

Vistas of change and adventure,
Thro' the green land   5
The gray roads go beckoning and winding
Peopled with wains, and melodious
With harness-bells jangling:
Jangling and twangling rough rhythms
To the slow march of the stately, great horses   10
Whistled and shouted along.
White fleets of cloud,
Argosies heavy with fruitfulness,
Sail the blue peacefully. Green flame the hedge-rows.
Blackbirds are bugling, and white in wet winds   15
Sway the tall poplars.

Pageants of colour and fragrance,
Pass the sweet meadows, and viewless
Walks the mild spirit of May,
Visibly blessing the world.   20

O, the brilliance of blossoming orchards!
O, the savour and thrill of the woods,
When the leafage is stirred
By the flight of the Angel of Rain!
Loud lows the steer; in the fallows   25
Rooks are alert; and the brooks
Gurgle and tinkle and trill. Thro' the gloamings,
Under the rare, shy stars,
Boy and girl wander,
Dreaming in darkness and dew.   30

It's the Spring.
A sprightliness feeble and squalid
Wakes in the ward, and I sicken,
Impotent, winter at heart.

IMPRESSIONS

OSCAR WILDE

1. LES SILHOUETTES

The sea is flecked with bars of gray,
The dull dead wind is out of tune,
And like a withered leaf the moon
Is blown across the stormy bay.

Etched clear upon the pallid sand   5
Lies the black boat; a sailor boy
Clambers aboard in careless joy
With laughing face and gleaming hand.

And overhead the curlews cry,
Where through the dusky upland grass   10
The young brown-throated reapers pass,
Like silhouettes against the sky.

2. LA FUITE DE LA LUNE

To outer senses there is peace,
A dreamy peace on either hand,
Deep silence in the shadowy land,   15
Deep silence where the shadows cease—

Save for a cry that echoes shrill
From some lone bird disconsolate;
A corncrake calling to its mate;
The answer from the misty hill.   20

And suddenly the moon withdraws
Her sickle from the lightening skies,
And to her somber cavern flies,
Wrapped in a veil of yellow gauze.

Le Fuite de la Lune—The Flight of the
Moon

A SHROPSHIRE LAD

A. E. HOUSMAN

XIX

TO AN ATHLETE DYING YOUNG

The time you won your town the race
We chaired you through the market-place;
Man and boy stood cheering by,
And home we brought you shoulder-high.

To-day, the road all runners come,   5
Shoulder-high we bring you home,
And set you at your threshold down,
Townsman of a stiller town.

Smart lad, to slip betimes away
From fields where glory does not stay   10
And early though the laurel grows
It withers quicker than the rose.

Eyes the shady night has shut
Cannot see the record cut,
And silence sounds no worse than cheers   15
After earth has stopped the ears:

Now you will not swell the rout
Of lads that wore their honours out,
Runners whom renown outran
And the name died before the man.   20

So set, before its echoes fade,
The fleet foot on the sill of shade,
And hold to the low lintel up
The still-defended challenge-cup.

And round that early-laurelled head   25
Will flock to gaze the strengthless dead,
And find unwithered on its curls
The garland briefer than a girl's.

XL

Into my heart an air that kills
From yon far country blows:

What are those blue remembered hills,
    What spires, what farms are those?

That is the land of lost content,   5
    I see it shining plain,
The happy highways where I went
    And cannot come again.

XLIII

THE IMMORTAL PART

When I meet the morning beam
Or lay me down at night to dream,
I hear my bones within me say,
'Another night, another day.

'When shall this slough of sense be cast,   5
This dust of thoughts be laid at last,
The man of flesh and soul be slain
And the man of bone remain?

'This tongue that talks, these lungs that shout,
These thews that hustle us about,   10
This brain that fills the skull with schemes,
And its humming hive of dreams,—

'These to-day are proud in power
And lord it in their little hour:
The immortal bones obey control   15
Of dying flesh and dying soul.

' 'Tis long till eve and morn are gone:
Slow the endless night comes on,
And late to fulness grows the birth
That shall last as long as earth.   20

'Wanderers eastward, wanderers west,
Know you why you cannot rest?
'Tis that every mother's son
Travails with a skeleton.

'Lie down in the bed of dust;   25
Bear the fruit that bear you must;

Bring the eternal seed to light,
And morn is all the same as night.

'Rest you so from trouble sore,
Fear the heat o' the sun no more,   30
Nor the snowing winter wild,
Now you labour not with child.

'Empty vessel, garment cast,
We that wore you long shall last.
—Another night, another day.'   35
So my bones within me say.

Therefore they shall do my will
To-day while I am master still,
And flesh and soul, now both are strong,
Shall hale the sullen slaves along,   40

Before this fire of sense decay,
This smoke of thought blow clean away,
And leave with ancient night alone
The steadfast and enduring bone.

THE KINGDOM OF GOD

FRANCIS THOMPSON

"IN NO STRANGE LAND"

O world invisible, we view thee,
O world intangible, we touch thee,
O world unknowable, we know thee,
Inapprehensible, we clutch thee!

Does the fish soar to find the ocean,   5
The eagle plunge to find the air—
That we ask of the stars in motion
If they have rumor of thee there?

"In no strange land"—see Exodus, 2:22.
Zipporah bore Moses a son, and he called
his name Gershom; for he said, "I have
been a stranger in a strange land"

Not where the wheeling systems darken.
And our benumbed conceiving soars!—   10
The drift of pinions, would we hearken.
Beats at our own clay-shuttered doors.

The angels keep their ancient places—
Turn but a stone and start a wing!
'Tis ye, 'tis your estrangéd faces,   15
That miss the many-splendored thing.

But (when so sad thou canst not sadder)
Cry—and upon thy so sore loss
Shall shine the traffic of Jacob's ladder
Pitched betwixt Heaven and Charing Cross.   20

Yea, in the night, my Soul, my daughter,
Cry—clinging Heaven by the hems;
And lo, Christ walking on the water,
Not of Genesareth, but Thames!

THE WAY THROUGH THE WOODS

RUDYARD KIPLING

They shut the road through the woods
Seventy years ago.
Weather and rain have undone it again,
And now you would never know
There was once a road through the woods   5
Before they planted the trees.
It is underneath the coppice and heath
And the thin anemones.
Only the keeper sees
That, where the ring-dove broods,   10
And the badgers roll at ease,
There was once a road through the woods.
Yet, if you enter the woods
Of a summer evening late,
When the night-air cools on the trout-ringed pools   15
Where the otter whistles his mate,
(They fear not men in the woods,
Because they see so few.)
You will hear the beat of a horse's feet,
And the swish of a skirt in the dew,   20
Steadily cantering through

The misty solitudes,
As though they perfectly knew
The old lost road through the woods. . . .
But there is no road through the woods.

TO THE ROSE UPON THE ROOD OF TIME

WILLIAM BUTLER YEATS

Red Rose, proud Rose, sad Rose of all my days!
Come near me, while I sing the ancient ways:
Cuchulain battling with the bitter tide;
The Druid, grey, wood-nurtured, quiet-eyed,
Who cast round Fergus dreams, and ruin untold;   5
And thine own sadness, whereof stars, grown old
In dancing silver-sandalled on the sea,
Sing in their high and lonely melody.
Come near, that no more blinded by man's fate,
I find under the boughs of love and hate,   10
In all poor foolish things that live a day,
Eternal beauty wandering on her way.

Come near, come near, come near—Ah, leave me still
A little space for the rose-breath to fill!
Lest I no more hear common things that crave;   15
The weak worm hiding down in its small cave,
The field-mouse running by me in the grass,
And heavy mortal hopes that toil and pass;
But seek alone to hear the strange things said
By God to the bright hearts of those long dead,   20
And learn to chaunt a tongue men do not know.
Come near; I would, before my time to go,
Sing of old Eire and the ancient ways;
Red Rose, proud Rose, sad Rose of all my days.

THE LOVER MOURNS FOR THE LOSS
OF LOVE

WILLIAM BUTLER YEATS

Pale brows, still hands and dim hair,
I had a beautiful friend
And dreamed that the old despair

Would end in love in the end:
She looked in my heart one day   5
And saw your image was there;
She has gone weeping away.

HE BIDS HIS BELOVED BE AT PEACE

WILLIAM BUTLER YEATS

I hear the Shadowy Horses, their long manes a-shake,
Their hoofs heavy with tumult, their eyes glimmering white;
The North unfolds above them clinging, creeping night,
The East her hidden joy before the morning break,
The West weeps in pale dew and sighs passing away,   5
The South is pouring down roses of crimson fire:
O vanity of Sleep, Hope, Dream, endless Desire,
The Horses of Disaster plunge in the heavy clay:
Beloved, let your eyes half close, and your heart beat
Over my heart, and your hair fall over my breast,   10
Drowning love's lonely hour in deep twilight of rest,
And hiding their tossing manes and their tumultuous feet.

THE FOLLY OF BEING COMFORTED

WILLIAM BUTLER YEATS

One that is ever kind said yesterday:
'Your well-belovèd's hair has threads of gray,
And little shadows come about her eyes;
Time can but make it easier to be wise
Though now it seems impossible, and so   5
All that you need is patience.'
                              Heart cries, 'No,
I have not a crumb of comfort, not a grain.
Time can but make her beauty over again:
Because of that great nobleness of hers   10
The fire that stirs about her, when she stirs,
Burns but more clearly. O she had not these ways
When all the wild summer was in her gaze.'

O heart! O heart! if she'd but turn her head,
You'd know the folly of being comforted.

ADAM'S CURSE

WILLIAM BUTLER YEATS

We sat together at one summer's end,
That beautiful mild woman, your close friend,
And you and I, and talked of poetry.
I said, 'A line will take us hours maybe;
Yet if it does not seem a moment's thought,   5
Our stitching and unstitching has been naught.

Better go down upon your marrow-bones
And scrub a kitchen pavement, or break stones
Like an old pauper, in all kinds of weather;
For to articulate sweet sounds together   10
Is to work harder than all these, and yet
Be thought an idler by the noisy set
Of bankers, schoolmasters, and clergymen
The martyrs call the world.'

                 And thereupon   15
That beautiful mild woman for whose sake
There's many a one shall find out all heartache
On finding that her voice is sweet and low
Replied, 'To be born woman is to know—
Although they do not talk of it at school—   20
That we must labour to be beautiful.'

I said, 'It's certain there is no fine thing
Since Adam's fall but needs much labouring.
There have been lovers who thought love should be
So much compounded of high courtesy   25
That they would sigh and quote with learned looks
Precedents out of beautiful old books;
Yet now it seems an idle trade enough.'

We sat grown quiet at the name of love;
We saw the last embers of daylight die,   30
And in the trembling blue-green of the sky
A moon, worn as if it had been a shell
Washed by time's waters as they rose and fell
About the stars and broke in days and years.

I had a thought for no one's but your ears: 35
That you were beautiful, and that I strove
To love you in the old high way of love;

That it had all seemed happy, and yet we'd grown
As weary-hearted as that hollow moon.

THE WILD SWANS AT COOLE

WILLIAM BUTLER YEATS

The trees are in their autumn beauty,
The woodland paths are dry,
Under the October twilight the water
Mirrors a still sky;
Upon the brimming water among the stones   5
Are nine-and-fifty swans.

The nineteenth autumn has come upon me
Since I first made my count;
I saw, before I had well finished,
All suddenly mount   10
And scatter wheeling in great broken rings
Upon their clamorous wings.

I have looked upon those brilliant creatures,
And now my heart is sore.
All's changed since I, hearing at twilight,   15
The first time on this shore,
The bell-beat of their wings above my head,
Trod with a lighter tread.

Unwearied still, lover by lover.
They paddle in the cold   20
Companionable streams or climb the air;
Their hearts have not grown old;
Passion or conquest, wander where they will,
Attend upon them still.

But now they drift on the still water,   25
Mysterious, beautiful;
Among what rushes will they build,
By what lake's edge or pool
Delight men's eyes when I awake some day
To find they have flown away?

HER PRAISE

WILLIAM BUTLER YEATS

She is foremost of those that I would hear praised.
I have gone about the house, gone up and down
As a man does who has published a new book,
Or a young girl dressed out in her new gown,
And though I have turned the talk by hook or crook   5
Until her praise should be the uppermost theme,
A woman spoke of some new tale she had read,
A man confusedly in a half dream
As though some other name ran in his head.
She is foremost of those that I would hear praised.   10
I will talk no more of books or the long war
But walk by the dry thorn until I have found
Some beggar sheltering from the wind, and there
Manage the talk until her name come round.
If there be rags enough he will know her name   15
And be well pleased remembering it, for in the old days,
Though she had young men's praise and old men's blame,
Among the poor both old and young gave her praise.

THE CAT AND THE MOON

WILLIAM BUTLER YEATS

The cat went here and there
And the moon spun round like a top,
And the nearest kin of the moon,
The creeping cat, looked up.
Black Minnaloushe stared at the moon,   5
For, wander and wail as he would,
The pure cold light in the sky
Troubled his animal blood.
Minnaloushe runs in the grass
Lifting his delicate feet.   10
Do you dance, Minnaloushe, do you dance?
When two close kindred meet,
What better than call a dance?
Maybe the moon may learn,
Tired of that courtly fashion,   15
A new dance turn.
Minnaloushe creeps through the grass
From moonlit place to place,

The sacred moon overhead
Has taken a new phase.   20
Does Minnaloushe know that his pupils
Will pass from change to change,
And that from round to crescent,
From crescent to round they range?
Minnaloushe creeps through the grass   25
Alone, important and wise,
And lifts to the changing moon
His changing eyes.

SAILING TO BYZANTIUM

WILLIAM BUTLER YEATS

I

That is no country for old men. The young
In one another's arms, birds in the trees
—Those dying generations—at their song,
The salmon-falls, the mackerel-crowded seas,
Fish, flesh, or fowl, commend all summer long   5
Whatever is begotten, born, and dies.
Caught in that sensual music all neglect
Monuments of unageing intellect.

II

An aged man is but a paltry thing,
A tattered coat upon a stick, unless   10
Soul clap its hands and sing, and louder sing
For every tatter in its mortal dress,
Nor is there singing school but studying
Monuments of its own magnificence;
And therefore I have sailed the seas and come   15
To the holy city of Byzantium.

III

O sages standing in God's holy fire
As in the gold mosaic of a wall,
Come from the holy fire, perne in a gyre,
And be the singing-masters of my soul.   20
Consume my heart away; sick with desire
And fastened to a dying animal
It knows not what it is; and gather me
Into the artifice of eternity.

IV

Once out of nature I shall never take   25
My bodily form from any natural thing,

But such a form as Grecian goldsmiths make
Of hammered gold and gold enamelling
To keep a drowsy Emperor awake;
Or set upon a golden bough to sing   30
To lords and ladies of Byzantium
Of what is past, or passing, or to come.

BYZANTIUM

WILLIAM BUTLER YEATS

The unpurged images of day recede;
The Emperor's drunken soldiery are abed;
Night resonance recedes, night-walkers' song
After great cathedral gong;
A starlit or a moonlit dome disdains   5
All that man is,
All mere complexities,
The fury and the mire of human veins.

Before me floats an image, man or shade,
Shade more than man, more image than a shade;   10
For Hades' bobbin bound in mummy-cloth
May unwind the winding path;
A mouth that has no moisture and no breath
Breathless mouths may summon;
I hail the superhuman;   15
I call it death-in-life and life-in-death.

Miracle, bird or golden handiwork,
More miracle than bird or handiwork,
Planted on the star-lit golden bough,
Can like the cocks of Hades crow,   20
Or, by the moon embittered, scorn aloud
In glory of changeless metal
Common bird or petal
And all complexities of mire or blood.

At midnight on the Emperor's pavement flit   25
Flames that no faggot feeds, nor steel has lit,
Nor storm disturbs, flames begotten of flame,
Where blood-begotten spirits come
And all complexities of fury leave,
Dying into a dance,   30
An agony of trance,
An agony of flame that cannot singe a sleeve.

Astraddle on the dolphin's mire and blood,
Spirit after spirit! The smithies break the flood,
The golden smithies of the Emperor!   35
Marbles of the dancing floor
Break bitter furies of complexity,
Those images that yet
Fresh images beget,
That dolphin-torn, that gong-tormented sea.   40

THE SECOND COMING

WILLIAM BUTLER YEATS

Turning and turning in the widening gyre
The falcon cannot hear the falconer;
Things fall apart; the centre cannot hold;
Mere anarchy is loosed upon the world,
The blood-dimmed tide is loosed, and everywhere   5
The ceremony of innocence is drowned;
The best lack all conviction, while the worst
Are full of passionate intensity.

Surely some revelation is at hand;
Surely the Second Coming is at hand.   10
The Second Coming! Hardly are those words out
When a vast image out of *Spiritus Mundi*
Troubles my sight: somewhere in sands of the desert
A shape with lion body and the head of a man,
A gaze blank and pitiless as the sun,   15
Is moving its slow thighs, while all about it
Reel shadows of the indignant desert birds.
The darkness drops again; but now I know
That twenty centuries of stony sleep
Were vexed to nightmare by a rocking cradle,   20
And what rough beast, its hour come round at last,
Slouches towards Bethlehem to be born?

A DIALOGUE OF SELF AND SOUL

WILLIAM BUTLER YEATS

I

My Soul. I summon to the winding ancient stair;
Set all your mind upon the steep ascent,

Upon the broken, crumbling battlement,
Upon the breathless starlit air,
Upon the star that marks the hidden pole;   5
Fix every wandering thought upon
That quarter where all thought is done:
Who can distinguish darkness from the soul?

My Self. The consecrated blade upon my knees
Is Sato's ancient blade, still as it was,   10
Still razor-keen, still like a looking-glass
Unspotted by the centuries;
That flowering, silken, old embroidery, torn
From some court-lady's dress and round
The wooden scabbard bound and wound,   15
Can, tattered, still protect, faded adorn.

My Soul. Why should the imagination of a man
Long past his prime remember things that are
Emblematical of love and war?
Think of ancestral night that can,   20
If but imagination scorn the earth
And intellect its wandering
To this and that and t'other thing,
Deliver from the crime of death and birth.

My Self. Montashigi, third of his family, fashioned it   25
Five hundred years ago, about it lie
Flowers from I know not what embroidery—
Heart's purple—and all these I set
For emblems of the day against the tower
Emblematical of the night,   30
And claim as by a soldier's right
A charter to commit the crime once more.

My Soul. Such fullness in that quarter overflows
And falls into the basin of the mind
That man is stricken deaf and dumb and blind,   35
For intellect no longer knows
Is from the *Ought,* or *Knower* from the *Known*—
That is to say, ascends to Heaven;
Only the dead can be forgiven;
But when I think of that my tongue's a stone.   40

II

My Self. A living man is blind and drinks his drop.
What matter if the ditches are impure?
What matter if I live it all once more?
Endure that toil of growing up;

289

The ignominy of boyhood; the distress   45
Of boyhood changing into man;
The unfinished man and his pain
Brought face to face with his own clumsiness;

The finished man among his enemies?—
How in the name of Heaven can he escape   50
That defiling and disfigured shape
The mirror of malicious eyes
Casts upon his eyes until at last
He thinks that shape must be his shape?
And what's the good of an escape   55
If honour find him in the wintry blast?

I am content to live it all again
And yet again, if it be life to pitch
Into the frog-spawn of a blind man's ditch,
A blind man battering blind men;   60
Or into that most fecund ditch of all,
The folly that man does
Or must suffer, if he woos
A proud woman not kindred of his soul.

I am content to follow to its source   65
Every event in action or in thought;
Measure the lot; forgive myself the lot!
When such as I cast out remorse
So great a sweetness flows into the breast
We must laugh and we must sing,   70
We are blest by everything,
Everything we look upon is blest.

LUKE HAVERGAL

EDWIN ARLINGTON ROBINSON

Go to the western gate, Luke Havergal,
There where the vines cling crimson on the wall,
And in the twilight wait for what will come.
The leaves will whisper there of her, and some,
Like flying words, will strike you as they fall;   5
But go, and if you listen she will call.
Go to the western gate, Luke Havergal—
Luke Havergal.

No, there is not a dawn in eastern skies
To rift the fiery night that's in your eyes;   **10**
But there, where western glooms are gathering,
The dark will end the dark, if anything:
God slays Himself with every leaf that flies,
And hell is more than half of paradise.
No, there is not a dawn in eastern skies—   **15**
In eastern skies.

Out of a grave I come to tell you this,
Out of a grave I come to quench the kiss
That flames upon your forehead with a glow
That blinds you to the way that you must go.   20
Yes, there is yet one way to where she is,
Bitter, but one that faith may never miss.
Out of a grave I come to tell you this—
To tell you this.

There is the western gate, Luke Havergal,   25
There are the crimson leaves upon the wall.
Go, for the winds are tearing them away,—
Nor think to riddle the dead words they say,
Nor any more to feel them as they fall;
But go, and if you trust her she will call.   30
There is the western gate, Luke Havergal—
Luke Havergal.

THE LISTENERS

WALTER DE LA MARE

"Is there anybody there?" said the Traveller,
  Knocking on the moonlit door;
And his horse in the silence champed the grasses
  Of the forest's ferny floor:
And a bird flew up out of the turret,   5
  Above the Traveller's head:
And he smote upon the door again a second time;
  "Is there anybody there?" he said.
But no one descended to the Traveller;
  No head from the leaf-fringed sill   10
Leaned over and looked into his grey eyes,
  Where he stood perplexed and still.

But only a host of phantom listeners
   That dwelt in the lone house then
Stood listening in the quiet of the moonlight   15
   To that voice from the world of men:
Stood thronging the faint moonbeams on the dark stair,
   That goes down to the empty hall,
Hearkening in an air stirred and shaken
   By the lonely Traveller's call.   20
And he felt in his heart their strangeness,
   Their stillness answering his cry,
While his horse moved, cropping the dark turf,
   'Neath the starred and leafy sky;
For he suddenly smote on the door, even   25
   Louder, and lifted his head:—
"Tell them I came, and no one answered,
   That I kept my word," he said.
Never the least stir made the listeners,
   Though every word he spake   30
Fell echoing through the shadowiness of the still house
   From the one man left awake:
Ay, they heard his foot upon the stirrup,
   And the sound of iron on stone,
And how the silence surged softly backward,   35
   When the plunging hoofs were gone.

DESIGN

ROBERT FROST

I found a dimpled spider, fat and white,
On a white heal-all, holding up a moth
Like a white piece of rigid satin cloth—
Assorted characters of death and blight
Mixed ready to begin the morning right,   5
Like the ingredients of a witches' broth—
A snow-drop spider, a flower like froth,
And dead wings carried like a paper kite.

What had that flower to do with being white,
The wayside blue and innocent heal-all?   10
What brought the kindred spider to that height,
Then steered the white moth thither in the night?
What but design of darkness to appall?—
If design govern in a thing so small.

THE OVEN BIRD

ROBERT FROST

There is a singer everyone has heard,
Loud, a mid-summer and a mid-wood bird,
Who makes the solid tree trunks sound again.
He says that leaves are old and that for flowers
Mid-summer is to spring as one to ten.   5
He says the early petal-fall is past
When pear and cherry bloom went down in showers
On sunny days a moment overcast;
And comes that other fall we name the fall.
He says the highway dust is over all.   10
The bird would cease and be as other birds
But that he knows in singing not to sing.
The question that he frames in all but words
Is what to make of a diminished thing.

RELUCTANCE

ROBERT FROST

Out through the fields and the woods
    And over the walls I have wended;
I have climbed the hills of view
    And looked at the world, and descended;
I have come by the highway home,   5
    And lo, it is ended.

The leaves are all dead on the ground,
    Save those that the oak is keeping
To ravel them one by one
    And let them go scraping and creeping   10
Out over the crusted snow,
    When others are sleeping.

And the dead leaves lie huddled and still,
    No longer blown hither and thither;
The last lone aster is gone;   15
    The flowers of the witch-hazel wither;

The heart is still aching to seek,
    But the feet question 'Whither?'

Ah, when to the heart of man
    Was it ever less than a treason   20
To go with the drift of things,
    To yield with a grace to reason,
And bow and accept the end
    Of a love or a season?

HOOF DUSK

CARL SANDBURG

The dusk of this box wood
is leather gold, buckskin gold,
and the hoofs of a dusk goat
leave their heel marks on it.

The cover of this wooden box   5
is a last-of-the-sunset red,
a red with a sandman sand
fixed in evening siftings—
late evening sands are here.

The gold of old clocks,   10
forgotten in garrets,
hidden out between battles
of long wars and short wars,
the smoldering ember gold
of old clocks found again—   15
here is the small smoke fadeout
of their slow loitering.

Feel me with your fingers,
measure me in fire and wind:
maybe I am buckskin gold, old clock gold,   20
late evening sunset sand—
          Let go
          and loiter
          in the smoke fadeout.

REDHAW RAIN

CARL SANDBURG

The red rain spatter under the redhaw
tree, the hut roof branches of the redhaw tree, the floor level loam under the
redhaw tree, the meeting place of the
fall red rain and loam of the first   5
fall frost—the Pottawatomies took this
into their understanding of why October
so seldom fails, why October so often
brings the red rain spatter under the red-
haw tree.   10

The slow rain soaks. The farmers fix
wagon axles, patch the barn roof shingles, peek in the thatch of the empty
swallow homes. The farm wives keep to
the kitchens cleaning pans. The slow   15
rain soaks.

The head at the end of a horse's neck
holds its bone and meat, teeth and eye-
balls, tongue and ears, to the west, to
the east, to the browse of the last of   20
the sweetgrass range this year. Snow
comes soon, out of the north, to the south
and south. The tongue of the head in
the sweetgrass knows.

The gray west opens for a spear of blue   25
longer than fifty, a hundred and fifty,
prairie miles.

The gray west opens a triangle silver,
an arch of bar clouds over the prairie.

And the sun washes the spear, the arch,   30
the triangle, over and over.

THE EAGLE THAT IS FORGOTTEN

VACHEL LINDSAY

(John P. Altgeld, Governor of Illinois and my next-door neighbor, 1893-1897. Born December 30, 1847; died March 12, 1902.)

Sleep softly . . . eagle forgotten . . . under the stone.
Time has its way with you there, and the clay has its own.

"We have buried him now," thought your foes, and in secret
　rejoiced.
They made a brave show of their mourning, their hatred unvoiced.
They had snarled at you, barked at you, foamed at you day after
　day.　　　　　　　　　　　　　　　　　　　　　　　　　　　　5
Now you were ended. They praised you. . . . and laid you away.

The others that mourned you in silence and terror and truth,
The widow bereft of her crust, and the boy without youth,
The mocked and the scorned and the wounded, the lame and the
　poor
That should have remembered forever. . . . remember no more.

Where are those lovers of yours, on what name do they call,　　11
The lost, that in armies wept over your funeral pall?
They call on the names of a hundred high-valiant ones,
A hundred white eagles have risen the sons of your sons,
The zeal in their wings is a zeal that your dreaming began　　15
The valor that wore out your soul in the service of man.

Sleep softly. . . . eagle forgotten. . . . under the stone,
Time has its way with you there and the clay has its own.
Sleep on, O brave-hearted, O wise man, that kindled the flame—
To live in mankind is far more than to live in a name,　　　　20
To live in mankind, far, far more . . . than to live in a name.

Altgeld—pardoned radicals convicted for
Haymarket riots

ANECDOTE OF MEN BY THE THOUSAND

WALLACE STEVENS

The soul, he said, is composed
Of the external world.

There are men of the East, he said,
Who are the East.
There are men of a province   5
Who are that province.
There are men of a valley
Who are that valley.

There are men whose words
Are as natural sounds   10
Of their places
As the cackle of toucans
In the place of toucans.
The mandoline is the instrument
Of a place.   15

Are there mandolines of western mountains?
Are there mandolines of northern moonlight?

The dress of a woman of Lhassa,
In its place,
Is an invisible element of that place   20
Made visible.

THE PEDIMENT OF APPEARANCE

WALLACE STEVENS

Young men go walking in the woods,
Hunting for the great ornament,
The pediment of appearance.

They hunt for a form which by its form alone,
Without diamond-blazons or flashing or   5
Chains of circumstance,

By its form alone, by being right,
By being high, is the stone
For which they are looking:

The savage transparence. They go crying   10
The world is myself, life is myself,
Breathing as if they breathed themselves,

Full of their ugly lord,
Speaking the phrases that follow the sight
Of this essential ornament   15

In the woods, in this full-blown May,
The month of understanding. The pediment
Lifts up its heavy scowl before them.

THE SNOW MAN

WALLACE STEVENS

One must have a mind of winter
To regard the frost and the boughs
Of the pine-trees crusted with snow;

And have been cold a long time
To behold the junipers shagged with ice,   5
The spruces rough in the distant glitter

Of the January sun; and not to think
Of any misery in the sound of the wind,
In the sound of a few leaves,

Which is the sound of the land   10
Full of the same wind
That is blowing in the same bare place

For the listener, who listens in the snow,
And, nothing himself, beholds
Nothing that is not there and the nothing that is.

CONNOISSEUR OF CHAOS

WALLACE STEVENS

I

A. A violent order is disorder; and
B. A great disorder is an order. These
Two things are one. (Pages of illustrations.)

II

If all the green of spring was blue, and it is;
If the flowers of South Africa were bright   5
On the tables of Connecticut, and they are;
If Englishmen lived without tea in Ceylon, and they do;
And if it all went on in an orderly way,
And it does; a law of inherent opposites,
Of essential unity, is as pleasant as port,   10
As pleasant as the brush-strokes of a bough,
An upper, particular bough in, say, Marchand.

III

After all the pretty contrast of life and death
Proves that these opposite things partake of one,
At least that was the theory, when bishops' books   15
Resolved the world. We cannot go back to that.
The squirming facts exceed the squamous mind,
If one may say so. And yet relation appears,
A small relation expanding like the shade
Of a cloud on sand, a shape on the side of a hill.   20

IV

A. Well, an old order is a violent one.
This proves nothing. Just one more truth, one more
Element in the immense disorder of truths.
B. It is April as I write. The wind
Is blowing after days of constant rain.   25
All this, of course, will come to summer soon.
But suppose the disorder of truths should ever come
To an order, most Plantagenet, most fixed . . .
A great disorder is an order. Now, A
And B are not like statuary, posed   30
For a vista in the Louvre. They are things chalked
On the sidewalk so that the pensive man may see.

squamous—scalelike

299

                                    V

The pensive man . . . He sees that eagle float
For which the intricate Alps are a single nest.

THE IDEA OF ORDER AT KEY WEST

WALLACE STEVENS

She sang beyond the genius of the sea.
The water never formed to mind or voice,
Like a body wholly body, fluttering
Its empty sleeves; and yet its mimic motion
Made constant cry, caused constantly a cry,   5
That was not ours although we understood,
Inhuman, of the veritable ocean.

The sea was not a mask. No more was she.
The song and water were not medleyed sound
Even if what she sang was what she heard,   10
Since what she sang was uttered word by word.
It may be that in all her phrases stirred
The grinding water and the gasping wind;
But it was she and not the sea we heard.
For she was the maker of the song she sang,   15
The ever-hooded, tragic-gestured sea
Was merely a place by which she walked to sing.
Whose spirit is this? we said, because we knew
It was the spirit that we sought and knew
That we should ask this often as she sang.   20

If it was only the dark voice of the sea
That rose, or even colored by many waves;
If it was only the outer voice of sky
And cloud, of the sunken coral water-walled,
However clear, it would have been deep air,   25
The heaving speech of air, a summer sound
Repeated in a summer without end
And sound alone. But it was more than that,
More even than her voice, and ours, among
The meaningless plungings of water and the wind,   30
Theatrical distances, bronze shadows heaped
On high horizons, mountainous atmospheres
Of sky and sea.

                    It was her voice that made
The sky acutest at its vanishing.   35
She measured to the hour its solitude.
She was the single artificer of the world
In which she sang. And when she sang, the sea,
Whatever self it had, became the self
That was her song, for she was the maker. Then we,   40
As we beheld her striding there alone,
Knew that there never was a world for her
Except the one she sang and, singing, made.

Ramon Fernandez, tell me, if you know,
Why, when the singing ended and we turned   45
Toward the town, tell why the glassy lights,
The lights in the fishing boats at anchor there,
As the night descended, tilting in the air,
Mastered the night and portioned out the sea,
Fixing emblazoned zones and fiery poles,   50
Arranging, deepening, enchanting night.
Oh! Blessed rage for order, pale Ramon,
The maker's rage to order words of the sea,
Words of the fragrant portals, dimly-starred,
And of ourselves and of our origins,   55
In ghostlier demarcations, keener sounds.

THE YACHTS

WILLIAM CARLOS WILLIAMS

contend in a sea which the land partly encloses
shielding them from the too heavy blows
of an ungoverned ocean which when it chooses

tortures the biggest hulls, the best man knows
to pit against its beatings, and sinks them pitilessly.   5
Mothlike in mists, scintillant in the minute

brilliance of cloudless days, with broad bellying sails
they glide to the wind tossing green water
from their sharp prows while over them the crew crawls

ant like, solicitously grooming them, releasing,   10
making fast as they turn, lean far over and having
caught the wind again, side by side, head for the mark.

In a well guarded arena of open water surrounded by
lesser and greater craft which, sycophant, lumbering
and flittering follow them, they appear youthful, rare   15

as the light of a happy eye, live with the grace
of all that in the mind is feckless, free and
naturally to be desired. Now the sea which holds them

is moody, lapping their glossy sides, as if feeling
for some slightest flaw but fails completely.   20
Today no race. Then the wind comes again. The yachts

move, jockeying for a start, the signal is set and they
are off. Now the waves strike at them but they are too
well made, they slip through, though they take in canvas.

Arms with hands grasping seek to clutch at the prows.   25
Bodies thrown recklessly in the way are cut aside.
It is a sea of faces about them in agony, in despair

until the horror of the race dawns staggering the mind,
the whole sea become an entanglement of watery bodies
lost to the world bearing what they cannot hold. Broken,   30

beaten, desolate, reaching from the dead to be taken up
they cry out, failing, failing! their cries rising
in waves still as the skillful yachts pass over.

LONDON SNOW

ROBERT BRIDGES

While men were all asleep the snow came flying,
In large white flakes falling on the city brown,
Stealthily and perpetually settling and loosely lying,
    Hushing the latest traffic of the drowsy town;
Deadening, muffling, stifling its murmurs failing;   5
Lazily and incessantly floating down and down;
    Silently sifting and veiling road, roof, and railing;
Hiding difference, making unevenness even,
Into angles and crevices softly drifting and sailing.
    All night it fell, and when full inches seven   10

302

It lay in the depth of its uncompacted lightness,
The clouds blew off from a high and frosty heaven;
    And all woke earlier for the unaccustomed brightness
Of the winter dawning, the strange unheavenly glare.
The eye marveled—marveled at the dazzling whiteness;   15
    The ear harkened to the stillness of the solemn air;
No sound of wheel rumbling nor of foot falling,
And the busy morning cries came thin and spare.
    Then boys I heard, as they went to school, calling;
They gathered up the crystal manna to freeze   20
Their tongues with tasting, their hands with snowballing;
    Or rioted in a drift, plunging up to the knees;
Or peering up from under the white-mossed wonder,
"O look at the trees!" they cried, "O look at the trees!"
With lessened load a few carts creak and blunder,   25
Following along the white deserted way,
A country company long dispersed asunder;
    When now already the sun, in pale display
Standing by Paul's high dome, spread forth below
His sparkling beams, and awoke the stir of the day.   30
    For now doors open, and war is waged with the snow;
And trains of somber men, past tale of number,
Tread along brown paths, as toward their toil they go;
    But even for them awhile no cares encumber
Their minds diverted; the daily word is unspoken,   35
The daily thoughts of labor and sorrow slumber
At the sight of the beauty that greets them, for the charm they have
    broken.

NIGHTINGALES

ROBERT BRIDGES

Beautiful must be the mountains whence ye come,
And bright in the fruitful valleys the streams, wherefrom
    Ye learn your song.
Where are those starry woods? Oh, might I wander there,
Among the flowers, which in that heavenly air   5
    Bloom the year long!
Nay, barren are those mountains and spent the streams;
Our song is the voice of desire, that haunts our dreams,
    A throe of the heart,
Whose pining visions dim, forbidden hopes profound,   10
No dying cadence nor long sigh can sound,
    For all our art.

Alone, aloud in the raptured ear of men
We pour our dark nocturnal secret; and then,
As night is withdrawn   15
From these sweet-springing meads and bursting boughs of May,
Dream, while the innumerable choir of day
Welcome the dawn.

TREES IN THE GARDEN

D. H. LAWRENCE

Ah in the thunder air
how still the trees are!

And the lime-tree, lovely and tall, every leaf silent
hardly looses even a last breath of perfume.

And the ghostly, creamy coloured little trees of leaves   5
white, ivory white among the rambling greens
how evanescent, variegated elder, she hesitates on the green grass
as if, in another moment, she would disappear
with all her grace of foam!

And the larch that is only a column, it goes up too tall to see: 10
and the balsam-pines that are blue with the grey-blue blueness of
        things from the sea,
and the young copper beech, its leaves red-rosy at the ends
how still they are together, they stand so still
in the thunder air, all strangers to one another
as the green grass glows upwards, strangers in the garden.

FIDELITY

D. H. LAWRENCE

Fidelity and love are two different things, like a flower and a gem.
And love, like a flower, will fade, will change into something else
or it would not be flowery.

O flowers they fade because they are moving swiftly; a little torrent
    of life

leaps up to the summit of the stem, gleams, turns over round the
    bend   5
of the parabola of curved flight,
sinks, and is gone, like a comet curving into the invisible.

O flowers they are all the time travelling
like comets, and they come into our ken
for a day, for two days, and withdraw, slowly vanish again.   10

And we, we must take them on the wing, and let them go.
Embalmed flowers are not flowers, immortelles are not flowers;
flowers are just a motion, a swift motion, a coloured gesture;
that is their loveliness. And that is love.

But a gem is different. It lasts so much longer than we do   15
so much much much longer
that it seems to last forever.
Yet we know it is flowing away
as flowers are, and we are, only slower.
The wonderful slow flowing of the sapphire!   20

All flows, and every flow is related to every other flow.
Flowers and sapphires and us, diversely streaming.
In the old days, when sapphires were breathed upon and brought
    forth
during the wild orgasms of chaos
time was much slower, when the rocks came forth.   25
It took æons to make a sapphire, æons for it to pass away.

And a flower it takes a summer.

And man and woman are like the earth, that brings forth flowers
in summer, and love, but underneath is rock.
Older than flowers, older than ferns, older than foraminiferæ   30
older than plasm altogether is the soul of a man underneath.

And when, throughout all the wild orgasms of love
slowly a gem forms, in the ancient, once-more-molten rocks
of two human hearts, two ancient rocks, a man's heart and a
    woman's,
that is the crystal of peace, the slow hard jewel of trust,   35
the sapphire of fidelity.
The gem of mutual peace emerging from the wild chaos of love.

A PACT

EZRA POUND

I make a pact with you, Walt Whitman—
I have detested you long enough.
I come to you as a grown child
Who has had a pig-headed father;
I am old enough now to make friends.   5
It was you that broke the new wood,
Now is a time for carving.
We have one sap and one root—
Let there be commerce between us.

THE SPRING

EZRA POUND

'Ηρι μεν ἀι τε κυδώνιαι.   Ibycus

Cydonian Spring with her attendant train,
Maelids and water-girls,
Stepping beneath a boisterous wind from Thrace,
Throughout this sylvan place
Spreads the bright tips,   5
And every vine-stock is
Clad in new brilliancies.
                  And wild desire
Falls like black lightning.
O bewildered heart,   10
Though every branch have back what last year lost,
She, who moved here amid the cyclamen,
Moves only now a clinging tenuous ghost.

CANTO XVII

EZRA POUND

So that the vines burst from my fingers
And the bees weighted with pollen
Move heavily in the vine-shoots:
    chirr—chirr—chir-rikk—a purring sound,

And the birds sleepily in the branches.   5
   ZAGREUS! IO ZAGREUS!
With the first pale-clear of the heaven
And the cities set in their hills,
And the goddess of the fair knees
Moving there, with the oak-wood behind her,   10
The green slope, with white hounds
       leaping about her;
And thence down to the creek's mouth, until evening,
Flat water before me,
   and the trees growing in water,   15
Marble trunks out of stillness,
On past the palazzi,
                    in the stillness,
The light now, not of the sun.
                              Chrysophrase,   20
And the water green clear, and blue clear;
On, to the great cliffs of amber.
                         Between them,
Cave of Nerea,
   she like a great shell curved,   25
And the boat drawn without sound,
Without odour of ship-work,
Nor bird-cry, nor any noise of wave moving,
Nor splash of porpoise, nor any noise of wave moving,
Within her cave, Nerea,   30
                    she like a great shell curved
In the suavity of the rock,
                    cliff green-gray in the far,
In the near, the gate-cliffs of amber,
And the wave   35
       green clear, and blue clear,
And the cave salt-white, and glare-purple,
       cool, porphyry smooth,
       the rock sea-worn.
No gull-cry, no sound of porpoise,   40
Sand as of malachite, and no cold there,
   the light not of the sun.

Zagreus, feeding his panthers,
   the turf clear as on hills under light.
And under the almond-trees, gods,   45
   with them, *choros nympharum*. Gods,
Hermes and Athene,
              As shaft of compass,

Zagreus—Dionysus

Between them, trembled—
To the left is the place of fauns,   50
        sylva nympharum;
The low wood, moor-scrub,
   the doe, the young spotted deer,
   leap up through the broom-plants,
      as dry leaf amid yellow.   55
And by one cut of the hills,
   the great alley of Memnons.
Beyond, sea, crests seen over dune
Night sea churning shingle,
To the left, the alley of cypress.   60
           A boat came,
One man holding her sail,
Guiding her with oar caught over gunwhale, saying:
"There, in the forest of marble,
"the stone trees—out of water—   65
"the arbours of stone—
"marble leaf, over leaf,
"silver, steel over steel,
"silver beaks rising and crossing,
"prow set against prow,   70
"stone, ply over ply,
"the gilt beams flare of an evening."
Borso, Carmagnola, the men of craft, *i vitrei,*
Thither, at one time, time after time,
And the waters richer than glass,   75
Bronze gold, the blaze over the silver,
Dye-pots in the torch-light,
The flash of wave under prows,
And the silver beaks rising and crossing.
   Stone trees, white and rose-white in the darkness,   80
Cypress there by the towers,
   Drift under hulls in the night.

   "In the gloom the gold
Gathers the light about it." . . .

Now supine in burrow, half over-arched bramble,   85
One eye for the sea, through that peek-hole,
Gray light, with Athene.
Zothar and her elephants, the gold loin-cloth,
The sistrum, shaken, shaken,
   the cohort of her dancers.   90
And Aletha, by bend of the shore,
   with her eyes seaward,
   and in her hands sea-wrack

Salt-bright with the foam.
Koré through the bright meadow,   95
    with green-gray dust in the grass:
"For this hour, brother of Circe."
Arm laid over my shoulder,
Saw the sun for three days, the sun fulvid,
As a lion lift over sand-plain;   100

              and that day,
And for three days, and none after,
Splendour, as the splendour of Hermes,
And shipped thence

           to the stone place,   105
Pale white, over water,

          known water,
And the white forest of marble, bent bough over bough,
The pleached arbour of stone,
Thither Borso, when they shot the barbed arrow at him,
And Carmagnola, between the two columns,
Sigismundo, after that wreck in Dalmatia.
    Sunset like the grasshopper flying.

EVENING

H. D. [HILDA DOOLITTLE]

The light passes
from ridge to ridge,
from flower to flower—
the hypaticas, wide-spread
under the light   5
grow faint—
the petals reach inward,
the blue tips bend
toward the bluer heart
and the flowers are lost.   10

The cornel-buds are still white,
but shadows dart
from the cornel-roots—

Sigismundo Malatesta—of family of pa-
trons of art, 15th century

black creeps from root to root,
each leaf   15
cuts another leaf on the grass,
shadow seeks shadow,
then both leaf
and leaf-shadow are lost.

ALL THE LITTLE HOOFPRINTS

ROBINSON JEFFERS

Farther up the gorge the sea's voice fainted and ceased.
We heard a new noise far away ahead of us, vague and metallic,
    it might have been some unpleasant bird's voice
Bedded in a matrix of long silences. At length we came to a little
    cabin lost in the redwoods,
An old man sat on a bench before the doorway filing a cross-cut
    saw; sometimes he slept,
Sometimes he filed. Two or three horses in the corral by the stream-
    side lifted their heads   5
To watch us pass, but the old man did not.

                                                          In the afternoon we
    returned the same way,
And had the picture in our minds of magnificent regions of space
    and mountain not seen before. (This was
The first time that we visited Pigeon Gap, whence you look down
    behind the great shouldering pyramid-
Edges of Pico Blanco through eagle-gulfs of air to a forest basin
Where two-hundred-foot redwoods look like the pile on a Turkish
    carpet.) With such extension of the idol-   11
Worshipping mind we came down the streamside. The old man
    was still at his post by the cabin doorway, but now
Stood up and stared, said angrily, "Where are you camping?" I
    said "We're not camping, we're going home." He said
From his flushed heavy face, "That's the way fires get started. Did
    you come at night?" "We passed you this morning.
You were half asleep, filing a saw." "I'll kill anybody that starts a
    fire here . . ." his voice quavered   15
Into bewilderment . . . "I didn't see you. Kind of feeble I guess.
My temperature's a hundred and two every afternoon." "Why,
    what's the matter?" He removed his hat
And rather proudly showed us a deep healed trench in the bald
    skull. "My horse fell at the ford,

I must 'a' cracked my head on a rock. Well, sir, I can't remember
    anything till next morning.
I woke in bed the pillow was soaked with blood, the horse was in
    the corral and had had his hay,"—   20
Singing the words as if he had told the story a hundred times. To
    whom? To himself, probably,—
"The saddle was on the rack and the bridle on the right nail. What
    do you think of *that* now?" He passed
His hand on his bewildered forehead and said, "Unless an angel or
    something came down and did it.
A basin of blood and water by the crick, I must 'a' washed myself."
    My wife said sharply, "Have you been to a doctor?"
"Oh yes," he said, "my boy happened down." She said "You
    oughtn't to be alone here: are you all alone here?"   25
"No," he answered, "horses. I've been all over the world: right here
    is the most beautiful place in the world.
I played the piccolo in ships' orchestras." We looked at the im-
    mense redwoods and dark
Fern-taken slip of land by the creek, where the horses were, and
    the yuccaed hillsides high in the sun
Flaring like torches; I said "Darkness comes early here." He an-
    swered with pride and joy, "Two hundred and eighty-
Five days in the year the sun never gets in here.   30
Like living under the sea, green all summer, beautiful." My wife
    said, "How do you know your temperature's
A hundred and two?" "Eh? The doctor. He said the bone
Presses my brain, he's got to cut out a piece. I said 'All right,
    you've got to wait till it rains,
I've got to guard my place through the fire-season.' By God," he
    said joyously,
"The quail on my roof wake me up every morning, then I look out
    the window and a dozen deer   35
Drift up the canyon with the mist on their shoulders. Look in the
    dust at your feet, all the little hoofprints."

OH, LOVELY ROCK

ROBINSON JEFFERS

We stayed the night in the pathless gorge of Ventana Creek, up
    the east fork.
The rock walls and the mountain ridges hung forest on forest above
    our heads, maple and redwood,

Laurel, oak, madrone, up to the high and slender Santa Lucian firs
    that stare up the cataracts
Of slide-rock to the star-color precipices.

We lay on gravel and

    kept a little camp-fire for warmth.   5
Past midnight only two or three coals glowed red in the cooling
    darkness; I laid a clutch of dead bay-leaves
On the ember ends and felted dry sticks across them and lay down
    again. The revived flame
Lighted my sleeping son's face and his companion's, and the verti-
    cal face of the great gorge-wall
Across the stream. Light leaves overhead danced in the fire's
    breath, tree-trunks were seen: it was the rock wall
That fascinated my eyes and mind. Nothing strange: light-gray
    diorite with two or three slanting seams in it,   10
Smooth-polished by the endless attrition of slides and floods; no
    fern nor lichen, pure naked rock . . . as if I were
Seeing rock for the first time. As if I were seeing through the
    flame-lit surface into the real and bodily
And living rock. Nothing strange . . . I cannot
Tell you how strange: the silent passion, the deep nobility and
    childlike loveliness: this fate going on
Outside our fates. It is here in the mountain like a grave smiling
    child. I shall die, and my boys   15
Will live and die, our world will go on through its rapid agonies
    of change and discovery; this age will die,
And wolves have howled in the snow around a new Bethlehem:
    this rock will be here, grave, earnest, not passive: the energies
That are its atoms will still be bearing the whole mountain above:
    and I, many packed centuries ago,
Felt its intense reality with love and wonder, this lonely rock.

THE WOOD-WEASEL

MARIANNE MOORE

emerges daintily, the skunk—
don't laugh—in sylvan black and white chipmunk
regalia. The inky thing
adaptively whited with glistening
goat-fur, is wood-warden. In his   5
ermined well-cuttlefish-inked wool, he is

determination's totem. Out-
lawed? His sweet face and powerful feet go about
in chieftain's coat of Chilcat cloth.
He is his own protection from the moth,   10

noble little warrior. That
otter-skin on it, the living pole-cat,
smothers anything that stings. Well,—
this same weasel's playful and his weasel
associates are too. Only   15
WOOD-weasels shall associate with me.

THE MIND IS AN ENCHANTING THING

MARIANNE MOORE

is an enchanted thing
      like the glaze on a
katydid-wing
            subdivided by sun
            till the nettings are legion.   5
Like Gieseking playing Scarlatti;

like the apteryx-awl
      as a beak, or the
kiwi's rain-shawl
            of haired feathers, the mind   10
            feeling its way as though blind,
walks along with its eyes on the ground.

It has memory's ear
      that can hear without
having to hear.   15
            Like the gyroscope's fall,
            truly unequivocal
because trued by regnant certainty,

it is a power of
      strong enchantment. It   20
is like the dove-
            neck animated by
            sun; it is memory's eye;
it's conscientious inconsistency.

313

It tears off the veil; tears   25
    the temptation, the
mist the heart wears,
        from its eyes,—if the heart
        has a face; it takes apart
dejection. It's fire in the dove-neck's   30

iridescence; in the
    inconsistencies
of Scarlatti.
        Unconfusion submits
        its confusion to proof; it's   35
not a Herod's oath that cannot change.

HEART AND MIND

EDITH SITWELL

Said the Lion to the Lioness—'When you are amber dust,—
No more a raging fire like the heat of the Sun
(No liking but all lust)—
Remember still the flowering of the amber blood and bone
The rippling of bright muscles like a sea,   5
Remember the rose-prickles of bright paws
Though we shall mate no more
Till the fire of that sun the heart and the moon-cold bone are one.'

Said the Skeleton lying upon the sands of Time—
'The great gold planet that is the mourning heat of the Sun   10
Is greater than all gold, more powerful
Than the tawny body of a Lion that fire consumes
Like all that grows or leaps . . . so is the heart
More powerful than all dust. Once I was Hercules
Or Samson, strong as the pillars of the seas: 15
But the flames of the heart consumed me, and the mind
Is but a foolish wind.'

Said the Sun to the Moon—'When you are but a lonely white crone,
And I, a dead King in my golden armour somewhere in a dark
        wood,
Remember only this of our hopeless love   20
That never till Time is done
Will the fire of the heart and the fire of the mind be one.'

THE LOVE SONG OF
J. ALFRED PRUFROCK

T. S. ELIOT

S'io credesse che mia risposta fosse
A persona che mai tornasse al mondo,
Questa fiamma staria senza piu scosse.
Ma perciocche giammai di questo fondo
Non torno vivo alcun, s'i'odo il vero,
Senza tema d'infamia ti rispondo.°

Let us go then, you and I,
When the evening is spread out against the sky
Like a patient etherised upon a table;
Let us go, through certain half-deserted streets,
The muttering retreats   5
Of restless nights in one-night cheap hotels
And sawdust restaurants with oyster-shells:
Streets that follow like a tedious argument
Of insidious intent
To lead you to an overwhelming question. . . .   10
Oh, do not ask, 'What is it?'
Let us go and make our visit.

In the room the women come and go
Talking of Michelangelo.

The yellow fog that rubs its back upon the window-panes,   15
The yellow smoke that rubs its muzzle on the window-panes
Licked its tongue into the corners of the evening,
Lingered upon the pools that stand in drains,
Let fall upon its back the soot that falls from chimneys,
Slipped by the terrace, made a sudden leap,   20
And seeing that it was a soft October night,
Curled once about the house, and fell asleep.
And indeed there will be time
For the yellow smoke that slides along the street
Rubbing its back upon the window-panes;   25
There will be time, there will be time
To prepare a face to meet the faces that you meet;
There will be time to murder and create,
And time for all the works and days of hands

---

* S'io . . . rispondo—"If I thought my answer were to one who ever could
return to the world, this flame should shake no more; but since none ever did
return alive from this depth, if what I hear be true, without fear of infamy I
answer thee." Dante, *Inferno*, xxvii, 61-66.

That lift and drop a question on your plate;   30
Time for you and time for me,
And time yet for a hundred indecisions,
And for a hundred visions and revisions,
Before the taking of a toast and tea.

In the room the women come and go   35
Talking of Michelangelo.

And indeed there will be time
To wonder, 'Do I dare?' and, 'Do I dare?'
Time to turn back and descend the stair,
With a bald spot in the middle of my hair—   40
[They will say: 'How his hair is growing thin!']
My morning coat, my collar mounting firmly to the chin,
My necktie rich and modest, but asserted by a simple pin—

[They will say: 'But how his arms and legs are thin!']
Do I dare   45
Disturb the universe?
In a minute there is time
For decisions and revisions which a minute will reverse.

For I have known them all already, known them all—
Have known the evenings, mornings, afternoons,   50
I have measured out my life with coffee spoons;
I know the voices dying with a dying fall
Beneath the music from a farther room.
    So how should I presume?

And I have known the eyes already, known them all—   55
The eyes that fix you in a formulated phrase,
And when I am formulated, sprawling on a pin,
When I am pinned and wriggling on the wall,
Then how should I begin
To spit out all the butt-ends of my days and ways?   60
    And how should I presume?

And I have known the arms already, known them all—
Arms that are braceleted and white and bare
[But in the lamplight, downed with light brown hair!]
Is it perfume from a dress   65
That makes me so digress?
Arms that lie along a table, or wrap about a shawl.
    And should I then presume?
    And how should I begin?

Shall I say, I have gone at dusk through narrow streets   70
And watched the smoke that rises from the pipes
Of lonely men in shirt-sleeves, leaning out of windows? . . .

I should have been a pair of ragged claws
Scuttling across the floors of silent seas.

. . . . .

And the afternoon, the evening, sleeps so peacefully!   75
Smoothed by long fingers,
Asleep . . . tired . . . or it malingers,
Stretched on the floor, here beside you and me.
Should I, after tea and cakes and ices,
Have the strength to force the moment to its crisis?   80
But though I have wept and fasted, wept and prayed,
Though I have seen my head [grown slightly bald] brought in upon
     a platter,
I am no prophet—and here's no great matter;
I have seen the moment of my greatness flicker,
And I have seen the eternal Footman hold my coat, and snicker,
And in short, I was afraid.   86
And would it have been worth it, after all,
After the cups, the marmalade, the tea,
Among the porcelain, among some talk of you and me,
Would it have been worth while,   90
To have bitten off the matter with a smile,
To have squeezed the universe into a ball
To roll it toward some overwhelming question,
To say: 'I am Lazarus, come from the dead,
Come back to tell you all, I shall tell you all'—   95
If one, settling a pillow by her head,
     Should say: 'That is not what I meant at all.
     That is not it, at all.'

And would it have been worth it, after all,
Would it have been worth while,   100
After the sunsets and the dooryards and the sprinkled streets,
After the novels, after the teacups, after the skirts that trail along
     the floor—
And this, and so much more?—
It is impossible to say just what I mean!
But as if a magic lantern threw the nerves in patterns on a screen:
Would it have been worth while   106
If one, settling a pillow or throwing off a shawl,
And turning toward the window, should say:

317

'That is not it at all,
That is not what I meant, at all.'   110

.   .   .   .   .

No! I am not Prince Hamlet, nor was meant to be;
Am an attendant lord, one that will do
To swell a progress, start a scene or two,
Advise the prince; no doubt, an easy tool,
Deferential, glad to be of use,   115
Politic, cautious, and meticulous;
Full of high sentence, but a bit obtuse;
At times, indeed, almost ridiculous—
Almost, at times, the Fool.

I grow old . . . I grow old . . .   120
I shall wear the bottoms of my trousers rolled.

Shall I part my hair behind? Do I dare to eat a peach?
I shall wear white flannel trousers, and walk upon the beach.
I have heard the mermaids singing, each to each.

I do not think that they will sing to me.   125

I have seen them riding seaward on the waves
Combing the white hair of the waves blown back
When the wind blows the water white and black.

We have lingered in the chambers of the sea
By sea-girls wreathed with seaweed red and brown   130
Till human voices wake us, and we drown.

THE HOLLOW MEN

T. S. ELIOT

Mistah Kurtz—he dead.

A penny for the Old Guy

I

We are the hollow men
We are the stuffed men
Leaning together
Headpiece filled with straw. Alas!

Old Guy—effigy of Guy Fawkes

318

Our dried voices, when 5
We whisper together
Are quiet and meaningless
As wind in dry grass
Or rats' feet over broken glass
In our dry cellar 10

Shape without form, shade without colour,
Paralysed force, gesture without motion;

Those who have crossed
With direct eyes, to death's other Kingdom
Remember us—if at all—not as lost 15
Violent souls, but only
As the hollow men
The stuffed men.

II

Eyes I dare not meet in dreams
In death's dream kingdom 20
These do not appear:
There, the eyes are
Sunlight on a broken column
There, is a tree swinging
And voices are 25
In the wind's singing
More distant and more solemn
Than a fading star.

Let me be no nearer
In death's dream kingdom 30
Let me also wear
Such deliberate disguises
Rat's coat, crowskin, crossed staves
In a field
Behaving as the wind behaves 35
No nearer—

Not that final meeting
In the twilight kingdom

III

This is the dead land
This is cactus land 40
Here the stone images
Are raised, here they receive

The supplication of a dead man's hand
Under the twinkling of a fading star.

Is it like this   45
In death's other kingdom
Waking alone
At the hour when we are
Trembling with tenderness
Lips that would kiss   50
Form prayers to broken stone.

IV

The eyes are not here
There are no eyes here
In this valley of dying stars
In this hollow valley   55
This broken jaw of our lost kingdoms

In this last of meeting places
We grope together
And avoid speech
Gathered on this beach of the tumid river   60

Sightless, unless
The eyes reappear
As the perpetual star
Multifoliate rose
Of death's twilight kingdom   65
The hope only
Of empty men.

V

Here we go round the prickly pear
Prickly pear prickly pear
Here we go round the prickly pear   70
At five o'clock in the morning.

Between the idea
And the reality
Between the motion
And the act   75
Falls the Shadow

For Thine is the Kingdom

Between the conception
And the creation

Between the emotion   80
And the response
Falls the Shadow

Life is very long

Between the desire
And the spasm   85
Between the potency
And the existence
Between the essence
And the descent
Falls the Shadow   90

For Thine is the Kingdom

For Thine is
Life is
For Thine is the

This is the way the world ends   95
This is the way the world ends
This is the way the world ends
Not with a bang but a whimper.

ASH-WEDNESDAY

T. S. ELIOT

I

Because I do not hope to turn again
Because I do not hope
Because I do not hope to turn
Desiring this man's gift and that man's scope
I no longer strive to strive towards such things   5
(Why should the agèd eagle stretch its wings?)
Why should I mourn
The vanished power of the usual reign?

Because I do not hope to know again
The infirm glory of the positive hour   10
Because I do not think
Because I know I shall not know
The one veritable transitory power

Because I cannot drink
There, where trees flower, and springs flow, for there is nothing
  again   15

Because I know that time is always time
And place is always and only place
And what is actual is actual only for one time
And only for one place
I rejoice that things are as they are and   20
I renounce the blessèd face
And renounce the voice
Because I cannot hope to turn again
Consequently, I rejoice, having to construct something
Upon which to rejoice   25
And pray to God to have mercy upon us
And I pray that I may forget
These matters that with myself I too much discuss
Too much explain
Because I do not hope to turn again   30
Let these words answer
For what is done, not to be done again
May the judgement not be too heavy upon us

Because these wings are no longer wings to fly
But merely vans to beat the air   35
The air which is now thoroughly small and dry
Smaller and dryer than the will
Teach us to care and not to care
Teach us to sit still.

Pray for us sinners now and at the hour of our death   40
Pray for us now and at the hour of our death.

                                        II

Lady, three white leopards sat under a juniper-tree
In the cool of the day, having fed to satiety
On my legs my heart my liver and that which had been contained
In the hollow round of my skull. And God said   45
Shall these bones live? shall these
Bones live? And that which had been contained
In the bones (which were already dry) said chirping:
Because of the goodness of this Lady
And because of her loveliness, and because   50
She honours the Virgin in meditation,
We shine with brightness. And I who am here dissembled
Proffer my deeds to oblivion, and my love
To the posterity of the desert and the fruit of the gourd.
It is this which recovers   55

My guts the strings of my eyes and the indigestible portions
Which the leopards reject. The Lady is withdrawn
In a white gown, to contemplation, in a white gown.
Let the whiteness of bones atone to forgetfulness.
There is no life in them. As I am forgotten   60
And would be forgotten, so I would forget
Thus devoted, concentrated in purpose. And God said
Prophesy to the wind, to the wind only for only
The wind will listen. And the bones sang chirping
With the burden of the grasshopper, saying   65

Lady of silences
Calm and distressed
Torn and most whole
Rose of memory
Rose of forgetfulness   70
Exhausted and life-giving
Worried reposeful
The single Rose
Is now the Garden
Where all loves end   75
Terminate torment
Of love unsatisfied
The greater torment
Of love satisfied
End of the endless   80
Journey to no end
Conclusion of all that
Is inconclusible
Speech without word and
Word of no speech   85
Grace to the Mother
For the Garden
Where all love ends.

Under a juniper-tree the bones sang, scattered and shining
We are glad to be scattered, we did little good to each other, 90
Under a tree in the cool of the day, with the blessing of sand,
Forgetting themselves and each other, united
In the quiet of the desert. This is the land which ye
Shall divide by lot. And neither division nor unity
Matters. This is the land. We have our inheritance.   95

III

At the first turning of the second stair
I turned and saw below
The same shape twisted on the banister

Under the vapour in the fetid air
Struggling with the devil of the stairs who wears   100
The deceitful face of hope and of despair.

At the second turning of the second stair
I left them twisting, turning below;
There were no more faces and the stair was dark,
Damp, jaggèd, like an old man's mouth drivelling, beyond re-
      pair,   105
Or the toothed gullet of an agèd shark.

At the first turning of the third stair
Was a slotted window bellied like the fig's fruit
And beyond the hawthorn blossom and a pasture scene
The broadbacked figure drest in blue and green   110
Enchanted the maytime with an antique flute.
Blown hair is sweet, brown hair over the mouth blown,
Lilac and brown hair;
Distraction, music of the flute, stops and steps of the mind over
      the third stair,
Fading, fading; strength beyond hope and despair   115
Climbing the third stair.
Lord, I am not worthy
Lord, I am not worthy

        but speak the word only.

IV

Who walked between the violet and the violet   120
Who walked between
The various ranks of varied green
Going in white and blue, in Mary's colour,
Talking of trivial things
In ignorance and in knowledge of eternal dolour   125
Who moved among the others as they walked,
Who then made strong the fountains and made fresh the springs

Made cool the dry rock and made firm the sand
In blue of larkspur, blue of Mary's colour,
Sovegna vos   130

Here are the years that walk between, bearing
Away the fiddles and the flutes, restoring
One who moves in the time between sleep and waking, wearing

White light folded, sheathed about her, folded.
The new years walk, restoring   135

Through a bright cloud of tears, the years, restoring
With a new verse the ancient rhyme. Redeem
The time. Redeem
The unread vision in the higher dream
While jewelled unicorns draw by the gilded hearse.　　　140
The silent sister veiled in white and blue
Between the yews, behind the garden god,
Whose flute is breathless, bent her head and signed but spoke no
　　　word

But the fountain sprang up and the bird sang down
Redeem the time, redeem the dream　　　145
The token of the word unheard, unspoken

Till the wind shake a thousand whispers from the yew

And after this our exile

V

If the lost word is lost, if the spent word is spent
If the unheard, unspoken　　　150
Word is unspoken, unheard;
Still is the unspoken word, the Word unheard,
The Word without a word, the Word within
The world and for the world;
And the light shone in darkness and　　　155
Against the Word the unstilled world still whirled
About the centre of the silent Word.

　O my people, what have I done unto thee.

Where shall the word be found, where will the word
Resound? Not here, there is not enough silence　　　160
Not on the sea or on the islands, not
On the mainland, in the desert or the rain land,
For those who walk in darkness
Both in the day time and in the night time
The right time and the right place are not here　　　165
No place of grace for those who avoid the face
No time to rejoice for those who walk among noise and deny the
　　　voice

Will the veiled sister pray for
Those who walk in darkness, who chose thee and oppose thee,
Those who are torn on the horn between season and season, time
　　　and time, between　　　170
Hour and hour, word and word, power and power, those who wait

325

In darkness? Will the veiled sister pray
For children at the gate
Who will not go away and cannot pray:
Pray for those who chose and oppose   175

O my people, what have I done unto thee.

Will the veiled sister between the slender
Yew trees pray for those who offend her
And are terrified and cannot surrender
And affirm before the world and deny between the rocks   180
In the last desert between the last blue rocks
The desert in the garden the garden in the desert
Of drouth, spitting from the mouth the withered apple-seed.

O my people.

VI

Although I do not hope to turn again   185
Although I do not hope
Although I do not hope to turn

Wavering between the profit and the loss
In this brief transit where the dreams cross
The dreamcrossed twilight between birth and dying   190
(Bless me father) though I do not wish to wish these things
From the wide window towards the granite shore
The white sails still fly seaward, seaward flying
Unbroken wings

And the lost heart stiffens and rejoices   195
In the lost lilac and the lost sea voices
And the weak spirit quickens to rebel
For the bent golden-rod and the lost sea smell
Quickens to recover
The cry of quail and the whirling plover   200
And the blind eye creates
The empty forms between the ivory gates
And smell renews the salt savour of the sandy earth

This is the time of tension between dying and birth
The place of solitude where three dreams cross   205
Between blue rocks
But when the voices shaken from the yew-tree drift away
Let the other yew be shaken and reply.
Blessed sister, holy mother, spirit of the fountain, spirit of the
        garden,

Suffer us not to mock ourselves with falsehood   210
Teach us to care and not to care
Teach us to sit still
Even among these rocks,
Our peace in His will
And even among these rocks   215
Sister, mother
And spirit of the river, spirit of the sea,
Suffer me not to be separated

And let my cry come unto Thee.

PIAZZA PIECE

JOHN CROWE RANSOM

—I am a gentleman in a dustcoat trying
To make you hear. Your ears are soft and small
And listen to an old man not at all,
They want the young men's whispering and sighing.
But see the roses on your trellis dying   5
And hear the spectral singing of the moon;
For I must have my lovely lady soon,
I am a gentleman in a dustcoat trying.

—I am a lady young in beauty waiting
Until my truelove comes, and then we kiss.   10
But what grey man among the vines is this
Whose words are dry and faint as in a dream?
Back from my trellis, Sir, before I scream!
I am a lady young in beauty waiting.

MEMORY GREEN

ARCHIBALD MacLEISH

Yes and when the warm unseasonable weather
Comes at the year's end of the next late year
And the southwest wind that smells of rain and summer
Strips the huge branches of their dying leaves,

And you at dusk along the Friedrichstrasse 5
Or you in Paris on the windy quay
Shuffle the shallow fallen leaves before you
Thinking the thoughts that like the grey clouds change,

You will not understand why suddenly sweetness
Fills in your heart nor the tears come to your eyes: 10
You will stand in the June-warm wind and the leaves falling:
When was it so before, you will say, With whom?

You will not remember this at all: you will stand there
Feeling the wind on your throat, the wind in your sleeves,
You will smell the dead leaves in the grass of a garden: 15
You will close your eyes: With whom, you will say,
                                                    Ah where?

EMPIRE BUILDERS

ARCHIBALD MaCLEISH

THE MUSEUM ATTENDANT:

This is *The Making of America in Five Panels:*

This is Mister Harriman making America:
Mister-Harriman-is-buying-the-Union-Pacific-at-Seventy:
The Santa Fé is shining on his hair.

This is Commodore Vanderbilt making America: 5
Mister-Vanderbilt-is-eliminating-the-short-interest-in-Hudson:
Observe the carving on the rocking chair.

This is J. P. Morgan making America:
(The Tennessee Coal is behind to the left of the Steel Company.)
Those in mauve are braces he is wearing. 10

This is Mister Mellon making America:
Mister-Mellon-is-represented-as-a-symbolical-figure-in-aluminum-
Strewing-bank-stocks-on-a-burnished-stair.

This is the Bruce is the Barton making America:
Mister-Barton-is-selling-us-Doctor's-Deliciousest-Dentifrice. 15
This is he in beige with the canary.

You have just beheld the Makers making America:
This is The Making of America in Five Panels:

America lies to the west-southwest of the switch-tower:
There is nothing to see of America but land.   20

THE ORIGINAL DOCUMENT UNDER THE PANEL PAINT:

"To Thos. Jefferson Esq. his obd't serv't
M. Lewis: captain: detached:
                                    Sir:

Having in mind your repeated commands in this matter,
And the worst half of it done and streams mapped,   25

And we here on the back of this beach beholding the
Other ocean—two years gone and the cold

Breaking with rain for the third spring since St. Louis,
The crows at the fishbones on the frozen dunes,

The first cranes going over from south north,   30
And the river down by a mark of the pole since the morning,

And time near to return, and a ship (Spanish)
Lying in for the salmon: and fearing chance or the

Drought or the Sioux should deprive you of these discoveries—
Therefore we send by sea in this writing.   35

Above the Platte there were long plains and a clay country:
Rim of the sky far off, grass under it,

Dung for the cook fires by the sulphur licks.
After that there were low hills and the sycamores,   40

And we poled up by the Great Bend in the skiffs:
The honey bees left us after the Osage River:

The wind was west in the evenings, and no dew and the
Morning Star larger and whiter than usual—

The winter rattling in the brittle haws.   45
The second year there was sage and the quail calling.

All that valley is good land by the river:
Three thousand miles and the clay cliffs and

Rue and beargrass by the water banks
And many birds and the brant going over and tracks of   50

brant—wild geese

329

Bear, elk, wolves, marten: the buffalo
Numberless so that the cloud of their dust covers them:

The antelope fording the fall creeks, and the mountains and
Grazing lands and the meadow lands and the ground

Sweet and open and well-drained.   55
                              We advise you to
Settle troops at the forks and to issue licenses:

Many men will have living on these lands.
There is wealth in the earth for them all and the wood standing

And wild birds on the water where they sleep.   60
There is stone in the hills for the towns of a great people . . ."

You have just beheld the Makers Making America:
They screwed her scrawny and gaunt with their seven-year
      panics:
They bought her back on their mortagages old-whore-cheap:

They fattened their bonds at her breasts till the thin blood ran
      from them.   65

Men have forgotten how full clear and deep
The Yellowstone moved on the gravel and the grass grew
When the land lay waiting for her westward people!

ANYONE LIVED IN A PRETTY
HOW TOWN

E. E. CUMMINGS

anyone lived in a pretty how town
(with up so floating many bells down)
spring summer autumn winter
he sang his didn't he danced his did.

Women and men(both little and small)   5
cared for anyone not at all
they sowed their isn't they reaped their same
sun moon stars rain

children guessed(but only a few
and down they forgot as up they grew   10
autumn winter spring summer)
that noone loved him more by more

when by now and tree by leaf
she laughed his joy she cried his grief
bird by snow and stir by still   15
anyone's any was all to her

someones married their everyones
laughed their cryings and did their dance
(sleep wake hope and then)they
said their nevers they slept their dream   20

stars rain sun moon
(and only the snow can begin to explain
how children are apt to forget to remember
with up so floating many bells down)

one day anyone died i guess   25
(and noone stooped to kiss his face)
busy folk buried them side by side
little by little and was by was

all by all and deep by deep
and more by more they dream their sleep   30
noone and anyone earth by april
wish by spirit and if by yes.

Women and men(both dong and ding)
summer autumn winter spring
reaped their sowing and went their came   35
sun moon stars rain

LOVE IS MORE THICKER
THAN FORGET

E. E. CUMMINGS

love is more thicker than forget
more thinner than recall

more seldom than a wave is wet
more frequent than to fail

it is most mad and moonly   5
and less it shall unbe
than all the sea which only
is deeper than the sea

love is less always than to win
less never than alive   10
less bigger than the least begin
less littler than forgive

it is most sane and sunly
and more it cannot die
than all the sky which only   15
is higher than the sky

LOVERS IN WINTER

ROBERT GRAVES

The posture of the tree
    Shows the prevailing wind;
And ours, long misery
    When you are long unkind.

But forward, look, we lean—   5
    Not backward as in doubt—
And still with branches green
    Ride our ill weather out.

THROUGH NIGHTMARE

ROBERT GRAVES

Never be disenchanted of
That place you sometimes dream yourself into,
Lying at large remove beyond all dream,
Or those you find there, though but seldom
In their company seated—   5

The untameable, the live, the gentle.
Have you not known them? Whom? They carry
Time looped so river-wise about their house
There's no way in by history's road
To name or number them.   10

In your sleepy eyes I read the journey
Of which disjointly you tell; which stirs
My loving admiration, that you should travel
Through nightmare to a lost and moated land,
Who are timorous by nature.

AT MELVILLE'S TOMB

HART CRANE

Often beneath the wave, wide from this ledge
The dice of drowned men's bones he saw bequeath
An embassy. Their numbers as he watched,
Beat on the dusty shore and were obscured.

And wrecks passed without sound of bells,   5
The calyx of death's bounty giving back
A scattered chapter, livid hieroglyph,
The portent wound in corridors of shells.

Then in the circuit calm of one vast coil,
Its lashings charmed and malice reconciled,   10
Frosted eyes there were that lifted altars;
And silent answers crept across the stars.

Compass, quadrant and sextant contrive
No farther tides . . . High in the azure steeps
Monody shall not wake the mariner.   15
This fabulous shadow only the sea keeps.

VOYAGES

HART CRANE

I.

Above the fresh ruffles of the surf
Bright striped urchins flay each other with sand.

They have contrived a conquest for shell shucks,
And their fingers crumble fragments of baked weed
Gaily digging and scattering.   5

And in answer to their treble interjections
The sun beats lightning on the waves,
The waves fold thunder on the sand;
And could they hear me I would tell them:

O brilliant kids, frisk with your dog,   10
Fondle your shells and sticks, bleached
By time and the elements; but there is a line
You must not cross nor ever trust beyond it
Spry cordage of your bodies to caresses
Too lichen-faithful from too wide a breast.   15
The bottom of the sea is cruel.

II.

And yet this great wink of eternity,
Of rimless floods, unfettered leewardings,
Samite sheeted and processioned where
Her undinal vast belly moonward bends,   20
Laughing the wrapt inflections of our love;

Take this Sea, whose diapason knells
On scrolls of silver snowy sentences,
The sceptred terror of whose sessions rends
As her demeanors motion well or ill,   25
All but the pieties of lovers' hands.

And onward, as bells off San Salvador
Salute the crocus lustres of the stars,
In these poinsettia meadows of her tides,—
Adagios of islands, O my Prodigal,   30
Complete the dark confessions her veins spell.

Mark how her turning shoulders wind the hours,
And hasten while her penniless rich palms
Pass superscription of bent foam and wave,—
Hasten, while they are true,—sleep, death, desire,   35
Close round one instant in one floating flower.

Bind us in time, O Seasons clear, and awe.
O minstrel galleons of Carib fire,
Bequeath us to no earthly shore until

Is answered in the vortex of our grave   40
The seal's wide spindrift gaze toward paradise.

III.

Infinite consanguinity it bears—
This tendered theme of you that light
Retrieves from sea plains where the sky
Resigns a breast that every wave enthrones;   45
While ribboned water lanes I wind
Are laved and scattered with no stroke
Wide from your side, whereto this hour
The sea lifts, also, reliquary hands.

And so, admitted through black swollen gates   50
That must arrest all distance otherwise,—
Past whirling pillars and lithe pediments,
Light wrestling there incessantly with light,
Star kissing star through wave on wave unto
Your body rocking!   55

              and where death, if shed,
Presumes no carnage, but this single change,—
Upon the steep floor flung from dawn to dawn
The silken skilled transmemberment of song;

Permit me voyage, love, into your hands . . .

BY THE ROAD TO THE AIR-BASE

YVOR WINTERS

The calloused grass lies hard
Against the cracking plain:
Life is a grayish stain;
The salt-marsh hems my yard.

Dry dikes rise hill on hill: 5
In sloughs of tidal slime
Shell-fish deposit lime,
Wild sea-fowl creep at will.

The highway, like a beach,
Turns whiter, shadowy, dry: 10
Loud, pale against the sky,
The bombing planes hold speech.

Yet fruit grows on the trees;
Here scholars pause to speak;
Through gardens bare and Greek,   15
I hear my neighbor's bees.

THE FURY OF AERIAL BOMBARDMENT

RICHARD EBERHART

You would think the fury of aerial bombardment
Would rouse God to relent; the infinite spaces
Are still silent. He looks on shock-pried faces.
History, even, does not know what is meant.

You would feel that after so many centuries   5
God would give man to repent; yet he can kill
As Cain could, but with multitudinous will,
No farther advanced than in his ancient furies.

Was man made stupid to see his own stupidity?
Is God by definition indifferent, beyond us all?   10
Is the eternal truth man's fighting soul
Wherein the Beast ravens in its own avidity?

Of Van Wettering I speak, and Averill,
Names on a list, whose faces I do not recall
But they are gone to early death, who late in school 15
Distinguished the belt feed lever from the belt holding pawl.

THE HORSE CHESTNUT TREE

RICHARD EBERHART

Boys in sporadic but tenacious droves
Come with sticks, as certainly as Autumn,
To assault the great horse chestnut tree.

There is a law governs their lawlessness.
Desire is in them for a shining amulet   5
And the best are those that are highest up.

They will not pick them easily from the ground.
With shrill arms they fling to the higher branches,
To hurry the work of nature for their pleasure.

I have seen them trooping down the street   10
Their pockets stuffed with chestnuts shucked, unshucked.
It is only evening keeps them from their wish.

Sometimes I run out in a kind of rage
To chase the boys away: I catch an arm,
Maybe, and laugh to think of being the lawgiver.   15

I was once such a young sprout myself
And fingered in my pocket the prize and trophy.
But still I moralize upon the day

And see that we, outlaws on God's property,
Fling out imagination beyond the skies,   20
Wishing a tangible good from the unknown.

And likewise death will drive us from the scene
With the great flowering world unbroken yet,
Which we held in idea, a little handful.

NOTHING IS GIVEN: WE MUST FIND OUR LAW

W. H. AUDEN

Nothing is given: we must find our law.
Great buildings jostle in the sun for domination;
Behind them stretch like sorry vegetation
The low recessive houses of the poor.

We have no destiny assigned us: 5
Nothing is certain but the body; we plan
To better ourselves; the hospitals alone remind us
Of the equality of man.

Children are really loved here, even by police:
They speak of years before the big were lonely,   10
And will be lost.

And only
The brass bands throbbing in the parks foretell
Some future reign of happiness and peace.

We learn to pity and rebel.

IN MEMORY OF W. B. YEATS
(d. Jan. 1939)

W. H. AUDEN

1

He disappeared in the dead of winter:
The brooks were frozen, the airports almost deserted,
And snow disfigured the public statues;
The mercury sank in the mouth of the dying day.
O all the instruments agree   5
The day of his death was a dark cold day.

Far from his illness
The wolves ran on through the evergreen forests,
The peasant river was untempted by the fashionable quays;
By mourning tongues   10
The death of the poet was kept from his poems.

But for him it was his last afternoon as himself,
An afternoon of nurses and rumours;
The provinces of his body revolted,
The squares of his mind were empty,   15
Silence invaded the suburbs,
The current of his feeling failed: he became his admirers.

Now he is scattered among a hundred cities
And wholly given over to unfamiliar affections;
To find his happiness in another kind of wood   20
And be punished under a foreign code of conscience.
The words of a dead man
Are modified in the guts of the living.

But in the importance and noise of tomorrow   24

When the brokers are roaring like beasts on the floor of the Bourse,
And the poor have the sufferings to which they are fairly ac-
    customed,
And each in the cell of himself is almost convinced of his freedom;
A few thousand will think of this day
As one thinks of a day when one did something slightly unusual.

O all the instruments agree   30
The day of his death was a dark cold day.

2

You were silly like us: your gift survived it all;
The parish of rich women, physical decay,
Yourself; mad Ireland hurt you into poetry.
Now Ireland has her madness and her weather still,   35
For poetry makes nothing happen: it survives
In the valley of its saying where executives
Would never want to tamper; it flows south
From ranches of isolation and the busy griefs,
Raw towns that we believe and die in; it survives,   40
A way of happening, a mouth.

3

Earth, receive an honoured guest;
William Yeats is laid to rest:
Let the Irish vessel lie
Emptied of its poetry.   45

Time that is intolerant
Of the brave and innocent,
And indifferent in a week
To a beautiful physique,

Worships language and forgives   50
Everyone by whom it lives;
Pardons cowardice, conceit,
Lays its honours at their feet.

Time that with this strange excuse
Pardoned Kipling and his views,   55
And will pardon Paul Claudel,
Pardons him for writing well.

In the nightmare of the dark
All the dogs of Europe bark,
And the living nations wait,   60
Each sequestered in its hate;

Intellectual disgrace
Stares from every human face,
And the seas of pity lie
Locked and frozen in each eye.   65

Follow, poet, follow right
To the bottom of the night,
With your unconstraining voice
Still persuade us to rejoice;

With the farming of a verse   70
Make a vineyard of the curse,
Sing of human unsuccess
In a rapture of distress;

In the deserts of the heart
Let the healing fountain start,   75
In the prison of his days
Teach the free man how to praise.

THE WAKING

THEODORE ROETHKE

I wake to sleep, and take my waking slow.
I feel my fate in what I cannot fear.
I learn by going where I have to go.

We think by feeling. What is there to know?
I hear my being dance from ear to ear.   5
I wake to sleep, and take my waking slow.

Of those so close beside me, which are you?
God bless the Ground! I shall walk softly there,
And learn by going where I have to go.

Light takes the Tree; but who can tell us how?   10
The lowly worm climbs up a winding stair;
I wake to sleep, and take my waking slow.

Great Nature has another thing to do
To you and me; so take the lively air,

And, lovely, learn by going where to go.   15
This shaking keeps me steady. I should know.
What falls away is always. And is near.
I wake to sleep, and take my waking slow.
I learn by going where I have to go.

RESPONSIBILITY: THE PILOTS WHO DESTROYED GERMANY IN THE SPRING OF 1945

STEPHEN SPENDER

I stood on a roof top and they wove their cage
Their murmuring, throbbing cage, in the air of blue crystal,
I saw them gleam above the town like diamond bolts
Conjoining invisible struts of wire,
Carrying through the sky their geometric cage   5
Woven by senses delicate as a shoal of flashing fish.

They went. They left a silence in our streets below
Which boys gone to schoolroom leave in their playground.
A silence of asphalt, of privet hedge, of staring wall.
In the glass emptied sky their diamonds had scratched   10
Long curving finest whitest lines.
These the day soon melted into satin ribbons
Falling over heaven's terraces near the golden sun.

Oh that April morning they carried my will
Exalted expanding singing in their aeriel cage.   15
They carried my will. They dropped it on a German town.
My will expanded and tall buildings fell down.

Then, when the ribbons faded and the sky forgot,
And April was concerned with building nests and being hot
I began to remember the lost names and faces.   20

Now I tie the ribbons torn down from those terraces
Around the most hidden image in my lines,
And my life, which never paid the price of their wounds,
Turns thoughts over and over like a propellor
Assumes their guilt, honours, repents, prays for them.

THE FISH

I caught a tremendous fish
and held him beside the boat
half out of water, with my hook
fast in a corner of his mouth.
He didn't fight.   5
He hadn't fought at all.
He hung a grunting weight,
battered and venerable
and homely. Here and there
his brown skin hung in strips   10
like ancient wall-paper,
and its pattern of darker brown
was like wall-paper:
shapes like full-blown roses
stained and lost through age.   15
He was speckled with barnacles,
fine rosettes of lime,
and infested
with tiny white sea-lice,
and underneath two or three   20
rags of green weed hung down.
While his gills were breathing in
the terrible oxygen
—the frightening gills,
fresh and crisp with blood,   25
that can cut so badly—
I thought of the coarse white flesh
packed in like feathers,
the big bones and the little bones,
the dramatic reds and blacks   30
of his shiny entrails,
and the pink swim-bladder
like a big peony.
I looked into his eyes
which were far larger than mine   35
but shallower, and yellowed,
the irises backed and packed
with tarnished tinfoil
seen through the lenses
of old scratched isinglass.   40
They shifted a little, but not
to return my stare.

342

—It was more like the tipping
of an object toward the light.
I admired his sullen face,   45
the mechanism of his jaw,
and then I saw
that from his lower lip
—if you could call it a lip—
grim, wet, and weapon-like,   50
hung five old pieces of fish-line,
or four and a wire leader
with the swivel still attached,
with all their five big hooks
grown firmly in his mouth.   55
A green line, frayed at the end
where he broke it, two heavier lines,
and a fine black thread
still crimped from the strain and snap
when it broke and he got away.   60
Like medals with their ribbons
frayed and wavering,
a five-haired beard of wisdom
trailing from his aching jaw.
I stared and stared   65
and victory filled up
the little rented boat,
from the pool of bilge
where oil had spread a rainbow
around the rusted engine   70
to the bailer rusted orange,
the sun-cracked thwarts,
the oarlocks on their strings,
the gunnels—until everything
was rainbow, rainbow, rainbow!   75
And I let the fish go.

THE ORIGIN OF BASEBALL

KENNETH PATCHEN

Someone had been walking in and out
Of the world without coming
To much decision about anything.
The sun seemed too hot most of the time.
There weren't enough birds around   5

And the hills had a silly look
When he got on top of one.
The girls in heaven, however, thought
Nothing of asking to see his watch
Like you would want someone to tell   10
A joke—'Time,' they'd say, 'what's
That mean—time?' laughing with the edges
Of their white mouths, like a flutter of paper
In a madhouse. And he'd stumble over
General Sherman or Elizabeth B.   15
Browning, muttering, 'Can't you keep
Your big wings out of the aisle?' But down
Again, there'd be millions of people without
Enough to eat and men with guns just
Standing there shooting each other.   20

So he wanted to throw something
And he picked up a baseball.

THE TWINS

KARL SHAPIRO

Likeness has made them animal and shy.
See how they turn their full gaze left and right,
Seeking the other, yet not moving close;
Nothing in their relationship is gross,
But soft, conspicuous, like giraffes. And why   5
Do they not speak except by sudden sight?

Sisters kiss freely and unsubtle friends
Wrestle like lovers; brothers loudly laugh:
These in a dreamier bondage dare not touch.
Each is the other's soul and hears too much   10
The heartbeat of the other; each apprehends
The sad duality and the imperfect half.

The one lay sick, the other wandered free,
But like a child to a small plot confined
Walked a short way and dumbly reappeared.   15
Is it not all-in-all of what they feared,
The single death, the obvious destiny
That maims the miracle their will designed?
For they go emptily from face to face,

Keeping the instinctive partnership of birth   20
A ponderous marriage and a sacred name;
Theirs is the pride of shouldering each the same
The old indignity of Esau's race
And Dromio's denouement of tragic-mirth.

WHO IN ONE LIFETIME

MURIEL RUKEYSER

Who in one lifetime sees all causes lost,
Herself dismayed and helpless, cities down,
Love made monotonous fear and the sad-faced
Inexorable armies and the falling plane,
Has sickness, sickness. Introspective and whole,   5
She knows how several madnesses are born,
Seeing the integrated never fighting well,
The flesh too vulnerable, the eyes tear-torn.

She finds a pre-surrender on all sides:
Treaty before the war, ritual impatience turn   10
The camps of ambush to chambers of imagery.
She holds belief in the world, she stays and hides
Life in her own defeat, stands, though her whole world burn,
A childless goddess of fertility.

THE FORCE THAT THROUGH THE GREEN FUSE DRIVES THE FLOWER

DYLAN THOMAS

The force that through the green fuse drives the flower
Drives my green age; that blasts the roots of trees
Is my destroyer.
And I am dumb to tell the crooked rose
My youth is bent by the same wintry fever.   5

Esau—sold birthright to brother Jacob
Dromios—twin servants in Shakespeare's
Comedy of Errors

The force that drives the water through the rocks
Drives my red blood; that dries the mouthing streams
Turns mine to wax.
And I am dumb to mouth unto my veins
How at the mountain spring the same mouth sucks.   10

The hand that whirls the water in the pool
Stirs the quicksand; that ropes the blowing wind
Mauls my shroud sail.
And I am dumb to tell the hanging man
How of my clay is made the hangman's lime.   15

The lips of time leech to the fountain head;
Love drips and gathers, but the fallen blood
Shall calm her sores.
And I am dumb to tell a weather's wind
How time has ticked a heaven round the stars.   20

And I am dumb to tell the lover's tomb
How at my sheet goes the same crooked worm.

DO NOT GO GENTLE INTO
THAT GOOD NIGHT

DYLAN THOMAS

Do not go gentle into that good night,
Old age should burn and rave at close of day;
Rage, rage against the dying of the light.

Though wise men at their end know dark is right,
Because their words have forked no lightning they   5
Do not go gentle into that good night.

Good men, the last wave by, crying how bright
Their frail deeds might have danced in a green bay,
Rage, rage against the dying of the light.

Wild men who caught and sang the sun in flight,   10
And learn, too late, they grieved it on its way,
Do not go gentle into that good night.

Grave men, near death, who see with blinding sight
Blind eyes could blaze like meteors and be gay,
Rage, rage against the dying of the light.   15

And you, my father, there on the sad height,
Curse, bless, me now with your fierce tears, I pray.
Do not go gentle into that good night.
Rage, rage against the dying of the light.

FERN HILL

DYLAN THOMAS

Now as I was young and easy under the apple boughs
About the lilting house and happy as the grass was green,
      The night above the dingle starry,
         Time let me hail and climb
      Golden in the heydays of his eyes,   5
And honoured among wagons I was prince of the apple towns
And once below a time I lordly had the trees and leaves
         Trail with daisies and barley
      Down the rivers of the windfall light.

And as I was green and carefree, famous among the barns 10
About the happy yard and singing as the farm was home,

In the sun that is young once only,
    Time let me play and be
    Golden in the mercy of his means,   14
And green and golden I was huntsman and herdsman, the calves
Sang to my horn, the foxes on the hills barked clear and cold,
    And the sabbath rang slowly
    In the pebbles of the holy streams.

All the sun long it was running, it was lovely, the hay-
Fields high as the house, the tunes from the chimneys, it was air
    And playing, lovely and watery   21
        And fire green as grass.
    And nightly under the simple stars
As I rode to sleep the owls were bearing the farm away,
All the moon long I heard, blessed among stables, the night-jars
    Flying with the ricks, and the horses   26
        Flashing into the dark.

And then to awake, and the farm, like a wanderer white
With the dew, come back, the cock on his shoulder: it was all
    Shining, it was Adam and maiden,   30
        The sky gathered again
    And the sun grew round that very day.
So it must have been after the birth of the simple light
In the first, spinning place, the spellbound horses walking warm
    Out of the whinnying green stable   35
        On to the fields of praise.

And honoured among foxes and pheasants by the gay house
Under the new made clouds and happy as the heart was long,
    In the sun born over and over,
        I ran my heedless ways,   40
    My wishes raced through the house-high hay
And nothing I cared, at my sky blue trades, that time allows
In all his tuneful turning so few and such morning songs
    Before the children green and golden
        Follow him out of grace,   45

Nothing I cared, in the lamb white days, that time would take me
Up to the swallow thronged loft by the shadow of my hand,
    In the moon that is always rising,
        Nor that riding to sleep
    I should hear him fly with the high fields   50
And wake to the farm forever fled from the childless land.
Oh as I was young and easy in the mercy of his means,
    Time held me green and dying
    Though I sang in my chains like the sea.

IN MY CRAFT OR SULLEN ART

DYLAN THOMAS

In my craft or sullen art
Exercised in the still night
When only the moon rages
And the lovers lie abed
With all their griefs in their arms,   5
I labour by singing light
Not for ambition or bread
Or the strut and trade of charms
On the ivory stages
But for the common wages   10
Of their most secret heart.
Not for the proud man apart
From the raging moon I write
On these spindrift pages
Not for the towering dead   15
With their nightingales and psalms
But for the lovers, their arms
Round the griefs of the ages,
Who pay no praise or wages
Nor heed my craft or art.

COLLOQUY IN BLACK ROCK

ROBERT LOWELL

Here the jack-hammer jabs into the ocean;
My heart, you race and stagger and demand
More blood-gangs for your nigger-brass percussions,
Till I, the stunned machine of your devotion,
Clanging upon this cymbal of a hand,   5
Am rattled screw and footloose. All discussions

End in the mud-flat detritus of death.
My heart, beat faster, faster. In Black Mud
Hungarian workmen give their blood
For the martyre Stephen, who was stoned to death.   10

Black Rock Harbor in Bridgeport, Conn.,
with large Hungarian population.
Martyr Stephen stoned to death 32 A.D.,
St. Stephen 1000–1038 introduced Chris-
tianity to Hungary.

Black Mud, a name to conjure with: O mud
For watermelons gutted to the crust,
Mud for the mole-tide harbor, mud for mouse,
Mud for the armored Diesel fishing tubs that thud
A year and a day to wind and tide; the dust   15
Is on this skipping heart that shakes my house,

House of our Savior who was hanged till death.
My heart, beat faster, faster. In Black Mud
Stephen the martyre was broken down to blood:
Our ransom is the rubble of his death.   20

Christ walks on the black water. In Black Mud
Darts the kingfisher. On Corpus Christi, heart,
Over the drum-beat of St. Stephen's choir
I hear him, *Stupor Mundi,* and the mud
Flies from his hunching wings and beak—my heart,   25
The blue kingfisher dives on you in fire.

CEREMONY

RICHARD WILBUR

A striped blouse in a clearing by Bazille
Is, you may say, a patroness of boughs
Too queenly kind toward nature to be kin.
But ceremony never did conceal,
Save to the silly eye, which all allows,   5
How much we are the woods we wander in.

Let her be some Sabrina fresh from stream,
Lucent as shallows slowed by wading sun,
Bedded on fern, the flowers' cynosure:
Then nymph and wood must nod and strive to dream   10
That she is airy earth, the trees, undone,
Must ape her languor natural and pure.

Ho-hum. I am for wit and wakefulness,
And love this feigning lady by Bazille.
What's lightly hid is deepest understood,   15
And when with social smile and formal dress
She teaches leaves to curtsey and quadrille,
I think there are most tigers in the wood.

ALL THESE BIRDS

RICHARD WILBUR

Agreed that all these birds,
Hawk or heavenly lark or heard-of nightingale,
Perform upon the kite-strings of our sight
In a false distance, that the day and night
Are full of wingèd words   5
                                gone rather stale,
That nothing is so worn
As Philomel's bosom-thorn,

That it is, in fact, the male
Nightingale which sings, and that all these creatures wear   10
Invisible armor such as Hébert beheld
His water-ousel through, as, wrapped or shelled
In a clear bellying veil
                                or bubble of air,
It bucked the flood to feed   15
At the stream-bottom. Agreed

That the sky is a vast claire
In which the gull, despite appearances, is not
Less claustral than the oyster in its beak
And dives like nothing human; that we seek   20
Vainly to know the heron
                                (but can plot
What angle of the light
Provokes its northern flight).

Let them be polyglot   25
And wordless then, those boughs that spoke with Solomon
In Hebrew canticles, and made him wise;
And let a clear and bitter wind arise
To storm into the hotbeds
                                of the sun,   30
And there, beyond a doubt,
Batter the Phoenix out.

Let us, with glass or gun,
Watch (from our clever blinds) the monsters of the sky
Dwindle to habit, habitat, and song,   35
And tell the imagination it is wrong
Till, lest it be undone,
                                it spin a lie

So fresh, so pure, so rare
As to possess the air.   40

Why should it be more shy
Than chimney-nesting storks, or sparrows on a wall?
Oh, let it climb wherever it can cling
Like some great trumpet-vine, a natural thing
To which all birds that fly   45
                    come natural.
Come, stranger, sister, dove:
Put on the reins of love.

THE NEGRO SPEAKS OF RIVERS

LANGSTON HUGHES

I've known rivers:
I've known rivers ancient as the world and older than the flow of
    human blood in human veins.

My soul has grown deep like the rivers.

I bathed in the Euphrates when dawns were young.
I built my hut near the Congo and it lulled me to sleep.   5
I looked upon the Nile and raised the pyramids above it.
I heard the singing of the Mississippi when Abe Lincoln went down
    to New Orleans, and I've seen its muddy bosom turn all golden
    in the sunset.

I've known rivers:
Ancient, dusky rivers.

My soul has grown deep like the rivers.   10

LA TORRE

CHARLES OLSON

The tower is broken, the house
where the head was used to lift,

where awe was
And the hands

      (It is broken!   5
      And the sounds
      are sweet, the air
      acrid, in the night fear
      is fragrant

             The end of something has a satisfaction.   10
             When the structures go, light
             comes through

To begin again. Lightning
is an axe, transfer
of force subject to object is   15
order: destroy!

      To destroy
      is to start again, is a factor of
      sun, fire is
      when the sun is out, dowsed   20

                  (To cause the jaws to grind
                  before the nostrils flare
                  to let breath in

Stand clear! Here
it comes down and with it the heart has   25
what was, what was
we do lament

      Let him who knows not how to pray
      go to sea

             Where there are no walls   30
             there are no laws, forms, sounds, odors
             to grab hold of

Let the tower fall!
Where space is born
man has a beach to ground on   35

      We have taken too little note of this:
      the sound of a hammer on a nail can be as clear as
      the blood a knife can make spurt from a round taut belly

2
In the laden air

we are no longer cold.   40
Birds spring up, and on the fragrant sea
rafts come toward us lashed of wreckage and young tree.
They bring the quarried stuff we need to try this new-found strength.
It will take new stone, new tufa, to finish off this rising tower.

MY MOTHER WOULD BE A FALCONRESS

ROBERT DUNCAN

My mother would be a falconress.
And I, her gay falcon treading her wrist,
would fly to bring back
from the blue of the sky to her, bleeding, a prize,
where I dream in my little hood with many bells   5
jangling when I'd turn my head.

My mother would be a falconress,
and she sends me as far as her will goes.
She lets me ride to the end of her curb
where I fall back in anguish.   10
I dread that she will cast me away,
for I fall, I mis-take, I fail in her mission.

She would bring down the little birds.
And I would bring down the little birds.
When will she let me bring down the little birds,   15
pierced from their flight with their necks broken,
their heads like flowers limp from the stem?

I tread my mother's wrist and would draw blood.
Behind the little hood my eyes are hooded.
I have gone back into my hooded silence,   20
talking to myself and dropping off to sleep.

For she has muffled my dreams in the hood she has made me,
sewn round with bells, jangling when I move.
She rides with her little falcon upon her wrist.
She uses a barb that brings me to cower.   25
She sends me abroad to try my wings
and I come back to her.   I would bring down
the little birds to her
I may not tear into, I must bring back perfectly.

I tear at her wrist with my beak to draw blood,   30
and her eye holds me, anguisht, terrifying.
She draws a limit to my flight.
Never beyond my sight, she says.
She trains me to fetch and to limit myself in fetching.
She rewards me with meat for my dinner.   35
But I must never eat what she sends me to bring her.

Yet it would have been beautiful, if she would have carried me,
always, in a little hood with the bells ringing,
at her wrist, and her riding
to the great falcon hunt, and me   40
flying up to the curb of my heart from her heart
to bring down the skylark from the blue to her feet,
straining, and then released for the flight.

My mother would be a falconress,
and I her gerfalcon, raised at her will,   45
from her wrist sent flying, as if I were her own
pride, as if her pride
knew no limits, as if her mind
sought in me flight beyond the horizon.

Ah, but high, high in the air I flew.   50
And far, far beyond the curb of her will,
were the blue hills where the falcons nest.
And then I saw west to the dying sun—
it seemed my human soul went down in flames.

I tore at her wrist, at the hold she had for me,   55
until the blood ran hot and I heard her cry out,
far, far beyond the curb of her will

to horizons of stars beyond the ringing hills of the world
    where the falcons nest
I saw, and I tore at her wrist with my savage beak.
I flew, as if sight flew from the anguish in her eye beyond
    her sight,   60
sent from my striking loose, from the cruel strike at her wrist,
striking out from the blood to be free of her.

My mother would be a falconress,
and even now, years after this,
when the wounds I left her had surely heald,   65
and the woman is dead,
her fierce eyes closed, and if her heart
were broken, it is stilld

I would be a falcon and go free.
I tread her wrist and wear the hood,   70
talking to myself, and would draw blood.

READING YEATS
(PICTURES OF THE GONE WORLD / #26)

LAWRENCE FERLINGHETTI

Reading Yeats I do not think
                                                of Ireland
but of midsummer New York
                                and of myself back then
reading that copy I found   5
                                on the Thirdavenue El

    the El
                        with its flyhung fans
    and its signs reading
                        SPITTING IS FORBIDDEN   10

    the El
                        careening thru its thirdstory world
    with its thirdstory people
                                in their thirdstory doors
    looking as if they had never heard   15
                                of the ground

    an old dame
                        watering her plant
    or a joker in a straw
                        putting a stickpin in his peppermint tie   20
    and looking just like he had nowhere to go
                                but coneyisland

    or an undershirted guy
                                rocking in his rocker
    watching the El pass by   25
                        as if he expected it to be different
        each time

356

Reading Yeats I do not think
                              of Arcady
    and of its woods which Yeats thought dead   30
                              I think instead
        of all the gone faces
                              getting off at midtown places
        with their hats and their jobs
        and of that lost book I had   35
                    with its blue cover and its white inside
    where a pencilhand had written
                    HORSEMAN, PASS BY!

THE SHARK'S PARLOR

JAMES DICKEY

Memory: I can take my head and strike it on a wall   on
    Cumberland Island
Where the night tide came crawling under the stairs   came up
    the first
Two or three steps   and the cottage stood on poles all night
With the sea sprawled under it   as we dreamed of the great
    fin circling
Under the bedroom floor. In daylight there was my first brassy   5
    taste of beer
And Payton Ford and I came back from the Glynn County
    slaughterhouse
With a bucket of entrails and blood. We tied one end of a hawser
To a spindling porch pillar and rowed straight out of the house
Three hundred yards into the vast front yard of windless blue water
The rope outslithering its coil   the two-gallon jug stoppered   10
    and sealed
With wax   and a ten-foot chain leader   a drop-forged
    shark hook nestling.
We cast our blood on the waters   the land blood easily passing
For sea blood   and we sat in it for a moment with the stain
    spreading
Out from the boat   sat in a new radiance   in the pond of
    blood in the sea
Waiting for fins   waiting to spill our guts also in the glowing   15
    water.
We dumped the bucket, and baited the hook with a run-over
    collie pup. The jug
Bobbed, trying to shake off the sun as a dog would shake off the sea.

We rowed to the house   feeling the same water lift the boat
   a new way,
All the time seeing where we lived rise and dip with the oars.
We tied up and sat down in rocking chairs, one eye or the other   20
   responding
To the blue-eye wink of the jug. Payton got us a beer and we sat

All morning sat there with blood on our minds   the red mark out
In the harbor slowly failing us   then   the house groaned   the
   rope
Sprang out of the water   splinters flew   we leapt from our chairs
And grabbed the rope   hauled   did nothing   the house
   coming subtly   25
Apart   all around us   underfoot   boards beginning to sparkle
   like sand
With the glinting of the bright hidden parts of ten-year-old nails
Pulling out   the tarred poles we slept propped-up on   leaning
   to sea
As in land wind   crabs scuttling from under the floor   as
   we took turns about
Two more porch pillars   and looked out and saw   something
   a fish-flash   30
An almighty fin in trouble   a moiling of secret forces   a false
   start
Of water   a round wave growing: in the whole of Cumberland
   Sound the one ripple.
Payton took off without a word   I could not hold him either

But clung to the rope anyway: it was the whole house bending
Its nails that held whatever it was   coming in a little and   35
   like a fool
I took up the slack on my wrist. The rope drew gently   jerked
   I lifted
Clean off the porch and hit the water   the same water it was in
I felt in blue blazing terror at the bottom of the stairs and scrambled
Back up looking desperately into the human house as deeply
   as I could
Stopping my gaze before it went out the wire screen of the   40
   back door
Stopped it on the thistled rattan   the rugs I lay on and read
On my mother's sewing basket with next winter's socks spilling
   from it
The flimsy vacation furniture   a bucktoothed picture of myself.
Payton came back with three men from a filling station   and
   glanced at me

Dripping water   inexplicable   then we all grabbed hold like a
    tug-of-war.   45

We were gaining a little   from us a cry went up   from
    everywhere
People came running. Behind us the house filled with men and boys.
On the third step from the sea I took my place   looking down
    the rope
Going into the ocean, humming and shaking off drops. A houseful
Of people put their backs into it   going up the steps from me   50
Into the living room   through the kitchen   down the back stairs
Up and over a hill of sand   across a dust road   and onto a
    raised field
Of dunes   we were gaining   the rope in my hands began
    to be wet
With deeper water   all other haulers retreated through the house
But Payton and I on the stairs   drawing hand over hand on   55
    our blood
Drawing into existence by the nose   a huge body   becoming
A hammerhead   rolling in beery shallows   and I began to let up
But the rope still strained behind me   the town had gone
Pulling-mad in our house: far away in a field of sand they struggled
They had turned their backs on the sea   bent double   60
    some on their knees
The rope over their shoulders like a bag of gold   they strove for the
    ideal
Esso station across the scorched meadow   with the distant fish
    coming up
The front stairs   the sagging boards   still coming in   up
    taking
Another step   toward the empty house   where the rope stood
    straining
By itself through the rooms   in the middle of the air. "Pass   65
    the word,"
Payton said, and I screamed it: "Let up, good God, let up!"   to no
    one there.
The shark flopped on the porch, grating with salt-sand   driving
    back in
The nails he had pulled out   coughing chunks of his formless blood.
The screen door banged and tore off   he scrambled on his tail
    slid
Curved   did a thing from another world   and was out of his
    element and in   70
Our vacation paradise   cutting all four legs from under the dinner
    table

With one deep-water move   he unwove the rugs in a moment
    throwing pints
Of blood over everything we owned   knocked the buck teeth out of
    my picture
His odd head full of crushed jelly-glass splinters and radio tubes
    thrashing
Among the pages of fan magazines   all the movie stars drenched in
    sea-blood.   75
Each time we thought he was dead   he struggled back and
    smashed
One more thing   in all coming back to die   three or four more
    times after death.
At last we got him out   log-rolling him   greasing his sandpaper
    skin
With lard to slide him   pulling on his chained lips as the tide came
Tumbled him down the steps as the first night wave went under   80
    the floor.
He drifted off   head back   belly white as the moon. What could
    I do but buy
That house   for the one black mark still there   against death
    a forehead-
toucher in the room he circles beneath   and has been invited to
    wreck?
Blood hard as iron on the wall   black with time   still bloodlike
Can be touched whenever the brow is drunk enough: all
    changes: Memory: 85
Something like three-dimensional dancing in the limbs   with age
Feeling more in two worlds than one   in all worlds the growing
    encounters.

LIVING

DENISE LEVERTOV

The fire in leaf and grass
so green it seems
each summer the last summer.

The wind blowing, the leaves
shivering in the sun,   5
each day the last day.

A red salamander
so cold and so
easy to catch, dreamily

360

moves his delicate feet   10
and long tail. I hold
my hand open for him to go.

Each minute the last minute.

THE WINGS

DENISE LEVERTOV

Something hangs in back of me,
I can't see it, can't move it.

I know it's black,
a hump on my back.

It's heavy. You   5
can't see it.

What's in it? Don't tell me
you don't know. It's

what you told me about—
black   10

inimical power, cold
whirling out of it and

around me and
sweeping you flat.

But what if,   15
like a camel, it's

pure energy I store,
and carry humped and heavy?

Not black, not
that terror, stupidity   20

of cold rage; or black
only for being pent there?

What if released in air
it became a white

source of light, a fountain   25
of light? Could all that weight

be the power of flight?
Look inward: see me

with embryo wings, one
feathered in soot, the other   30

blazing ciliations of ember, pale
flare-pinions. Well—

could I go
on one wing,

the white one?   35

AT THE BOMB TESTING SITE

WILLIAM STAFFORD

At noon in the desert a panting lizard
waited for history, its elbows tense,
watching the curve of a particular road
as if something might happen.

It was looking for something farther off   5
than people could see, an important scene
acted in stone for little selves
at the flute end of consequences.

There was just a continent without much on it
under a sky that never cared less.   10
Ready for a change, the elbows waited.
The hands gripped hard on the desert.

WALKING WEST

WILLIAM STAFFORD

Anyone with quiet pace who
walks a gray road in the West

may hear a badger underground where
in deep flint another time is

Caught by flint and held forever,   5
the quiet pace of God stopped still.
Anyone who listens walks on
time that dogs him single file,

To mountains that are far from people,
the face of the land gone gray like flint.   10
Badgers dig their little lives there,
quiet-paced the land lies gaunt,

The railroad dies by a yellow depot,
town falls away toward a muddy creek.
Badger-gray the sod goes under   15
a river of wind, a hawk on a stick.

TRAVELING THROUGH THE DARK

WILLIAM STAFFORD

Traveling through the dark I found a deer
dead on the edge of the Wilson River road.
It is usually best to roll them into the canyon:
that road is narrow; to swerve might make more dead.

By glow of the tail-light I stumbled back of the car   5
and stood by the heap, a doe, a recent killing;
she had stiffened already, almost cold.
I dragged her off; she was large in the belly.

My fingers touching her side brought me the reason—
her side was warm; her fawn lay there waiting,   10
alive, still, never to be born.
Beside that mountain road I hesitated.

The car aimed ahead its lowered parking lights;
under the hood purred the steady engine.
I stood in the glare of the warm exhaust turning red;   15
around our group I could hear the wilderness listen.

I thought hard for us all—my only swerving—,
then pushed her over the edge into the river.

A READING OF HISTORY

LEONARD NATHAN

The good guys lost the city first;
The bad guys never should have won that battle,
But did and turned the good guys out to starve
Or butchered them as they had butchered cattle.

The bad guys lost the city next;   5
The worse guys swarmed the walls from land and sea
Till heroes of evil parcelled out the widows.
O then how good the bad guys seemed to be!

The worse guys lost the city next;
Shaggy brutes slashed in from west and east   10
To drag them from their temples by the hair,
For worse guys were too gentle for this beast.

Yet who but this beast assembled later,
Three to a corner, stricken by whispered fact
That powers of darkness hovered off the coast   15
And nothing could prevent their being sacked.

The future plainly belongs to evil;
To good, the past; and for the present—well,
Good guys and bad guys mingle in the market;
Business was never better. Time will tell.   20

HARDWEED PATH GOING

A. R. AMMONS

          Every evening, down into the hardweed
going,
the slop bucket heavy, held-out, wire handle
freezing in the hand, put it down a minute, the jerky
smooth unspilling levelness of the knees,
          meditation of a bucket rim,
lest the wheat meal,   5
floating on clear greasewater, spill,
down the grown-up path:

          don't forget to slop the hogs,
          feed the chickens,

                    water the mule,   10
                    cut the kindling,
                    build the fire,
                    call up the cow:

                    supper is over, it's starting to get
dark early,
better get the scraps together, mix a little meal in,   15
nothing but swill.

                    The dead-purple woods hover on the west.
I know those woods.
Under the tall, ceiling-solid pines, beyond the edge of
field and brush, where the wild myrtle grows,
                    I let my jo-reet loose.
A jo-reet is a bird. Nine weeks of summer he   20
sat on the well bench in a screened box,
a stick inside to walk on,
                    "jo-reet," he said, "jo-reet."
                    and I
would come up to the well and draw the bucket down
deep into the cold place where red and white marbled
clay oozed the purest water, water celebrated   25
throughout the county:
                    "Grits all gone?"
                    "jo-reet."
Throw a dipper of cold water on him. Reddish-black
flutter.
                    "reet, reet, reet!"   30

                    Better turn him loose before
cold weather comes on.
                    Doom caving in
                    inside
                    any pleasure, pure
                    attachment
                    of love.

Beyond the wild myrtle away from cats I turned him loose
and his eye asked me what to do, where to go;   35
he hopped around, scratched a little, but looked up at me.
Don't look at me. Winter is coming.
Disappear in the bushes. I'm tired of you and will
be alone hereafter. I will go dry in my well.
                    I will turn still.
Go south. Grits is not available in any natural form.   40
Look under leaves, try mushy logs, the floors of pinywoods.
South into the dominion of bugs.

They're good woods.
But lay me out if a mourning dove far off in the dusky pines
    starts.

        Down the hardweed path going,
leaning, balancing, away from the bucket, to   45
Sparkle, my favorite hog, sparse, fine black hair,
grunted while feeding if rubbed,
scratched against the hair, or if talked to gently:
got the bottom of the slop bucket:
            "Sparkle   50
            "You hungry?
            "Hungry, girly?"
blowing, bubbling in the trough.

        Waiting for the first freeze:
"Think it's going to freeze tonight?" say the neighbors,   55
the neighbors, going by.

        Hog-killing.

Sparkle, when the axe tomorrow morning falls
and the rush is made to open your throat,
I will sing, watching dry-eyed as a man, sing my   60
        love for you in the tender feedings.

        She's nothing but a hog, boy.

Bleed out, Sparkle, the moon-chilled bleaches
        of your body hanging upside-down
hardening through the mind and night of the first freeze. 65

FANCY

ROBERT CREELEY

Do you know what
the truth is,
what's rightly
or wrongly said,

what is wiseness,   5
or rightness, what
wrong, or well-
done if it is,

or is not, done.
I thought.   10
I thought and
thought and thought.

In a place
I was sitting,
and there   15
it was, a little

faint thing
hardly felt, a
kind of small
nothing.   20

THE RYTHM

ROBERT CREELEY

It is all a rhythm,
from the shutting
door, to the window
opening,

the seasons, the sun's   5
light, the moon,
the oceans, the
growing of things,

the mind in men
personal, recurring   10
in them again,
thinking the end

is not the end, the
time returning,
themselves dead, but   15
someone else coming.

If in death I am dead,
then in life also
dying, dying . . .
And the women cry and die.   20

The little children
grow only to old men.
The grass dries,
the force goes.

But is met by another   25
returning, oh not mine,
not mine, and
in turn dies.

The rhythm which projects
from itself continuity   30
bending all to its force
from window to door,
from ceiling to floor,
light at the opening,
dark at the closing.   35

THE SHAME

ROBERT CREELEY

What will
the shame be,
what
cost to pay.

We are walking   5
in a wood,
wood of stones,
boulders for trees.

The sky
is a black   10
sudden cloud,
a sun.

Speak
to me, say
what things   15
were forgotten.

SUNFLOWER SUTRA

I walked on the banks of the tincan banana dock and sat down
　　under the huge shade of a Southern Pacific locomotive to
　　look at the sunset over the box house hills and cry.
Jack Kerouac sat beside me on a busted rusty iron pole,
　　companion, we thought the same thoughts of the soul,　5
　　bleak and blue and sad-eyed, surrounded by the gnarled
　　steel roots of trees of machinery.
The oily water on the river mirrored the red sky, sun sank on top
　　of final Frisco peaks, no fish in that stream, no hermit in
　　those mounts, just ourselves rheumy-eyed and hungover　10
　　like old bums on the riverbank, tired and wily.
Look at the Sunflower, he said, there was a dead gray shadow
　　against the sky, big as a man, sitting dry on top of a pile of
　　ancient sawdust—
—I rushed up enchanted—it was my first sunflower, memories　15
　　of Blake—my visions—Harlem
and Hells of the Eastern rivers, bridges clanking, Joes Greasy
　　Sandwiches, dead baby carriages, black treadless tires
　　forgotten and unretreaded, the poem of the riverbank,
　　condoms & pots, steel knives, nothing stainless, only the　20
　　dank muck and the razor sharp artifacts passing into the
　　past--
and the gray Sunflower poised against the sunset, crackly bleak
　　and dusty with the smut and smog and smoke of olden
　　locomotives in its eye—　　　　　　　　　　　　　　　25
corolla of bleary spikes pushed down and broken like a battered
　　crown, seeds fallen out of its face, soon-to-be-toothless
　　mouth of sunny air, sunrays obliterated on its hairy head
　　like a dried wire spiderweb,
leaves stuck out like arms out of the stem, gestures from the　30
　　sawdust root, broke pieces of plaster fallen out of the black
　　twigs, a dead fly in its ear,
Unholy battered old thing you were, my sunflower O my soul,
　　I loved you then!
The grime was no man's grime but death and human loco-　35
　　motives,
all that dress of dust, that veil of darkened railroad skin, that
　　smog of cheek, that eyelid of black mis'ry, that sooty hand
　　or phallus or protuberance of artificial worse-than-dirt—
　　industrial—modern—all that civilization spotting your　40
　　crazy golden crown—

and those blear thoughts of death and dusty loveless eyes and ends
and withered roots below, in the home-pile of sand and
sawdust, rubber dollar bills, skin of machinery, the guts
and innards of the weeping coughing car, the empty lonely 45
tincans with their rusty tongues alack, what more could I
name, the smoked ashes of some cock cigar, the c . . . s of
wheelbarrows and the milky breasts of cars, wornout asses
out of chairs & sphincters of dynamos—all these
entangled in your mummied roots—and you there standing before 50
me in the sunset, all your glory in your form!
A perfect beauty of a sunflower! a perfect excellent lovely
sunflower existence! a sweet natural eye to the new hip
moon, woke up alive and excited grasping in the sunset
shadow sunrise golden monthly breeze! 55
How many flies buzzed round you innocent of your grime, while
you cursed the heavens of the railroad and your flower
soul?
Poor dead flower? when did you forget you were a flower? when
did you look at your skin and decide you were an impotent
dirty old locomotive? the ghost of a locomotive? the 60
specter and shade of a once powerful mad American
locomotive?
You were never no locomotive, Sunflower, you were a sunflower!
And you Locomotive, you are a locomotive, forget me not!
So I grabbed up the skeleton thick sunflower and stuck it at my 65
side like a scepter,
and deliver my sermon to my soul, and Jack's soul too, and anyone
who'll listen,
—We're not our skin of grime, we're not our dread bleak dusty
imageless locomotive, we're all beautiful golden sun- 70
flowers inside, we're blessed by our own seed & golden
hairy naked accomplishment-bodies growing into mad
black formal sunflowers in the sunset, spied on by our
eyes under the shadow of the mad locomotive riverbank
sunset Frisco hilly tincan evening sitdown vision. 75

SUNLIGHT

THOM GUNN

Some things, by their affinity light's token,
Are more than shown: steel glitters from a track;
Small glinting scoops, after a wave has broken,
Dimple the water in its draining back;

Water, glass, metal, match light in their raptures,   5
Flashing their many answers to the one.
What captures light belongs to what it captures:
The whole side of a world facing the sun,

Re-turned to woo the original perfection,
Giving itself to what created it,   10
And wearing green in sign of its subjection.
It is as if the sun were infinite.

But angry flaws are swallowed by the distance;
It varies, moves, its concentrated fires
Are slowly dying—the image of persistence   15
Is an image, only, of our own desires:

Desires and knowledge touch without relating.
The system of which sun and we are part
Is both imperfect and deteriorating.
And yet the sun outlasts us at the heart.   20

Great seedbed, yellow center of the flower,
Flower on its own, without a root or stem,
Giving all color and all shape their power,
Still recreating in defining them,

Enable us, altering like you, to enter   25
Your passionless love, impartial but intense,
And kindle in acceptance round your center,
Petals of light lost in your innocence.

BULLFROG

TED HUGHES

With their lithe long strong legs
Some frogs are able
To thump upon double-
Bass strings though pond-water deadens and clogs.

But you, bullfrog, you pump out   5
Whole fogs full of horn—a threat
As of a liner looming. True
That, first hearing you
Disgorging your gouts of darkness like a wounded god,

Not utterly fantastical I expected   10
(As in some antique tale depicted)
A broken-down bull up to its belly in mud,
Sucking black swamp up, belching out black cloud

And a squall of gudgeon and lilies.
                                                A surprise,   15
To see you, a boy's prize,
No bigger than a rat—all dumb silence
In your little old woman hands.

HAWK ROOSTING

TED HUGHES

I sit in the top of the wood, my eyes closed.
Inaction, no falsifying dream
Between my hooked head and hooked feet:
Or in sleep rehearse perfect kills and eat.

The convenience of the high trees!   5
The air's buoyancy and the sun's ray
Are of advantage to me;
And the earth's face upward for my inspection.

My feet are locked upon the rough bark.
It took the whole of Creation   10
To produce my foot, my each feather:
Now I hold Creation in my foot

Or fly up, and revolve it all slowly—
I kill where I please because it is all mine.
There is no sophistry in my body: 15
My manners are tearing off heads—

The allotment of death.
For the one path of my flight is direct
Through the bones of the living.
No arguments assert my right: 20

The sun is behind me.
Nothing has changed since I began.
My eye has permitted no change.
I am going to keep things like this.

AMITABHA'S VOW

"If, after obtaining Buddhahood, anyone in my land
  gets tossed in jail on a vagrancy rap, may I
  not attain highest perfect enlightenment.

  wild geese in the orchard
  frost on the new grass   5

"If, after obtaining Buddhahood, anyone in my land
  loses a finger coupling boxcars, may I
  not attain highest perfect enlightenment.

  mare's eye flutters
  jerked by the lead-rope   10
  stone-bright shoes flick back
  ankles trembling: down steep rock

"If, after obtaining Buddhahood, anyone in my land
  can't get a ride hitch-hiking all directions, may I
  not attain highest perfect enlightenment.   15

  wet rocks buzzing
  rain and thunder southwest
  hair, beard, tingle
  wind whips bare legs
  we should go back   20
  we don't

ALGERIEN REVEUR

"In time,
When earth has become a paradise, it will be
A paradise full of assassins."

Wallace Stevens

They have been asking me
for seven days

—*Who blew up the road?*

373

I ask *what road* and lose a tooth.
I ask *when road* and lose an eye.   5
I ask *why me* and cannot determine
the loss.

For seven days they have been
unmaking me

—Who blew up the road?   10

Awed by their stone masks, pressed
to hemorrhage by their premonitions, the
flux of their certainty (o god, what
republicans), I construct a road in the
drained cavern of my mind. I put   15
saboteurs with jeweled beards and scarless
backs to work on its foundation. I try
to discover their names.

Work faster, shadows:
in the name of the tongueless prophet   20
kiss off the fuse—
surrender yourselves at once.

Until I answer questions out of my fantasy
as sanely as they ask
out of their dream.   25

But dialectic flags:
flesh and bone going, eyes and teeth
a gruel, after enough of questioning
I become disinterested—
and they are left to frown   30
above a huddle of bloody clothes,
to quarrel about miscalculated stress.
Until, beyond the garbled ashes
still warm and shuddering
in the wake of my escape,   35
a grand thug in blinding white,
immersed in clouds of nitre,
grins from the pantry of judgment,
from behind angels with copper eyes
and feathered parachutes,   40
asking:

—Who Blew Up The Road?

EACH MORNING

(Section 4 from "Hymn for Lanie Poo")

LE ROI JONES

Each morning
I go down
to Gansevoort St.
and stand on the docks.
I stare out   5
at the horizon
until it gets up
and comes to embrace
me. I
make believe   10
it is my father.
This is known
as genealogy.

BEFORE AN OLD PAINTING
OF THE CRUCIFIXION

The Mission Carmel
June 1960

N. SCOTT MOMADAY

I ponder how He died, despairing once.
I've heard the cry subside in vacant skies,
In clearings where no other was. Despair,
Which, in the vibrant wake of utterance,
Resides in desolate calm, preoccupies,   5
Though it is still. There is no solace there.

That calm inhabits wilderness, the sea,
And where no peace inheres but solitude;
Near death it most impends. It was for Him,
Absurd and public in His agony,   10
Inscrutably itself, nor misconstrued,
Nor metaphrased in art or pseudonym:

A vague contagion. Old, the mural fades . . .
Reminded of the fainter sea I scanned,
I recollect: How mute in constancy!   15
I could not leave the wall of palisades
Till cormorants returned my eyes on land.
The mural but implies eternity:

Not death, but silence after death is change.
Judean hills, the endless afternoon,   20
The farther groves and arbors seasonless
But fix the mind within the moment's range.
Where evening would obscure our sorrow soon,
There shines too much a sterile loveliness.

No imprecisions of commingled shade,   25
No shimmering deceptions of the sun,
Herein no semblances remark the cold
Unhindered swell of time, for time is stayed.
The Passion wanes into oblivion,
And time and timelessness confuse, I'm told.   30

These centuries removed from either fact
Have lain upon the critical expanse
And been of little consequence. The void
Is calendared in stone; the human act,
Outrageous, is in vain. The hours advance   35
Like flecks of foam borne landward and destroyed.

THE CHINESE CHECKER PLAYERS

RICHARD BRAUTIGAN

When I was six years old
I played Chinese checkers
   with a woman
who was ninety-three years old.
She lived by herself   5
in an apartment down the hall
   from ours.
We played Chinese checkers
every Monday and Thursday nights.
While we played she usually talked   10
about her husband
who had been dead for seventy years,

and we drank tea and ate cookies
and cheated.

ALL WATCHED OVER BY MACHINES
OF LOVING GRACE

RICHARD BRAUTIGAN

I like to think (and
the sooner the better!)
of a cybernetic meadow
where mammals and computers
live together in mutually   5
programming harmony
like pure water
touching clear sky.

I like to think
    (right now, please!)   10
of a cybernetic forest
filled with pines and electronics
where deer stroll peacefully
past computers
as if they were flowers   15
with spinning blossoms.

I like to think
    (it has to be!)
of a cybernetic ecology
where we are free of our labors   20
and joined back to nature,
returned to our mammal
brothers and sisters,
and all watched over
by machines of loving grace.   25

LEMONS, LEMONS

AL YOUNG

Hanging from fresh trees
or yellow against green

in a soft blaze of afternoon
while I eat dutifully
my cheese & apple lunch   5
or the coolness of twilight
in some of these California towns
I inhabited a lifetime ago

Hung that way
filled up with sunlight   10
like myself ripe with light
brown with light & ripe with shadow
the apple red & gold & green with it
cheese from the insides of
sun-loving cows   15

Sweet goldeness of light
& life itself
sunny at the core
lasting all day long
into night   20
into sleep
permeating dream shapes
forming tingly little words
my 2¢ squeezed out
photosynthetically   25
in hasty praise
of lemon/light

THE BICYCLE

STANLEY RICE

That which *is*, for example,
the *bicycle*
stands out
among things its *wheels*, fierce,
its substance   5
is present and works the air. For example
the spokes *are*. Spinning
they are even more surely, by which
we recognize the life-light around the hub
and under the brain's thin skin work   10
a thought for the rightness with which
its fenders join with the frame,

the handlebars, the accuracy, the *pureness*.
In the same radiance most things
stand, ugly, harmonic, *stand*   15
for us to mount
and ride out, clicking, handbrakes cool steel
handbrakes, alive more than ever
to what *is*, our eyeness fashioned to please
the legs, the way things   20
devicelessly wreck us with their perfect chains
on two oily wheels and wreck our
bodies, that we should somehow
rise out of this twofold spinning or leaning,
happy at last, at rest, furiously at rest,   25
a thing so rightly joined
the chain and frame
will never pull, for example, apart
from where we are *going*.

ON THE MURDER
OF MARTIN LUTHER KING

STANLEY RICE

I.   The young Texan reads a book.
Each night has new meaning
in it. Tonight. Aeschylus, I hear your black and gold mask
thunk in the yard, where each leaf of ivy
comes up;
reaching and sparkling.   5

It's like a . . . like a . . . party:
the terror hosting the terror hosting
the tendrils. They are white,
their strength coils through the black yard like
a snake around a chicken egg   10
it swallows without breaking.
Gold souls in fragile things: I'm watching the stars
in the black branches and I'm thinking of the meaning
this man's death has.
If it will last.
If any.   15

It's April.
The guests in my garden

stick out their white tongues under the dirt.
Light gives them color.
It changes the complexion of the mask.   20
Aeschylus, I hear in my brain rather than in my ears
your deathmask clink against the gravel.
This night means I am in it
up to my lips. Kick me.
I am beginning.   25

His head stuck up
because the hero is always more visible. Or rather,
he was a hero and therefore his head
stuck up above the sludge we call the flow we live in.
BANG!   30
    Aeschylus, you said:
    God marks that man with watchful eyes
    Who counts his killed by companies;
    And when his luck, his proud success,
    Forgets the law of righteousness,   35
    Then the dark Furies launch at length
    A counter-blow to crush his strength
    And cloud his brightness, till the dim
    Pit of oblivion swallows him.

But this is not a Literary Poem.   40
I am aware that this is a Poem.
I am singing but I am sinking
into the little black hole
in Martin Luther King's black jaw.
Or, as one of his friends put it: "His face just exploded."   45
The language got too much.
His life stopped working.

So what is a dead Greek to this dead nigger?
At the Vice-President's fund raising dinner where the news
came out the Chaplain said: 50
    "The-king-is-dead-long-live-the-king-of-Peace-on-Earth."
Meaning: each night has new meaning in it.
Meaning: we have heard that soft language before and it grew
        white ivy.
Meaning: I am. My black roots are hair; are   55
showing.

II.   The young Texan sees the children with the crushed souls
    for the first time.

Suave children black and brown

stand in my ivy patch
knocking on the openings in bottles
with their palms.   60
Standing in the wide leaves
each still an ear of dew
making the bottles sound like
they are grief stricken. Children without real eyes
   in their heads I think   65
standing in my ivy patch
if I struck their faces with my palm lightly
would thunk like bottles
so pure is their emptiness.

The physical world around them a mystery,   70
no lit animals,
no yellow,
just holes in their faces.

Give them many bottles,
wet their lips with Coke,   75
suave black and brown bodies full of echoes,
scarey as Death in the ivy standing
knee-deep in the green ivy,
beating on the mouths of bottles with their palms,
grieving and smiling.   80

III.   The young Texan returns to the Texas State Fair and sees
       the source of his racism sitting in a glass cage over a tank
       of water.

And here is where the niggers wash.
You can kill a nigger at last.
You can throw a baseball at the target hooked to his body.
Now you can pay him back for his sensual blackness.
You can drown him and drown him but still   85
he will laugh like a sleek, stupid, ape,
because that's what he is;
sleek; shiney; the whites of his eyes are yellow;
the brown pupils covered with a mucous blue film;
the teeth. You can make his seat snap open   90
and down into the white filthy water he drops,
his black hands and feet mixed in the foam,
staring at you through the glass tank
like an animal that you can't kill,
you can't kill him,   95
he keeps rising all oily and fresh, like a seal,
taunting you, virile, soiling you, soiled, your victim, your master.

IV.   The young Texan re-reads a book.

Agamemnon's slit jaws on the floor's Lord blooms
like a beautiful idea about freedom.
My-vacuumed-room-will-not-grow-ivy.   100
April-to-it-is-merely-a-season.
So, what?
So let the ears of ivy hear me
knock on my ears until the gunfire
forces a bloodred rain from the thunder.   105
I'm sure that Agamemnon's golden deathmask is a fake.
Martin Luther King's skin is awake in my garden.
It talks.
It says: your uncle's, your father's, your brother's, your own
bones   bones   bones   110
are pale and rotten and crushed and swallowed.
The little black hole in his cheek
sprouts water.   Tonight.
I see.
I am.   115
My own.
Skin's father.

FELIX OF THE SILENT FOREST

to Felix the Cat/Noveltytoons, USA
& Ed Krasnow

DAVID HENDERSON

Felix   you horizon dancer
Who are these people who say
they have known you a long time?
who are those friends
who attack you by the same handle?   5

In this age of debarkment
          epoch of mass inter-regimentation
     no longer have we cause to stay away

382

for not diving in
        it is the age of epaulet & picket line   10
        vertigo and alliance

Felix walks here and there
Felix walks the City
sometimes fast sometimes slow
like a dying man wanting everything he sees   15
not wanting to desist   to leave
never to allow Fate Palance
to have his way

Felix stops & then goes on

Often   20
Felix walks the City hungry in every sense
of every gastric salivating phenomenon
thighs   to eyes   to mouth
        He is wooed by Tad's $1.19 steaks
as well as 2 for 25¢ Hamburgers on forty-second street   25
                        the Crossroads—
He has bent in supplication
over 25¢ potato & gravy meals
in Pole Town Avenue "A"
as often as fried chicken fantasies   30
down Avenue "D"—the downtown Harlem
        On upper Seventh Avenue
he watches his plate being piled high
with fish & fried potatoes
the oil soaks and drips down   35
Felix thinks of cholesterol   chest pains   heart spasms
            yet   he passes fish
        to watered-down hot sauce   to mouth with gladness
    plus joy to the plastic-blotter bread
which picks up the grease   40

Felix
sits in Martin's Bar   Smiths   Blarney Stones
Bowery deformed men's bars   the Silver Rail Harlem
Shalomar-by-Randolph's   Regan's on Staten Island
the Jerome Avenue Spa or Sylvia's Blue Morocco Bronx NY 45
        Felix sits in any bar 3 or 4 for a dollar
wondering if
anyone he loves
wonders where he is

THE LOST PILOT

for my father, 1922–1944

JAMES TATE

Your face did not rot
like the others—the co-pilot,
for example, I saw him

yesterday. His face is corn-
mush: his wife and daughter, 5
the poor ignorant people, stare

as if he will compose soon.
He was more wronged than Job.
But your face did not rot

like the others—it grew dark, 10
and hard like ebony;
the features progressed in their

distinction. If I could cajole
you to come back for an evening, 15
down from your compulsive

orbiting, I would touch you,
read your face as Dallas,
your hoodlum gunner, now,

with the blistered eyes, reads 20
his braille editions. I would
touch your face as a disinterested

scholar touches an original page.
However frightening, I would
discover you, and I would not 25

turn you in, I would not make
you face your wife, or Dallas,
or the co-pilot, Jim. You

could return to your crazy
orbiting, and I would not try 30
to fully understand what

it means to you. All I know
is this: when I see you,
as I have seen you at least

once every year of my life,   35
spin across the wilds of the sky
like a tiny, African god,

I feel dead. I feel as if I were
the residue of a stranger's life,
that I should pursue you.   40

My head cocked toward the sky,
I cannot get off the ground,
and, you, passing over again,

fast, perfect, and unwilling
to tell me that you are doing   45
well, or that it was mistake

that placed you in that world,
and me in this; or that misfortune
placed these worlds in us.

WALKING ON THE LIPS OF THE BRONX

VICTOR H. CRUZ

1

the frightened bartender hit their heads on the south bronx
police of pipes & cans   iron strings
rides the south bronx   cars full of beer & mafia &
mafia loves   the bridge   under the bridge   by the water
J&B   & the Daily News   news of death   cars broken on the   5
highway
the man he walked up by the store   in his hands / he had
a big wall   the big walls   he knew   he knew
who would teach him anything   anything
you got to teach   10
teach me the ways   O teach me the ways   but what can
you, teacher,
teach the man with the walls / drop the wall on the corner

by the police   O   yeah   what can you teach the man with the
wall   15
look at him / walk & talk   look at him / he snagged the wall
out   what can you do
what can you do
talk about a wall / stare at a wall   the man he took the wall
down & threw it against the cars   20
the big red lips of the south bronx / right over the water
mr. machine got his head kicked / by the man with the wall
in his hands.

2

open his hands / what he will give you.
brooke avenue could be another thing   25
or willis   what you find   everything
happens   or what will / walking away
stores in the walls / talk / something
is happening / the man's eyes were deep
& had ways / to the train & go like   30
water
kissing the big red lips of the south bronx.

LATIN & SOUL

for Joe Bataan

VICTOR H. CRUZ

1
some waves
          a wave of now
                    a trombone speaking to you
a piano is trying to break a molecule
is trying to lift the stage into orbit   5
around the red spotlights

a shadow
the shadows   of dancers
dancers   they are dancing   falling
out that space   made for dancing   10

they should dance
on the tables   they should
dance inside of their drinks

they should dance on the
ceiling they should dance / dance 15

thru universes
leaning-moving
   we are traveling

where are we going
if we only knew 20

with this rhythm with
this banging with fire
with this all this O
my god i wonder where are
we going 25
    sink into a room full of laughter
    full of happiness full of life
    those dancers
    the dancers
       are clapping their hands 30
       stomping their feet

hold back them tears
       all those sentimental stories
cooked uptown   if you can hold it for after
we are going 35
    away-away-away
    beyond these wooden tables
    beyond these red lights
    beyond these rugs & paper
    walls beyond way past 40
    i mean way past them clouds
    over the buildings over the
    rivers over towns over cities
    like on rails but faster like
    a train but smoother 45
    away past stars
    bursting with drums.

2
a sudden misunderstanding
     a cloud
     full of grayness 50
a body thru a store window
     a hand reaching
     into the back
     pocket

a piano is talking to you
thru all this
why don't you answer it.

Index of Terms

Abstract terms: for ideas or concepts considered apart from material objects; *invention, justice; p. 24.*

Accent: the stress or emphasis given to certain syllables. Stress-'; un-stress-˘. Degrees of stress between these may be discerned. *p. 26.*

Allegory: a metaphor systematically extended, item by item, as the progression of the seasons may be treated as an allegory of human life; see *Metaphor, p. 24.*

Alliteration: the repetition of consonants, particularly in initial stressed syllables, as in the words *seven sorrows.* In Anglo-Saxon, the basic organizing principle of the line. See Auden's "Look, Stranger," for a modified Anglo-Saxon use. And *p. 24.*

Ambiguity: a double or mixed meaning. *p. 29.*

Amplification: enlarging or adding particulars to a statement. *p. 24.*

Anapest: two unaccented syllables followed by an accented syllable, as in *on the beat, p. 27.*

Art: the production of goodness and truth in the shape of the beautiful. *pp. 3, 31.*

Assonance: the identity of vowel sounds, as in the words *peal* and *beach. p. 24.*

Ballad: a popular narrative poem in simple stanzas, 4a3b4c3b. The folk ballad, of which the literary ballad is an imitation, is a poem of unknown authorship which passes orally from one generation to another. *p. 6.*

Blank verse: unrhymed iambic pentameter lines, without formal stanza units. *p. 29.*

Cadence: rhythmical flow of language, by phrases. *p. 27.*

Caesura: the main pause within a line of poetry. "He came to call, (*pause*) but found nobody home." *p. 27.*

Classic: having a coherent system embodying principles and methods accepted as authoritative; or, conforming to the models and rules of the Greeks and Romans; here specifically used for objective, balanced style. *pp. 51-52 and ff.*

389

Cliché: an expression which has lost freshness and vitality because of continued use; a trite, "rubber-stamp" expression. *p. 24.*

Climax: the peak of complication and suspense; see *narrative* and *dramatic, p. 3.*

Coinage (Neologism): a new or invented or newly applied term, to suit a new need. *p. 24.*

Conceit: a witty thought or turn of expression; a strongly conceptual metaphor. *p. 24.*

Concrete terms: names of substances, actions, people, events, with sensory qualities. *p. 24.*

Connotation: implied meanings and associations. Contrasted to *denotation,* the particular signification of a term. In logic: the set of attributes constituting the meaning of a term. *p. 24.*

Consonance: identity of consonants, as in *pine, plain. p. 24.*

Content: the actions, objects, concepts referred to; see *Substance, p. 24.*

Context: the larger whole in which a word or passage occurs. *p. 30.*

Convention: a rule, practice, or form which has its sanction in custom or usage. *p. 29.*

Couplet: two rhymed lines. A couplet is *closed* when the sense is completed within its compass. *p. 29.*

Dactyl: one accented syllable followed by two unaccented syllables, as in *fóllowĕd bў, and sýllăblĕ. p. 27.*

Denotation: the specific signification of a word. *p. 24.*

Dialogue: a conversation between two or more persons or personified objects; see *drama, p. 3.*

Diction: levels and specializations of usage in language: of time, place, formality, and technicality. *p. 24.*

Elegy: a poem of subjective and meditative nature, especially a poem of grief. *p. 29.*

Epic: a long narrative poem dealing with persons of heroic stature and actions of significance and observing certain epic conventions. *p. 29.*

Epigram: a short, pithy, and pointed remark often in couplet verse form. *p. 29.*

Episode: a separate but not unrelated incident in narration; see *narrative, p. 3.*

Evaluative: stressing some quality or set of qualities considered valuable, intrinsic, essential; distinguished from *implicative,* stressing associated rather than intrinsic qualities, as in symbol; and from *interchange,* the transposition of traits, as in metaphor. *p. 24.*

Figure of speech: stylistic form or expression—such as allegory, hyperbole, metaphor, simile, personification—which by its unusual combination of ideas suggests two ideas in one, an unusual likeness. *p. 24.*

Foot: a metrical unit of poetry, a combination of one accented and one or more unaccented syllables. See specifically *iamb, trochee, anapest, dactyl, spondee. p 27.*

Form: metrical, stanzaic, structural, or thematic arrangement, or all these in one. Traditional *verse forms* or *stanza forms* are based on certain repeated patterns: blank verse—basic unit, one line iambic pentameter without rhyme ("Bishop Orders His Tomb"); free verse—one line irregular length based on cadence without rhyme (Henley, H. D., Pound); mixed verse—one line metered and rhymed irregularly (Eliot); Anglo-Saxon—one line four-stressed, alliterated across medial caesura (Birney's "World Winter"); couplet verse—sequence of two units joined by rhyme, closed as statement coincides and is not run on or carried up to the next couplet (Dryden's "Mac Flecknoe"); tercet—stanza of three lines often rhymed aaa, bbb, (Rochester, Stevens) or interweaving as in terza rima aba, bcb; Japanese Haiku—three lines of 5,7,5 syllables respectively (Basho's "Haiku"); quatrain—four line rhymed abcb ballad or song, abab, abba; also various 5,6,7,9, and larger stanza units as for example, limerick—five lines 3′a, 3′a, 2′b, 2′b, 3′a; rhyme royal—seven lines 5′ ababbcc; triolet—eight line ABaAabAB with capitals indicating repeated lines (Bridges' "When First We Met"); sonnet—fourteen line iambic pentameter Petrarchan (Milton) rhyming abba abba cdecde, with break in meaning between octave and sestet, Shakespearean rhyming abab cdcd efef gg in a series of quatrains concluded by a couplet; villanelle—six terza rima stanzas with alternate refrain line summarized in final quatrain (Thomas' "Do not go gentle" and Roethke's "Waking"). Other forms not represented in this collection are the French rondeau and rondel combined line and refrain and sestina, six stanzas of six lines plus envoy, each stanza repeating similar line-ends in different order. Note also forms based on syllable length and count like Bridges' "London Snow," and "Nightingales," and Swinburne's "Sapphics" and Marianne Moore's two poems.

General: pertaining to all members of a class or group; distinguished from *specific, individual, single, particular.*

Genre: a traditional kind or category based on a complex of traits: for example, heroic, tragic, comic, lyric, elegiac, epigrammatic, pastoral. *p. 29.*

Heroic Couplet: a closed iambic pentameter couplet, coinciding with statement. *p. 27.*

Hexameter: six feet in a line; also, as twelve syllables, called *alexandrine. p. 27.*

Hyperbole: exaggeration; see metaphor, *p. 24.*

Iamb: an unaccented followed by an accented syllable, as in thĕ béat. *p. 27.*

Image: a representation of sense experience, most commonly of sight or sound; consciously emphasized since about 1700, especially by the "Imagist" poets of this century in England and America. *p. 25.*

Irony: an ironical statement, indicating a meaning other than the one it professes to give; an ironical event or situation, one in which there is a contrast between expectation and fulfilment; dramatic irony, the discrepancy between the understanding of those on stage and those in the audience.

Language: a system of spoken and written signs for the representation, expression, and communication of meanings. *p. 3.*

Literal: conveying the usual and primary meaning of words; distinguished from metaphoric, evaluative, and symbolic, as *is* from *as if, should,* and *may be. p. 24.*

Lyric: a poem with some of the form and musical quality of song, distinguished by its unity of mood from narrative and dramatic, but possibly sharing in either. *p. 24.*

Metaphor: an interchange and identification of one thing or idea with another not usually related, reshaping the thought of both to be held in mind, *as if* the two were one. *p. 24.*

Metaphysical: in literary history, the intellectual, colloquial, and dramatic style of the poets of the early 17th century, especially Donne. *pp. 25, 50-52 and ff.*

Meter: the systematization of rhythm as determined by the relationships of accented and unaccented syllables. Line measures are named for the metrical units or feet: dimeter, two feet; trimeter, three; tetrameter, four; pentameter, five; hexameter, six; and so on. Alternative measure by syllables is, for example, octosyllabic for eight, decasyllabic for ten. *p. 26-28.*

Motif: the recurrent theme or dominant feature of a poem; see *theme*, *p. 30.*

Octave: the first eight lines of a Petrarchan, or Italian, sonnet; see *Sonnet*.

Ode: a serious and formally emotional poem of invocation or celebration, usually complicated in metrical and stanzaic form, often divided into the three sections: strophe, antistrophe, and epode. *p. 29.*

Onomatopoeia: words imitating the sounds which they designate, for example *hiss, hum;* tones imitating moods. *p. 24.*

Paradox: a statement apparently self-contradictory or contrary to general opinion: "in the end is the beginning"; see *Metaphor, p. 24.*

Parody: the mimicking of the style or language of an author. See G. K. Chesterton's parody of Whitman, for example. *p. 29.*

Pastoral: poetry based on the conventions descended from the classic poetry of shepherd life. The persons involved are presented as shepherds, although they may be poets, scholars, or churchmen, and the subjects treated may have no reference to rural life. *p. 29.*

Pathetic fallacy: the practice of ascribing human traits or feelings to inanimate nature. The term was coined by Ruskin; see *Metaphor, p. 24.*

Personification: abstract qualities treated as if they were persons, as in *Justice, with eyes blindfolded;* see *Metaphor, p. 24.*

Plot: the plan or main story, the interrelationship of events; see *narrative* and *dramatic, p. 3.*

Poem: the art of language in line. *p. 3.*

Projective verse: term used by Charles Olson to call attention to projection of energy of sense across breaks in line. *p. 352*

Prose poetry: possessing many of the characteristics of poetry as art, but not its closely organized linear pattern. *p. 3.*

Quantity: the number and stress of syllables (in more limited usage, the length or brevity of vowel sounds or syllables, important in classical verse). *p. 24.*

Quatrain: a four-line stanza, rhyming in various patterns, such as abab, abba. See *Form.*

Refrain: words or phrases repeated, usually at the end of the stanza or a group of lines. *p. 24.*

Rhetoric: the classical rules of literary style. The purposive use of language in relation to audience, as distinguished from logic, relation to truth; and from grammar, interrelation of words. *pp. 6, 24.*

Rhyme: the identity, in the last words of two or more lines, of the accented vowels and of all consonants and vowels following: *give, live, pp. 28.*

Rhythm: motion measured by stress recurrent with some degree of regularity; in rising rhythm, units end with stressed syllables; in falling, with unstressed; in sprung rhythm, with stressed syllables juxtaposed. *pp. 26-28.*

Romantic: implying the personal, dramatic, or individual, as distinguished from the general norms of the classic. *pp. 50-52 and ff.*

Run-on lines: lines the ends of which do not coincide with a normal speech pause. *p. 28.*

Satire: a work holding up human vices or social follies to ridicule or scorn, by indirect means—imitation and exaggeration. *pp. 50-52 and ff.*

Scansion: the process of marking off the stresses as they occur in verse, coinciding or contrasting with their occurrence in normal speech. *p. 28.*

Sestet: six lines; in a Petrarchan sonnet, the last six lines, in which the poet presents the conclusion he has drawn from the theme; see *Sonnet.*

Simile: an unusual yet explicit comparison, generally announced by *like* or *as*; see *Metaphor, p. 24.*

Slant rhyme: use of either assonance or consonance, but not both, in final syllables. *pp. 24, 28.*

Sonnet: a poem in fourteen lines of iambic pentameter. The *Petrarchan sonnet* rhymes abbaabba-cdecde, with variations, and is divided into the *octave* and the *sestet.* The Shakespearean sonnet rhymes ababcdcdefefgg and consists of three quatrains and a couplet. *p. 100-102, 79-80.*

Sound: the basis of form in the poetic line, in the quantity (number and stress) and quality (tone-color) of syllables. *pp. 24, 27;* see *Rhythm* and *Rhyme.*

Spondee: a foot composed of two stressed syllables, as in *mán's fáte. p. 27.*

Stanza: a fixed pattern of lines, usually also involving a fixed *rhyme scheme,* or pattern of rhymes; see *verse. p. 24.*

Stress: accent, emphasis. *p. 24.*

Structure: relationship of statements or sentences and of the words within them. *pp. 3, 24.*

Style: manner; the poet's choice and arrangement of language. *p. 26.*

Sublime: a style high and ceremonious, invocative and implicative, characteristic of the 18th century. *pp. 50-52 and ff.*

Substance: word-reference, literal and extended. *pp. 3, 24.*

Symbol: an object which is used to stand for a concept; a token. Symbolist poetry, that which emphasizes the use of symbols; especially characteristic of late 19th-century France. *p. 24.*

Syntax: mutual relations of words in a sentence. *p. 24.*

Tercet: a group of three successive verses rhyming together or interlaced in rhyming with an adjoining tercet. *p. 29.*

Theme: prevailing idea, implicit or explicit. *p. 29.*

Tone: character and quality of sound; modulation of meaning and feeling. Whole Tone: prevailing tenor of sound in relation to substance and structure. *p. 24.*

Trochee: one accented followed by one unaccented syllable, as in *tróchĕe. p. 27.*

Trope: a figure of speech; see *metaphor, p. 24.*

Verse: line, or line-group; the regularized "turn" or recurrence of rhythm. Names of standard groups are: free verse, blank verse, couplet, tercet, quatrain, sestet, and so on; see *p. 27.*

Wit: the ability to perceive and express associations between ideas not usually connected; thus apt to use metaphor. *p. 53.*

Index of Poets

For almost every one of the poets included, there is an inexpensive yet carefully edited edition in one of the pocket or paperback series, as well as a standard scholarly text. And again for almost every poet, there is a recent biographical and critical study, like Lionel Trilling's of Matthew Arnold, Helen Darbishire's of Wordsworth, James R. Caldwell's of Keats. For most of the major poets, there is such helpful technical analysis as the concordance-tabulations of words in context; and for some, variorum editions which show variant versions and interpretations of the work.

As guides to poetry in general, there are a few helpful handbooks like Brooks and Warren's *Understanding Poetry,* Perrine's *Sound and Sense,* and Untermeyer's and Clement Woods' handbook of verse forms.

For theoretical discussions of poetry, the basic traditional works are by Aristotle, Horace, Longinus, available in translation from Greek and Latin, and by Sidney, Dryden, Coleridge, Arnold, in earlier eras of English poetry, as well as by European critics, especially those of the 19th century. Interesting modern works on poetry are I. A. Richards' *Practical Criticism,* Kenneth Burke's *Philosophy of Literary Form,* R. P. Blackmur's *Language as Gesture,* John Crowe Ransom's *The World's Body,* T. S. Eliot's *Selected Essays,* Ezra Pound's *ABC of Reading,* Donald Davie's *Articulate Energy,* Suzanne Langer's *Feeling and Form,* Morse Peckham's *Rage for Chaos,* Barbara Smith's *Poetic Closure,* W. K. Wimsatt's *Verbal Icon* and Isabel Hungerland's *Poetic Discourse.*

Especially good or lively translations of poetry, in bilingual texts, are those by Arthur Waley and Kenneth Rexroth of

Chinese and Japanese, C. F. MacIntyre of French and German, Richmond Lattimore of Greek, Babette Deutsch of Russian, Rolfe Humphries and H. R. Hays of Spanish, and Pound of several languages—and note Marianne Moore's translation of La Fontaine, Mary Barnard's of Sappho, and the selected translations of Baudelaire published by New Directions in 1955, as well as Stanley Burnshaw's *The Poem Itself* and others of its kind.

7925

UNIVERSITY-TEXARKANA